CIVIL WAR

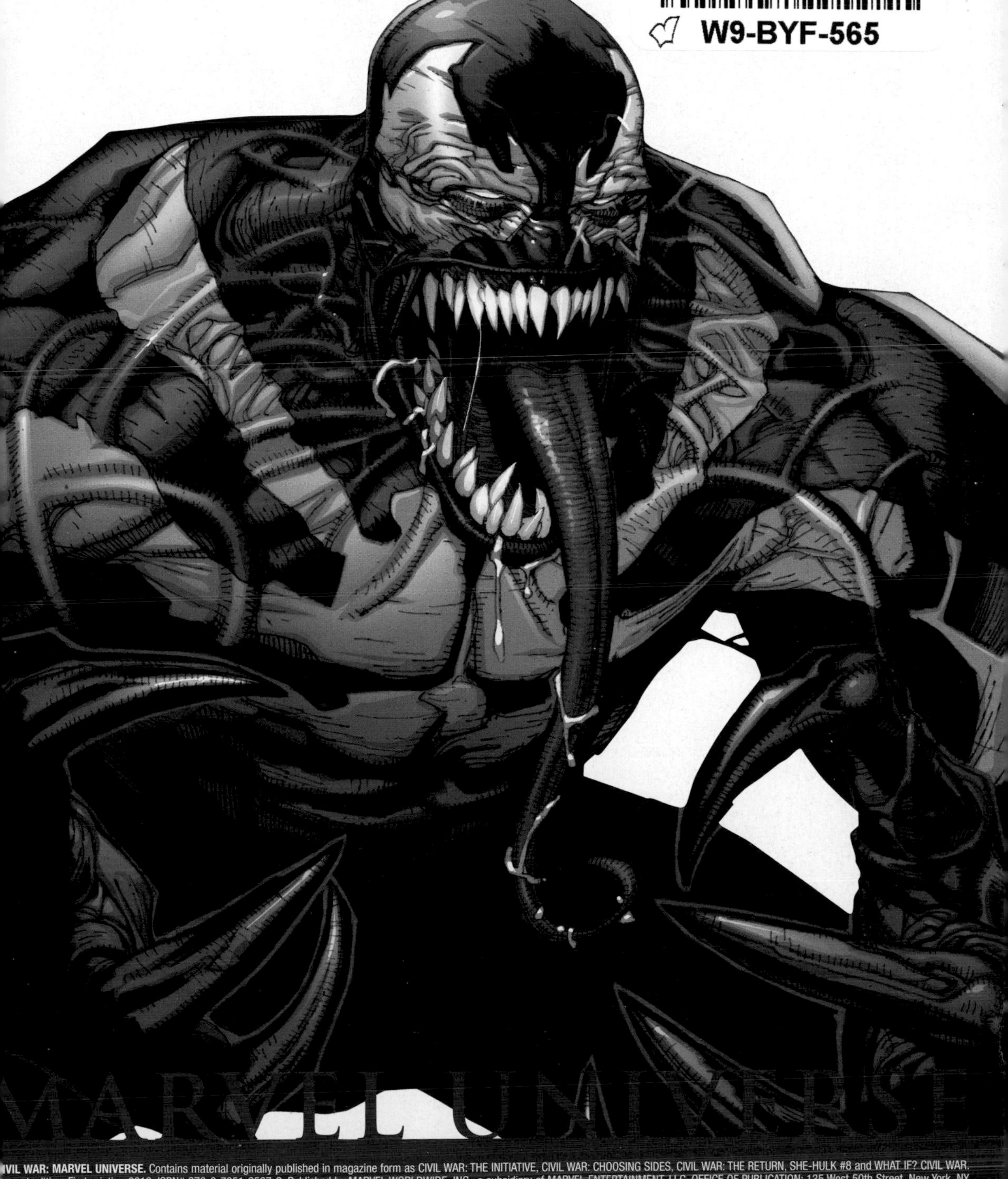

MARVEL UNIVERSE

IVIL WAR: MARVEL UNIVERSE. Contains material originally published in magazine form as CIVIL WAR: THE INITIATIVE, CIVIL WAR: CHOOSING SIDES, CIVIL WAR: THE RETURN, SHE-HULK #8 and WHAT IF? CIVIL WAR. econd edition. First printing 2016. ISBN# 978-0-7851-9567-2. Published by MARVEL WORLDWIDE, INC., a subsidiary of MARVEL ENTERTAINMENT, LLC. OFFICE OF PUBLICATION: 135 West 50th Street, New York, NY 0020. **Printed in the U.S.A.** ALAN FINE, President, Marvel Entertainment; DAN BUCKLEY, President, TV, Publishing & Brand Management; JOE QUESADA, Chief Creative Officer; TOM REVOORT, SVP of Publishing; DAVID BOGART, SVP of Business Affairs & Operations, Publishing & Partnership; C.B. CEBULSKI, VP of Brand Management & Development, Asia; DAVID GABRIEL, SVP of Sales & Marketing, ublishing; JEFF YOUNGQUIST, VP of Production & Special Projects; DAN CARR, Executive Director of Publishing Technology; ALEX MORALES, Director of Publishing Operations; SUSAN CRESPI, Production Manager; STAN EE, Chairman Emeritus. For information regarding advertising in Marvel Comics or on Marvel.com, please contact Vit DeBellis, Integrated Sales Manager, at vdebellis@marvel.com. For Marvel subscription inquiries, lease call 888-511-5480. **Manufactured between 1/29/2016 and 3/7/2016 by R.R. DONNELLEY, INC., SALEM, VA, USA.**

A
MARVEL COMICS
PRESENTATION

CIVIL WAR
MARVEL UNIVERSE

SHE-HULK #8
WRITER: DAN SLOTT
ARTIST: PAUL SMITH
COLORIST: AVALON'S DAVE KEMP
LETTERER: DAVE SHARPE
COVER ART: GREG HORN
ASSISTANT EDITORS: MOLLY LAZER
& AUBREY SITTERSON
EDITOR: TOM BREVOORT

CIVIL WAR: CHOOSING SIDES
WRITERS: MARC GUGGENHEIM,
ROBERT KIRKMAN, ED BRUBAKER &
MATT FRACTION, MICHAEL AVON OEMING
AND TY TEMPLETON
ARTISTS: LEINIL YU, PHIL HESTER &
ANDE PARKS, DAVID AJA, SCOTT KOLINS
& ROGER LANGRIDGE
COLORISTS: DAVE MCCAIG,
BILL CRABTREE, MATT HOLLINGSWORTH,
BRIAN REBER & SOTOCOLOR'S J. BROWN
LETTERERS: VC'S JOE CARAMAGNA &
ARTMONKEYS' DAVE LANPHEAR
EDITORS: MOLLY LAZER, AUBREY SITTERSON,
WARREN SIMONS, ANDY SCHMIDT &
TOM BREVOORT

CIVIL WAR: THE RETURN
WRITER: PAUL JENKINS
PENCILER: TOM RANEY
INKER: SCOTT HANNA
COLORISTS: GINA GOING (PP. 1-13) &
SOTOCOLOR'S A. CROSSLEY (PP. 14-23)
LETTERER: DAVE SHARPE
ASSISTANT EDITORS: MOLLY LAZER
& AUBREY SITTERSON
EDITOR: STEVE WACKER

CIVIL WAR: THE INITIATIVE
WRITERS: BRIAN MICHAEL BENDIS
& WARREN ELLIS
PENCILER: MARC SILVESTRI
ART & LETTERS: TOP COW PRODUCTIONS
COLORIST: FRANK D'ARMATA
ASSISTANT EDITORS: MOLLY LAZER &
AUBREY SITTERSON
EDITOR: TOM BREVOORT

WHAT IF? CIVIL WAR
WRITERS: ED BRUBAKER, KEVIN GREVIOUX
& CHRISTOS GAGE
ARTISTS: MARKO DJURDJEVIC; GUSTAVO,
SANDU FLOREA, VICTOR OLAZABA & SCOTT
KOBLISH; AND HARVEY TOLIBAO
COLORISTS: GURU-EFX, AVALON'S ED TADEO
& JAY DAVID RAMOS
LETTERER: VC'S JOE CARAMAGNA
EDITORIAL ASSISTANCE: MICHAEL HORWITZ
ASSISTANT EDITORS: CHRIS ALLO & NATE COSBY
CONSULTING EDITORS: TOM BREVOORT
& MARK PANICCIA
EDITOR: JUSTIN GABRIE

COLLECTION EDITOR
JENNIFER GRÜNWALD

ASSOCIATE EDITOR
SARAH BRUNSTAD

ASSOCIATE MANAGING EDITOR
ALEX STARBUCK

EDITOR, SPECIAL PROJECTS
MARK D. BEAZLEY

VP, PRODUCTION & SPECIAL PROJECTS
JEFF YOUNGQUIST

SVP PRINT, SALES & MARKETING
DAVID GABRIEL

BOOK DESIGNER
DAYLE CHESLER

EDITOR IN CHIEF
AXEL ALONSO

CHIEF CREATIVE OFFICER
JOE QUESADA

PUBLISHER
DAN BUCKLEY

EXECUTIVE PRODUCER
ALAN FINE

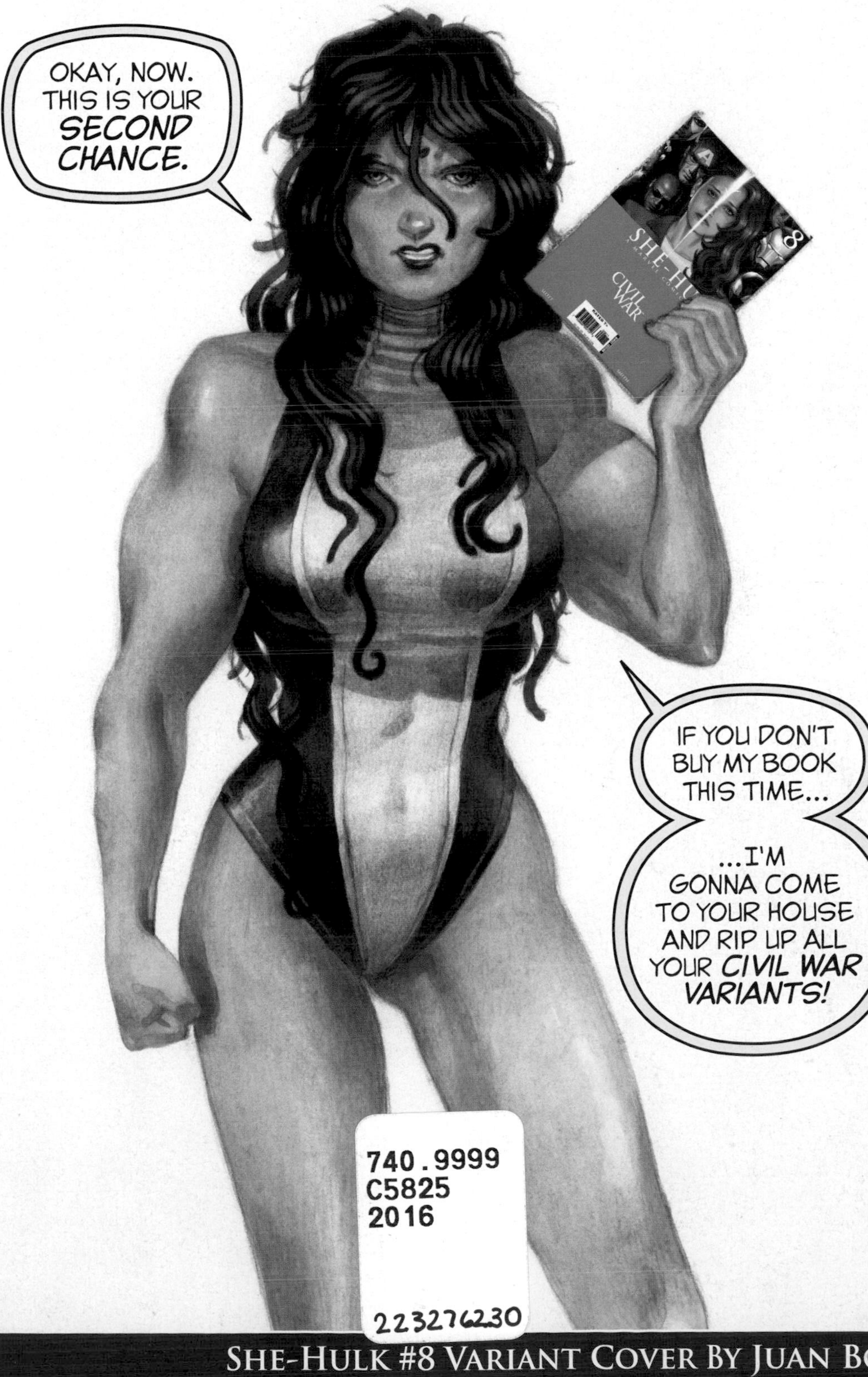
OKAY, NOW. THIS IS YOUR SECOND CHANCE.
IF YOU DON'T BUY MY BOOK THIS TIME...
...I'M GONNA COME TO YOUR HOUSE AND RIP UP ALL YOUR CIVIL WAR VARIANTS!

SHE-HULK #8 VARIANT COVER BY JUAN BOBILLO

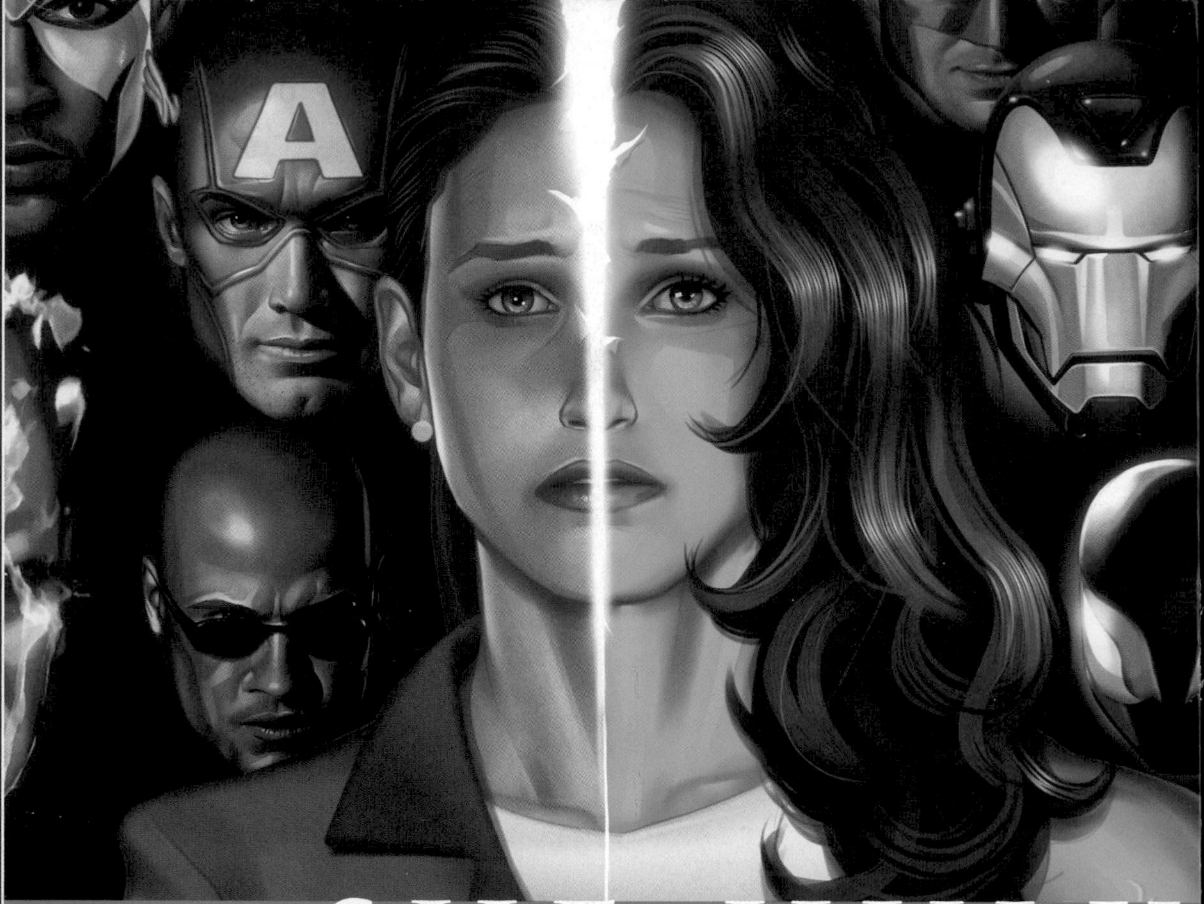

SHE-HULK

A MARVEL COMICS EVENT

CIVIL WAR

SHE-HULK #8

R WALTERS HAD ALWAYS THOUGHT THAT BEING A LAWYER WAS IN HER BLOOD... UNTIL A GAMMA-IRRADIATED BLOOD TRANSFUS
HER THE ABILITY TO CHANGE INTO THE WORLD'S SEXIEST, SASSIEST, AND STRONGEST SUPER HEROINE:

She-Hulk

PREVIOUSLY IN CIVIL WAR

g to boost their ratings, four New Warriors, young super heroes and reality television stars, attempted to appr rtet of villains holed up in Stamford, Connecticut. Unfortunately, when confronted, the explosive Nitro employ etonation ability, blowing the New Warriors and a large chunk of Stamford to oblivion. The entire incident was on tape.

Casualties number in the hundreds.

eaction to this tragedy, public outcry calls for reform in the way super heroes conduct their affairs. On Capitol human Registration Act is debated which would require all those possessing paranormal abilities to register w rnment, divulging their true identities to the authorities and submitting to training and sanctioning in the man federal agents.

e heroes, such as Iron Man, see this as a natural evolution of the role of super heroes in society, and a reasor request. Others, embodied by Captain America, take umbrage at this assault on their civil liberties.

Captain America is called upon to hunt down his fellow heroes who are in defiance of the Registration Act, he to go AWOL, becoming a public enemy in the process.

wake of the tragedy in Stamford, She-Hulk appears on CNN advocating the training and licensing of super her

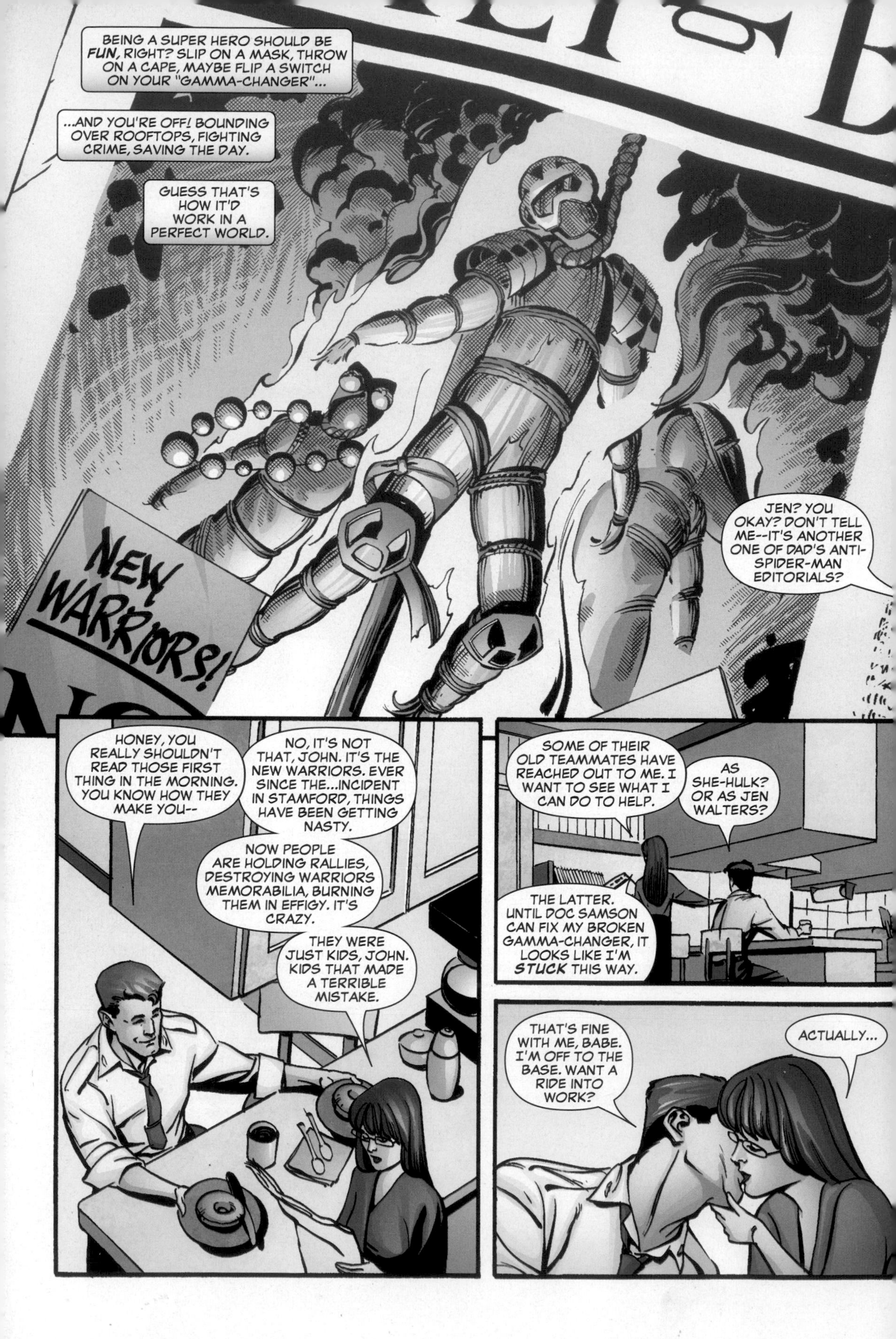
BEING A SUPER HERO SHOULD BE *FUN*, RIGHT? SLIP ON A MASK, THROW ON A CAPE, MAYBE FLIP A SWITCH ON YOUR "GAMMA-CHANGER"...
...AND YOU'RE OFF! BOUNDING OVER ROOFTOPS, FIGHTING CRIME, SAVING THE DAY.
GUESS THAT'S HOW IT'D WORK IN A PERFECT WORLD.
NEW WARRIORS!
JEN? YOU OKAY? DON'T TELL ME--IT'S ANOTHER ONE OF DAD'S ANTI-SPIDER-MAN EDITORIALS?
HONEY, YOU REALLY SHOULDN'T READ THOSE FIRST THING IN THE MORNING. YOU KNOW HOW THEY MAKE YOU--
NO, IT'S NOT THAT, JOHN. IT'S THE NEW WARRIORS. EVER SINCE THE...INCIDENT IN STAMFORD, THINGS HAVE BEEN GETTING NASTY.
NOW PEOPLE ARE HOLDING RALLIES, DESTROYING WARRIORS MEMORABILIA, BURNING THEM IN EFFIGY. IT'S CRAZY.
THEY WERE JUST KIDS, JOHN. KIDS THAT MADE A TERRIBLE MISTAKE.
SOME OF THEIR OLD TEAMMATES HAVE REACHED OUT TO ME. I WANT TO SEE WHAT I CAN DO TO HELP.
AS SHE-HULK? OR AS JEN WALTERS?
THE LATTER. UNTIL DOC SAMSON CAN FIX MY BROKEN GAMMA-CHANGER, IT LOOKS LIKE I'M *STUCK* THIS WAY.
THAT'S FINE WITH ME, BABE. I'M OFF TO THE BASE. WANT A RIDE INTO WORK?
ACTUALLY...

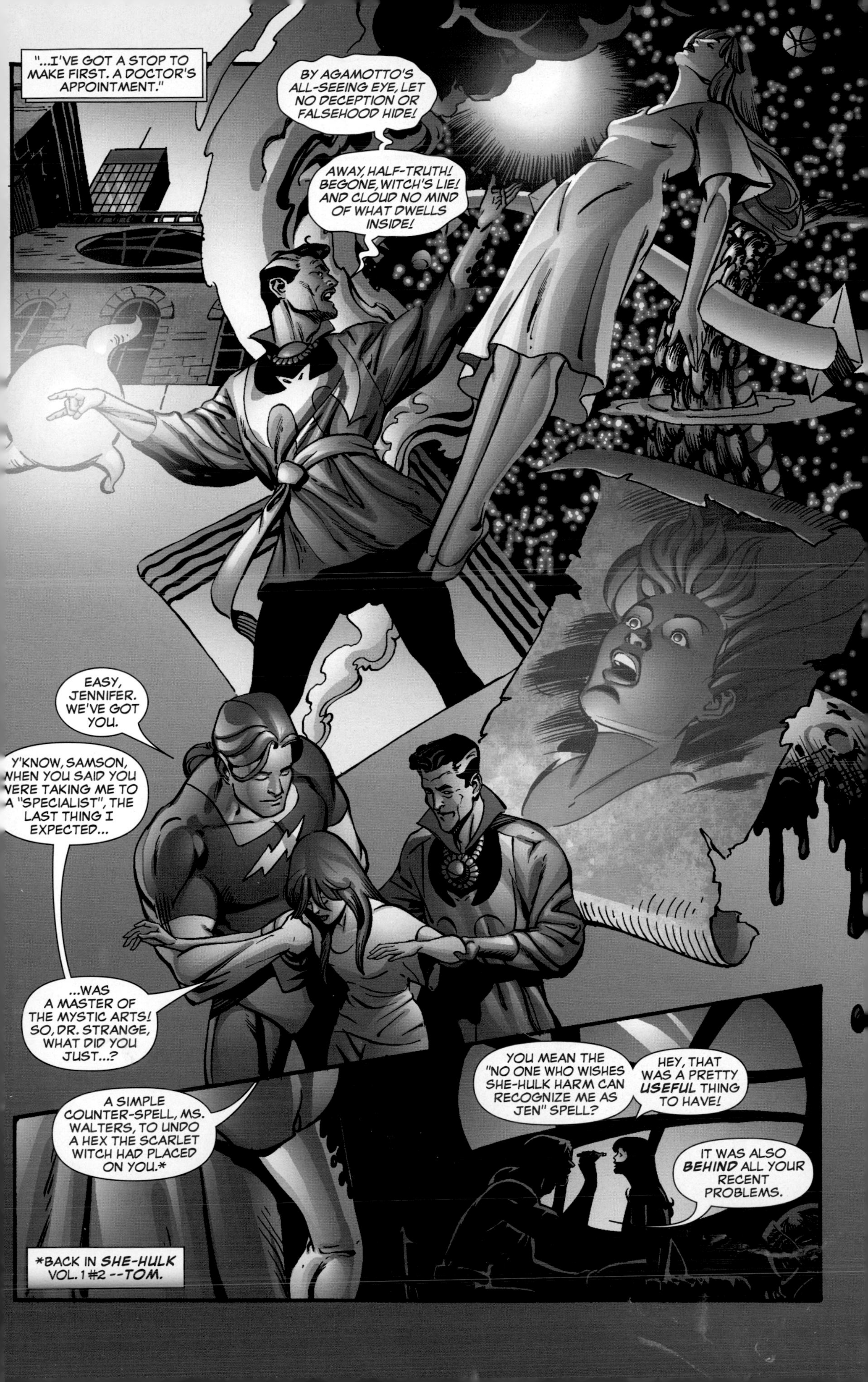
"...I'VE GOT A STOP TO MAKE FIRST. A DOCTOR'S APPOINTMENT."
BY AGAMOTTO'S ALL-SEEING EYE, LET NO DECEPTION OR FALSEHOOD HIDE!
AWAY, HALF-TRUTH! BEGONE, WITCH'S LIE! AND CLOUD NO MIND OF WHAT DWELLS INSIDE!
EASY, JENNIFER. WE'VE GOT YOU.
Y'KNOW, SAMSON, WHEN YOU SAID YOU WERE TAKING ME TO A "SPECIALIST", THE LAST THING I EXPECTED...
...WAS A MASTER OF THE MYSTIC ARTS! SO, DR. STRANGE, WHAT DID YOU JUST...?
A SIMPLE COUNTER-SPELL, MS. WALTERS, TO UNDO A HEX THE SCARLET WITCH HAD PLACED ON YOU.*
YOU MEAN THE "NO ONE WHO WISHES SHE-HULK HARM CAN RECOGNIZE ME AS JEN" SPELL?
HEY, THAT WAS A PRETTY USEFUL THING TO HAVE!
IT WAS ALSO BEHIND ALL YOUR RECENT PROBLEMS.
*BACK IN SHE-HULK VOL. 1 #2 --TOM.

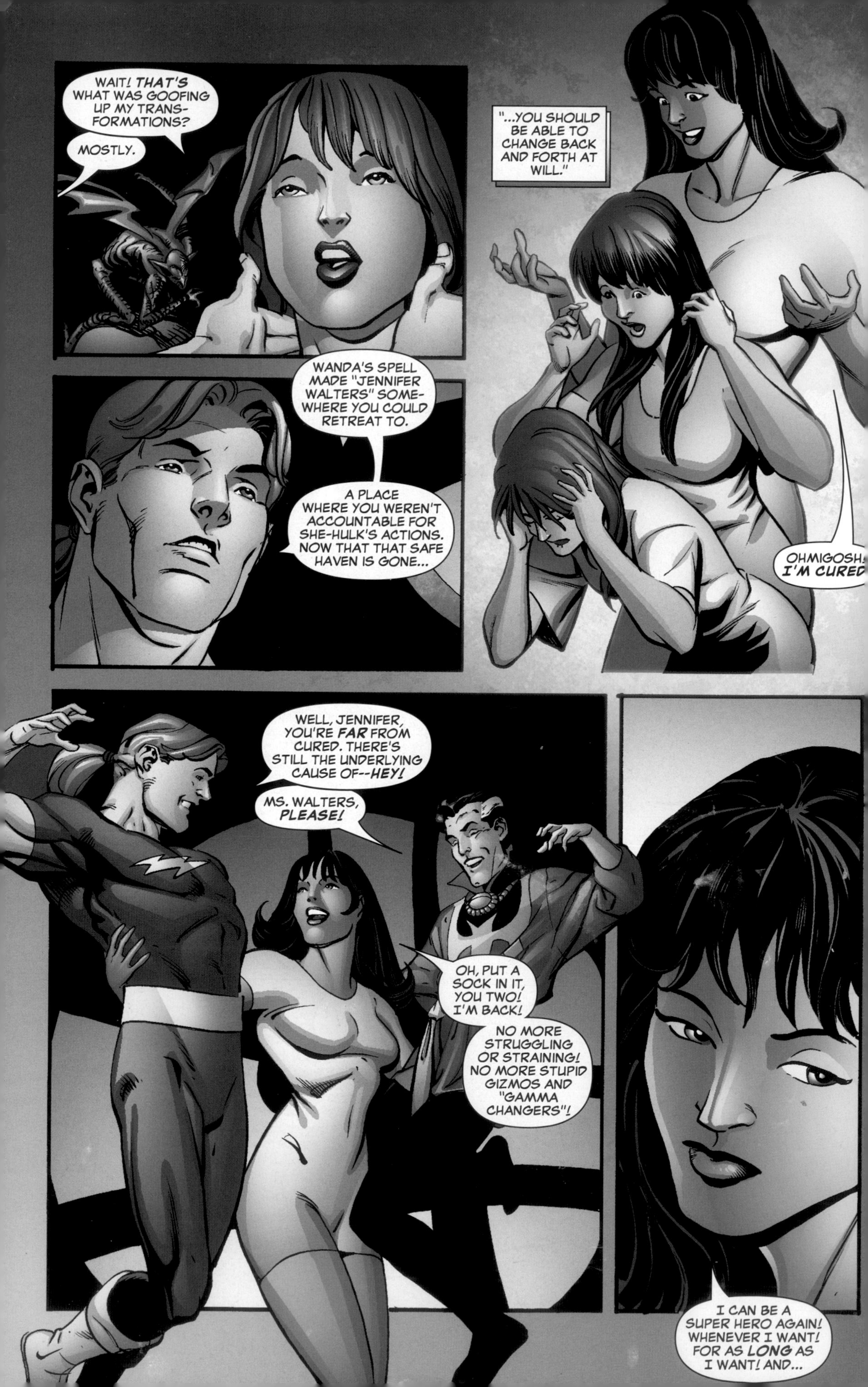
WAIT! THAT'S WHAT WAS GOOFING UP MY TRANS-FORMATIONS?
MOSTLY.
"...YOU SHOULD BE ABLE TO CHANGE BACK AND FORTH AT WILL."
WANDA'S SPELL MADE "JENNIFER WALTERS" SOME-WHERE YOU COULD RETREAT TO.
A PLACE WHERE YOU WEREN'T ACCOUNTABLE FOR SHE-HULK'S ACTIONS. NOW THAT THAT SAFE HAVEN IS GONE...
OHMIGOSH! I'M CURED
WELL, JENNIFER, YOU'RE FAR FROM CURED. THERE'S STILL THE UNDERLYING CAUSE OF--HEY!
MS. WALTERS, PLEASE!
OH, PUT A SOCK IN IT, YOU TWO! I'M BACK!
NO MORE STRUGGLING OR STRAINING! NO MORE STUPID GIZMOS AND "GAMMA CHANGERS"!
I CAN BE A SUPER HERO AGAIN! WHENEVER I WANT! FOR AS LONG AS I WANT! AND...

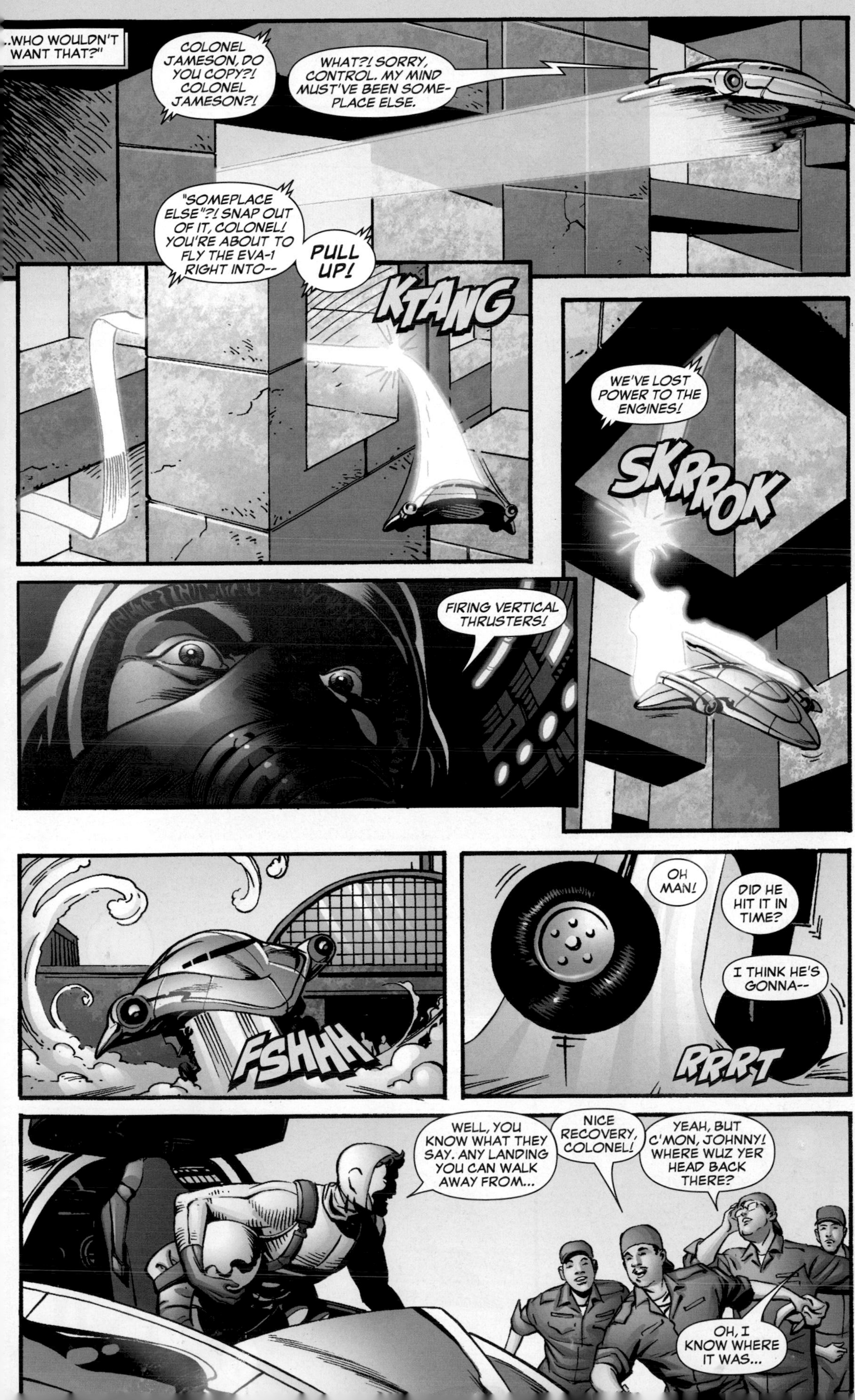
..WHO WOULDN'T WANT THAT?"
COLONEL JAMESON, DO YOU COPY?! COLONEL JAMESON?!
WHAT?! SORRY, CONTROL. MY MIND MUST'VE BEEN SOME-PLACE ELSE.
"SOMEPLACE ELSE"?! SNAP OUT OF IT, COLONEL! YOU'RE ABOUT TO FLY THE EVA-1 RIGHT INTO--
PULL UP!
KTANG
WE'VE LOST POWER TO THE ENGINES!
SKRROK
FIRING VERTICAL THRUSTERS!
FSHHH
OH MAN!
DID HE HIT IT IN TIME?
I THINK HE'S GONNA--
RRRT
WELL, YOU KNOW WHAT THEY SAY. ANY LANDING YOU CAN WALK AWAY FROM...
NICE RECOVERY, COLONEL!
YEAH, BUT C'MON, JOHNNY! WHERE WUZ YER HEAD BACK THERE?
OH, I KNOW WHERE IT WAS...

...THINKING ABOUT HIS BIG, GREEN GIRL-FRIEND!

AW, LAY OFF, NED. YOU KNOW JAMESON DON'T LIKE US TALKIN' ABOUT THE "LITTLE WOMAN."

AIN'T THAT RIGHT, "MRS. SHE-HULK"?

GUYS...

COLONEL JAMESON, A MOMENT OF YOUR TIME.

YES, SIR, GENERAL. I TAKE FULL RESPONSI-BILITY FOR--

IN *PRIVATE*, COLONEL.

JOHN, IT'S WELL KNOWN THAT YOU HAVE STRONG TIES TO THE SUPERHUMAN COMMUNITY.

FRIENDS WITH SPIDER-MAN. BEEN CAPTAIN AMERICA'S PILOT. NOW YOU'RE DATING THE HULK'S COUSIN.

FOR YOUR OWN GOOD, IT'D BE BEST IF YOU SEVER THOSE TIES. BIG THINGS ARE BREWING, COLONEL.

WORD ON HIGH SAYS THE SUPERHUMAN REGISTRATION ACT IS GOING TO PASS. AND IF ANY OF THOSE "CAPE-FLAPPERS" DON'T FALL IN LINE...

...WELL, WHY DO YOU THINK WE'RE PUSHING FORWARD WITH THE EVA INTERCEPTOR?

SIR? I THOUGHT THE EXTREME VERTICAL ASSAULT CRAFT WAS FOR TAKING OUT SMALL, LOW-FLYING VEHICLES IN URBAN AREAS.

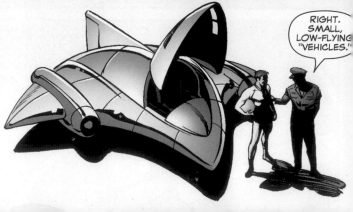

RIGHT. SMALL, LOW-FLYING "VEHICLES."

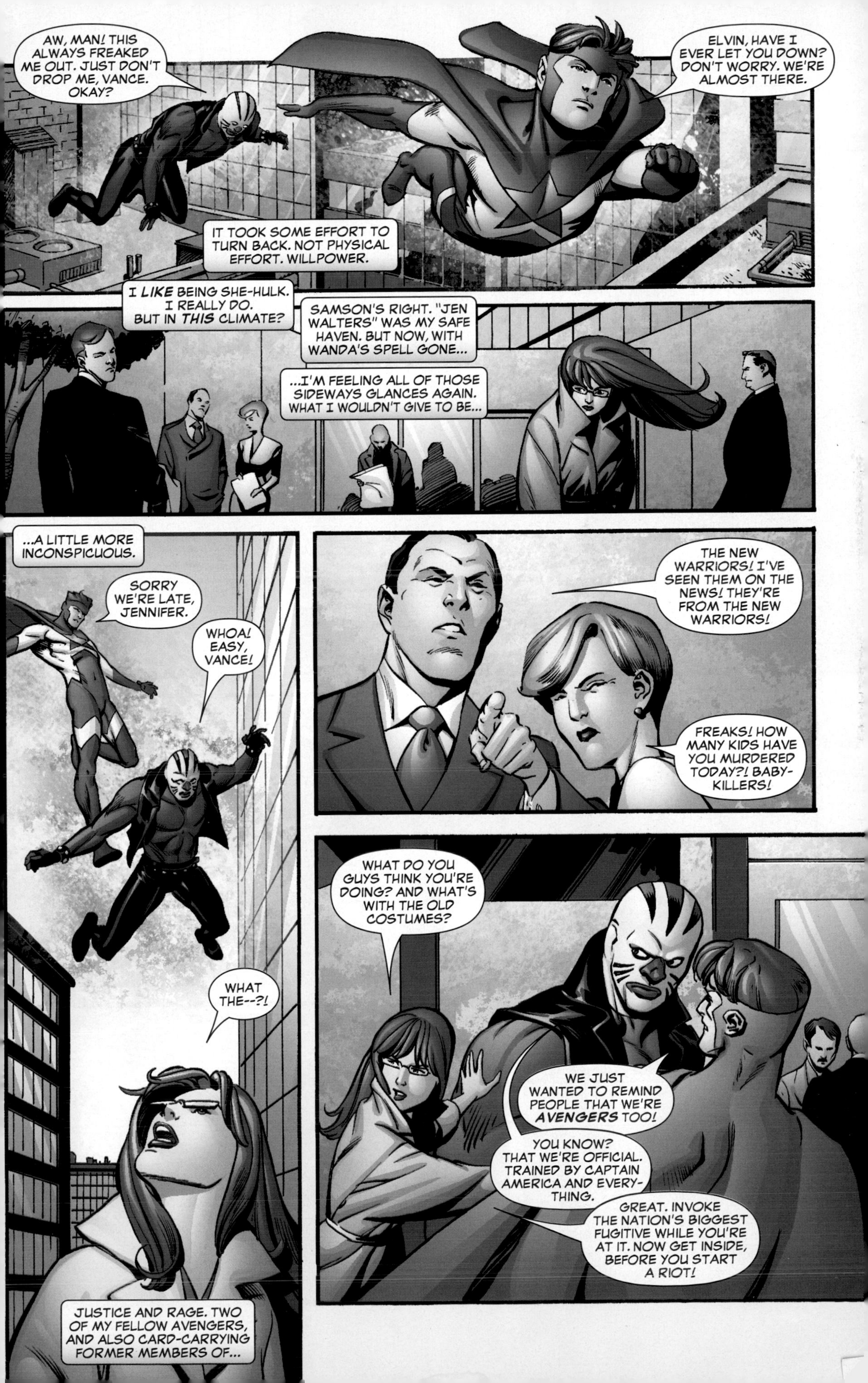
AW, MAN! THIS ALWAYS FREAKED ME OUT. JUST DON'T DROP ME, VANCE. OKAY?
ELVIN, HAVE I EVER LET YOU DOWN? DON'T WORRY. WE'RE ALMOST THERE.
IT TOOK SOME EFFORT TO TURN BACK. NOT PHYSICAL EFFORT. WILLPOWER.
I LIKE BEING SHE-HULK. I REALLY DO. BUT IN THIS CLIMATE?
SAMSON'S RIGHT. "JEN WALTERS" WAS MY SAFE HAVEN. BUT NOW, WITH WANDA'S SPELL GONE...
...I'M FEELING ALL OF THOSE SIDEWAYS GLANCES AGAIN. WHAT I WOULDN'T GIVE TO BE...
...A LITTLE MORE INCONSPICUOUS.
SORRY WE'RE LATE, JENNIFER.
WHOA! EASY, VANCE!
WHAT THE--?!
JUSTICE AND RAGE. TWO OF MY FELLOW AVENGERS, AND ALSO CARD-CARRYING FORMER MEMBERS OF...
THE NEW WARRIORS! I'VE SEEN THEM ON THE NEWS! THEY'RE FROM THE NEW WARRIORS!
FREAKS! HOW MANY KIDS HAVE YOU MURDERED TODAY?! BABY-KILLERS!
WHAT DO YOU GUYS THINK YOU'RE DOING? AND WHAT'S WITH THE OLD COSTUMES?
WE JUST WANTED TO REMIND PEOPLE THAT WE'RE AVENGERS TOO!
YOU KNOW? THAT WE'RE OFFICIAL. TRAINED BY CAPTAIN AMERICA AND EVERY-THING.
GREAT. INVOKE THE NATION'S BIGGEST FUGITIVE WHILE YOU'RE AT IT. NOW GET INSIDE, BEFORE YOU START A RIOT!

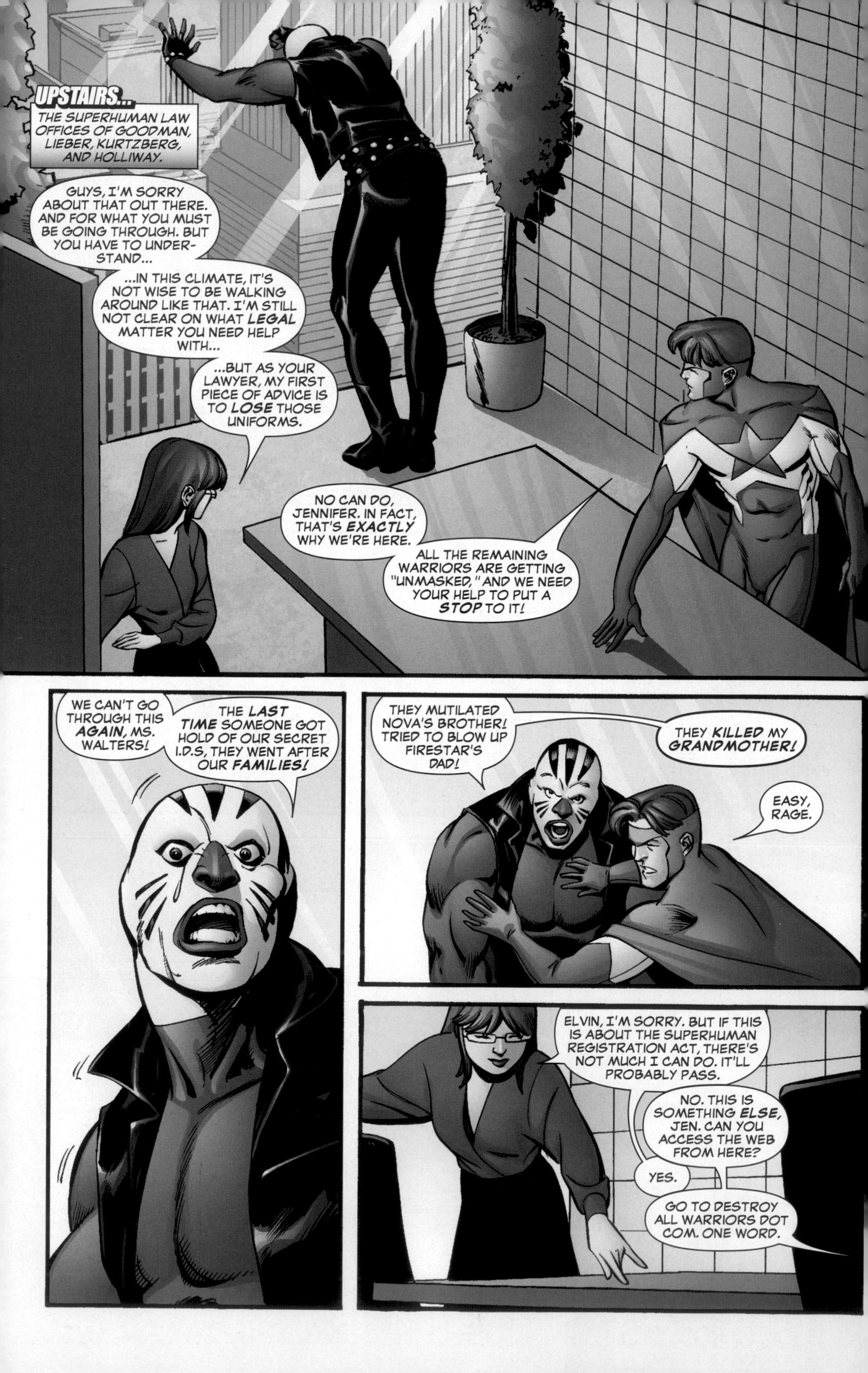
UPSTAIRS...
THE SUPERHUMAN LAW OFFICES OF GOODMAN, LIEBER, KURTZBERG, AND HOLLIWAY.
GUYS, I'M SORRY ABOUT THAT OUT THERE. AND FOR WHAT YOU MUST BE GOING THROUGH. BUT YOU HAVE TO UNDER-STAND...
...IN THIS CLIMATE, IT'S NOT WISE TO BE WALKING AROUND LIKE THAT. I'M STILL NOT CLEAR ON WHAT LEGAL MATTER YOU NEED HELP WITH...
...BUT AS YOUR LAWYER, MY FIRST PIECE OF ADVICE IS TO LOSE THOSE UNIFORMS.
NO CAN DO, JENNIFER. IN FACT, THAT'S EXACTLY WHY WE'RE HERE.
ALL THE REMAINING WARRIORS ARE GETTING "UNMASKED," AND WE NEED YOUR HELP TO PUT A STOP TO IT!
WE CAN'T GO THROUGH THIS AGAIN, MS. WALTERS!
THE LAST TIME SOMEONE GOT HOLD OF OUR SECRET I.D.S, THEY WENT AFTER OUR FAMILIES!
THEY MUTILATED NOVA'S BROTHER! TRIED TO BLOW UP FIRESTAR'S DAD!
THEY KILLED MY GRANDMOTHER!
EASY, RAGE.
ELVIN, I'M SORRY. BUT IF THIS IS ABOUT THE SUPERHUMAN REGISTRATION ACT, THERE'S NOT MUCH I CAN DO. IT'LL PROBABLY PASS.
NO. THIS IS SOMETHING ELSE, JEN. CAN YOU ACCESS THE WEB FROM HERE?
YES.
GO TO DESTROY ALL WARRIORS DOT COM. ONE WORD.

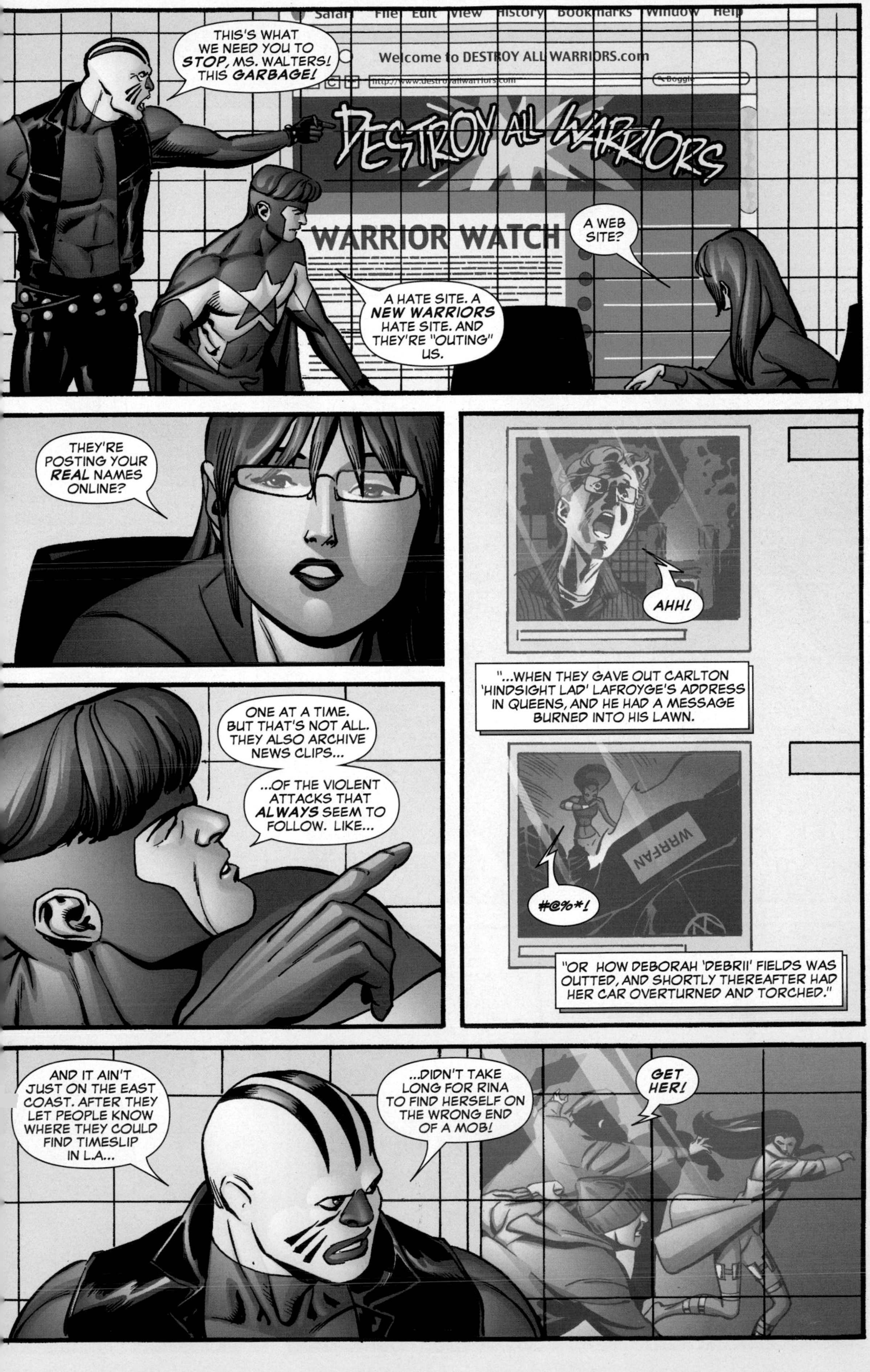
Safari File Edit View History Bookmarks Window Help
Welcome to DESTROY ALL WARRIORS.com
THIS'S WHAT WE NEED YOU TO STOP, MS. WALTERS! THIS GARBAGE!
DESTROY ALL WARRIORS
WARRIOR WATCH
A WEB SITE?
A HATE SITE. A NEW WARRIORS HATE SITE. AND THEY'RE "OUTING" US.
THEY'RE POSTING YOUR REAL NAMES ONLINE?
AHH!
"...WHEN THEY GAVE OUT CARLTON 'HINDSIGHT LAD' LAFROYGE'S ADDRESS IN QUEENS, AND HE HAD A MESSAGE BURNED INTO HIS LAWN.
ONE AT A TIME. BUT THAT'S NOT ALL. THEY ALSO ARCHIVE NEWS CLIPS...
...OF THE VIOLENT ATTACKS THAT ALWAYS SEEM TO FOLLOW. LIKE...
WARRFAN
#@%*!
"OR HOW DEBORAH 'DEBRII' FIELDS WAS OUTTED, AND SHORTLY THEREAFTER HAD HER CAR OVERTURNED AND TORCHED."
AND IT AIN'T JUST ON THE EAST COAST. AFTER THEY LET PEOPLE KNOW WHERE THEY COULD FIND TIMESLIP IN L.A...
...DIDN'T TAKE LONG FOR RINA TO FIND HERSELF ON THE WRONG END OF A MOB!
GET HER!

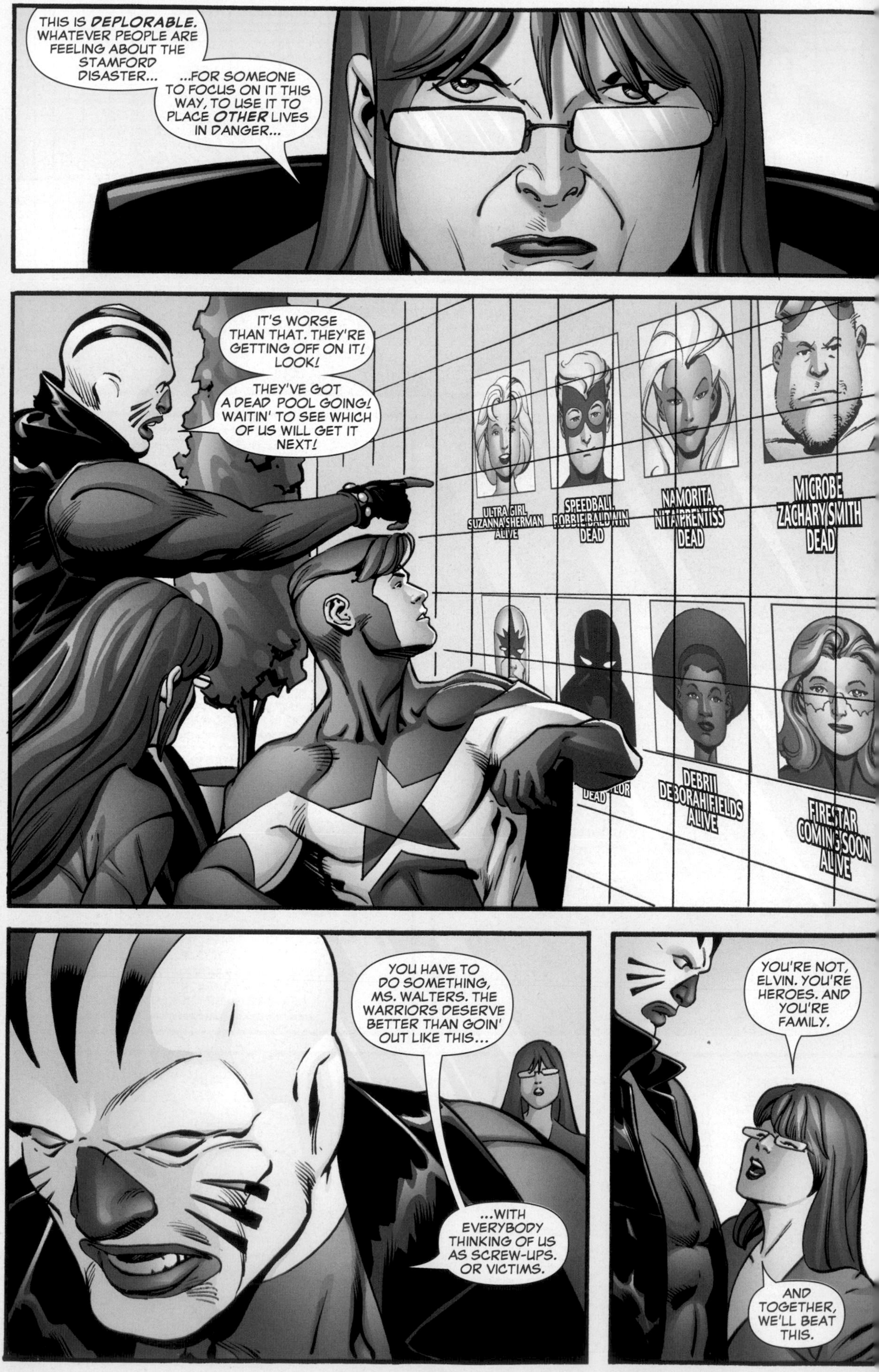
THIS IS DEPLORABLE. WHATEVER PEOPLE ARE FEELING ABOUT THE STAMFORD DISASTER...
...FOR SOMEONE TO FOCUS ON IT THIS WAY, TO USE IT TO PLACE OTHER LIVES IN DANGER...
IT'S WORSE THAN THAT. THEY'RE GETTING OFF ON IT! LOOK!
THEY'VE GOT A DEAD POOL GOING! WAITIN' TO SEE WHICH OF US WILL GET IT NEXT!
ULTRA GIRL SUZANNA SHERMAN ALIVE
SPEEDBALL ROBBIE BALDWIN DEAD
NAMORITA NITA PRENTISS DEAD
MICROBE ZACHARY SMITH DEAD
DEBRII DEBORAH FIELDS ALIVE
FIRESTAR COMING SOON ALIVE
YOU HAVE TO DO SOMETHING, MS. WALTERS. THE WARRIORS DESERVE BETTER THAN GOIN' OUT LIKE THIS...
...WITH EVERYBODY THINKING OF US AS SCREW-UPS. OR VICTIMS.
YOU'RE NOT, ELVIN. YOU'RE HEROES. AND YOU'RE FAMILY.
AND TOGETHER, WE'LL BEAT THIS.

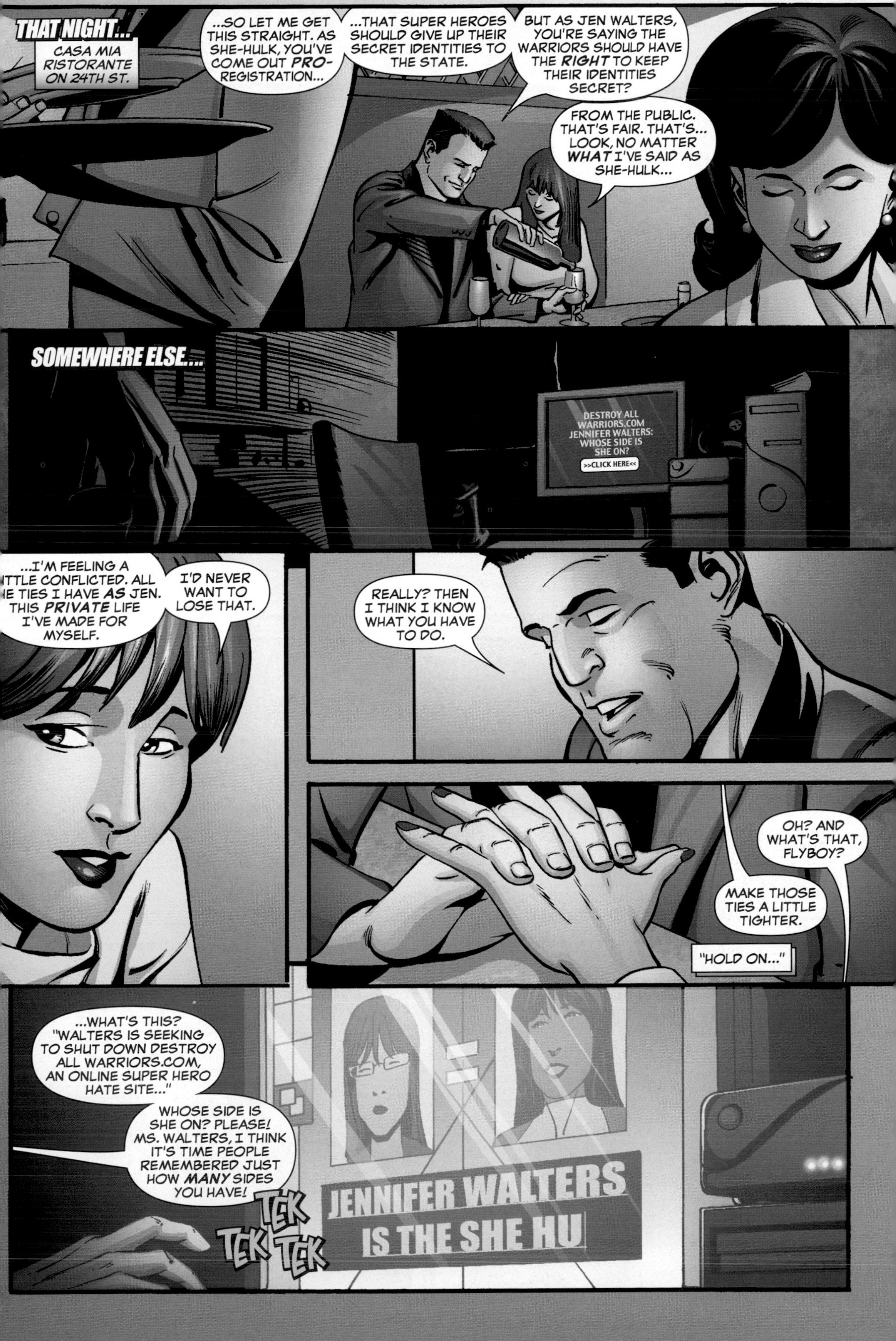
THAT NIGHT...
CASA MIA RISTORANTE ON 24TH ST.
...SO LET ME GET THIS STRAIGHT. AS SHE-HULK, YOU'VE COME OUT PRO-REGISTRATION...
...THAT SUPER HEROES SHOULD GIVE UP THEIR SECRET IDENTITIES TO THE STATE.
BUT AS JEN WALTERS, YOU'RE SAYING THE WARRIORS SHOULD HAVE THE RIGHT TO KEEP THEIR IDENTITIES SECRET?
FROM THE PUBLIC. THAT'S FAIR. THAT'S... LOOK, NO MATTER WHAT I'VE SAID AS SHE-HULK...
SOMEWHERE ELSE...
DESTROY ALL WARRIORS.COM
JENNIFER WALTERS: WHOSE SIDE IS SHE ON?
>>CLICK HERE<<
...I'M FEELING A LITTLE CONFLICTED. ALL THE TIES I HAVE AS JEN. THIS PRIVATE LIFE I'VE MADE FOR MYSELF.
I'D NEVER WANT TO LOSE THAT.
REALLY? THEN I THINK I KNOW WHAT YOU HAVE TO DO.
OH? AND WHAT'S THAT, FLYBOY?
MAKE THOSE TIES A LITTLE TIGHTER.
"HOLD ON..."
...WHAT'S THIS? "WALTERS IS SEEKING TO SHUT DOWN DESTROY ALL WARRIORS.COM, AN ONLINE SUPER HERO HATE SITE..."
WHOSE SIDE IS SHE ON? PLEASE! MS. WALTERS, I THINK IT'S TIME PEOPLE REMEMBERED JUST HOW MANY SIDES YOU HAVE!
TEK TEK TEK
JENNIFER WALTERS IS THE SHE HU

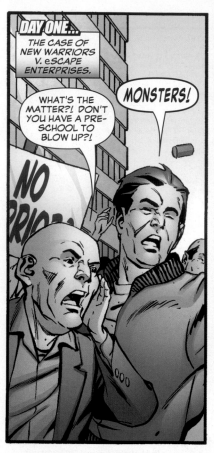

DAY ONE...

THE CASE OF NEW WARRIORS V. eSCAPE ENTERPRISES.

WHAT'S THE MATTER?! DON'T YOU HAVE A PRE-SCHOOL TO BLOW UP?!

MONSTERS!

THAT'S IT! JUSTICE, DROP YOUR TELEKINETIC SHIELD! I AIN'T AFRAID OF ANYTHING THESE JERKS THROW MY WAY!

YEAH, RIGHT. YOU THINK THIS SHIELD'S IN PLACE TO KEEP THEM FROM YOU?

OH, THIS IS UGLY. (AND I'VE SEEN CROWDS THAT'VE LITERALLY BEEN ZAPPED BY HATE RAYS!)

BETTER MOVE THIS ALL INSIDE THE COURTHOUSE BEFORE THINGS GET...

...OUT OF CONTROL.

THAT'S HER! THEIR LAWYER! THE ONE FROM THE WEB PAGE!

GUYS, OVER HERE! I GOT SHE-HULK!

AH!

SHRRRIP

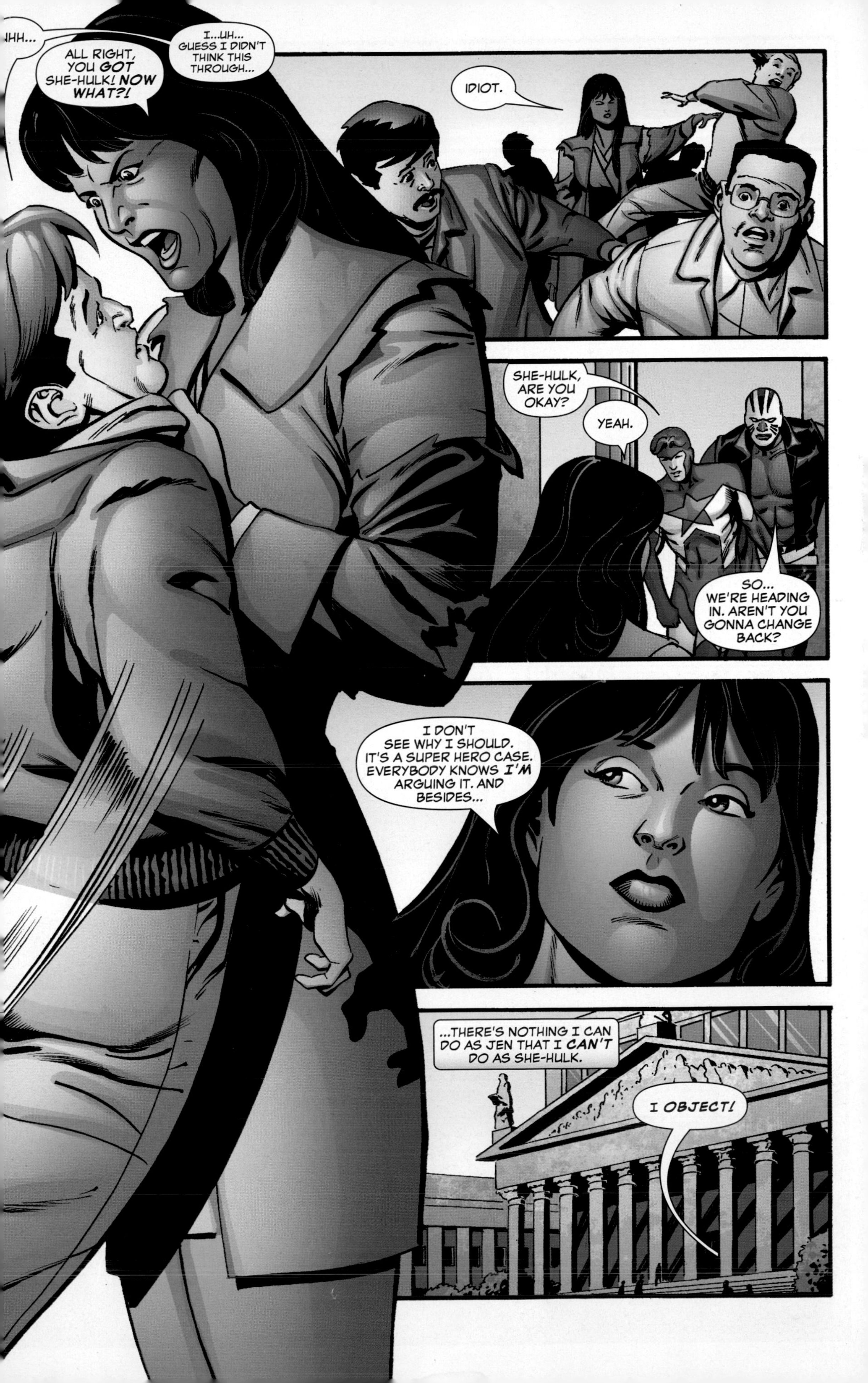
HHH...
ALL RIGHT, YOU GOT SHE-HULK! NOW WHAT?!
I...UH... GUESS I DIDN'T THINK THIS THROUGH...
IDIOT.
SHE-HULK, ARE YOU OKAY?
YEAH.
SO... WE'RE HEADING IN. AREN'T YOU GONNA CHANGE BACK?
I DON'T SEE WHY I SHOULD. IT'S A SUPER HERO CASE. EVERYBODY KNOWS I'M ARGUING IT. AND BESIDES...
...THERE'S NOTHING I CAN DO AS JEN THAT I CAN'T DO AS SHE-HULK.
I OBJECT!

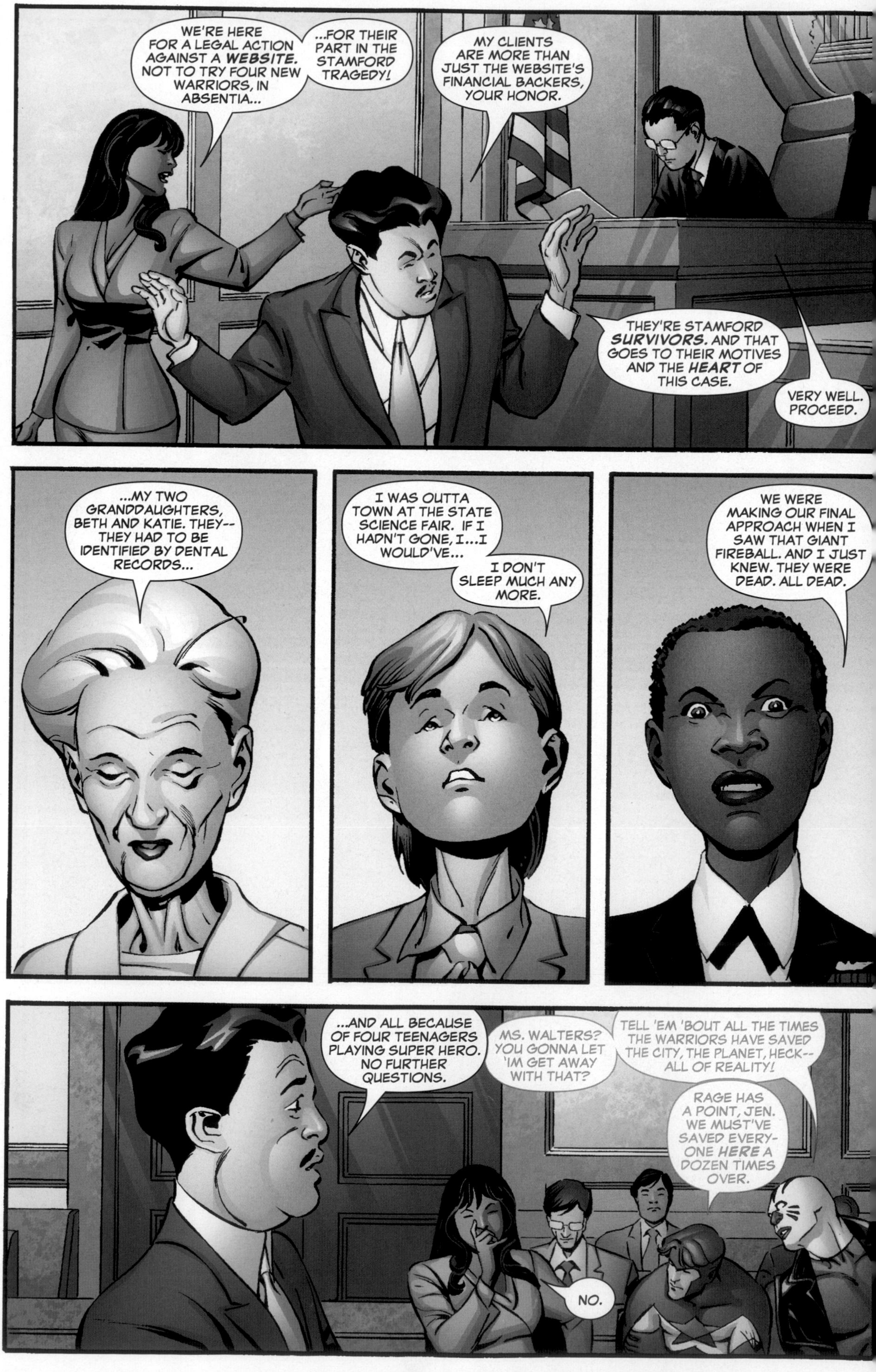
WE'RE HERE FOR A LEGAL ACTION AGAINST A **WEBSITE.** NOT TO TRY FOUR NEW WARRIORS, IN ABSENTIA...
...FOR THEIR PART IN THE STAMFORD TRAGEDY!
MY CLIENTS ARE MORE THAN JUST THE WEBSITE'S FINANCIAL BACKERS, YOUR HONOR.
THEY'RE STAMFORD **SURVIVORS.** AND THAT GOES TO THEIR MOTIVES AND THE **HEART** OF THIS CASE.
VERY WELL. PROCEED.
...MY TWO GRANDDAUGHTERS, BETH AND KATIE. THEY--THEY HAD TO BE IDENTIFIED BY DENTAL RECORDS...
I WAS OUTTA TOWN AT THE STATE SCIENCE FAIR. IF I HADN'T GONE, I...I WOULD'VE...
I DON'T SLEEP MUCH ANY MORE.
WE WERE MAKING OUR FINAL APPROACH WHEN I SAW THAT GIANT FIREBALL. AND I JUST KNEW. THEY WERE DEAD. ALL DEAD.
...AND ALL BECAUSE OF FOUR TEENAGERS PLAYING SUPER HERO. NO FURTHER QUESTIONS.
MS. WALTERS? YOU GONNA LET 'IM GET AWAY WITH THAT?
TELL 'EM 'BOUT ALL THE TIMES THE WARRIORS HAVE SAVED THE CITY, THE PLANET, HECK--ALL OF REALITY!
RAGE HAS A POINT, JEN. WE MUST'VE SAVED EVERYONE **HERE** A DOZEN TIMES OVER.
NO.

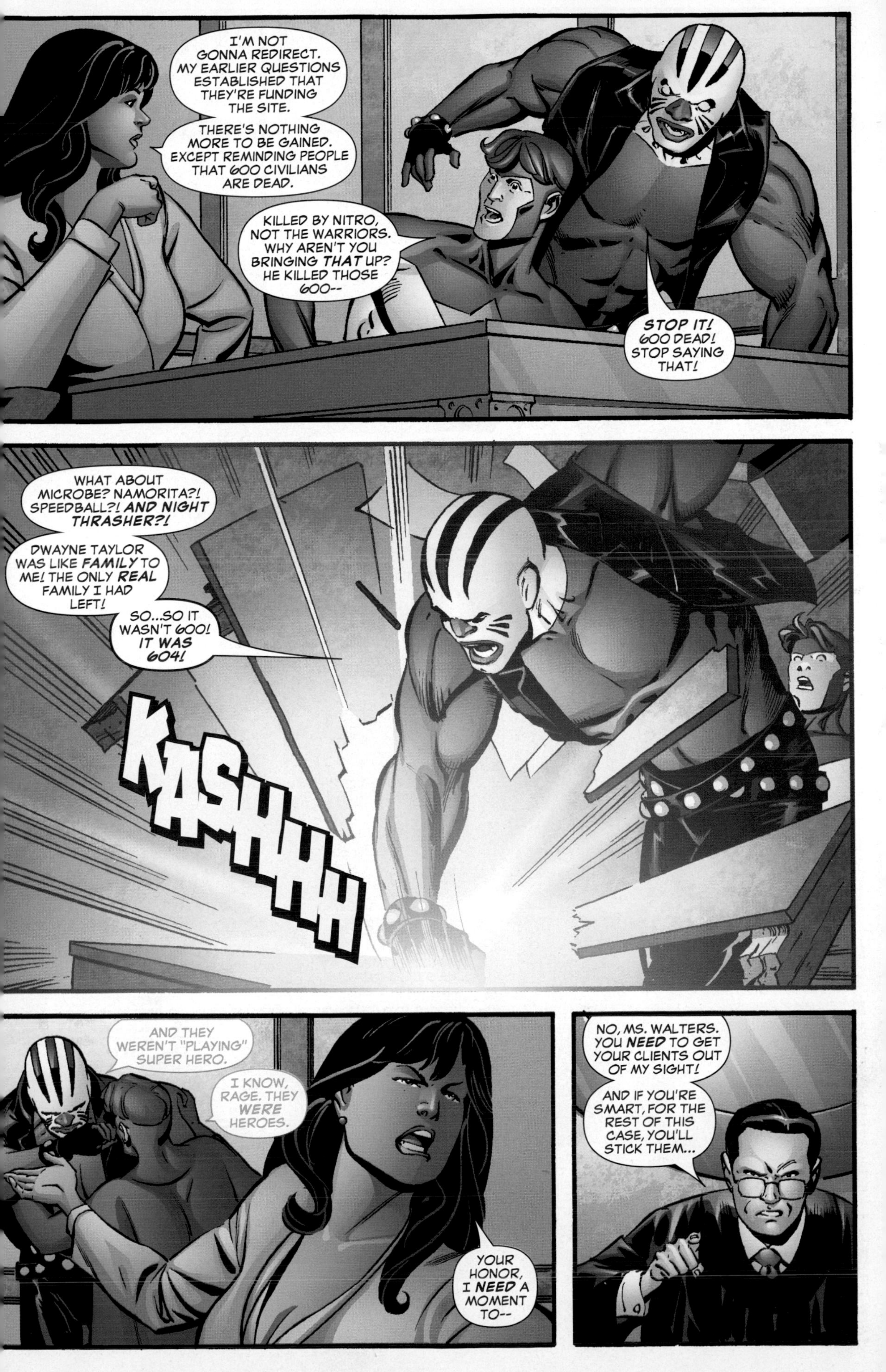
I'M NOT GONNA REDIRECT. MY EARLIER QUESTIONS ESTABLISHED THAT THEY'RE FUNDING THE SITE.
THERE'S NOTHING MORE TO BE GAINED. EXCEPT REMINDING PEOPLE THAT 600 CIVILIANS ARE DEAD.
KILLED BY NITRO, NOT THE WARRIORS. WHY AREN'T YOU BRINGING THAT UP? HE KILLED THOSE 600--
STOP IT! 600 DEAD! STOP SAYING THAT!
WHAT ABOUT MICROBE? NAMORITA?! SPEEDBALL?! AND NIGHT THRASHER?!
DWAYNE TAYLOR WAS LIKE FAMILY TO ME! THE ONLY REAL FAMILY I HAD LEFT!
SO...SO IT WASN'T 600! IT WAS 604!
KASHHHH
AND THEY WEREN'T "PLAYING" SUPER HERO.
I KNOW, RAGE. THEY WERE HEROES.
YOUR HONOR, I NEED A MOMENT TO--
NO, MS. WALTERS. YOU NEED TO GET YOUR CLIENTS OUT OF MY SIGHT!
AND IF YOU'RE SMART, FOR THE REST OF THIS CASE, YOU'LL STICK THEM...

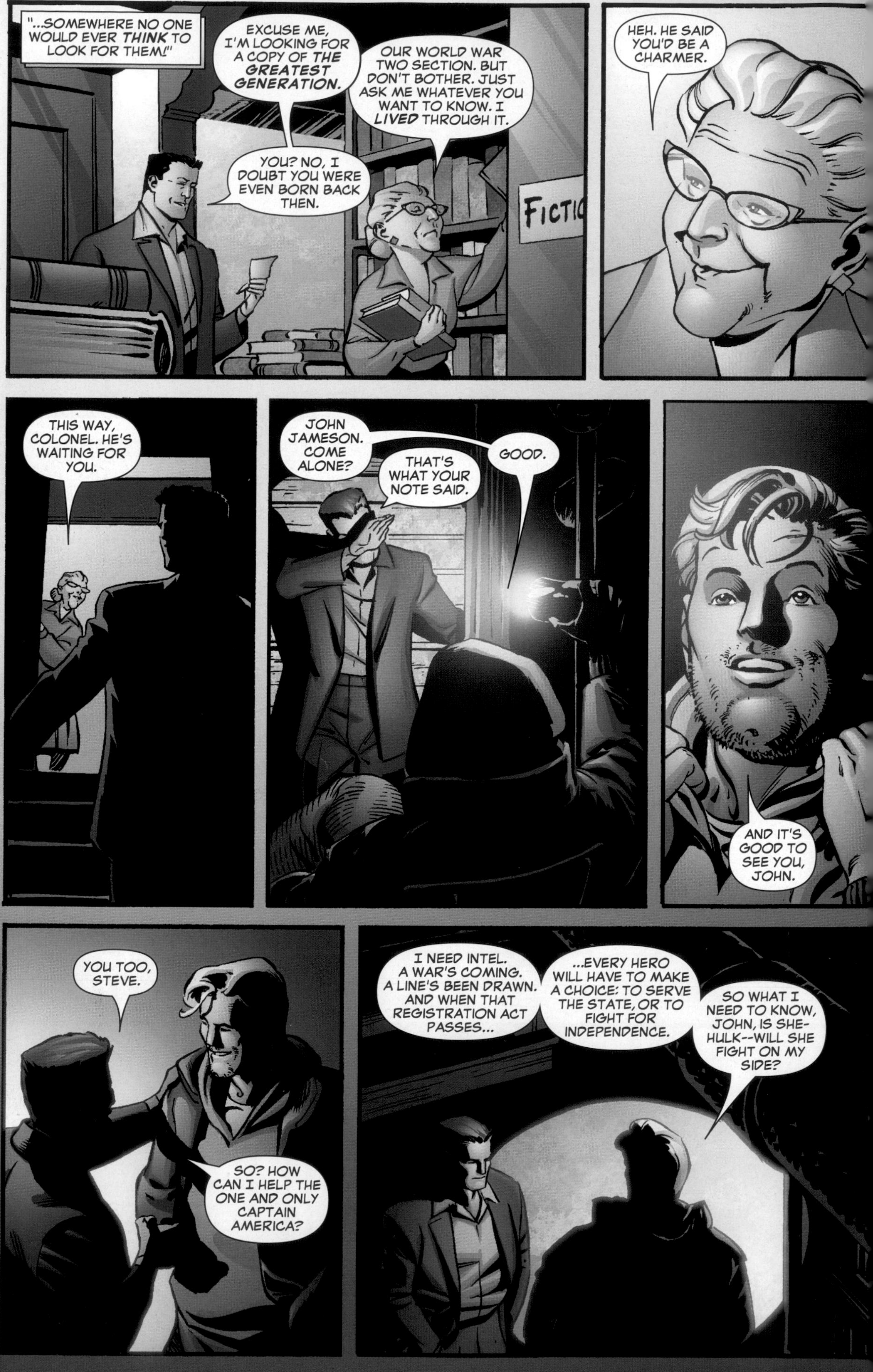
"...SOMEWHERE NO ONE WOULD EVER THINK TO LOOK FOR THEM!"
EXCUSE ME, I'M LOOKING FOR A COPY OF THE GREATEST GENERATION.
OUR WORLD WAR TWO SECTION. BUT DON'T BOTHER. JUST ASK ME WHATEVER YOU WANT TO KNOW. I LIVED THROUGH IT.
YOU? NO, I DOUBT YOU WERE EVEN BORN BACK THEN.
FICTI
HEH. HE SAID YOU'D BE A CHARMER.
THIS WAY, COLONEL. HE'S WAITING FOR YOU.
JOHN JAMESON. COME ALONE?
THAT'S WHAT YOUR NOTE SAID.
GOOD.
AND IT'S GOOD TO SEE YOU, JOHN.
YOU TOO, STEVE.
SO? HOW CAN I HELP THE ONE AND ONLY CAPTAIN AMERICA?
I NEED INTEL. A WAR'S COMING. A LINE'S BEEN DRAWN. AND WHEN THAT REGISTRATION ACT PASSES...
...EVERY HERO WILL HAVE TO MAKE A CHOICE: TO SERVE THE STATE, OR TO FIGHT FOR INDEPENDENCE.
SO WHAT I NEED TO KNOW, JOHN, IS SHE-HULK--WILL SHE FIGHT ON MY SIDE?

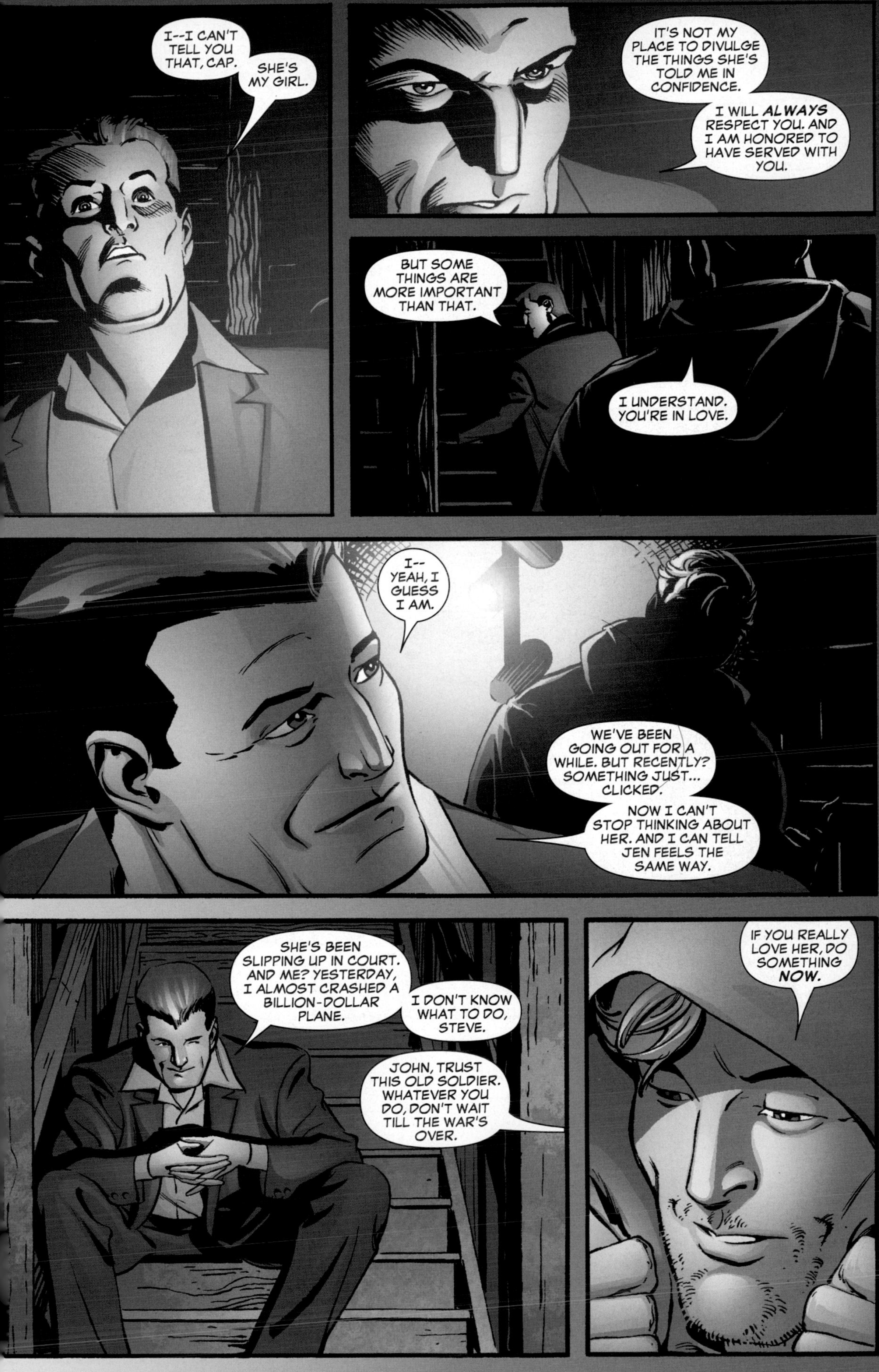
I--I CAN'T TELL YOU THAT, CAP.
SHE'S MY GIRL.
IT'S NOT MY PLACE TO DIVULGE THE THINGS SHE'S TOLD ME IN CONFIDENCE.
I WILL ALWAYS RESPECT YOU. AND I AM HONORED TO HAVE SERVED WITH YOU.
BUT SOME THINGS ARE MORE IMPORTANT THAN THAT.
I UNDERSTAND. YOU'RE IN LOVE.
I-- YEAH, I GUESS I AM.
WE'VE BEEN GOING OUT FOR A WHILE. BUT RECENTLY? SOMETHING JUST... CLICKED.
NOW I CAN'T STOP THINKING ABOUT HER. AND I CAN TELL JEN FEELS THE SAME WAY.
SHE'S BEEN SLIPPING UP IN COURT. AND ME? YESTERDAY, I ALMOST CRASHED A BILLION-DOLLAR PLANE.
I DON'T KNOW WHAT TO DO, STEVE.
JOHN, TRUST THIS OLD SOLDIER. WHATEVER YOU DO, DON'T WAIT TILL THE WAR'S OVER.
IF YOU REALLY LOVE HER, DO SOMETHING NOW.

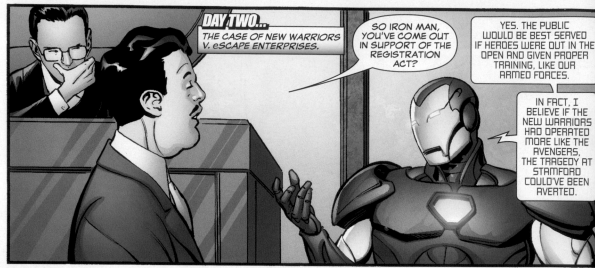

DAY TWO...
THE CASE OF NEW WARRIORS V. eSCAPE ENTERPRISES.

SO IRON MAN, YOU'VE COME OUT IN SUPPORT OF THE REGISTRATION ACT?

YES. THE PUBLIC WOULD BE BEST SERVED IF HEROES WERE OUT IN THE OPEN AND GIVEN PROPER TRAINING, LIKE OUR ARMED FORCES.

IN FACT, I BELIEVE IF THE NEW WARRIORS HAD OPERATED MORE LIKE THE AVENGERS, THE TRAGEDY AT STAMFORD COULD'VE BEEN AVERTED.

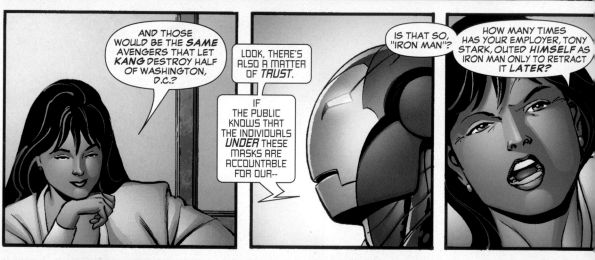

AND THOSE WOULD BE THE **SAME** AVENGERS THAT LET **KANG** DESTROY HALF OF WASHINGTON, D.C.?

LOOK, THERE'S ALSO A MATTER OF **TRUST.**

IF THE PUBLIC KNOWS THAT THE INDIVIDUALS **UNDER** THESE MASKS ARE ACCOUNTABLE FOR OUR--

IS THAT SO, "IRON MAN"?

HOW MANY TIMES HAS YOUR EMPLOYER, TONY STARK, OUTED **HIMSELF** AS IRON MAN ONLY TO RETRACT IT **LATER**?

IN FACT, I RECALL HE ONCE USED AN **ILLEGAL** SATELLITE TO BRAINWASH **ALL** OF EARTH INTO FORGETTING HIS SECRET!

DOES HE PLAN TO DO SOMETHING LIKE THAT **AGAIN** IF ALL OF THIS BLOWS UP IN HIS FACE?!

THAT'S ENOUGH! WE'RE TAKING A RECESS TILL YOU ALL SIMMER DOWN!

JENNIFER!

SMAK

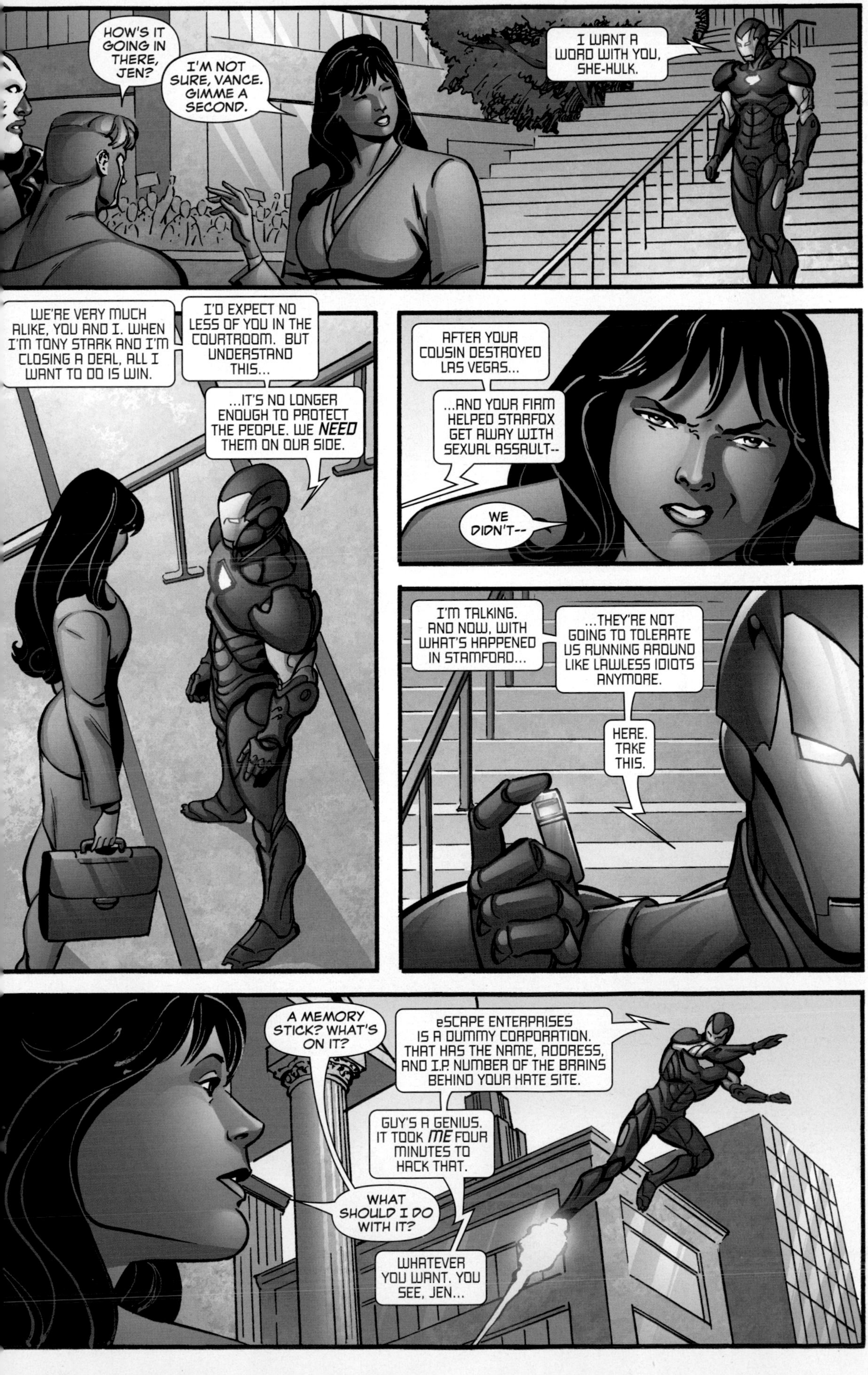
HOW'S IT GOING IN THERE, JEN?
I'M NOT SURE, VANCE. GIMME A SECOND.
I WANT A WORD WITH YOU, SHE-HULK.
WE'RE VERY MUCH ALIKE, YOU AND I. WHEN I'M TONY STARK AND I'M CLOSING A DEAL, ALL I WANT TO DO IS WIN.
I'D EXPECT NO LESS OF YOU IN THE COURTROOM. BUT UNDERSTAND THIS...
...IT'S NO LONGER ENOUGH TO PROTECT THE PEOPLE. WE NEED THEM ON OUR SIDE.
AFTER YOUR COUSIN DESTROYED LAS VEGAS...
...AND YOUR FIRM HELPED STARFOX GET AWAY WITH SEXUAL ASSAULT--
WE DIDN'T--
I'M TALKING. AND NOW, WITH WHAT'S HAPPENED IN STAMFORD...
...THEY'RE NOT GOING TO TOLERATE US RUNNING AROUND LIKE LAWLESS IDIOTS ANYMORE.
HERE. TAKE THIS.
A MEMORY STICK? WHAT'S ON IT?
eSCAPE ENTERPRISES IS A DUMMY CORPORATION. THAT HAS THE NAME, ADDRESS, AND I.P. NUMBER OF THE BRAINS BEHIND YOUR HATE SITE.
GUY'S A GENIUS. IT TOOK ME FOUR MINUTES TO HACK THAT.
WHAT SHOULD I DO WITH IT?
WHATEVER YOU WANT. YOU SEE, JEN...

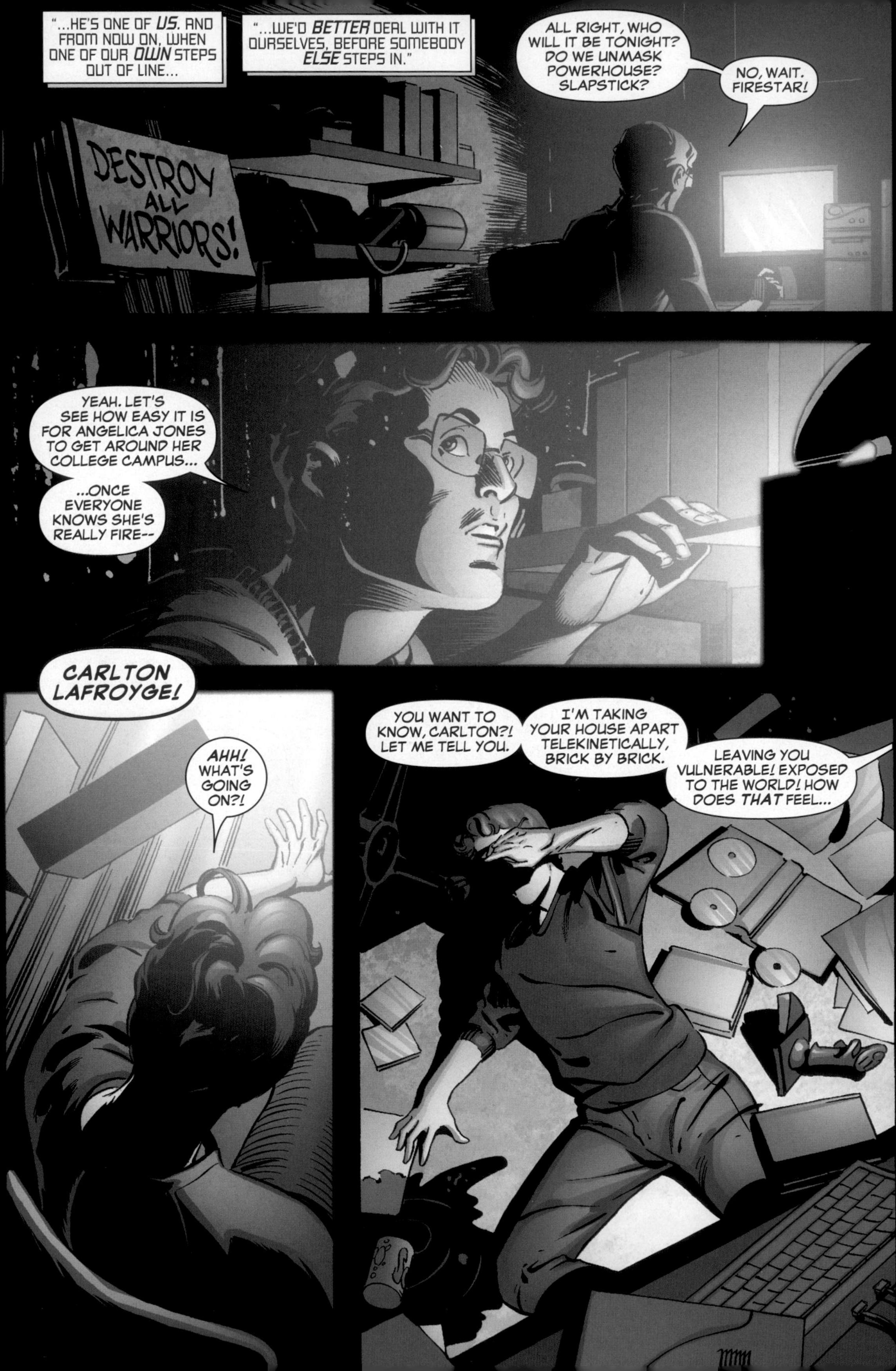
"...HE'S ONE OF US. AND FROM NOW ON, WHEN ONE OF OUR OWN STEPS OUT OF LINE...
"...WE'D BETTER DEAL WITH IT OURSELVES, BEFORE SOMEBODY ELSE STEPS IN."
DESTROY ALL WARRIORS!
ALL RIGHT, WHO WILL IT BE TONIGHT? DO WE UNMASK POWERHOUSE? SLAPSTICK?
NO, WAIT. FIRESTAR!
YEAH. LET'S SEE HOW EASY IT IS FOR ANGELICA JONES TO GET AROUND HER COLLEGE CAMPUS...
...ONCE EVERYONE KNOWS SHE'S REALLY FIRE--
CARLTON LAFROYGE!
AHH! WHAT'S GOING ON?!
YOU WANT TO KNOW, CARLTON?! LET ME TELL YOU.
I'M TAKING YOUR HOUSE APART TELEKINETICALLY, BRICK BY BRICK.
LEAVING YOU VULNERABLE! EXPOSED TO THE WORLD! HOW DOES THAT FEEL...

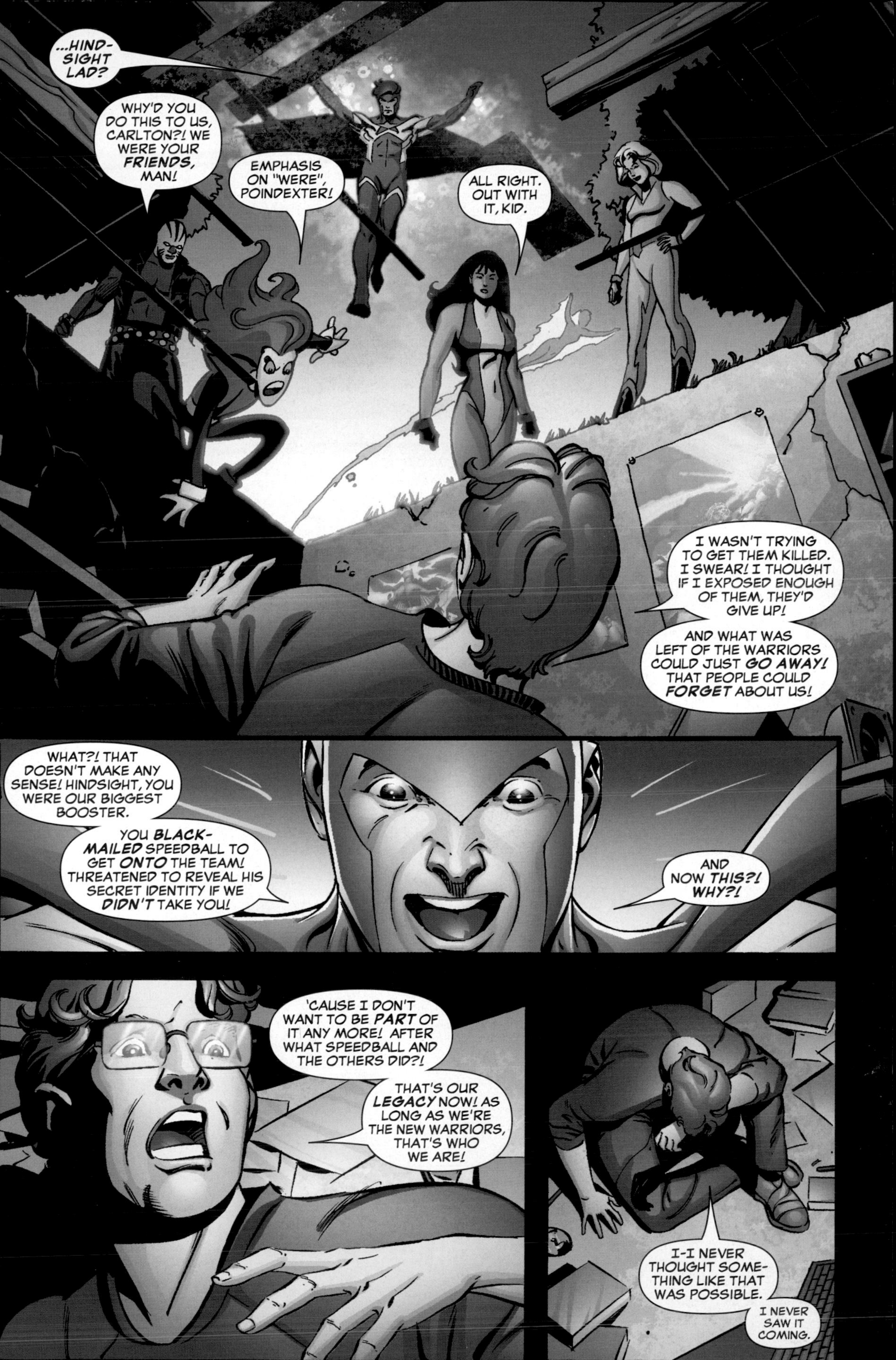
...HIND-SIGHT LAD?
WHY'D YOU DO THIS TO US, CARLTON?! WE WERE YOUR **FRIENDS**, MAN!
EMPHASIS ON "WERE", POINDEXTER!
ALL RIGHT. OUT WITH IT, KID.
I WASN'T TRYING TO GET THEM KILLED. I SWEAR! I THOUGHT IF I EXPOSED ENOUGH OF THEM, THEY'D GIVE UP!
AND WHAT WAS LEFT OF THE WARRIORS COULD JUST **GO AWAY!** THAT PEOPLE COULD **FORGET** ABOUT US!
WHAT?! THAT DOESN'T MAKE ANY SENSE! HINDSIGHT, YOU WERE OUR BIGGEST BOOSTER.
YOU **BLACK-MAILED** SPEEDBALL TO GET **ONTO** THE TEAM! THREATENED TO REVEAL HIS SECRET IDENTITY IF WE **DIDN'T** TAKE YOU!
AND NOW **THIS?! WHY?!**
'CAUSE I DON'T WANT TO BE **PART** OF IT ANY MORE! AFTER WHAT SPEEDBALL AND THE OTHERS DID?!
THAT'S OUR **LEGACY** NOW! AS LONG AS WE'RE THE NEW WARRIORS, THAT'S WHO WE ARE!
I-I NEVER THOUGHT SOME-THING LIKE THAT WAS POSSIBLE.
I NEVER SAW IT COMING.

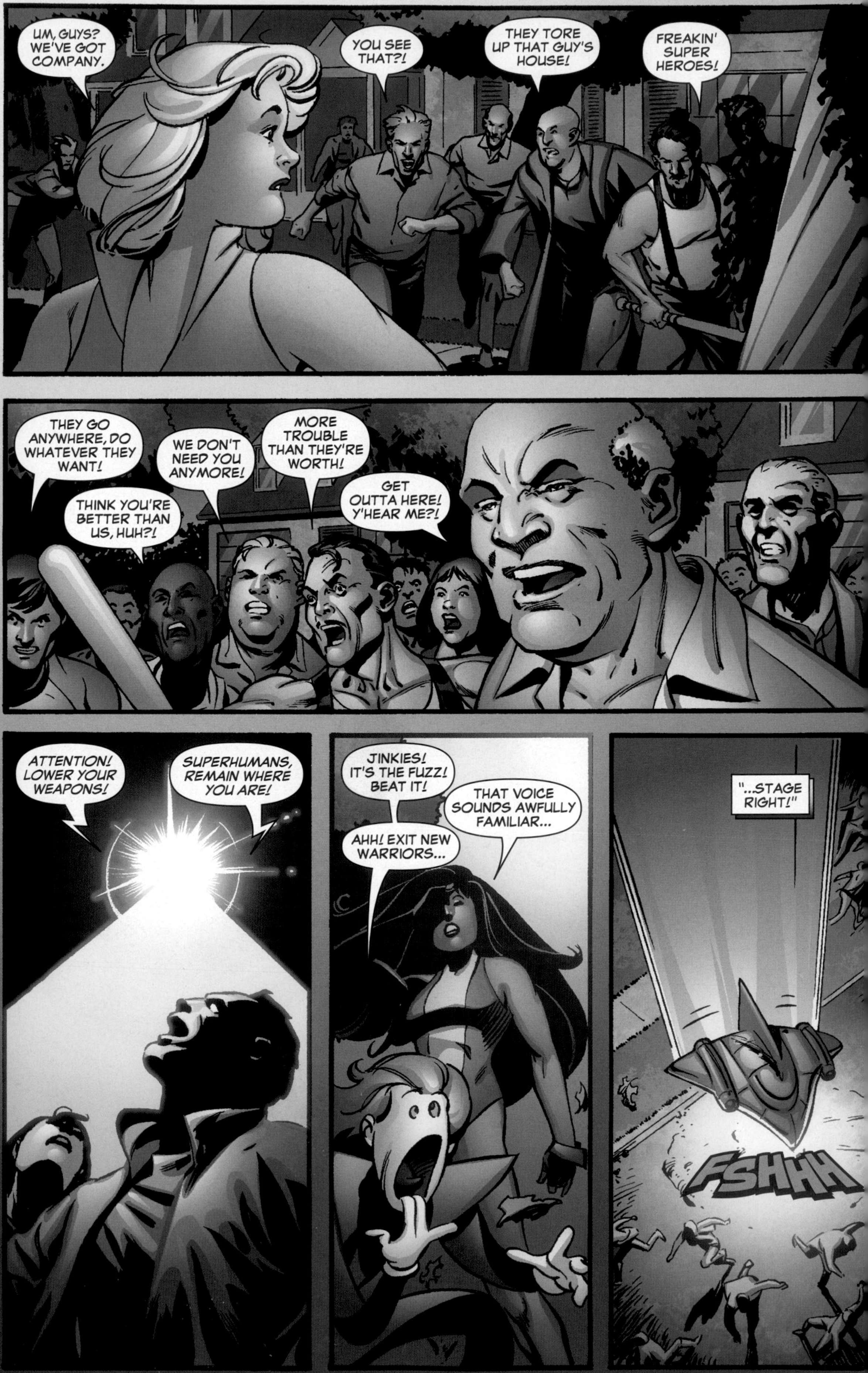
UM, GUYS? WE'VE GOT COMPANY.
YOU SEE THAT?!
THEY TORE UP THAT GUY'S HOUSE!
FREAKIN' SUPER HEROES!
THEY GO ANYWHERE, DO WHATEVER THEY WANT!
THINK YOU'RE BETTER THAN US, HUH?!
WE DON'T NEED YOU ANYMORE!
MORE TROUBLE THAN THEY'RE WORTH!
GET OUTTA HERE! Y'HEAR ME?!
ATTENTION! LOWER YOUR WEAPONS!
SUPERHUMANS, REMAIN WHERE YOU ARE!
JINKIES! IT'S THE FUZZ! BEAT IT!
AHH! EXIT NEW WARRIORS...
THAT VOICE SOUNDS AWFULLY FAMILIAR...
"...STAGE RIGHT!"
FSHHH

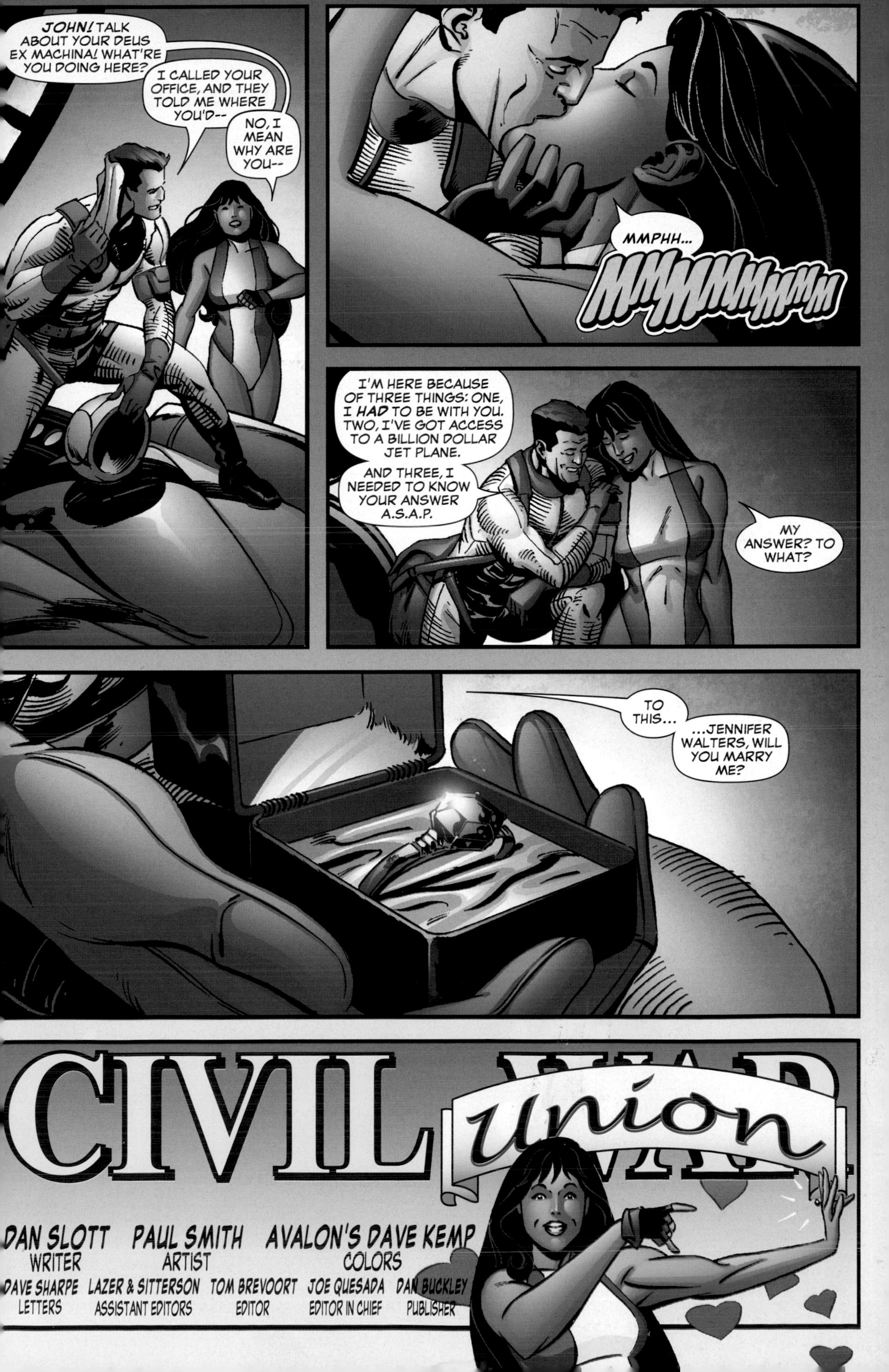

JOHN! TALK ABOUT YOUR DEUS EX MACHINA! WHAT'RE YOU DOING HERE?
I CALLED YOUR OFFICE, AND THEY TOLD ME WHERE YOU'D--
NO, I MEAN WHY ARE YOU--
MMPHH...
MMMMMMMMMM
I'M HERE BECAUSE OF THREE THINGS: ONE, I HAD TO BE WITH YOU. TWO, I'VE GOT ACCESS TO A BILLION DOLLAR JET PLANE.
AND THREE, I NEEDED TO KNOW YOUR ANSWER A.S.A.P.
MY ANSWER? TO WHAT?
TO THIS...
...JENNIFER WALTERS, WILL YOU MARRY ME?
CIVIL WAR union
DAN SLOTT WRITER
PAUL SMITH ARTIST
AVALON'S DAVE KEMP COLORS
DAVE SHARPE LETTERS
LAZER & SITTERSON ASSISTANT EDITORS
TOM BREVOORT EDITOR
JOE QUESADA EDITOR IN CHIEF
DAN BUCKLEY PUBLISHER

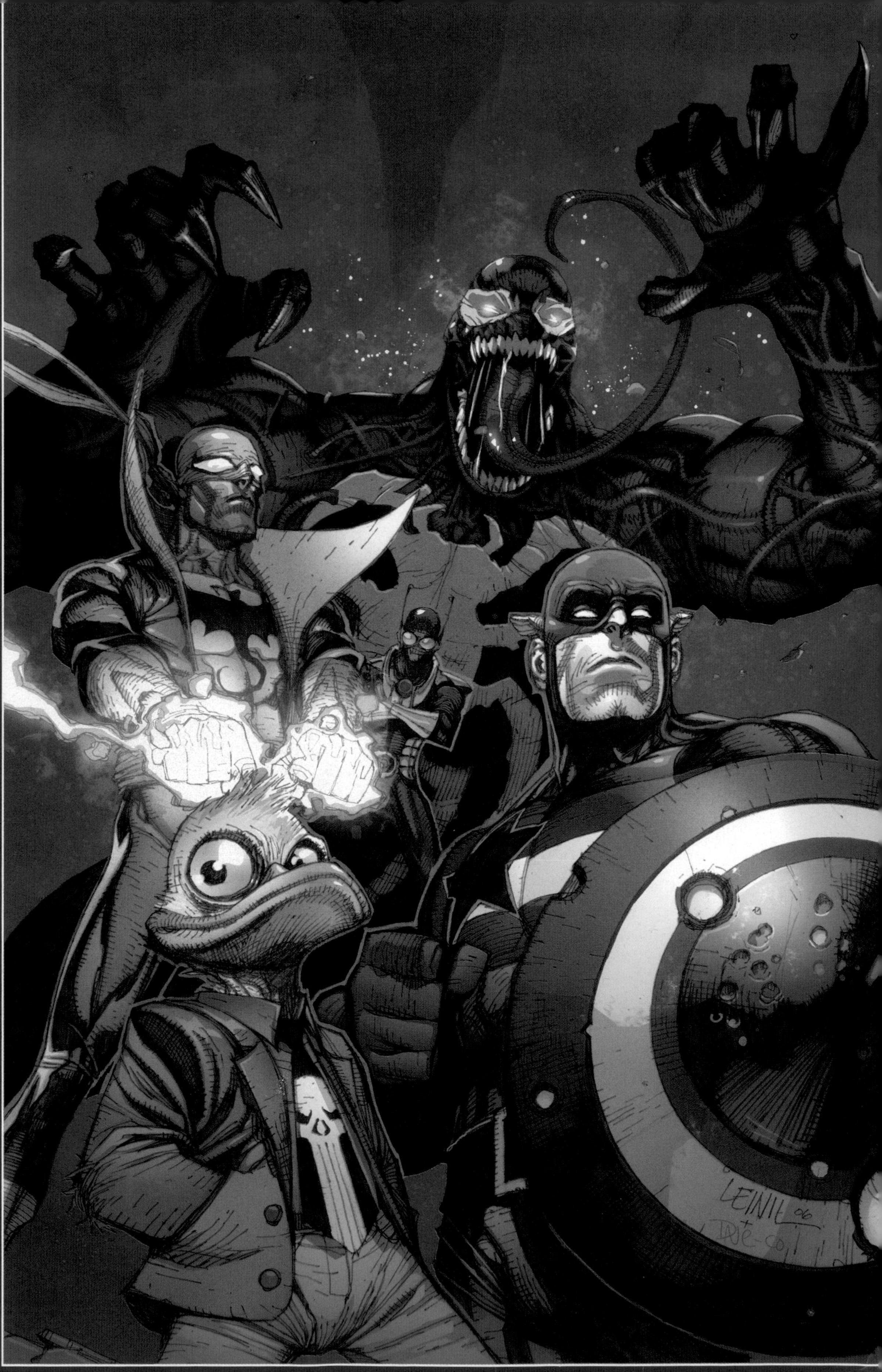

CIVIL WAR: CHOOSING SIDES

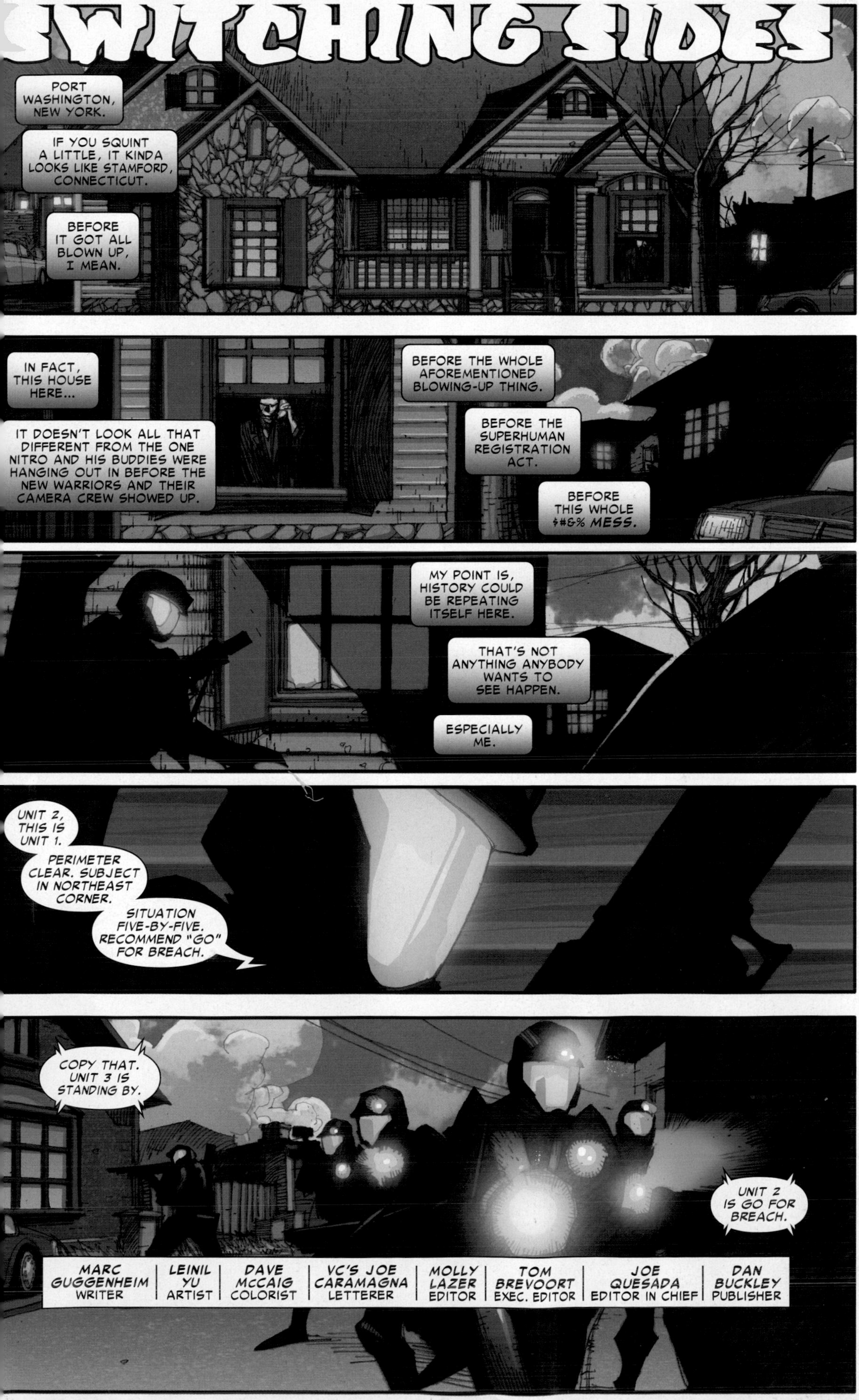
SWITCHING SIDES
PORT WASHINGTON, NEW YORK.
IF YOU SQUINT A LITTLE, IT KINDA LOOKS LIKE STAMFORD, CONNECTICUT.
BEFORE IT GOT ALL BLOWN UP, I MEAN.
IN FACT, THIS HOUSE HERE...
IT DOESN'T LOOK ALL THAT DIFFERENT FROM THE ONE NITRO AND HIS BUDDIES WERE HANGING OUT IN BEFORE THE NEW WARRIORS AND THEIR CAMERA CREW SHOWED UP.
BEFORE THE WHOLE AFOREMENTIONED BLOWING-UP THING.
BEFORE THE SUPERHUMAN REGISTRATION ACT.
BEFORE THIS WHOLE $#&% MESS.
MY POINT IS, HISTORY COULD BE REPEATING ITSELF HERE.
THAT'S NOT ANYTHING ANYBODY WANTS TO SEE HAPPEN.
ESPECIALLY ME.
UNIT 2, THIS IS UNIT 1.
PERIMETER CLEAR. SUBJECT IN NORTHEAST CORNER.
SITUATION FIVE-BY-FIVE. RECOMMEND "GO" FOR BREACH.
COPY THAT. UNIT 3 IS STANDING BY.
UNIT 2 IS GO FOR BREACH.
MARC GUGGENHEIM WRITER | LEINIL YU ARTIST | DAVE McCAIG COLORIST | VC'S JOE CARAMAGNA LETTERER | MOLLY LAZER EDITOR | TOM BREVOORT EXEC. EDITOR | JOE QUESADA EDITOR IN CHIEF | DAN BUCKLEY PUBLISHER

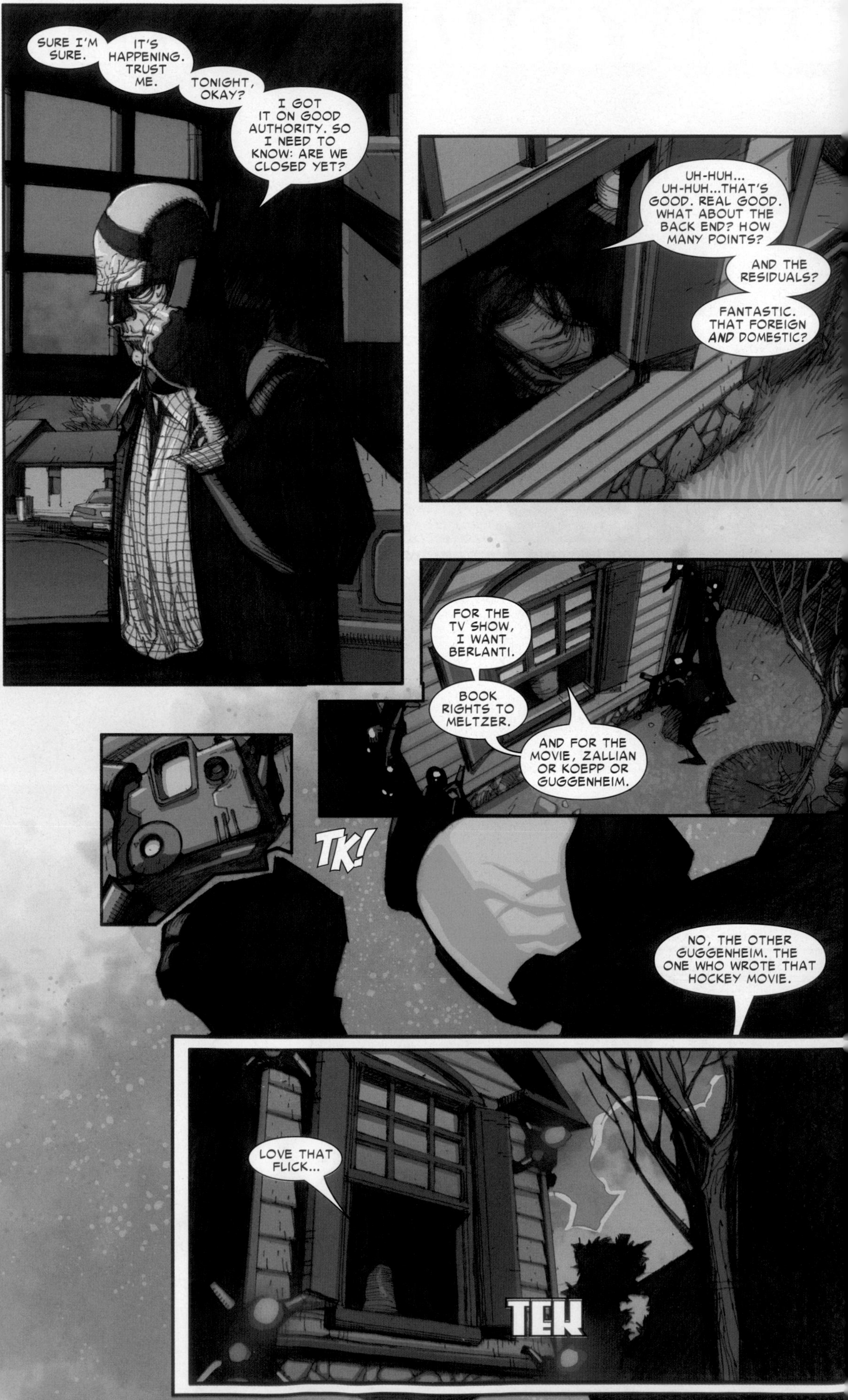
SURE I'M SURE.
IT'S HAPPENING. TRUST ME.
TONIGHT, OKAY?
I GOT IT ON GOOD AUTHORITY. SO I NEED TO KNOW: ARE WE CLOSED YET?
UH-HUH... UH-HUH...THAT'S GOOD. REAL GOOD. WHAT ABOUT THE BACK END? HOW MANY POINTS?
AND THE RESIDUALS?
FANTASTIC. THAT FOREIGN AND DOMESTIC?
FOR THE TV SHOW, I WANT BERLANTI.
BOOK RIGHTS TO MELTZER.
AND FOR THE MOVIE, ZALLIAN OR KOEPP OR GUGGENHEIM.
TK!
NO, THE OTHER GUGGENHEIM. THE ONE WHO WROTE THAT HOCKEY MOVIE.
LOVE THAT FLICK...
TEK

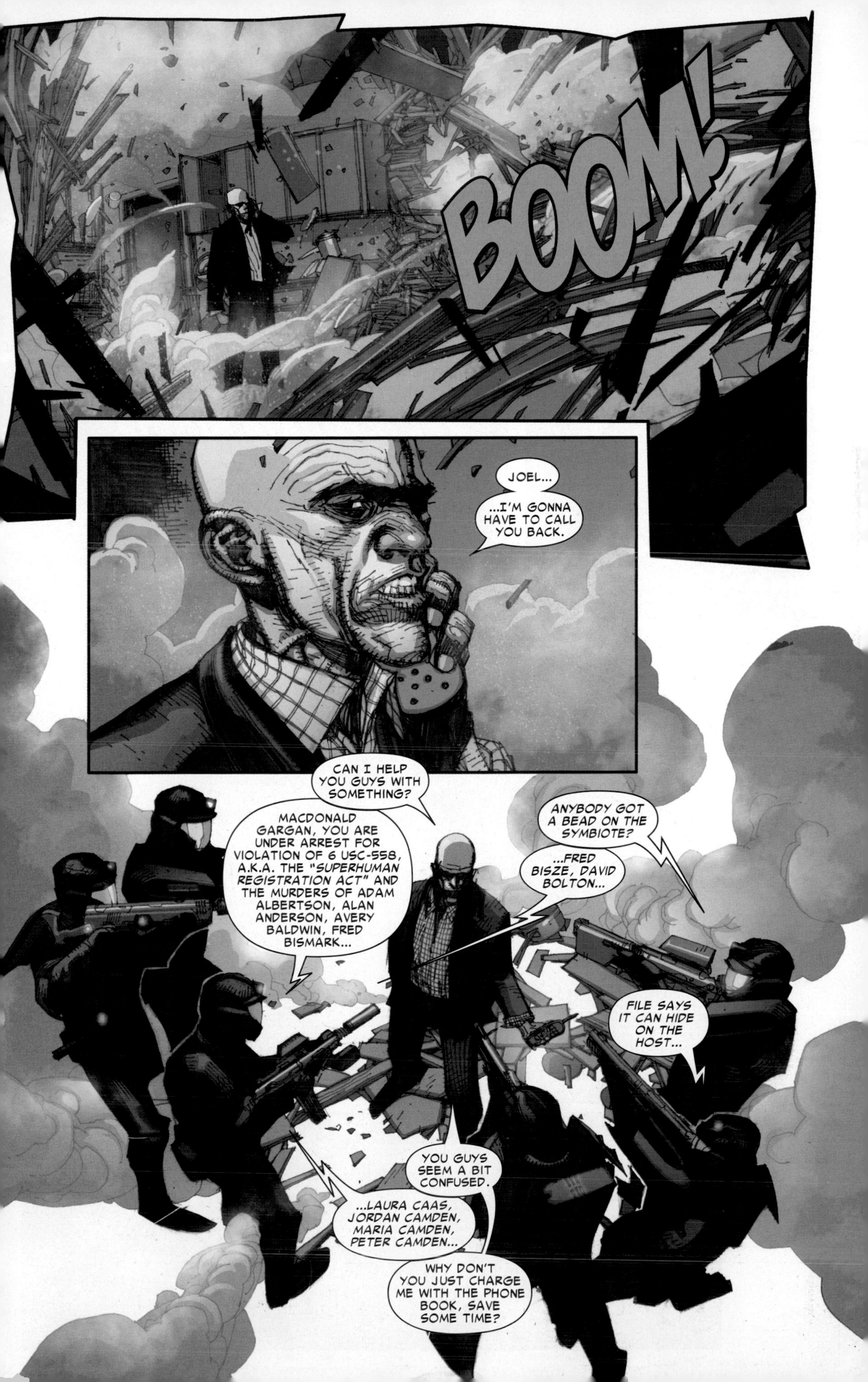
BOOM!
JOEL...
...I'M GONNA HAVE TO CALL YOU BACK.
CAN I HELP YOU GUYS WITH SOMETHING?
MACDONALD GARGAN, YOU ARE UNDER ARREST FOR VIOLATION OF 6 USC-558, A.K.A. THE "SUPERHUMAN REGISTRATION ACT" AND THE MURDERS OF ADAM ALBERTSON, ALAN ANDERSON, AVERY BALDWIN, FRED BISMARK...
ANYBODY GOT A BEAD ON THE SYMBIOTE?
...FRED BISZE, DAVID BOLTON...
FILE SAYS IT CAN HIDE ON THE HOST...
YOU GUYS SEEM A BIT CONFUSED.
...LAURA CAAS, JORDAN CAMDEN, MARIA CAMDEN, PETER CAMDEN...
WHY DON'T YOU JUST CHARGE ME WITH THE PHONE BOOK, SAVE SOME TIME?

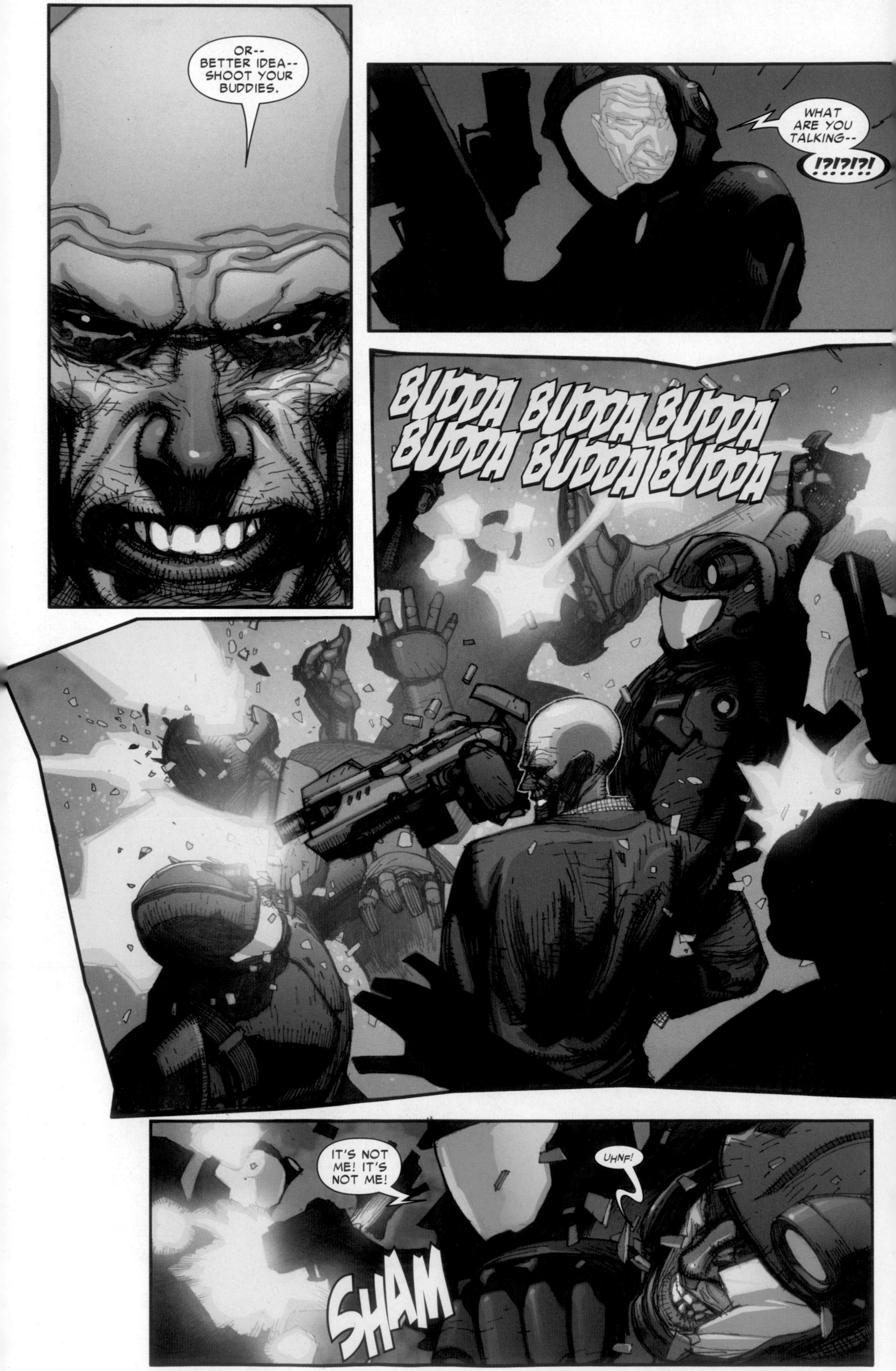
OR-- BETTER IDEA-- SHOOT YOUR BUDDIES.
WHAT ARE YOU TALKING--
!?!?!?!
BUDDA BUDDA BUDDA
BUDDA BUDDA BUDDA
IT'S NOT ME! IT'S NOT ME!
UHNF!
SHAM

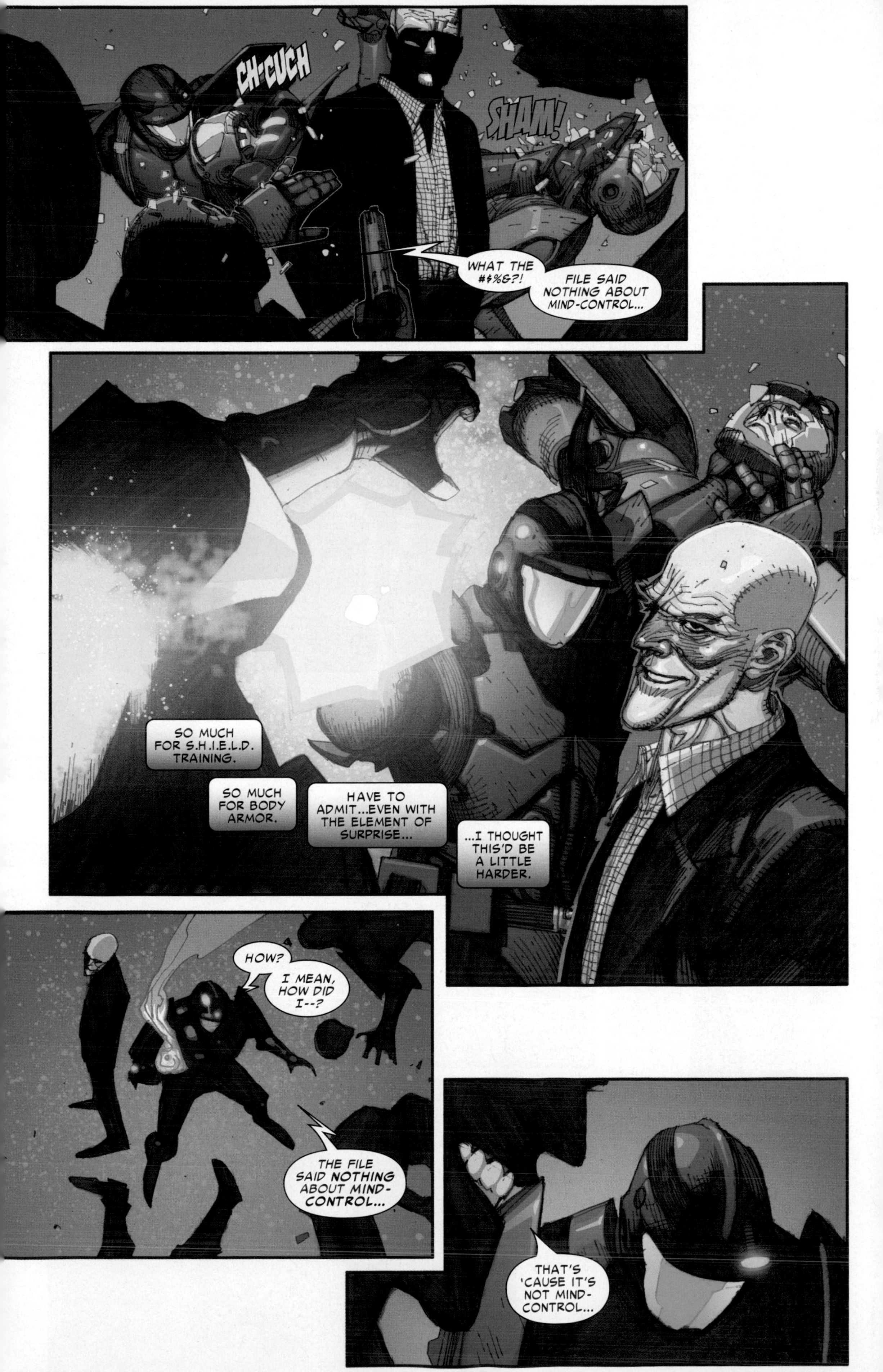
CH-CUCH
SHAM!
WHAT THE #$%&?!
FILE SAID NOTHING ABOUT MIND-CONTROL...
SO MUCH FOR S.H.I.E.L.D. TRAINING.
SO MUCH FOR BODY ARMOR.
HAVE TO ADMIT...EVEN WITH THE ELEMENT OF SURPRISE...
...I THOUGHT THIS'D BE A LITTLE HARDER.
HOW?
I MEAN, HOW DID I--?
THE FILE SAID NOTHING ABOUT MIND-CONTROL...
THAT'S 'CAUSE IT'S NOT MIND-CONTROL...

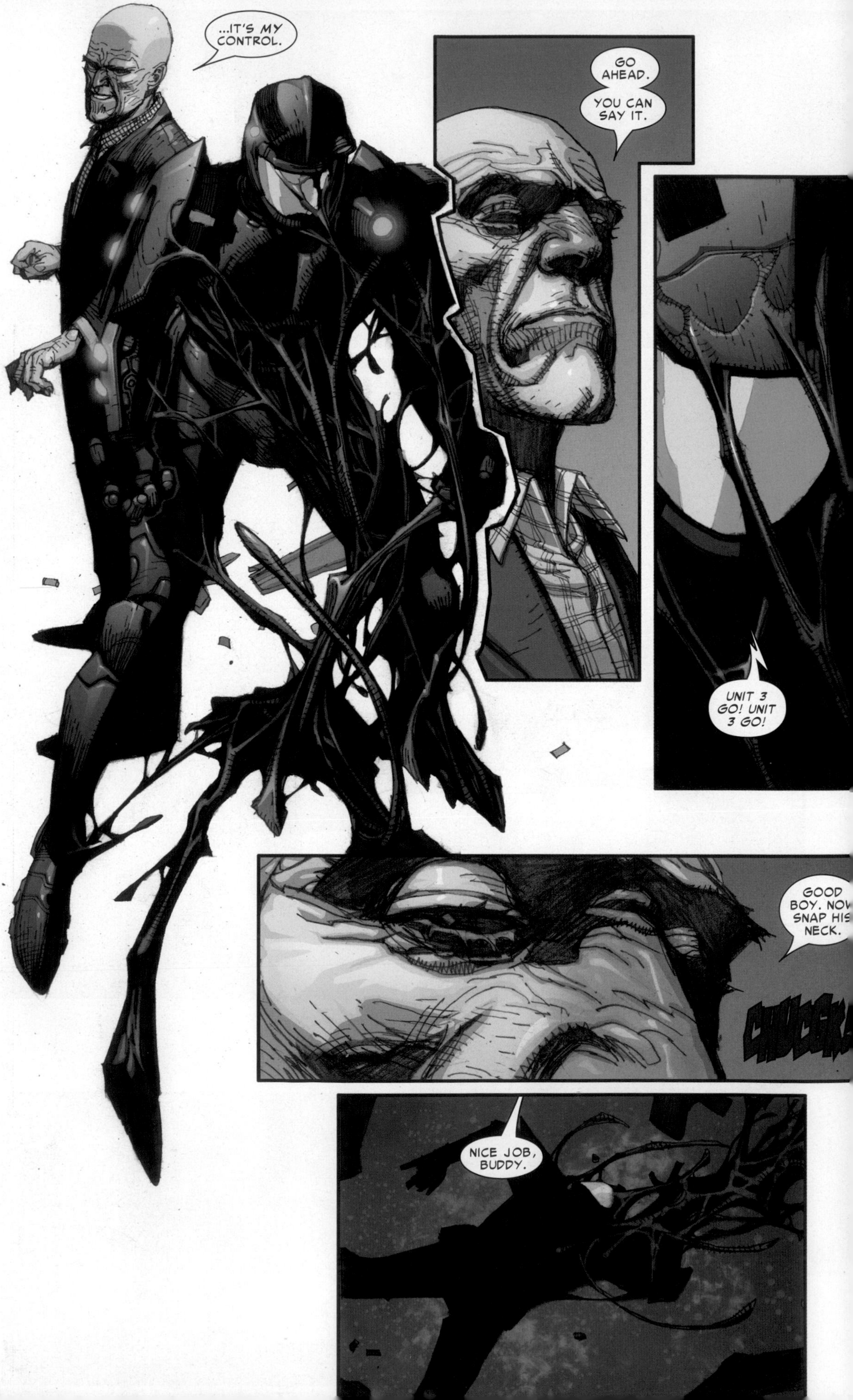
...IT'S MY CONTROL.
GO AHEAD.
YOU CAN SAY IT.
UNIT 3 GO! UNIT 3 GO!
GOOD BOY. NOW SNAP HIS NECK.
NICE JOB, BUDDY.

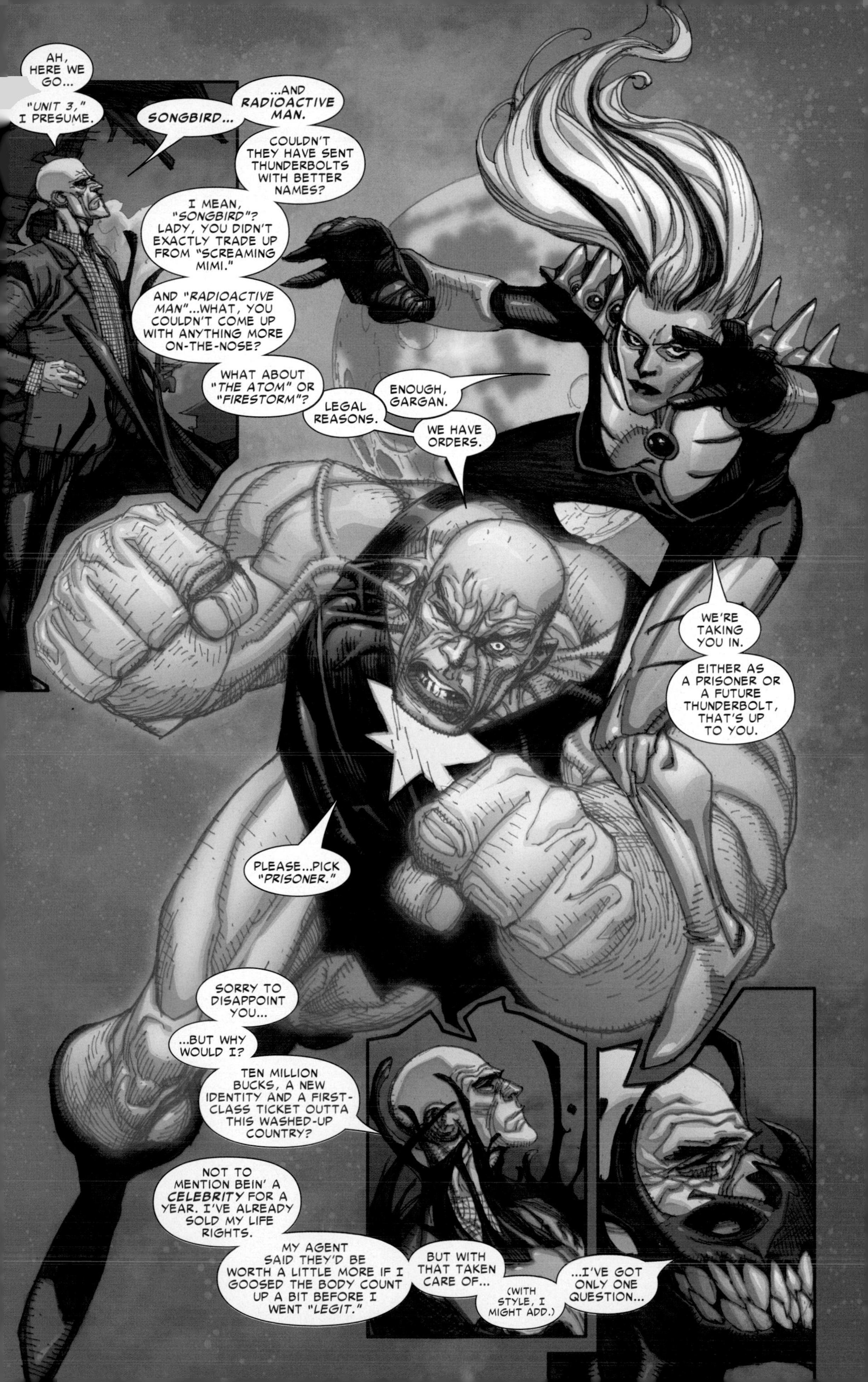

AH, HERE WE GO...
"UNIT 3," I PRESUME.
SONGBIRD...
...AND RADIOACTIVE MAN.
COULDN'T THEY HAVE SENT THUNDERBOLTS WITH BETTER NAMES?
I MEAN, "SONGBIRD"? LADY, YOU DIDN'T EXACTLY TRADE UP FROM "SCREAMING MIMI."
AND "RADIOACTIVE MAN"...WHAT, YOU COULDN'T COME UP WITH ANYTHING MORE ON-THE-NOSE?
WHAT ABOUT "THE ATOM" OR "FIRESTORM"?
LEGAL REASONS.
ENOUGH, GARGAN.
WE HAVE ORDERS.
WE'RE TAKING YOU IN.
EITHER AS A PRISONER OR A FUTURE THUNDERBOLT, THAT'S UP TO YOU.
PLEASE...PICK "PRISONER."
SORRY TO DISAPPOINT YOU...
...BUT WHY WOULD I?
TEN MILLION BUCKS, A NEW IDENTITY AND A FIRST-CLASS TICKET OUTTA THIS WASHED-UP COUNTRY?
NOT TO MENTION BEIN' A CELEBRITY FOR A YEAR. I'VE ALREADY SOLD MY LIFE RIGHTS.
MY AGENT SAID THEY'D BE WORTH A LITTLE MORE IF I GOOSED THE BODY COUNT UP A BIT BEFORE I WENT "LEGIT."
BUT WITH THAT TAKEN CARE OF...
(WITH STYLE, I MIGHT ADD.)
...I'VE GOT ONLY ONE QUESTION...

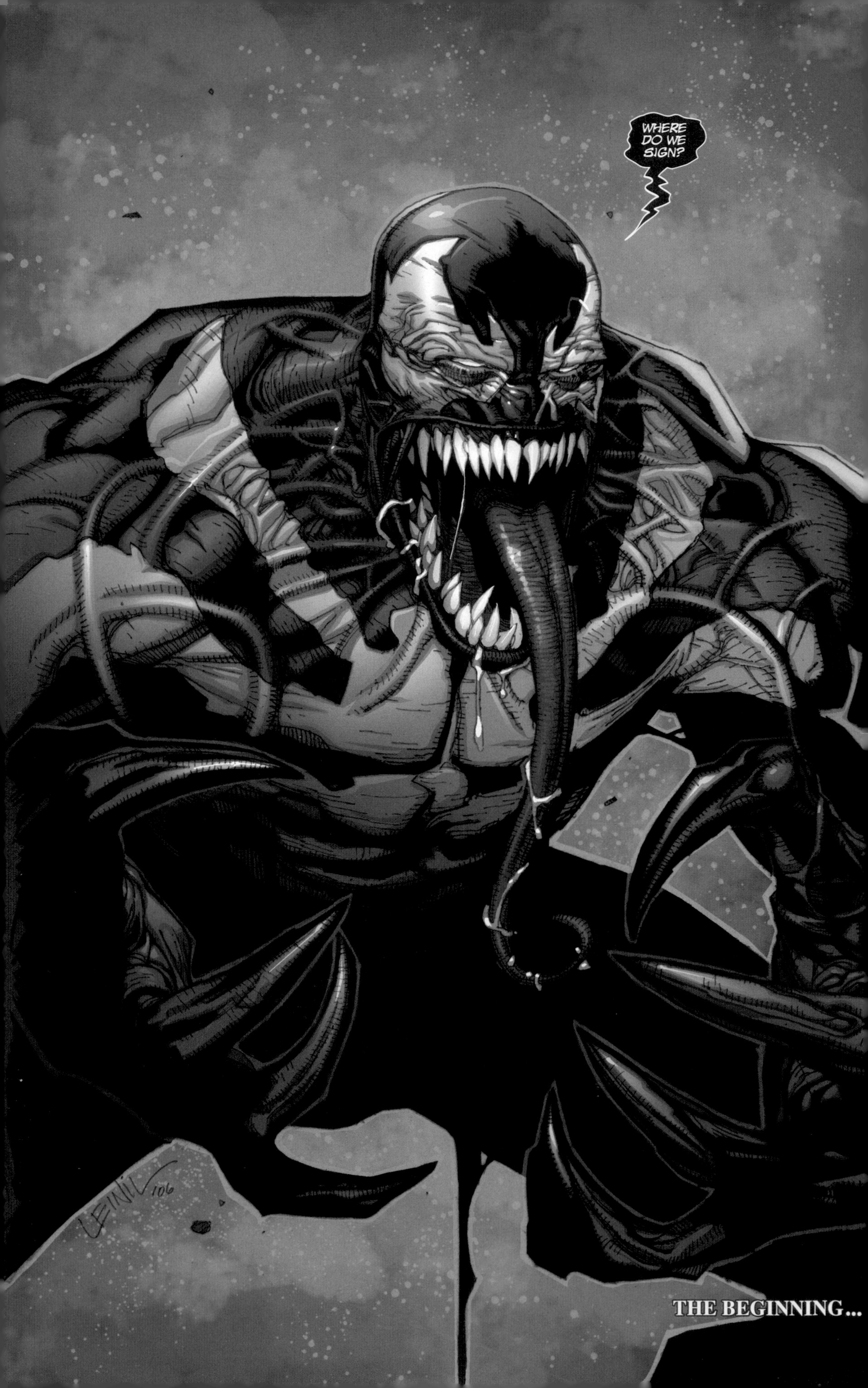
WHERE DO WE SIGN?
THE BEGINNING...

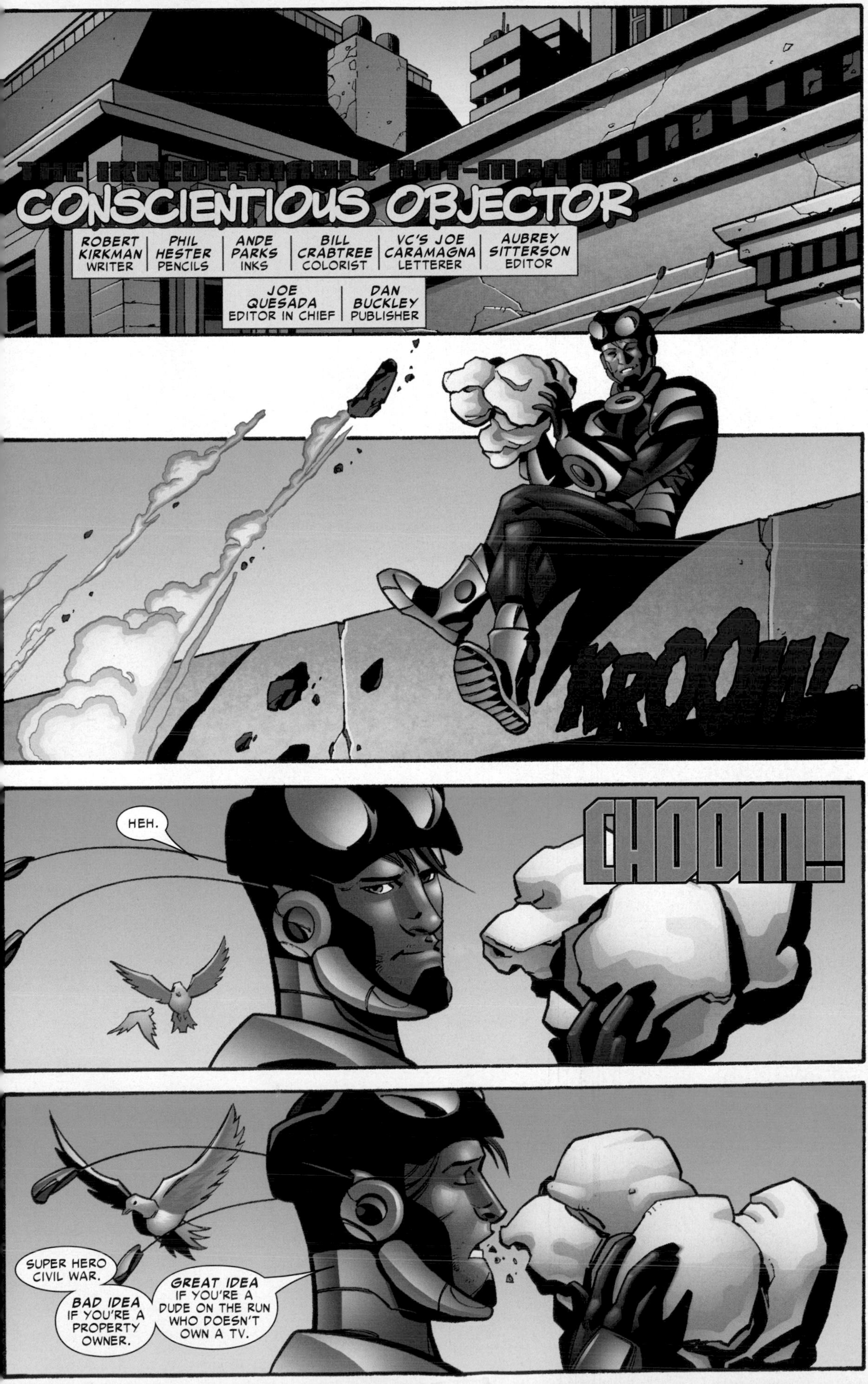
THE IRREDEEMABLE ANT-MAN IN:
CONSCIENTIOUS OBJECTOR
ROBERT KIRKMAN WRITER
PHIL HESTER PENCILS
ANDE PARKS INKS
BILL CRABTREE COLORIST
VC'S JOE CARAMAGNA LETTERER
AUBREY SITTERSON EDITOR
JOE QUESADA EDITOR IN CHIEF
DAN BUCKLEY PUBLISHER
KROOM!!
HEH.
CHOOM!!
SUPER HERO CIVIL WAR.
BAD IDEA IF YOU'RE A PROPERTY OWNER.
GREAT IDEA IF YOU'RE A DUDE ON THE RUN WHO DOESN'T OWN A TV.

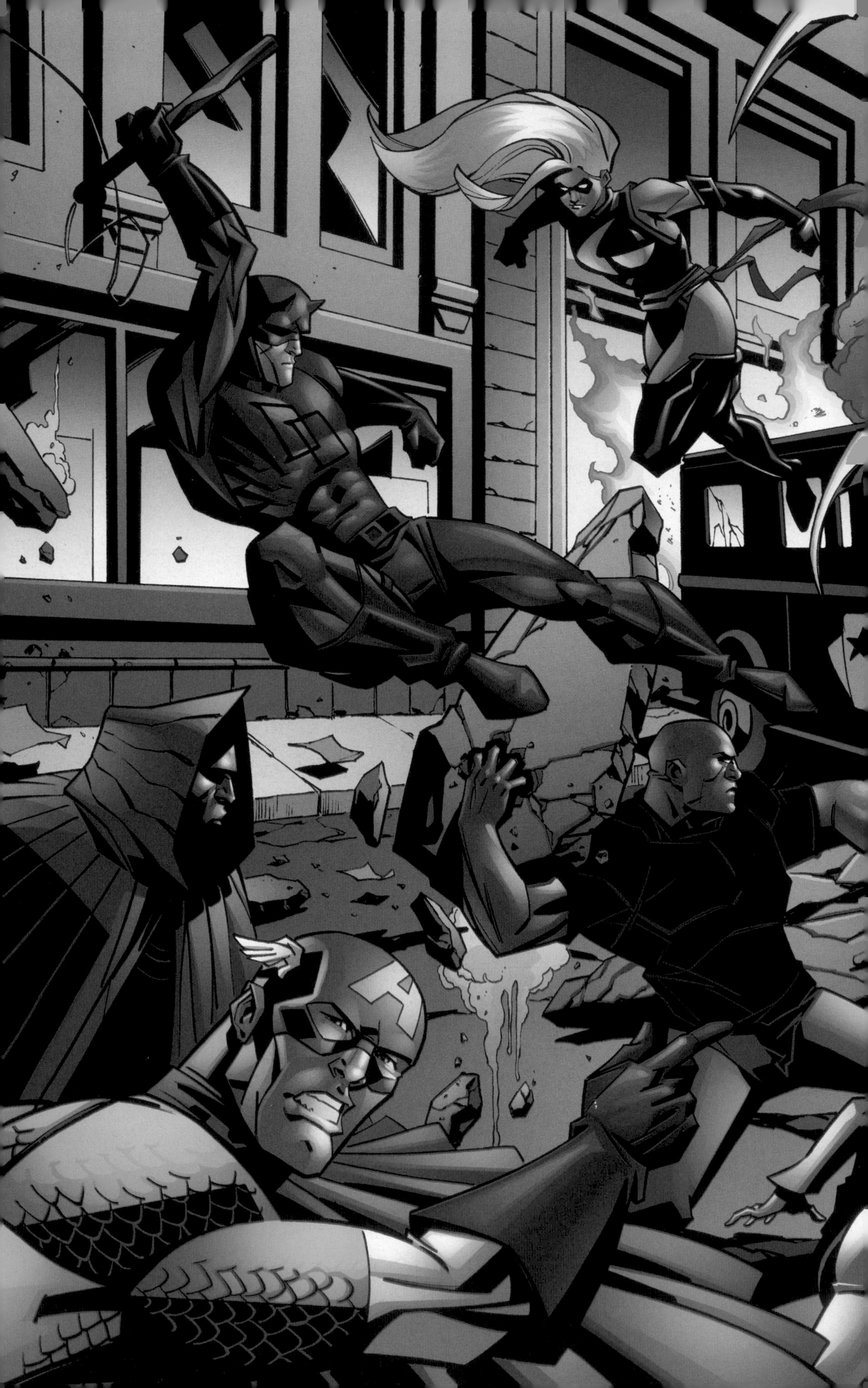

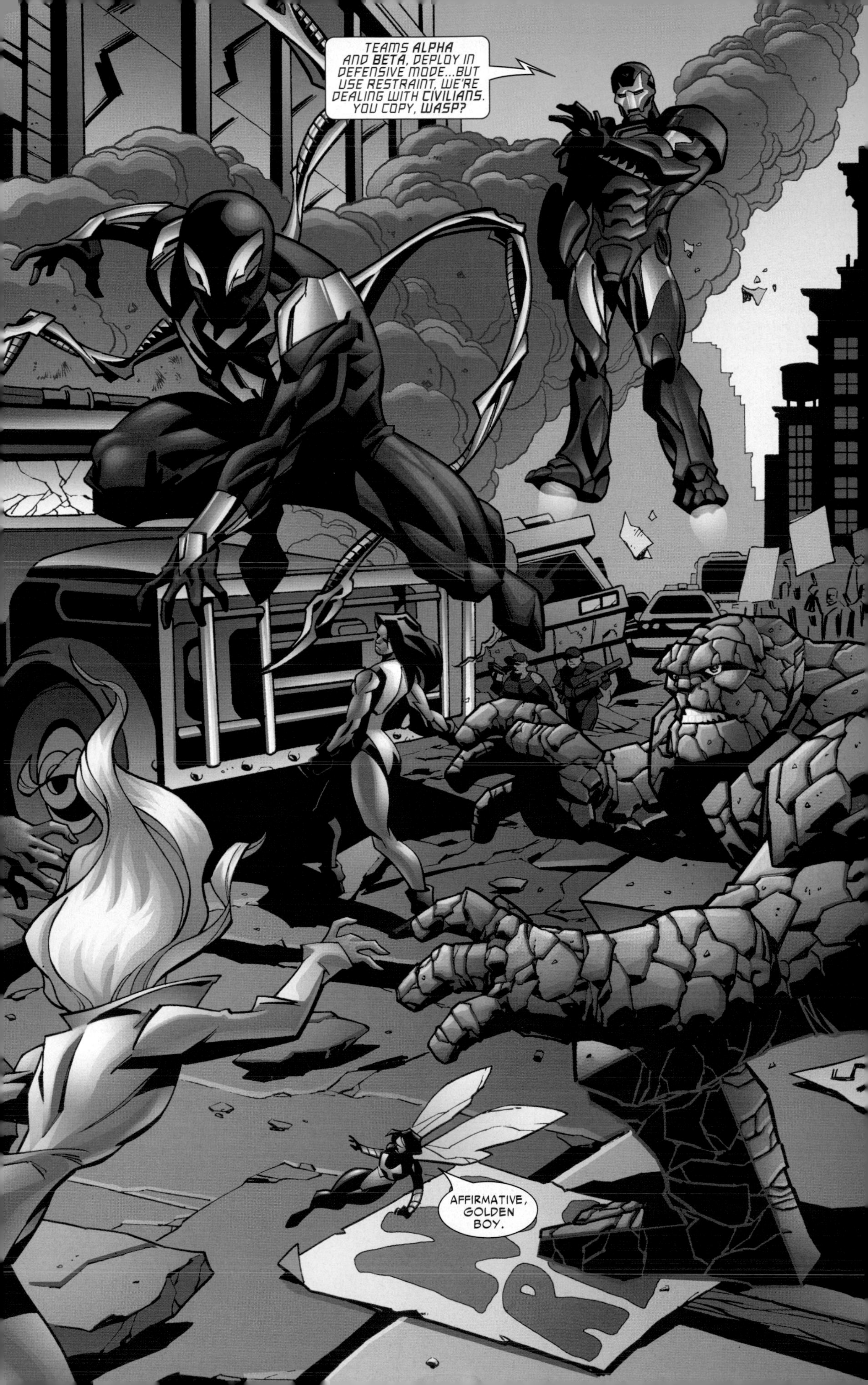
TEAMS ALPHA AND BETA, DEPLOY IN DEFENSIVE MODE...BUT USE RESTRAINT. WE'RE DEALING WITH CIVILIANS. YOU COPY, WASP?
AFFIRMATIVE, GOLDEN BOY.

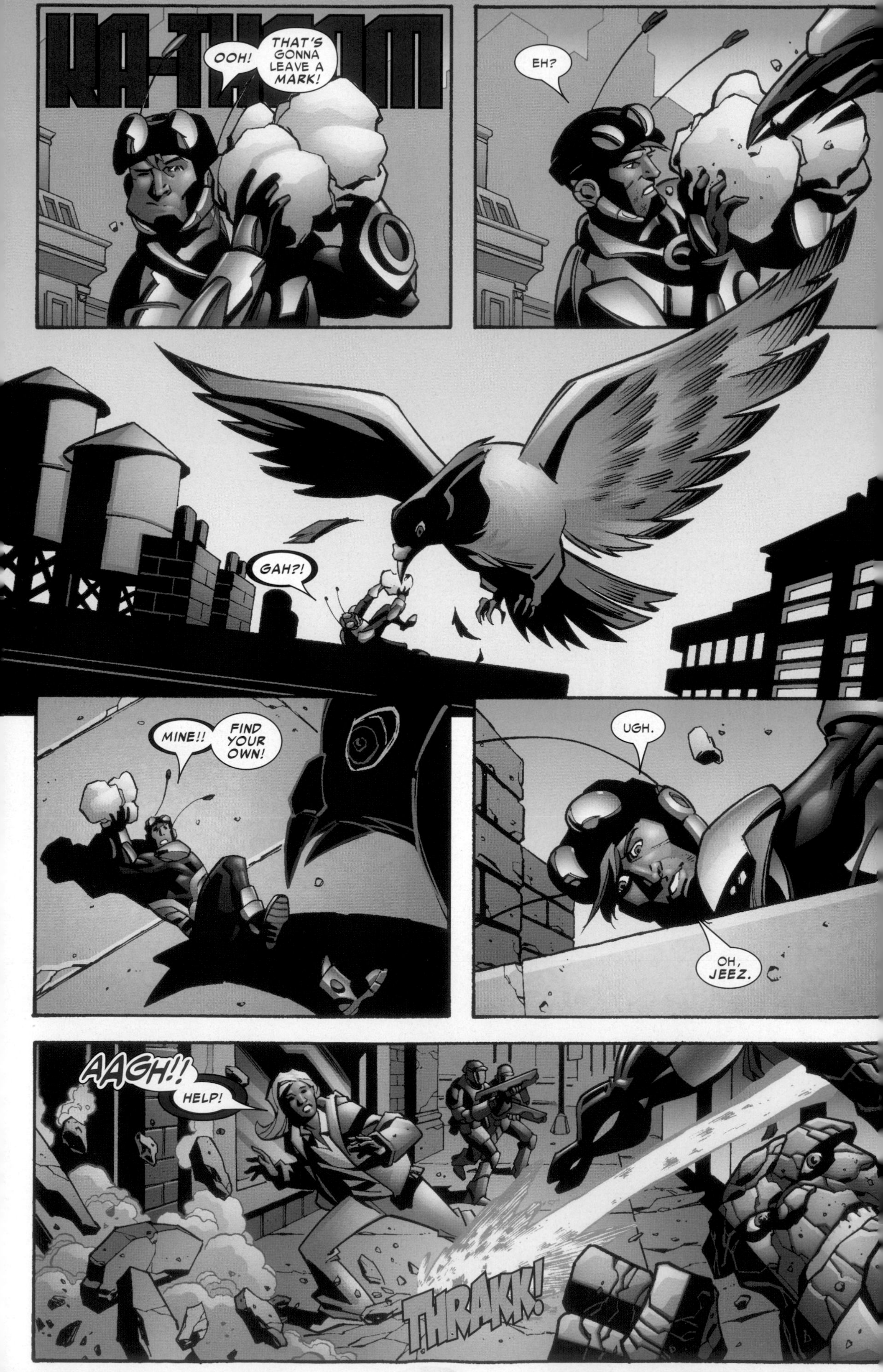
KA-THOOM
OOH!
THAT'S GONNA LEAVE A MARK!
EH?
GAH?!
MINE!!
FIND YOUR OWN!
UGH.
OH, JEEZ.
AAGH!!
HELP!
THRAKK!

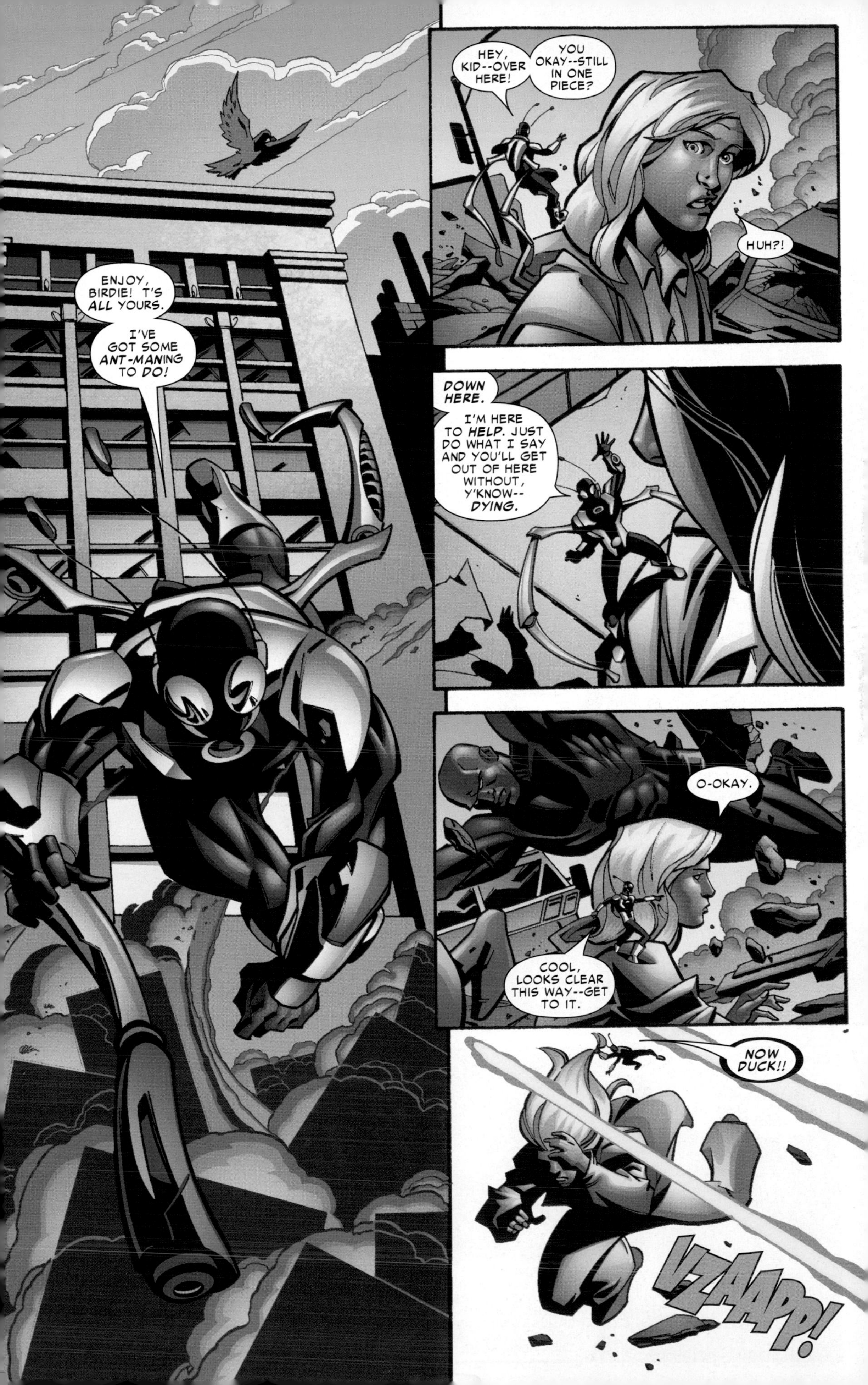
ENJOY, BIRDIE! T'S ALL YOURS.
I'VE GOT SOME ANT-MANING TO DO!
HEY, KID--OVER HERE!
YOU OKAY--STILL IN ONE PIECE?
HUH?!
DOWN HERE.
I'M HERE TO HELP. JUST DO WHAT I SAY AND YOU'LL GET OUT OF HERE WITHOUT, Y'KNOW--DYING.
O-OKAY.
COOL, LOOKS CLEAR THIS WAY--GET TO IT.
NOW DUCK!!
VZAAPP!

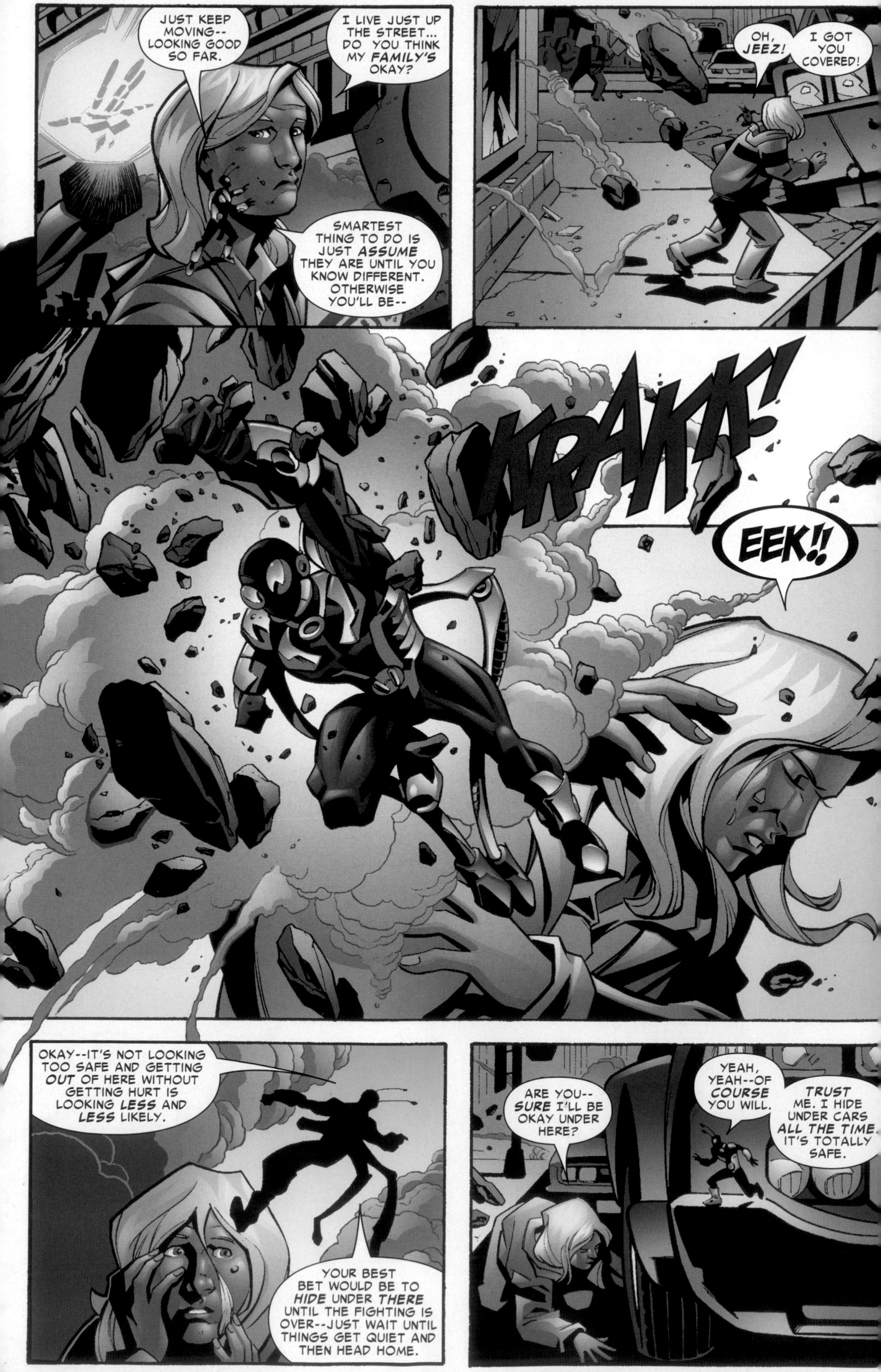
JUST KEEP MOVING--LOOKING GOOD SO FAR.
I LIVE JUST UP THE STREET... DO YOU THINK MY FAMILY'S OKAY?
SMARTEST THING TO DO IS JUST ASSUME THEY ARE UNTIL YOU KNOW DIFFERENT. OTHERWISE YOU'LL BE--
OH, JEEZ!
I GOT YOU COVERED!
KRAKK!
EEK!!
OKAY--IT'S NOT LOOKING TOO SAFE AND GETTING OUT OF HERE WITHOUT GETTING HURT IS LOOKING LESS AND LESS LIKELY.
YOUR BEST BET WOULD BE TO HIDE UNDER THERE UNTIL THE FIGHTING IS OVER--JUST WAIT UNTIL THINGS GET QUIET AND THEN HEAD HOME.
ARE YOU-- SURE I'LL BE OKAY UNDER HERE?
YEAH, YEAH--OF COURSE YOU WILL.
TRUST ME. I HIDE UNDER CARS ALL THE TIME. IT'S TOTALLY SAFE.

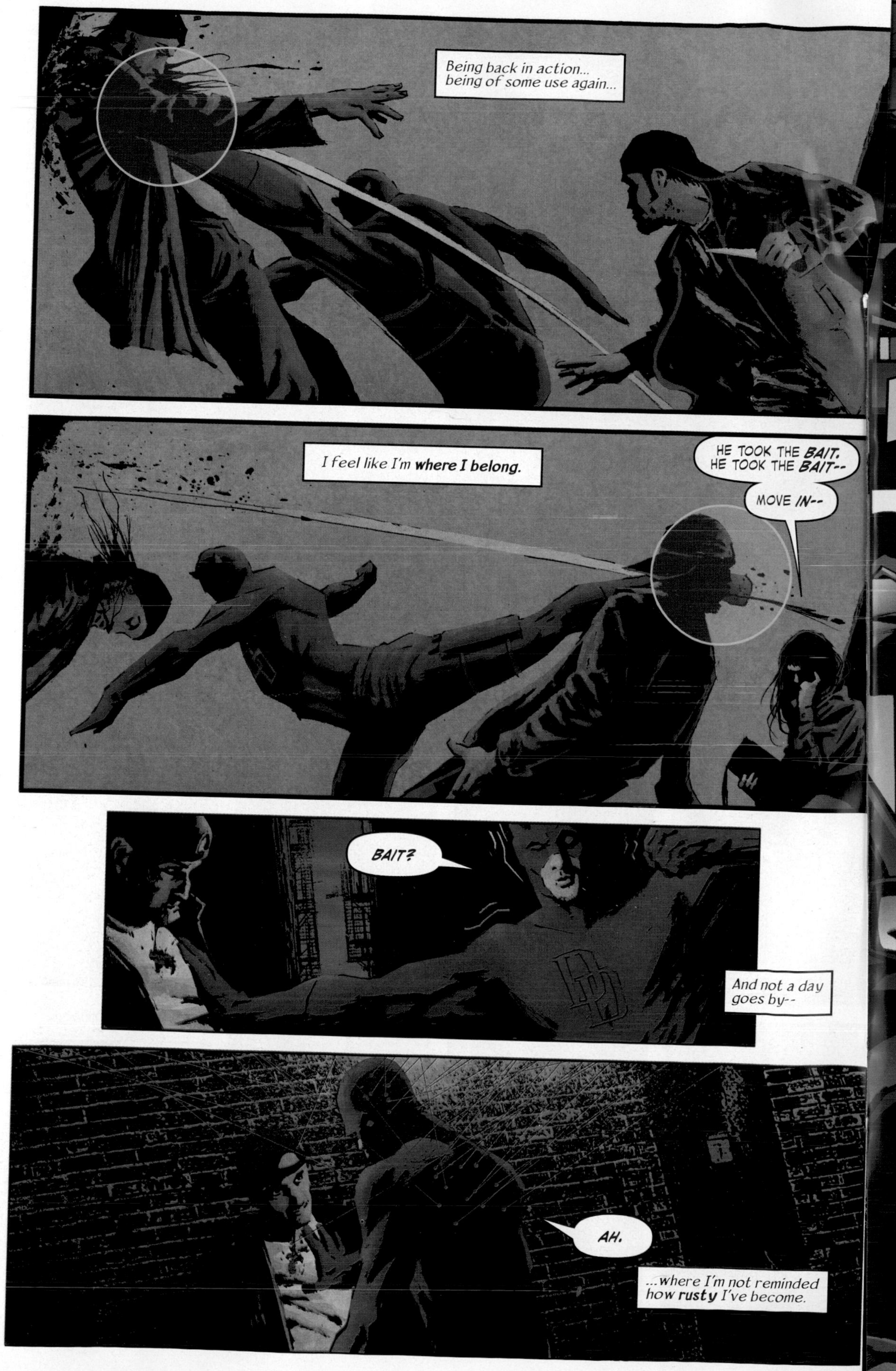

Being back in action...
being of some use again...
I feel like I'm where I belong.
HE TOOK THE BAIT. HE TOOK THE BAIT--
MOVE IN--
BAIT?
And not a day goes by--
AH.
...where I'm not reminded how rusty I've become.

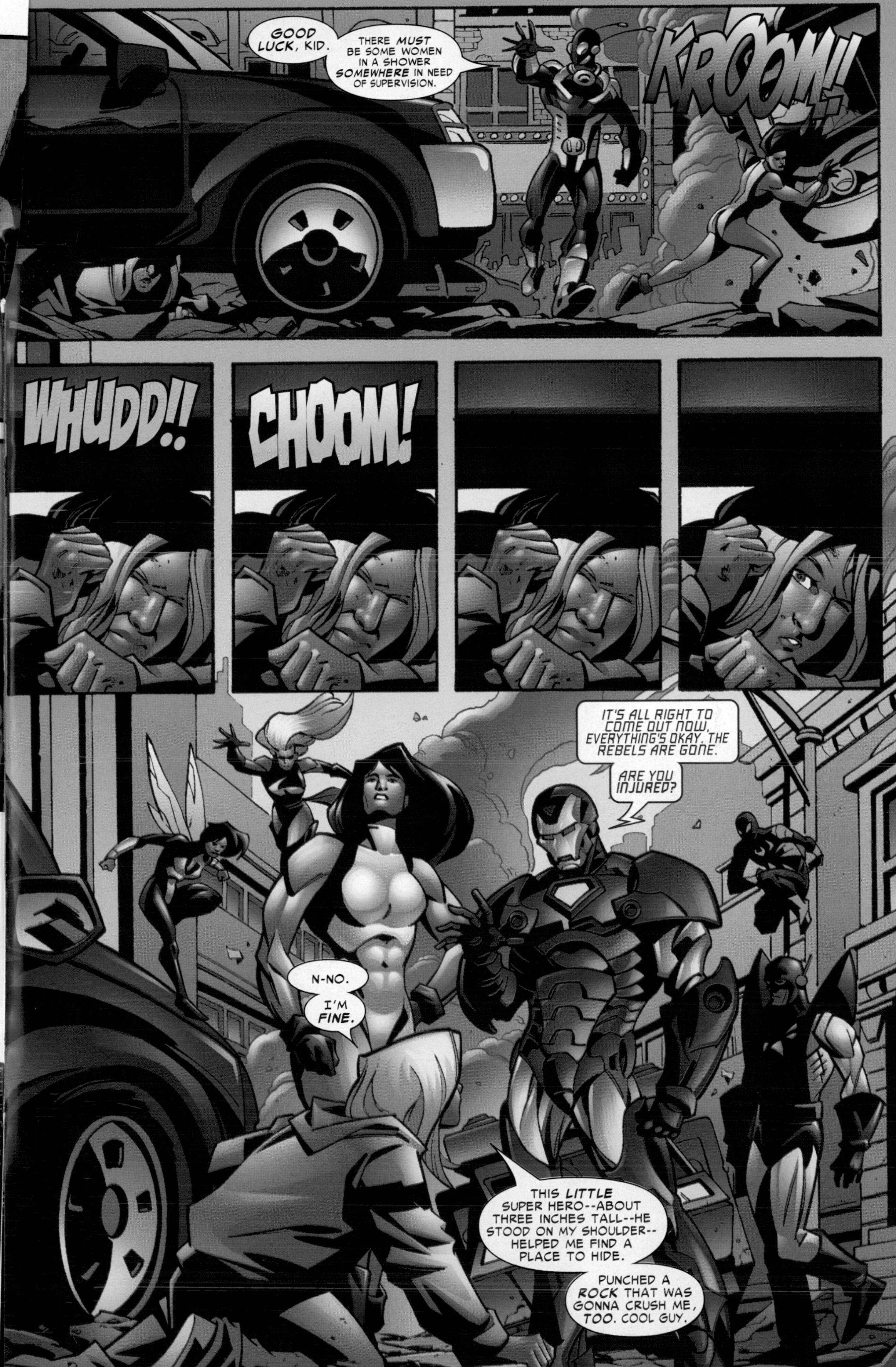

GOOD LUCK, KID.
THERE MUST BE SOME WOMEN IN A SHOWER SOMEWHERE IN NEED OF SUPERVISION.
KROOM!!
WHUDD!!
CHOOM!
IT'S ALL RIGHT TO COME OUT NOW, EVERYTHING'S OKAY. THE REBELS ARE GONE.
ARE YOU INJURED?
N-NO.
I'M FINE.
THIS LITTLE SUPER HERO--ABOUT THREE INCHES TALL--HE STOOD ON MY SHOULDER--HELPED ME FIND A PLACE TO HIDE.
PUNCHED A ROCK THAT WAS GONNA CRUSH ME, TOO. COOL GUY.

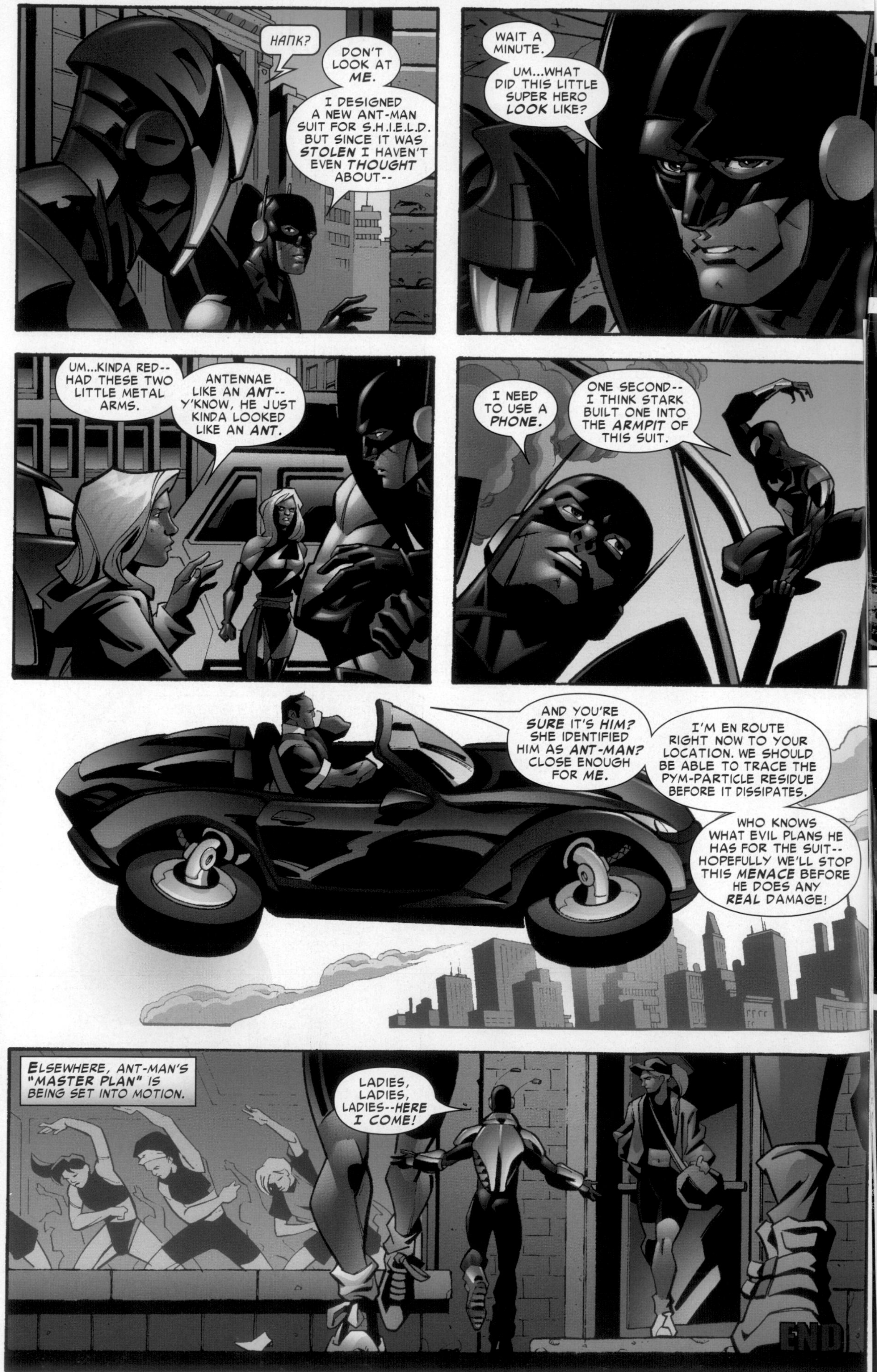
HANK?
DON'T LOOK AT ME.
I DESIGNED A NEW ANT-MAN SUIT FOR S.H.I.E.L.D. BUT SINCE IT WAS STOLEN I HAVEN'T EVEN THOUGHT ABOUT--
WAIT A MINUTE.
UM...WHAT DID THIS LITTLE SUPER HERO LOOK LIKE?
UM...KINDA RED-- HAD THESE TWO LITTLE METAL ARMS.
ANTENNAE LIKE AN ANT-- Y'KNOW, HE JUST KINDA LOOKED LIKE AN ANT.
I NEED TO USE A PHONE.
ONE SECOND-- I THINK STARK BUILT ONE INTO THE ARMPIT OF THIS SUIT.
AND YOU'RE SURE IT'S HIM? SHE IDENTIFIED HIM AS ANT-MAN? CLOSE ENOUGH FOR ME.
I'M EN ROUTE RIGHT NOW TO YOUR LOCATION. WE SHOULD BE ABLE TO TRACE THE PYM-PARTICLE RESIDUE BEFORE IT DISSIPATES.
WHO KNOWS WHAT EVIL PLANS HE HAS FOR THE SUIT-- HOPEFULLY WE'LL STOP THIS MENACE BEFORE HE DOES ANY REAL DAMAGE!
ELSEWHERE, ANT-MAN'S "MASTER PLAN" IS BEING SET INTO MOTION.
LADIES, LADIES, LADIES--HERE I COME!
END

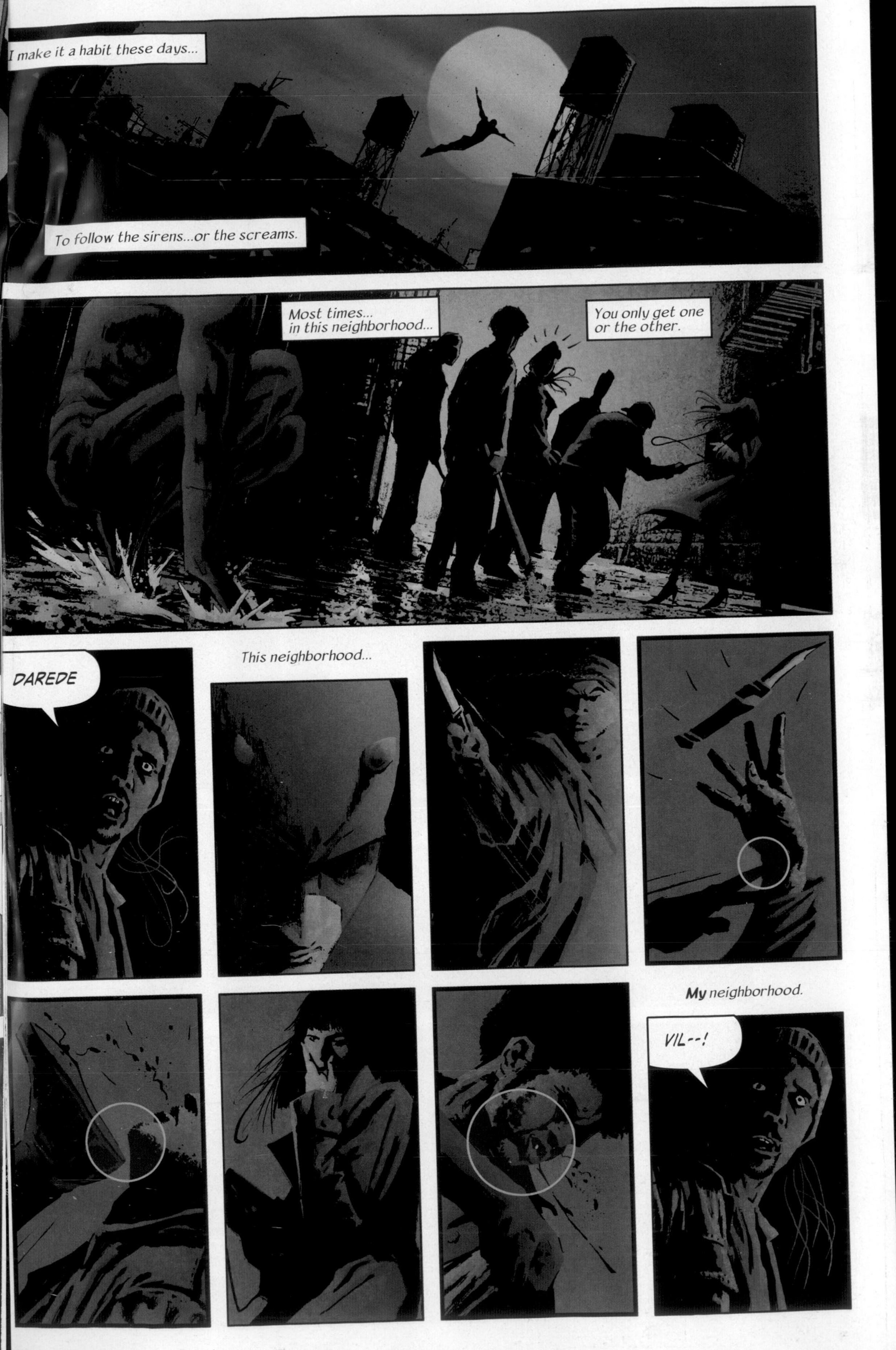
I make it a habit these days...
To follow the sirens...or the screams.
Most times... in this neighborhood...
You only get one or the other.
DAREDE
This neighborhood...
My neighborhood.
VIL--!

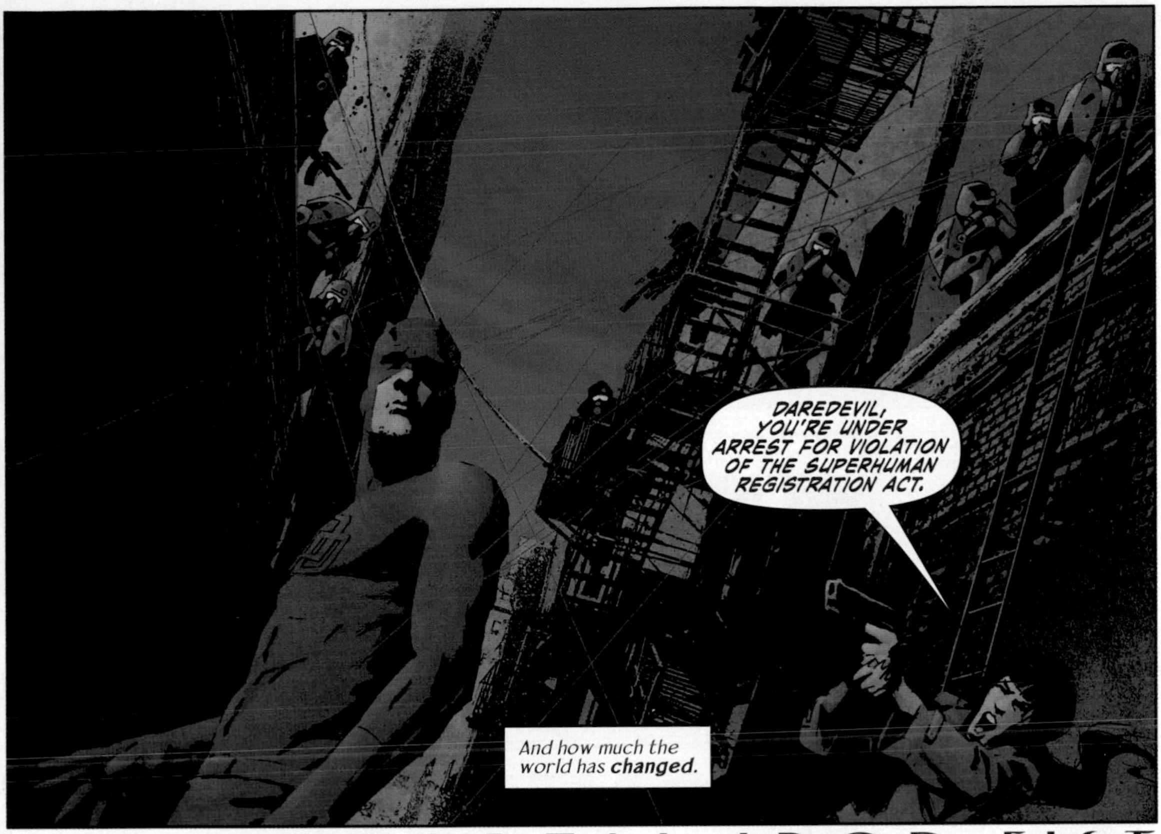
DAREDEVIL, YOU'RE UNDER ARREST FOR VIOLATION OF THE SUPERHUMAN REGISTRATION ACT.
And how much the world has changed.

THE IMMORTAL IRON FIST

"CHOOSING SIDES"

ED BRUBAKER & MATT FRACTION – WRITERS
DAVID AJA – ARTIST / **MATT HOLLINGSWORTH** – COLORIST
DAVE LANPHEAR – LETTERER / **WARREN SIMONS** – EDITOR

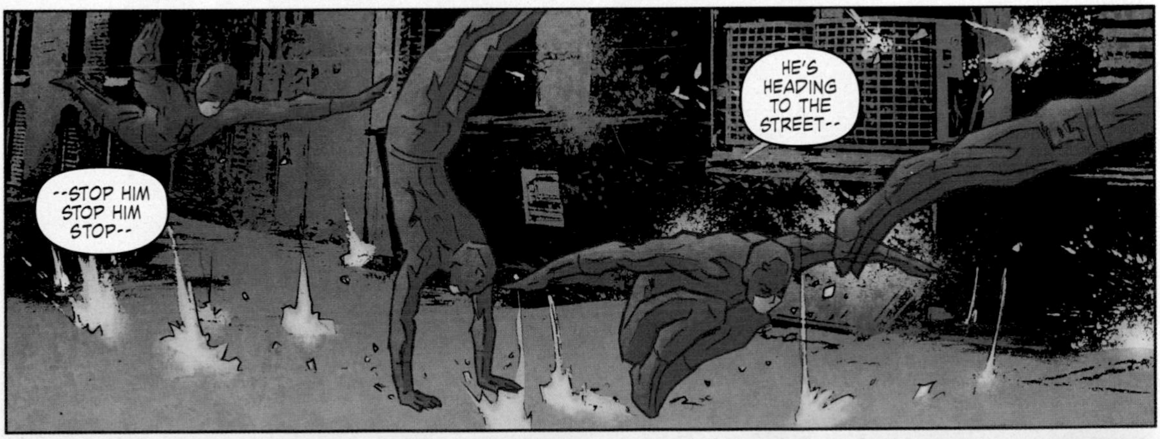
HE'S HEADING TO THE STREET--
--STOP HIM STOP HIM STOP--

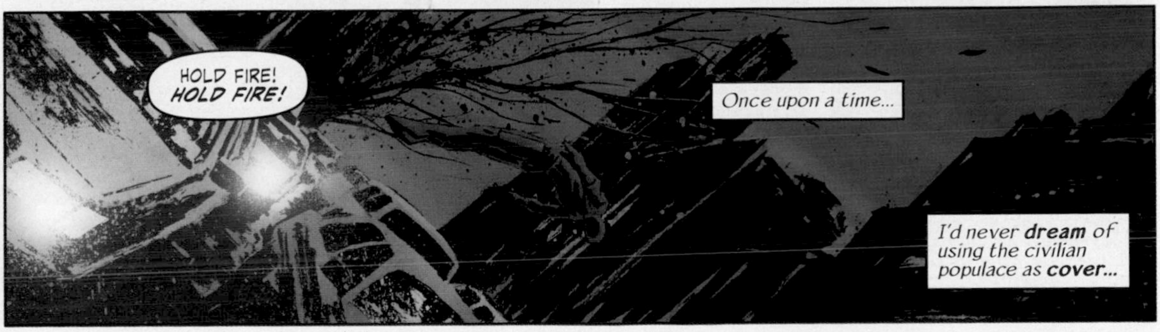
HOLD FIRE! HOLD FIRE!
Once upon a time...
I'd never dream of using the civilian populace as cover...

...but **war** changes everything.

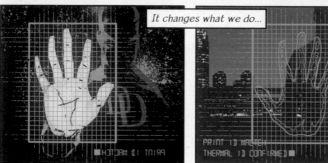

It changes what we do...

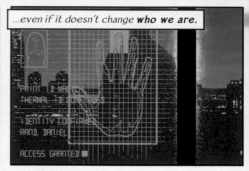

...even if it doesn't change **who we are.**

PRINT ID MATCH
THERMAL ID CONFIRMED
IDENTITY CONFIRMED
RAND, DANIEL
ACCESS GRANTED

YOU HAVE **ONE** MESSAGE.

DANNY, IT'S **JERYN.** LOOK, THIS **THING** COMING UP NEXT WEEK, IT'S PRETTY BIG FOR US. LIKE, **BIG** WITH CAPITAL **BILLIONS**...

IT'S BIG FOR ME, IT'S BIG FOR YOU. IT'S BIG FOR RAND...HELL, DANNY, IT'S BIG FOR **ALL OF CHINA**...

...AND EVERY-BODY HERE CAN APPRECIATE THAT YOU WANT TO **GET INVOLVED** AND MAKE AN APPEARANCE AT THE **FINISH LINE,** BUT...

...WELL, DANNY, IT'S NOT LIKE YOU'VE MADE ANY **SECRET** OF NOT BEING AROUND FOR THE LAST, UH, **FEW YEARS** OR ANYTHING...

AND IF YOU'RE COMING INTO **THE ROOM** ON THIS THING...

...I WANT YOU TO REMEMBER WHO YOU ARE...

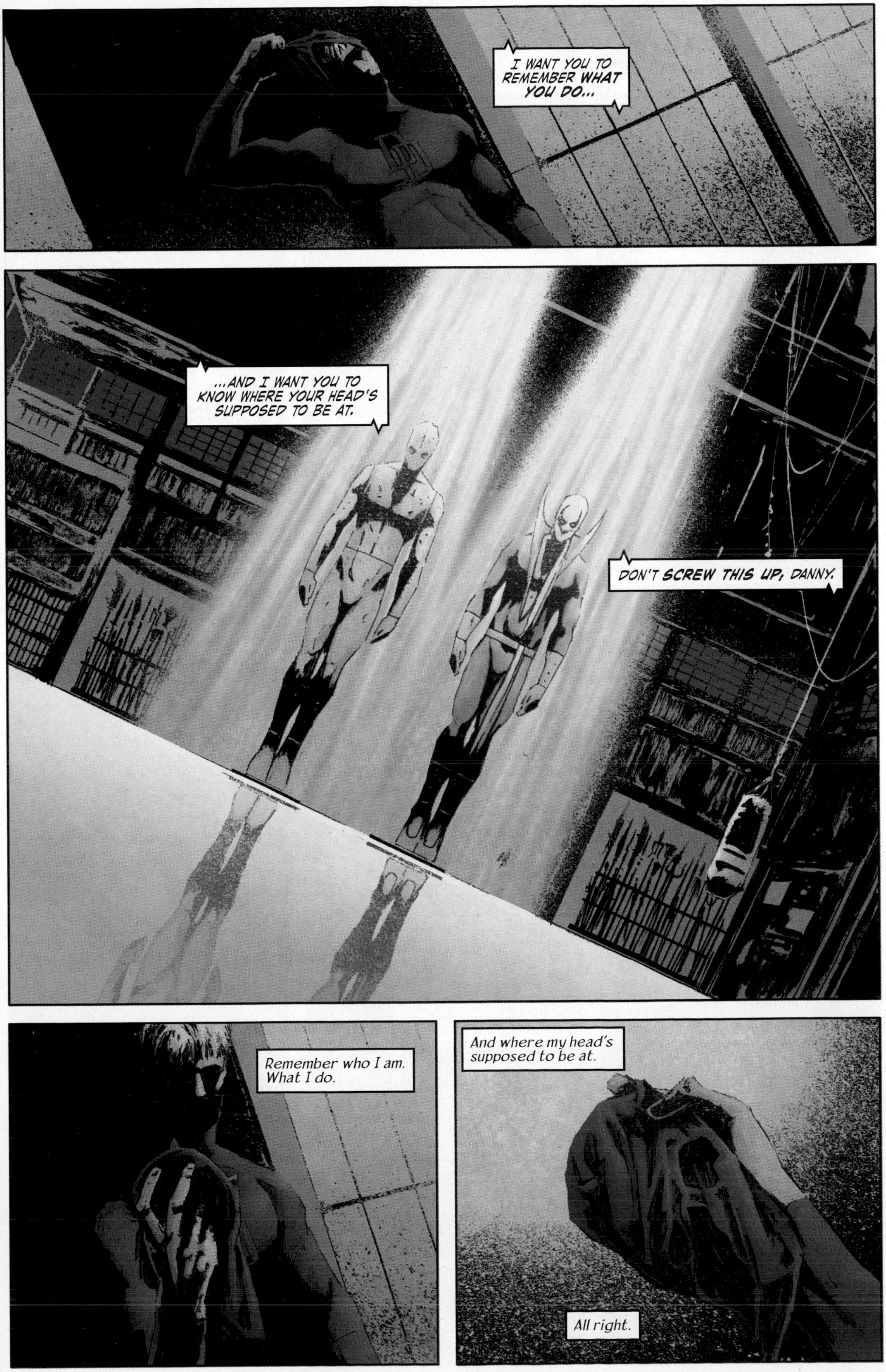
I WANT YOU TO REMEMBER WHAT YOU DO...
...AND I WANT YOU TO KNOW WHERE YOUR HEAD'S SUPPOSED TO BE AT.
DON'T SCREW THIS UP, DANNY.
Remember who I am. What I do.
And where my head's supposed to be at.
All right.

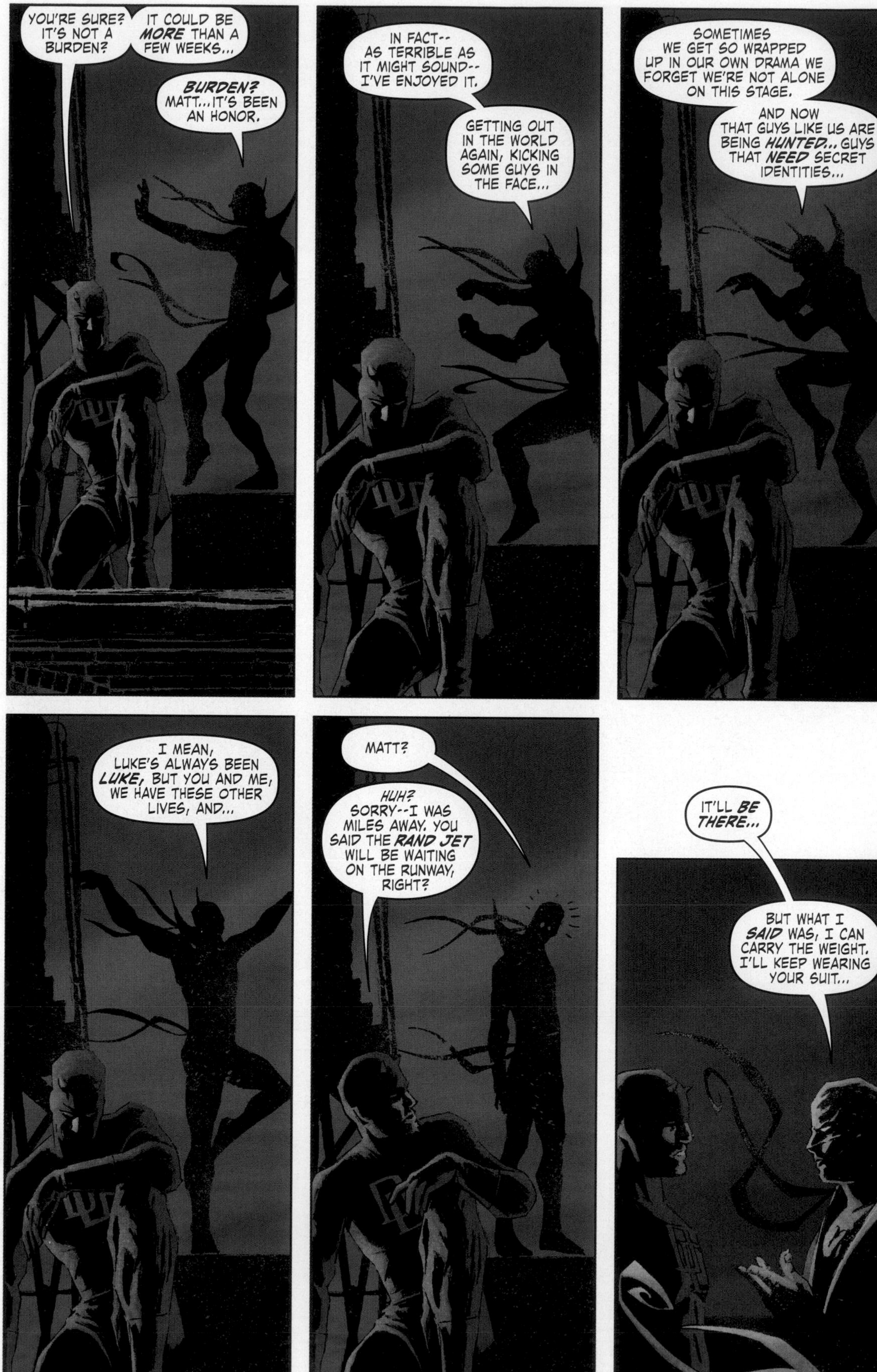
YOU'RE SURE? IT'S NOT A BURDEN?
IT COULD BE MORE THAN A FEW WEEKS...
BURDEN? MATT...IT'S BEEN AN HONOR.
IN FACT-- AS TERRIBLE AS IT MIGHT SOUND-- I'VE ENJOYED IT.
GETTING OUT IN THE WORLD AGAIN, KICKING SOME GUYS IN THE FACE...
SOMETIMES WE GET SO WRAPPED UP IN OUR OWN DRAMA WE FORGET WE'RE NOT ALONE ON THIS STAGE.
AND NOW THAT GUYS LIKE US ARE BEING HUNTED... GUYS THAT NEED SECRET IDENTITIES...
I MEAN, LUKE'S ALWAYS BEEN LUKE, BUT YOU AND ME, WE HAVE THESE OTHER LIVES, AND...
MATT?
HUH? SORRY--I WAS MILES AWAY. YOU SAID THE RAND JET WILL BE WAITING ON THE RUNWAY, RIGHT?
IT'LL BE THERE...
BUT WHAT I SAID WAS, I CAN CARRY THE WEIGHT. I'LL KEEP WEARING YOUR SUIT...

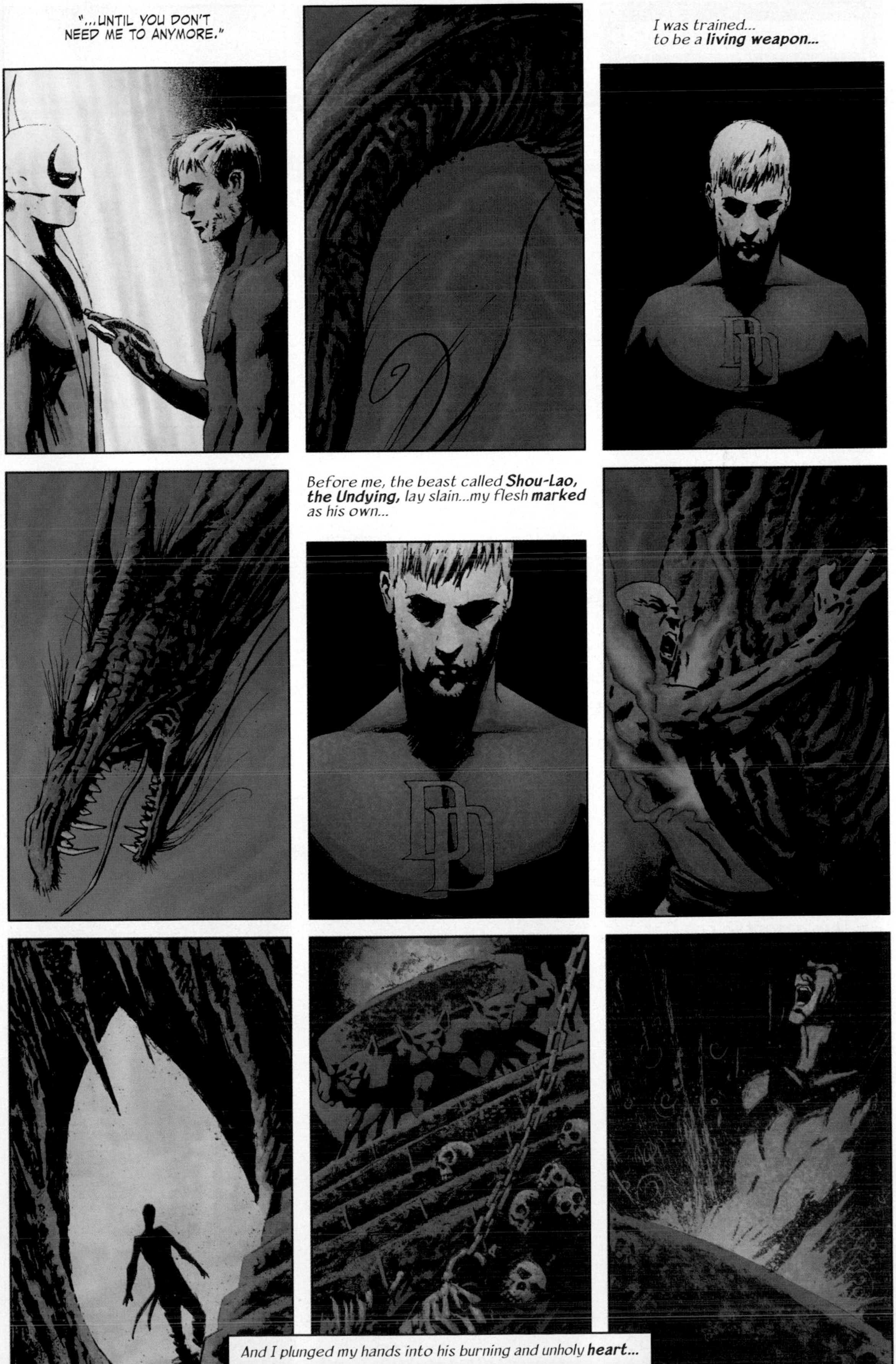
"...UNTIL YOU DON'T NEED ME TO ANYMORE."
I was trained... to be a **living weapon...**
Before me, the beast called **Shou-Lao, the Undying,** lay slain...my flesh **marked** as his own...
And I plunged my hands into his burning and unholy **heart...**

And my fist became like unto...

..a thing of **iron**.

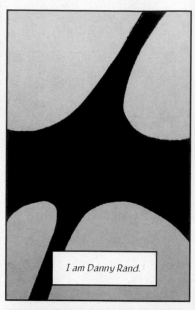

I am Danny Rand.

The Immortal Iron Fist.

I made a promise to Matt Murdock to wear his mask...I've fought this war in his place... And I'll continue to.

But I haven't **forgotten** who I am...

...and soon it will be time to carry my **own** burdens again.

END

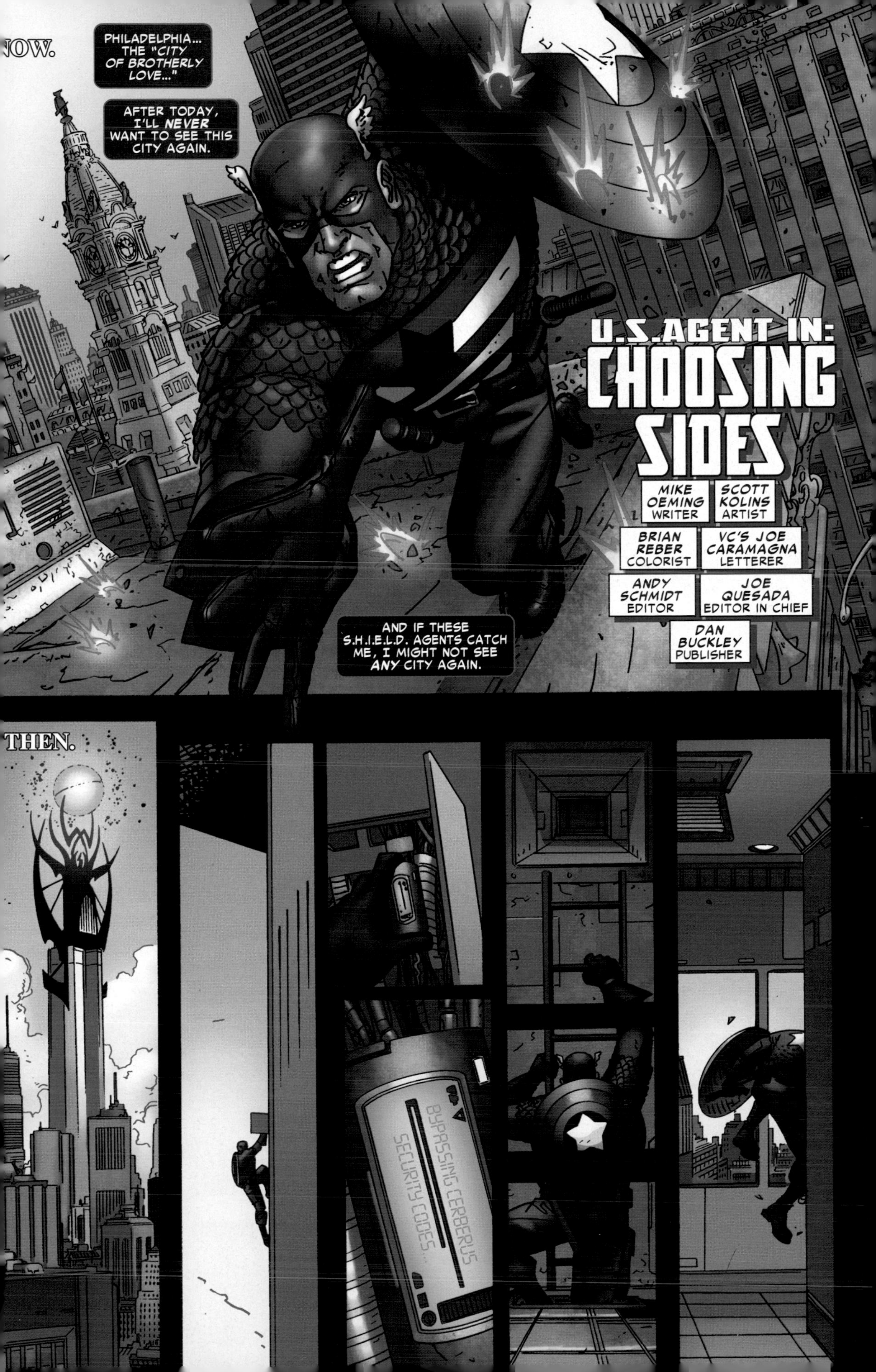
NOW.
PHILADELPHIA... THE "CITY OF BROTHERLY LOVE..."
AFTER TODAY, I'LL NEVER WANT TO SEE THIS CITY AGAIN.
U.S. AGENT IN:
CHOOSING SIDES
MIKE OEMING WRITER
SCOTT KOLINS ARTIST
BRIAN REBER COLORIST
VC'S JOE CARAMAGNA LETTERER
ANDY SCHMIDT EDITOR
JOE QUESADA EDITOR IN CHIEF
DAN BUCKLEY PUBLISHER
AND IF THESE S.H.I.E.L.D. AGENTS CATCH ME, I MIGHT NOT SEE ANY CITY AGAIN.
THEN.
BYPASSING CERBERUS SECURITY CODES...

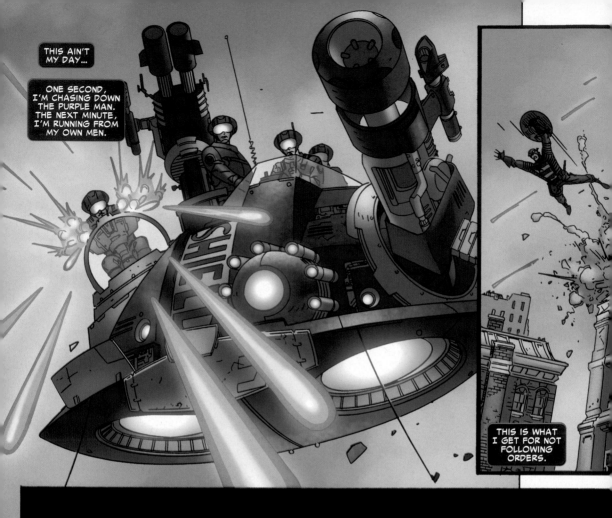

THIS AIN'T MY DAY...

ONE SECOND, I'M CHASING DOWN THE PURPLE MAN. THE NEXT MINUTE, I'M RUNNING FROM MY OWN MEN.

THIS IS WHAT I GET FOR NOT FOLLOWING ORDERS.

...AND HERE'S A MEMO FROM THE PRESIDENT, MR. STARK. JUST CAME IN.

...GET CAPTAIN WALKER A PROPER SECURITY PASS.

THANKS... OH, AND ONE MORE THING...

I'D HATE FOR HIM TO BE A VICTIM OF A MISUNDERSTANDING WITH OUR SECURITY SYSTEM.

CRUD.

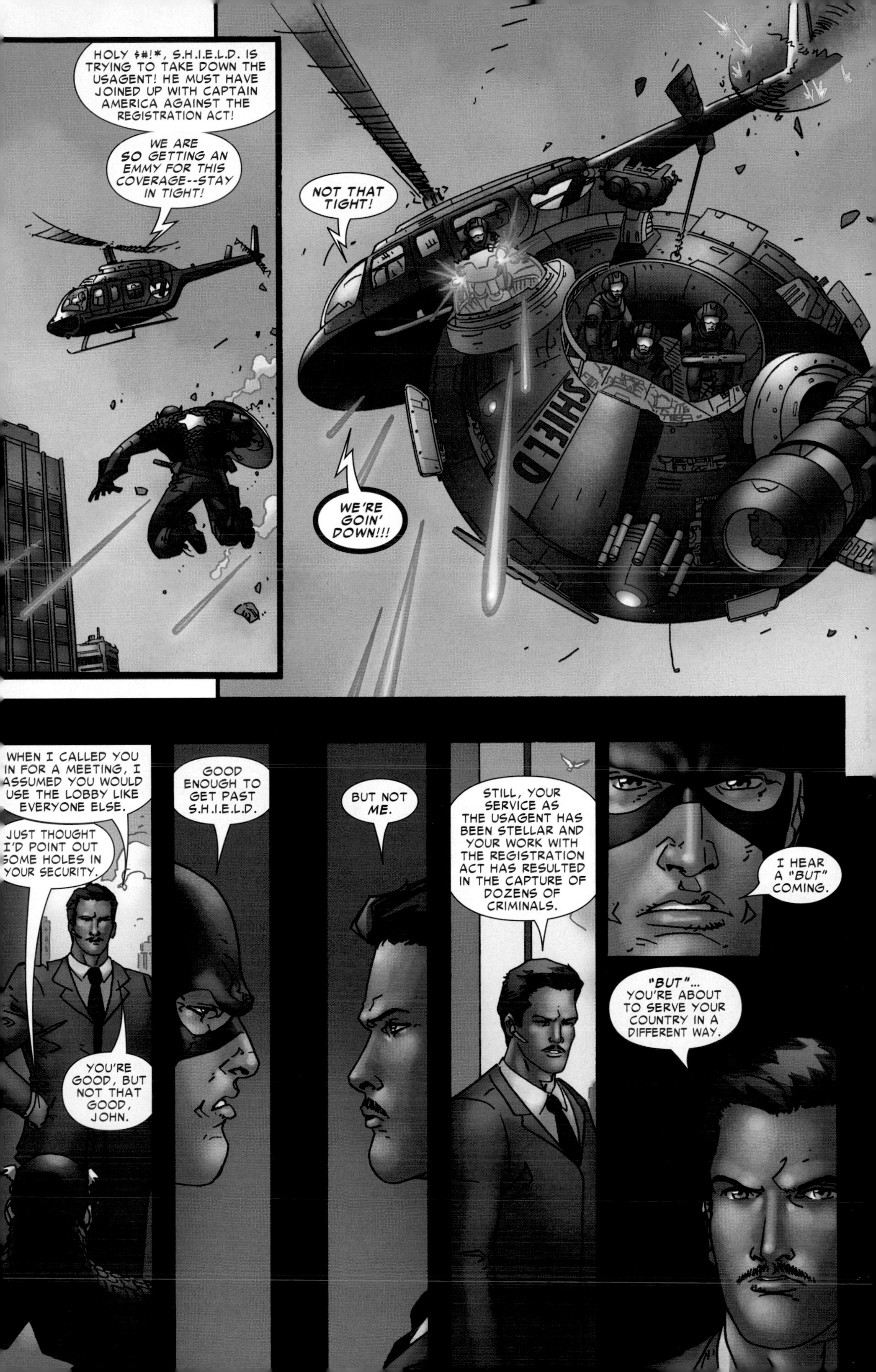
HOLY $#!*, S.H.I.E.L.D. IS TRYING TO TAKE DOWN THE USAGENT! HE MUST HAVE JOINED UP WITH CAPTAIN AMERICA AGAINST THE REGISTRATION ACT!
WE ARE SO GETTING AN EMMY FOR THIS COVERAGE--STAY IN TIGHT!
NOT THAT TIGHT!
SHIELD
WE'RE GOIN' DOWN!!!
WHEN I CALLED YOU IN FOR A MEETING, I ASSUMED YOU WOULD USE THE LOBBY LIKE EVERYONE ELSE.
JUST THOUGHT I'D POINT OUT SOME HOLES IN YOUR SECURITY.
YOU'RE GOOD, BUT NOT THAT GOOD, JOHN.
GOOD ENOUGH TO GET PAST S.H.I.E.L.D.
BUT NOT ME.
STILL, YOUR SERVICE AS THE USAGENT HAS BEEN STELLAR AND YOUR WORK WITH THE REGISTRATION ACT HAS RESULTED IN THE CAPTURE OF DOZENS OF CRIMINALS.
I HEAR A "BUT" COMING.
"BUT"... YOU'RE ABOUT TO SERVE YOUR COUNTRY IN A DIFFERENT WAY.

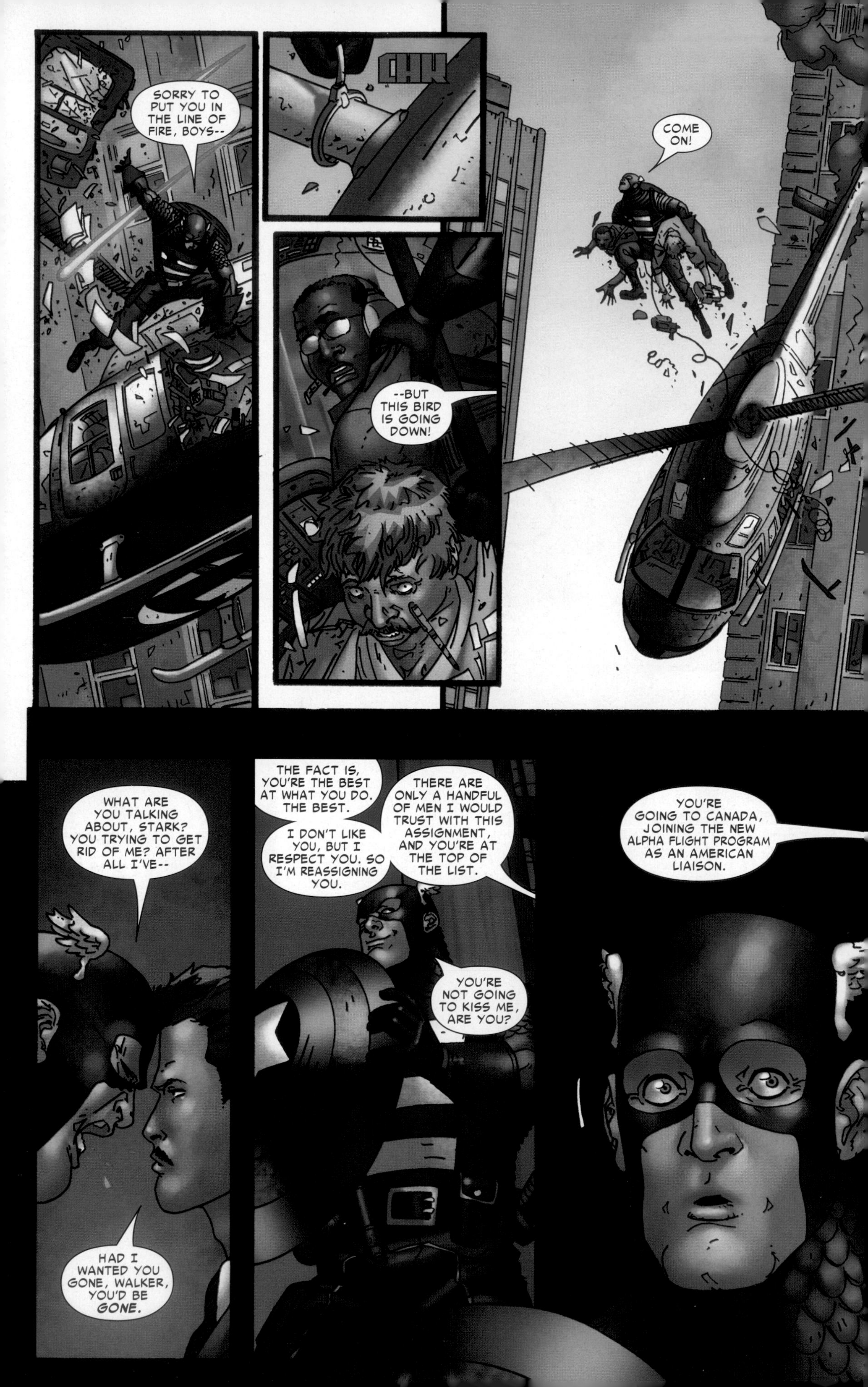
SORRY TO PUT YOU IN THE LINE OF FIRE, BOYS--
CHK
--BUT THIS BIRD IS GOING DOWN!
COME ON!
WHAT ARE YOU TALKING ABOUT, STARK? YOU TRYING TO GET RID OF ME? AFTER ALL I'VE--
HAD I WANTED YOU GONE, WALKER, YOU'D BE GONE.
THE FACT IS, YOU'RE THE BEST AT WHAT YOU DO. THE BEST.
I DON'T LIKE YOU, BUT I RESPECT YOU. SO I'M REASSIGNING YOU.
THERE ARE ONLY A HANDFUL OF MEN I WOULD TRUST WITH THIS ASSIGNMENT, AND YOU'RE AT THE TOP OF THE LIST.
YOU'RE NOT GOING TO KISS ME, ARE YOU?
YOU'RE GOING TO CANADA, JOINING THE NEW ALPHA FLIGHT PROGRAM AS AN AMERICAN LIAISON.

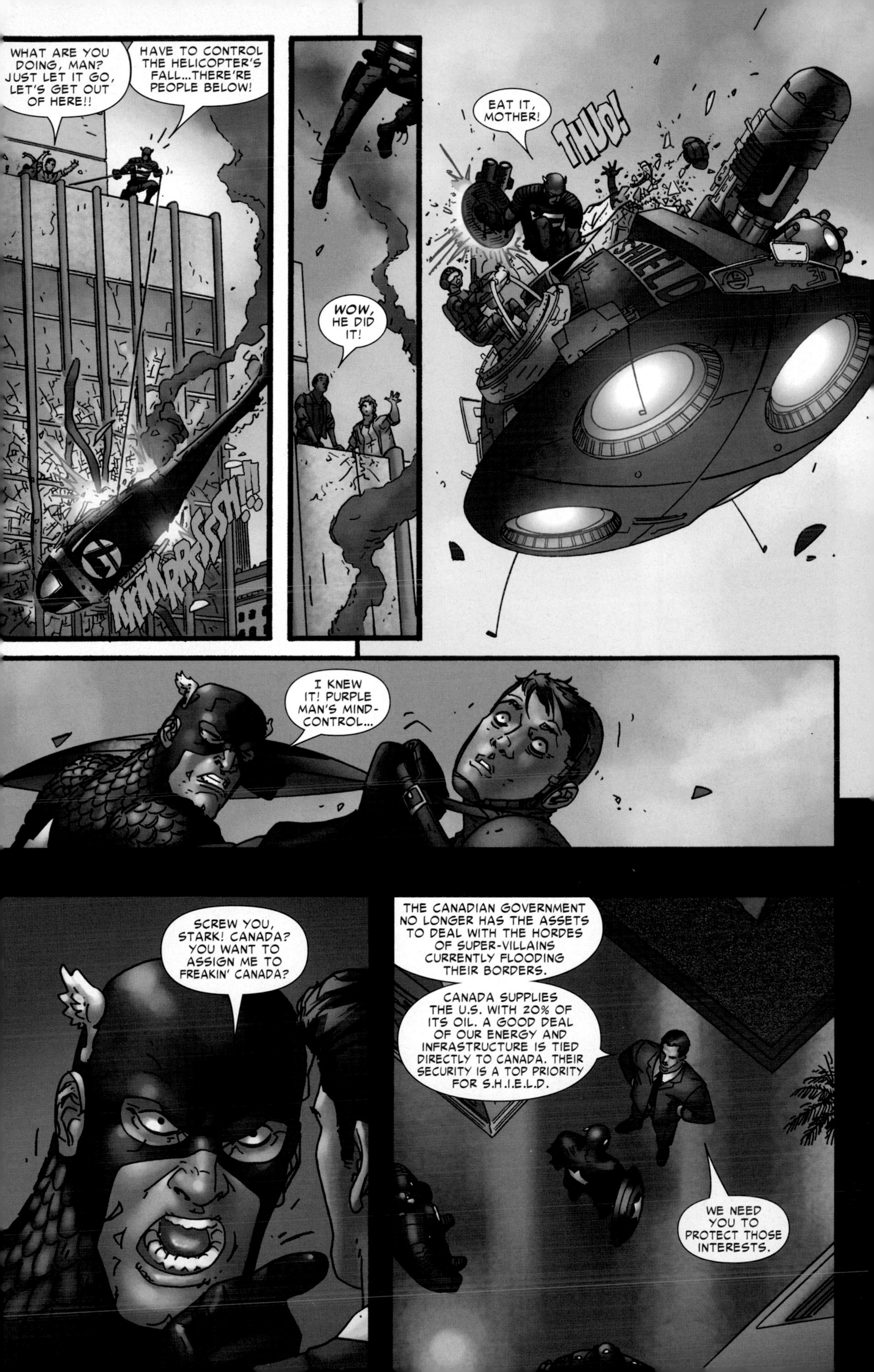
WHAT ARE YOU DOING, MAN? JUST LET IT GO, LET'S GET OUT OF HERE!!
HAVE TO CONTROL THE HELICOPTER'S FALL...THERE'RE PEOPLE BELOW!
KKKKRRSSSH!!!
WOW, HE DID IT!
EAT IT, MOTHER!
THUD!
SHIELD
I KNEW IT! PURPLE MAN'S MIND-CONTROL...
SCREW YOU, STARK! CANADA? YOU WANT TO ASSIGN ME TO FREAKIN' CANADA?
THE CANADIAN GOVERNMENT NO LONGER HAS THE ASSETS TO DEAL WITH THE HORDES OF SUPER-VILLAINS CURRENTLY FLOODING THEIR BORDERS.
CANADA SUPPLIES THE U.S. WITH 20% OF ITS OIL. A GOOD DEAL OF OUR ENERGY AND INFRASTRUCTURE IS TIED DIRECTLY TO CANADA. THEIR SECURITY IS A TOP PRIORITY FOR S.H.I.E.L.D.
WE NEED YOU TO PROTECT THOSE INTERESTS.

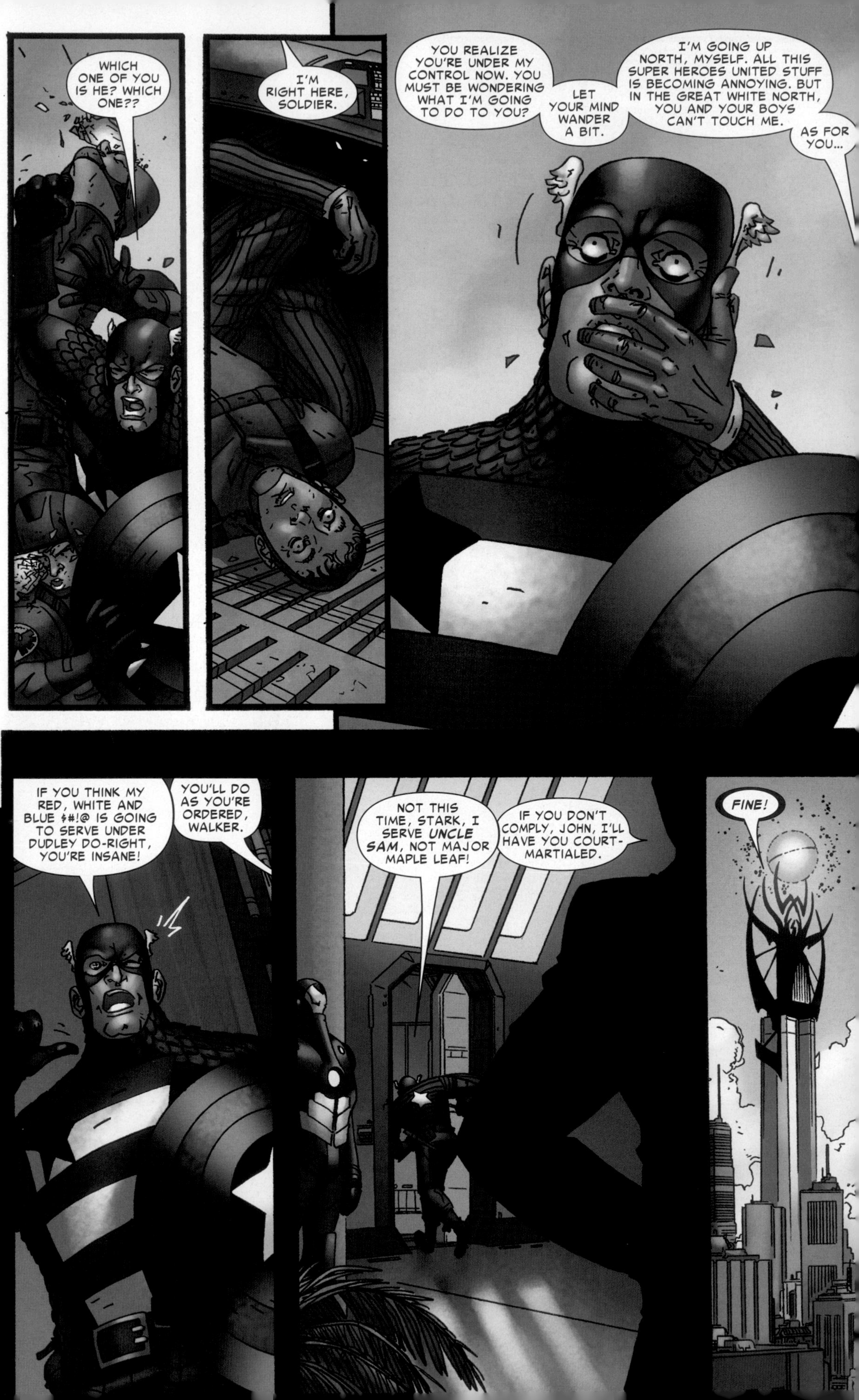
WHICH ONE OF YOU IS HE? WHICH ONE??
I'M RIGHT HERE, SOLDIER.
YOU REALIZE YOU'RE UNDER MY CONTROL NOW. YOU MUST BE WONDERING WHAT I'M GOING TO DO TO YOU?
LET YOUR MIND WANDER A BIT.
I'M GOING UP NORTH, MYSELF. ALL THIS SUPER HEROES UNITED STUFF IS BECOMING ANNOYING. BUT IN THE GREAT WHITE NORTH, YOU AND YOUR BOYS CAN'T TOUCH ME.
AS FOR YOU...
IF YOU THINK MY RED, WHITE AND BLUE $#!@ IS GOING TO SERVE UNDER DUDLEY DO-RIGHT, YOU'RE INSANE!
YOU'LL DO AS YOU'RE ORDERED, WALKER.
NOT THIS TIME, STARK, I SERVE *UNCLE SAM*, NOT MAJOR MAPLE LEAF!
IF YOU DON'T COMPLY, JOHN, I'LL HAVE YOU COURT-MARTIALED.
FINE!

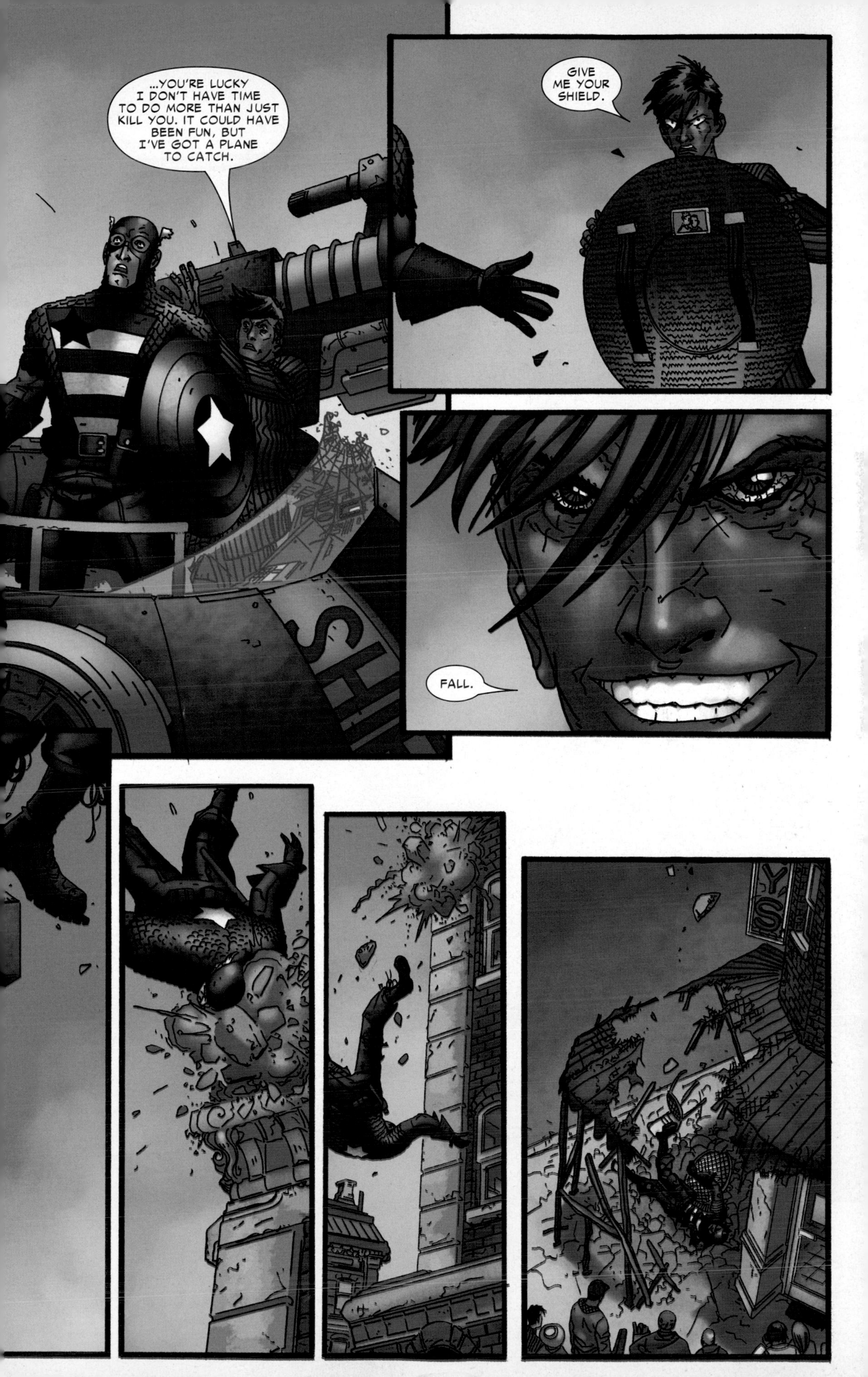
...YOU'RE LUCKY I DON'T HAVE TIME TO DO MORE THAN JUST KILL YOU. IT COULD HAVE BEEN FUN, BUT I'VE GOT A PLANE TO CATCH.
GIVE ME YOUR SHIELD.
FALL.

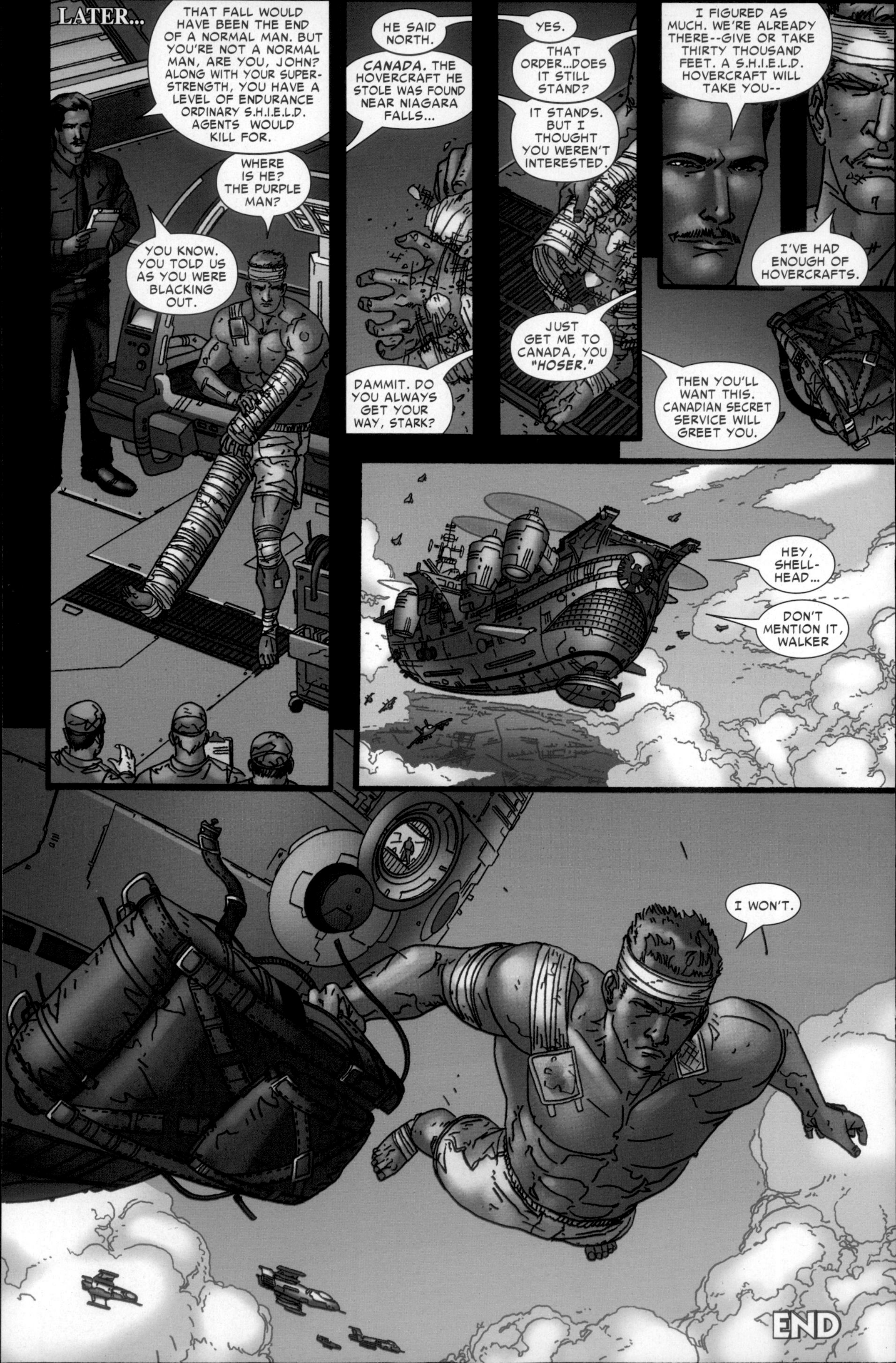
LATER...
THAT FALL WOULD HAVE BEEN THE END OF A NORMAL MAN. BUT YOU'RE NOT A NORMAL MAN, ARE YOU, JOHN? ALONG WITH YOUR SUPER-STRENGTH, YOU HAVE A LEVEL OF ENDURANCE ORDINARY S.H.I.E.L.D. AGENTS WOULD KILL FOR.
WHERE IS HE? THE PURPLE MAN?
YOU KNOW. YOU TOLD US AS YOU WERE BLACKING OUT.
HE SAID NORTH.
CANADA. THE HOVERCRAFT HE STOLE WAS FOUND NEAR NIAGARA FALLS...
YES.
THAT ORDER...DOES IT STILL STAND?
IT STANDS. BUT I THOUGHT YOU WEREN'T INTERESTED.
I FIGURED AS MUCH. WE'RE ALREADY THERE--GIVE OR TAKE THIRTY THOUSAND FEET. A S.H.I.E.L.D. HOVERCRAFT WILL TAKE YOU--
I'VE HAD ENOUGH OF HOVERCRAFTS.
JUST GET ME TO CANADA, YOU "HOSER."
DAMMIT. DO YOU ALWAYS GET YOUR WAY, STARK?
THEN YOU'LL WANT THIS. CANADIAN SECRET SERVICE WILL GREET YOU.
HEY, SHELL-HEAD...
DON'T MENTION IT, WALKER
I WON'T.
END

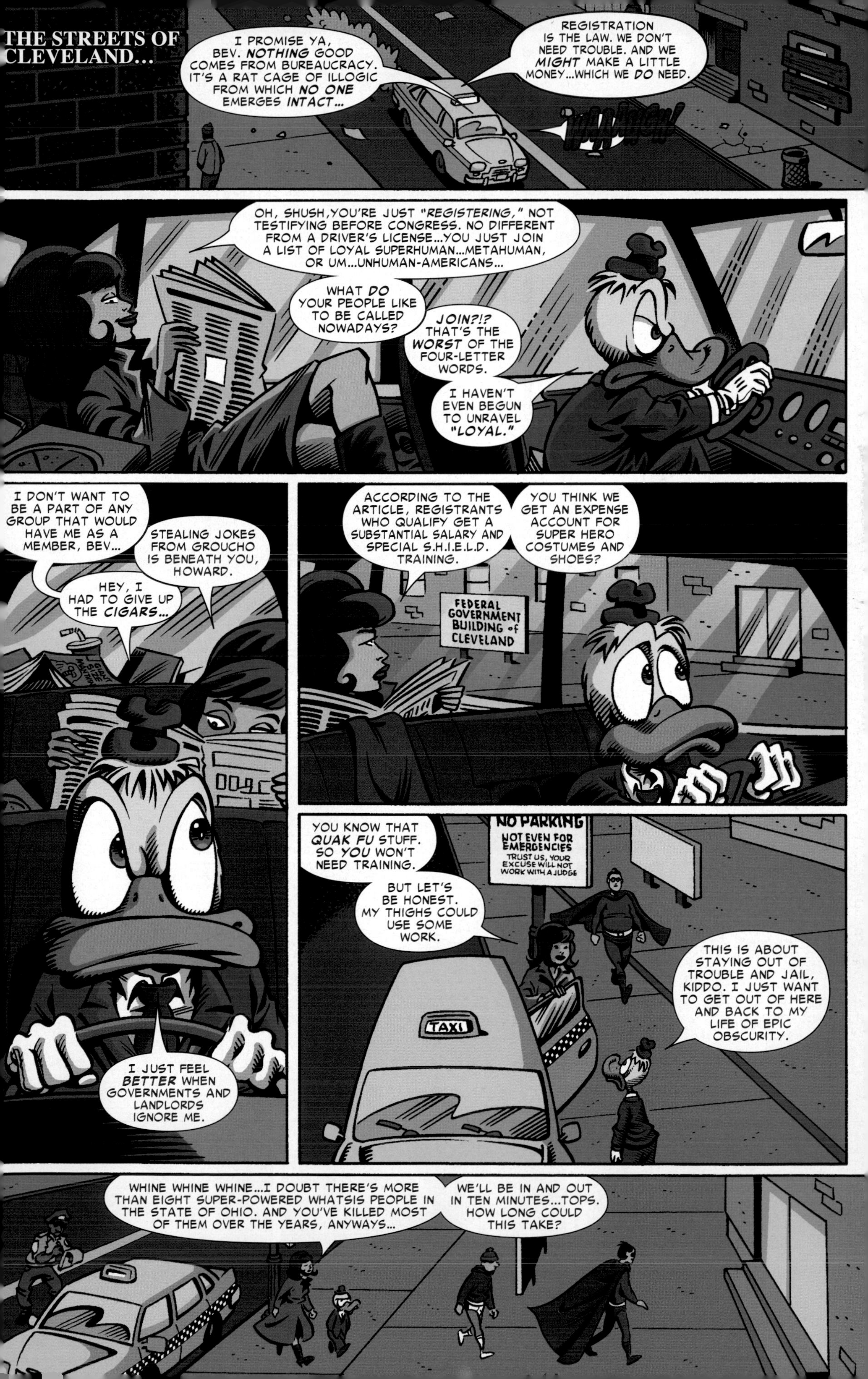
THE STREETS OF CLEVELAND…
I PROMISE YA, BEV. NOTHING GOOD COMES FROM BUREAUCRACY. IT'S A RAT CAGE OF ILLOGIC FROM WHICH NO ONE EMERGES INTACT…
REGISTRATION IS THE LAW. WE DON'T NEED TROUBLE. AND WE MIGHT MAKE A LITTLE MONEY…WHICH WE DO NEED.
OH, SHUSH, YOU'RE JUST "REGISTERING," NOT TESTIFYING BEFORE CONGRESS. NO DIFFERENT FROM A DRIVER'S LICENSE…YOU JUST JOIN A LIST OF LOYAL SUPERHUMAN…METAHUMAN, OR UM…UNHUMAN-AMERICANS…
WHAT DO YOUR PEOPLE LIKE TO BE CALLED NOWADAYS?
JOIN?!? THAT'S THE WORST OF THE FOUR-LETTER WORDS.
I HAVEN'T EVEN BEGUN TO UNRAVEL "LOYAL."
I DON'T WANT TO BE A PART OF ANY GROUP THAT WOULD HAVE ME AS A MEMBER, BEV…
STEALING JOKES FROM GROUCHO IS BENEATH YOU, HOWARD.
HEY, I HAD TO GIVE UP THE CIGARS…
I JUST FEEL BETTER WHEN GOVERNMENTS AND LANDLORDS IGNORE ME.
ACCORDING TO THE ARTICLE, REGISTRANTS WHO QUALIFY GET A SUBSTANTIAL SALARY AND SPECIAL S.H.I.E.L.D. TRAINING.
YOU THINK WE GET AN EXPENSE ACCOUNT FOR SUPER HERO COSTUMES AND SHOES?
FEDERAL GOVERNMENT BUILDING of CLEVELAND
NO PARKING NOT EVEN FOR EMERGENCIES TRUST US, YOUR EXCUSE WILL NOT WORK WITH A JUDGE
YOU KNOW THAT QUAK FU STUFF. SO YOU WON'T NEED TRAINING.
BUT LET'S BE HONEST. MY THIGHS COULD USE SOME WORK.
THIS IS ABOUT STAYING OUT OF TROUBLE AND JAIL, KIDDO. I JUST WANT TO GET OUT OF HERE AND BACK TO MY LIFE OF EPIC OBSCURITY.
TAXI
WHINE WHINE WHINE…I DOUBT THERE'S MORE THAN EIGHT SUPER-POWERED WHATSIS PEOPLE IN THE STATE OF OHIO. AND YOU'VE KILLED MOST OF THEM OVER THE YEARS, ANYWAYS…
WE'LL BE IN AND OUT IN TEN MINUTES…TOPS. HOW LONG COULD THIS TAKE?

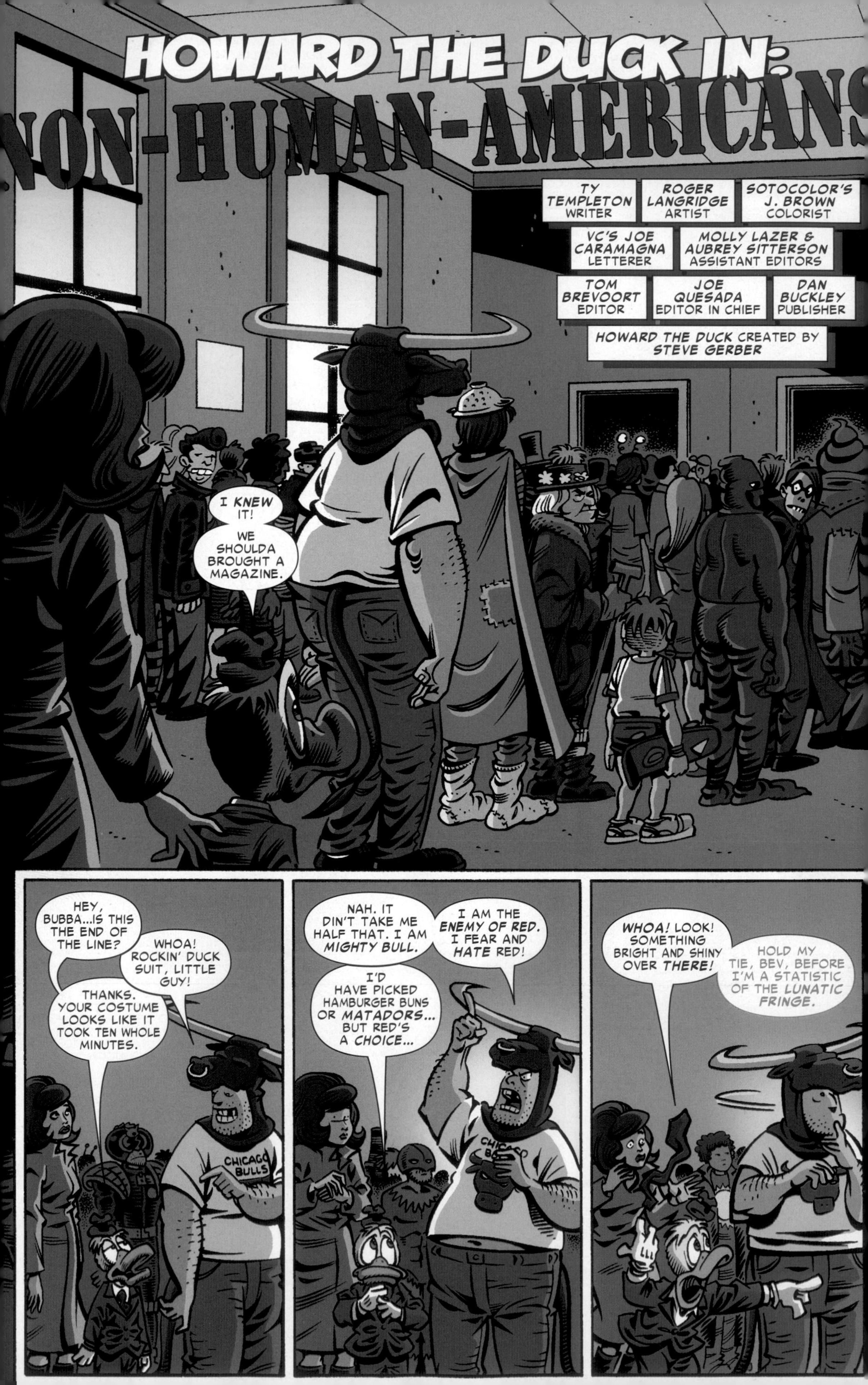
HOWARD THE DUCK IN:
NON-HUMAN-AMERICANS
TY TEMPLETON WRITER
ROGER LANGRIDGE ARTIST
SOTOCOLOR'S J. BROWN COLORIST
VC'S JOE CARAMAGNA LETTERER
MOLLY LAZER & AUBREY SITTERSON ASSISTANT EDITORS
TOM BREVOORT EDITOR
JOE QUESADA EDITOR IN CHIEF
DAN BUCKLEY PUBLISHER
HOWARD THE DUCK CREATED BY STEVE GERBER
I KNEW IT!
WE SHOULDA BROUGHT A MAGAZINE.
HEY, BUBBA...IS THIS THE END OF THE LINE?
WHOA! ROCKIN' DUCK SUIT, LITTLE GUY!
THANKS. YOUR COSTUME LOOKS LIKE IT TOOK TEN WHOLE MINUTES.
CHICAGO BULLS
NAH. IT DIN'T TAKE ME HALF THAT. I AM MIGHTY BULL.
I AM THE ENEMY OF RED. I FEAR AND HATE RED!
I'D HAVE PICKED HAMBURGER BUNS OR MATADORS... BUT RED'S A CHOICE...
WHOA! LOOK! SOMETHING BRIGHT AND SHINY OVER THERE!
HOLD MY TIE, BEV, BEFORE I'M A STATISTIC OF THE LUNATIC FRINGE.

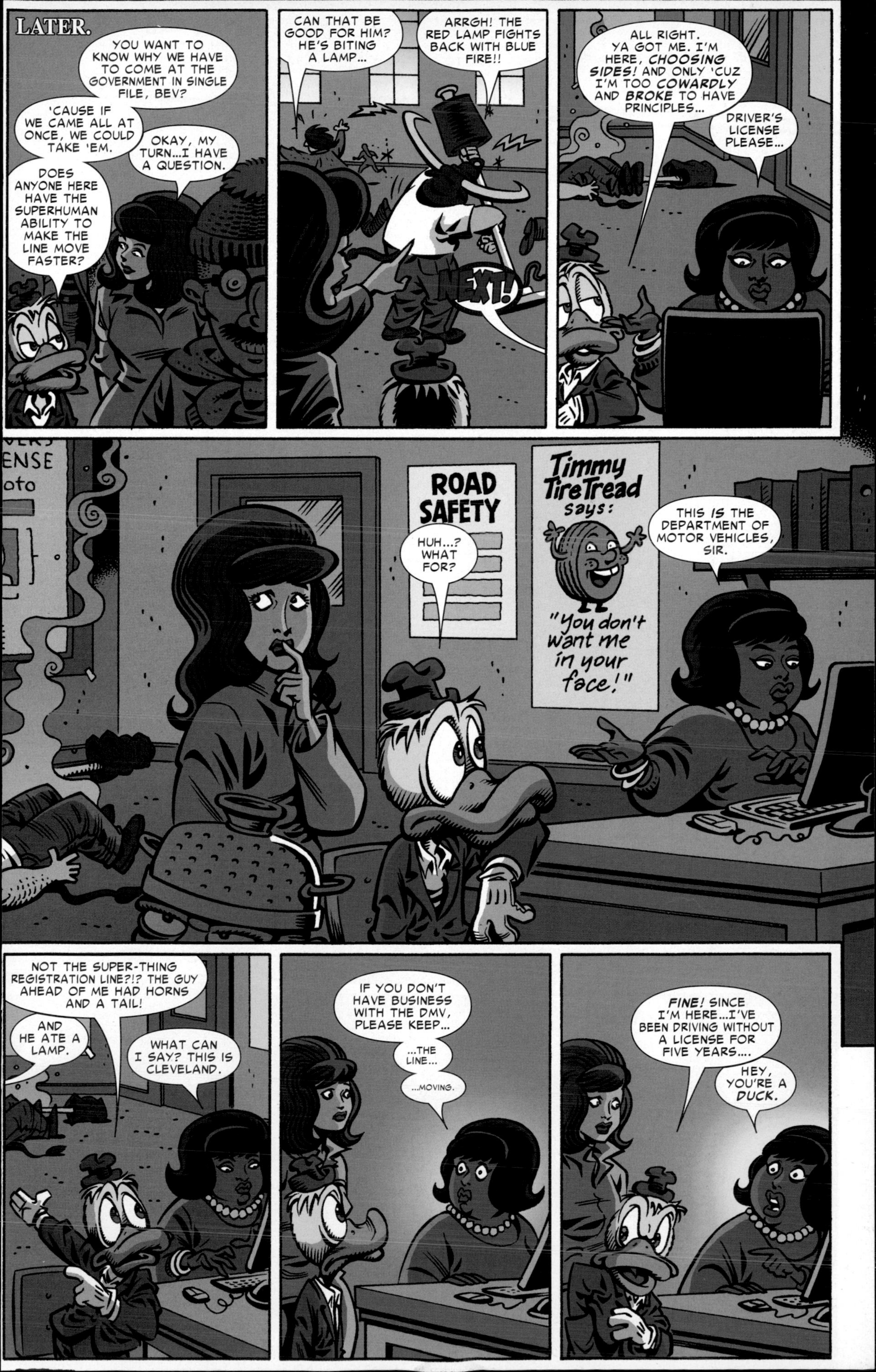
LATER.
YOU WANT TO KNOW WHY WE HAVE TO COME AT THE GOVERNMENT IN SINGLE FILE, BEV?
'CAUSE IF WE CAME ALL AT ONCE, WE COULD TAKE 'EM.
OKAY, MY TURN...I HAVE A QUESTION.
DOES ANYONE HERE HAVE THE SUPERHUMAN ABILITY TO MAKE THE LINE MOVE FASTER?
CAN THAT BE GOOD FOR HIM? HE'S BITING A LAMP...
ARRGH! THE RED LAMP FIGHTS BACK WITH BLUE FIRE!!
NEXT!
ALL RIGHT. YA GOT ME. I'M HERE, CHOOSING SIDES! AND ONLY 'CUZ I'M TOO COWARDLY AND BROKE TO HAVE PRINCIPLES...
DRIVER'S LICENSE PLEASE...
ROAD SAFETY
Timmy TireTread says: "You don't want me in your face!"
HUH...? WHAT FOR?
THIS IS THE DEPARTMENT OF MOTOR VEHICLES, SIR.
NOT THE SUPER-THING REGISTRATION LINE?!? THE GUY AHEAD OF ME HAD HORNS AND A TAIL!
AND HE ATE A LAMP.
WHAT CAN I SAY? THIS IS CLEVELAND.
IF YOU DON'T HAVE BUSINESS WITH THE DMV, PLEASE KEEP...
...THE LINE...
...MOVING.
FINE! SINCE I'M HERE...I'VE BEEN DRIVING WITHOUT A LICENSE FOR FIVE YEARS....
HEY, YOU'RE A DUCK.

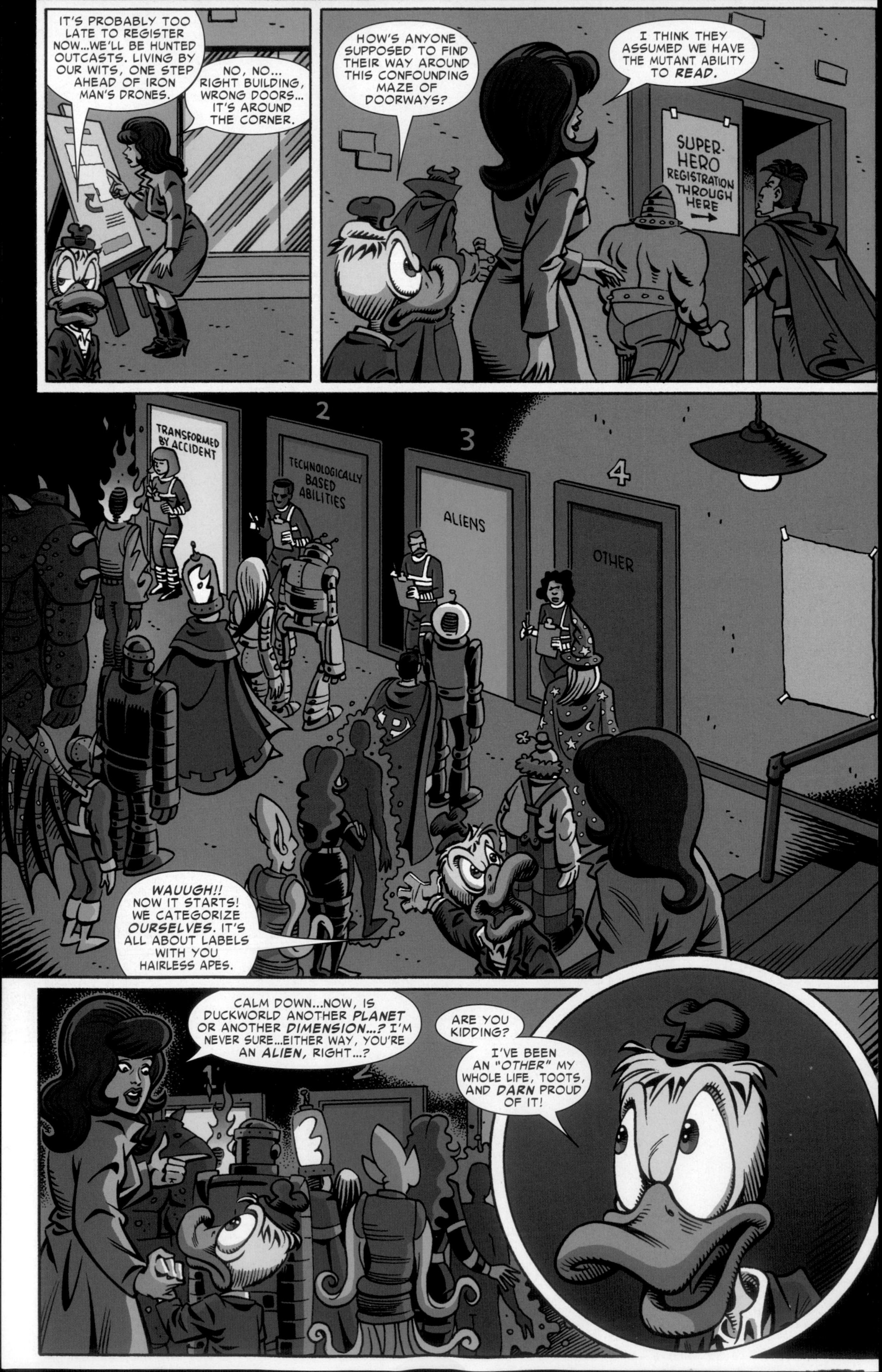
IT'S PROBABLY TOO LATE TO REGISTER NOW...WE'LL BE HUNTED OUTCASTS. LIVING BY OUR WITS, ONE STEP AHEAD OF IRON MAN'S DRONES.
NO, NO... RIGHT BUILDING, WRONG DOORS... IT'S AROUND THE CORNER.
HOW'S ANYONE SUPPOSED TO FIND THEIR WAY AROUND THIS CONFOUNDING MAZE OF DOORWAYS?
I THINK THEY ASSUMED WE HAVE THE MUTANT ABILITY TO READ.
SUPER-HERO REGISTRATION THROUGH HERE →
TRANSFORMED BY ACCIDENT
2
TECHNOLOGICALLY BASED ABILITIES
3
ALIENS
4
OTHER
WAUUGH!! NOW IT STARTS! WE CATEGORIZE OURSELVES. IT'S ALL ABOUT LABELS WITH YOU HAIRLESS APES.
CALM DOWN...NOW, IS DUCKWORLD ANOTHER PLANET OR ANOTHER DIMENSION...? I'M NEVER SURE...EITHER WAY, YOU'RE AN ALIEN, RIGHT...?
ARE YOU KIDDING?
I'VE BEEN AN "OTHER" MY WHOLE LIFE, TOOTS, AND DARN PROUD OF IT!

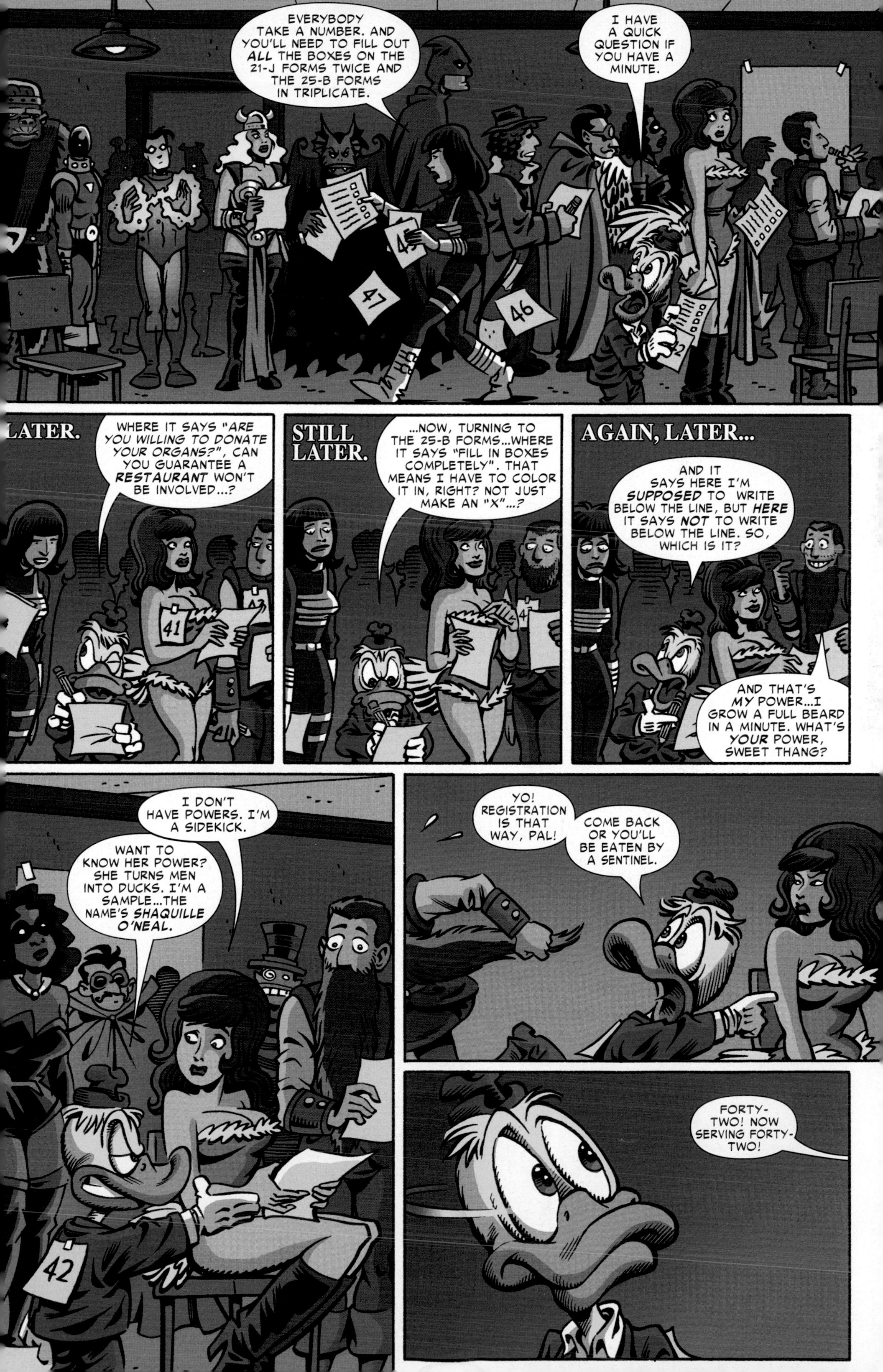
EVERYBODY TAKE A NUMBER. AND YOU'LL NEED TO FILL OUT ALL THE BOXES ON THE 21-J FORMS TWICE AND THE 25-B FORMS IN TRIPLICATE.
I HAVE A QUICK QUESTION IF YOU HAVE A MINUTE.
LATER.
WHERE IT SAYS "ARE YOU WILLING TO DONATE YOUR ORGANS?", CAN YOU GUARANTEE A RESTAURANT WON'T BE INVOLVED...?
STILL LATER.
...NOW, TURNING TO THE 25-B FORMS...WHERE IT SAYS "FILL IN BOXES COMPLETELY". THAT MEANS I HAVE TO COLOR IT IN, RIGHT? NOT JUST MAKE AN "X"...?
AGAIN, LATER...
AND IT SAYS HERE I'M SUPPOSED TO WRITE BELOW THE LINE, BUT HERE IT SAYS NOT TO WRITE BELOW THE LINE. SO, WHICH IS IT?
AND THAT'S MY POWER...I GROW A FULL BEARD IN A MINUTE. WHAT'S YOUR POWER, SWEET THANG?
I DON'T HAVE POWERS. I'M A SIDEKICK.
WANT TO KNOW HER POWER? SHE TURNS MEN INTO DUCKS. I'M A SAMPLE...THE NAME'S SHAQUILLE O'NEAL.
YO! REGISTRATION IS THAT WAY, PAL!
COME BACK OR YOU'LL BE EATEN BY A SENTINEL.
FORTY-TWO! NOW SERVING FORTY-TWO!

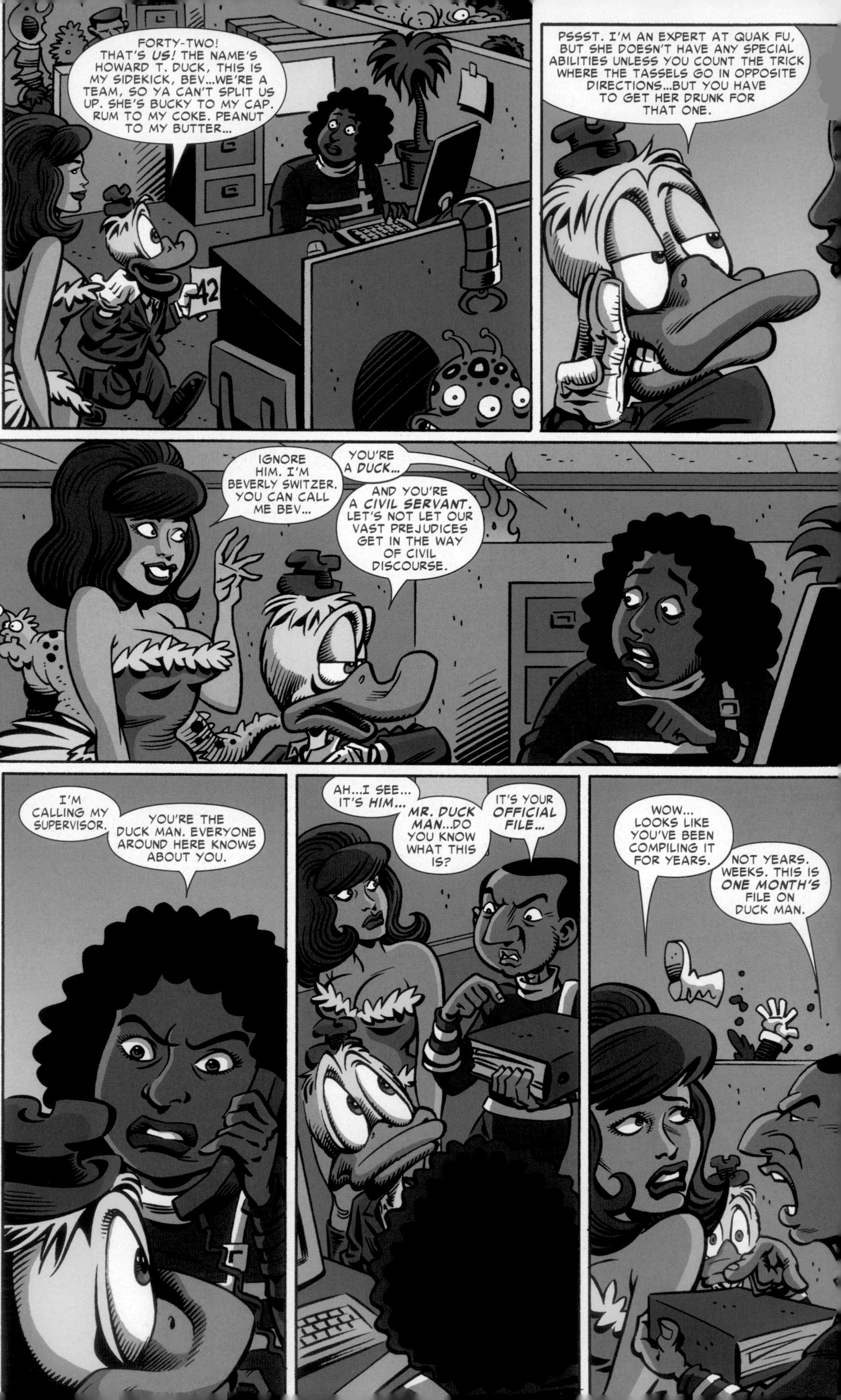

FORTY-TWO! THAT'S US! THE NAME'S HOWARD T. DUCK, THIS IS MY SIDEKICK, BEV...WE'RE A TEAM, SO YA CAN'T SPLIT US UP. SHE'S BUCKY TO MY CAP. RUM TO MY COKE. PEANUT TO MY BUTTER...
42
PSSST. I'M AN EXPERT AT QUAK FU, BUT SHE DOESN'T HAVE ANY SPECIAL ABILITIES UNLESS YOU COUNT THE TRICK WHERE THE TASSELS GO IN OPPOSITE DIRECTIONS...BUT YOU HAVE TO GET HER DRUNK FOR THAT ONE.
IGNORE HIM. I'M BEVERLY SWITZER. YOU CAN CALL ME BEV...
YOU'RE A DUCK...
AND YOU'RE A CIVIL SERVANT. LET'S NOT LET OUR VAST PREJUDICES GET IN THE WAY OF CIVIL DISCOURSE.
I'M CALLING MY SUPERVISOR.
YOU'RE THE DUCK MAN. EVERYONE AROUND HERE KNOWS ABOUT YOU.
AH...I SEE... IT'S HIM...
MR. DUCK MAN...DO YOU KNOW WHAT THIS IS?
IT'S YOUR OFFICIAL FILE...
WOW... LOOKS LIKE YOU'VE BEEN COMPILING IT FOR YEARS.
NOT YEARS. WEEKS. THIS IS ONE MONTH'S FILE ON DUCK MAN.

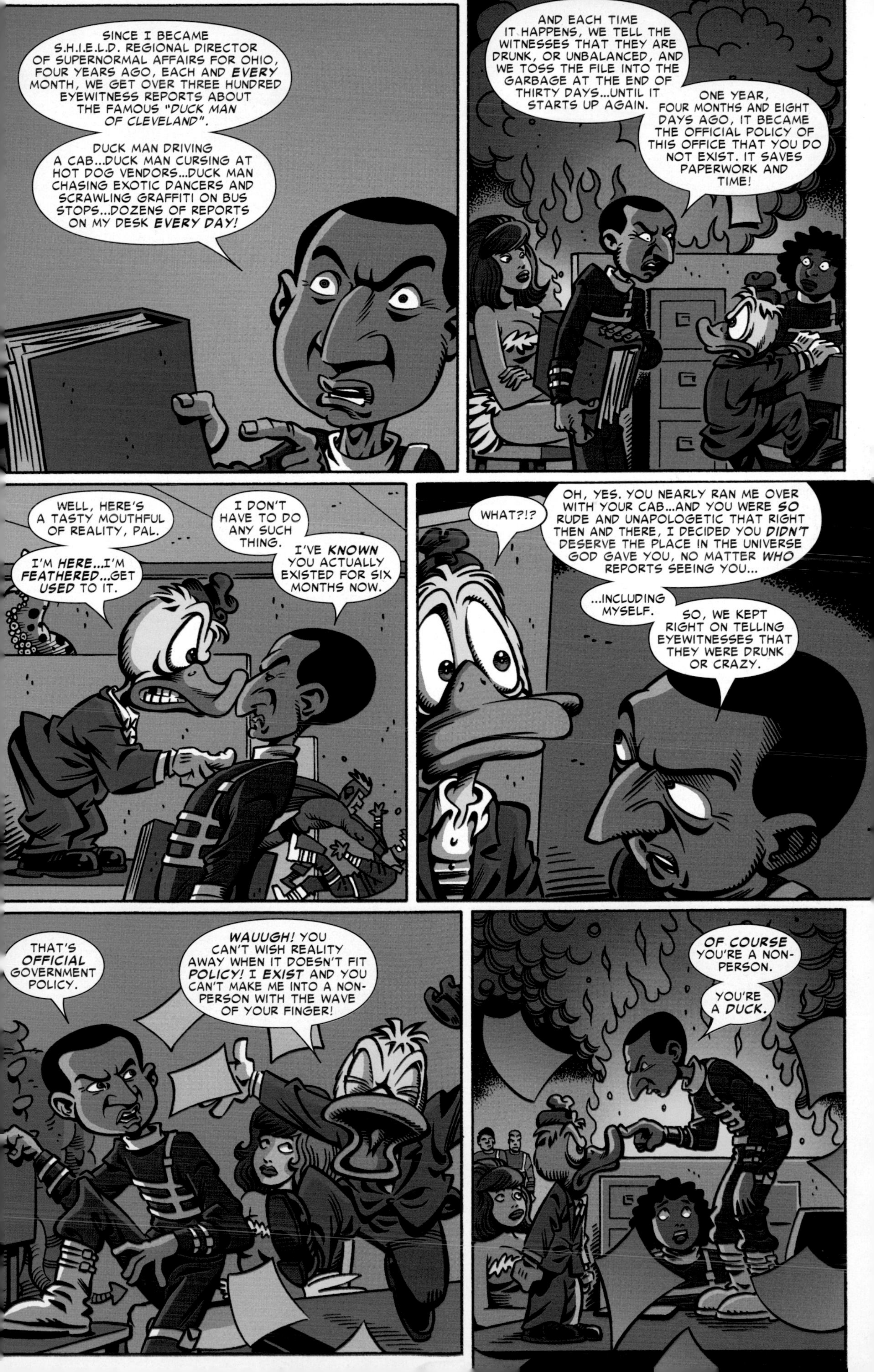

SINCE I BECAME S.H.I.E.L.D. REGIONAL DIRECTOR OF SUPERNORMAL AFFAIRS FOR OHIO, FOUR YEARS AGO, EACH AND EVERY MONTH, WE GET OVER THREE HUNDRED EYEWITNESS REPORTS ABOUT THE FAMOUS "DUCK MAN OF CLEVELAND".
DUCK MAN DRIVING A CAB...DUCK MAN CURSING AT HOT DOG VENDORS...DUCK MAN CHASING EXOTIC DANCERS AND SCRAWLING GRAFFITI ON BUS STOPS...DOZENS OF REPORTS ON MY DESK EVERY DAY!
AND EACH TIME IT HAPPENS, WE TELL THE WITNESSES THAT THEY ARE DRUNK, OR UNBALANCED, AND WE TOSS THE FILE INTO THE GARBAGE AT THE END OF THIRTY DAYS...UNTIL IT STARTS UP AGAIN.
ONE YEAR, FOUR MONTHS AND EIGHT DAYS AGO, IT BECAME THE OFFICIAL POLICY OF THIS OFFICE THAT YOU DO NOT EXIST. IT SAVES PAPERWORK AND TIME!
WELL, HERE'S A TASTY MOUTHFUL OF REALITY, PAL.
I'M HERE...I'M FEATHERED...GET USED TO IT.
I DON'T HAVE TO DO ANY SUCH THING.
I'VE KNOWN YOU ACTUALLY EXISTED FOR SIX MONTHS NOW.
WHAT?!?
OH, YES. YOU NEARLY RAN ME OVER WITH YOUR CAB...AND YOU WERE SO RUDE AND UNAPOLOGETIC THAT RIGHT THEN AND THERE, I DECIDED YOU DIDN'T DESERVE THE PLACE IN THE UNIVERSE GOD GAVE YOU, NO MATTER WHO REPORTS SEEING YOU...
...INCLUDING MYSELF.
SO, WE KEPT RIGHT ON TELLING EYEWITNESSES THAT THEY WERE DRUNK OR CRAZY.
THAT'S OFFICIAL GOVERNMENT POLICY.
WAUUGH! YOU CAN'T WISH REALITY AWAY WHEN IT DOESN'T FIT POLICY! I EXIST AND YOU CAN'T MAKE ME INTO A NON-PERSON WITH THE WAVE OF YOUR FINGER!
OF COURSE YOU'RE A NON-PERSON.
YOU'RE A DUCK.

MMAHCH!

I'LL KILL HIM!

IN TRIPLICATE!

LET ME AT HIM.

AND STAY OUT!

HAA! HAAA!

BOOT!

NO PARKING
NOT EVEN FOR EMERGENCIES
TRUST US, YOUR EXCUSE WILL NOT WORK WITH A JUDGE

YOU OKAY, HOWARD? I THOUGHT YOU WERE GOING TO MOLT, YOU WERE SO ANGRY...

ANGRY?!? ARE YOU KIDDING?!? THIS IS THE GREATEST THING THAT COULD EVER HAPPEN TO ME.

FOR THE REST OF MY LIFE...NO MORE PARKING TICKETS...NO MORE TAXES... OR JURY DUTY. HECK, I COULDN'T EVEN VOTE IF I WANTED TO!

THIS IS BETTER THAN CHRISTMAS IN VEGAS. I NO LONGER OFFICIALLY EXIST!

HEY! BULL BOY! YOU LOOKING FOR THE PLACE FOR THE SUPER HERO REGISTRATION?!?

I AM MIGHTY BULL! I CRUSH RED!

LET ME GIVE YOU SOME ADVICE, AND TRUST ME ON THIS...

...HEAD FOR LINE FOUR...

SUPER HERO REGISTRATION THROUGH HERE

THE END.

THE RETURN
A MARVEL COMICS EVENT

CIVIL WAR

THE RETURN

A Superhuman Registration Act has been passed which requires all people possessing paranormal abilities to register with the government. Those who do not register are considered criminals. Some heroes, such as Iron Man, see this as a natural evolution of the role of superhumans in society and a reasonable request. Others view the Act as an assault on their civil liberties. Captain America currently leads an underground resistance movement against the new law.

After a brutal battle, Bill Foster--the anti-registration hero known as Goliath--has been killed. Other members of Captain America's resistance have been captured and brought to the pro-registration faction's holding facility in the Negative Zone. Both sides have retreated in order to regroup and plan their next move.

Meanwhile, across the country, super heroes continue to weigh the cost of registering against the price of freedom...

PAUL JENKINS
WRITER

TOM RANEY
PENCILER

SCOTT HANNA
INKER

GINA GOING (PAGES 1-13)
SOTOCOLOR'S A. CROSSLEY (PAGES 14-23)
COLORISTS

DAVE SHARPE
LETTERER

ANTHONY DIAL
PRODUCTION

MOLLY LAZER & AUBREY SITTERSON
ASSISTANT EDITORS

STEPHEN WACKER
EDITOR

JOE QUESADA
EDITOR IN CHIEF

DAN BUCKLEY
PUBLISHER

VARIANT COVER **BY ED MCGUINNESS & DAVE MCCAIG**

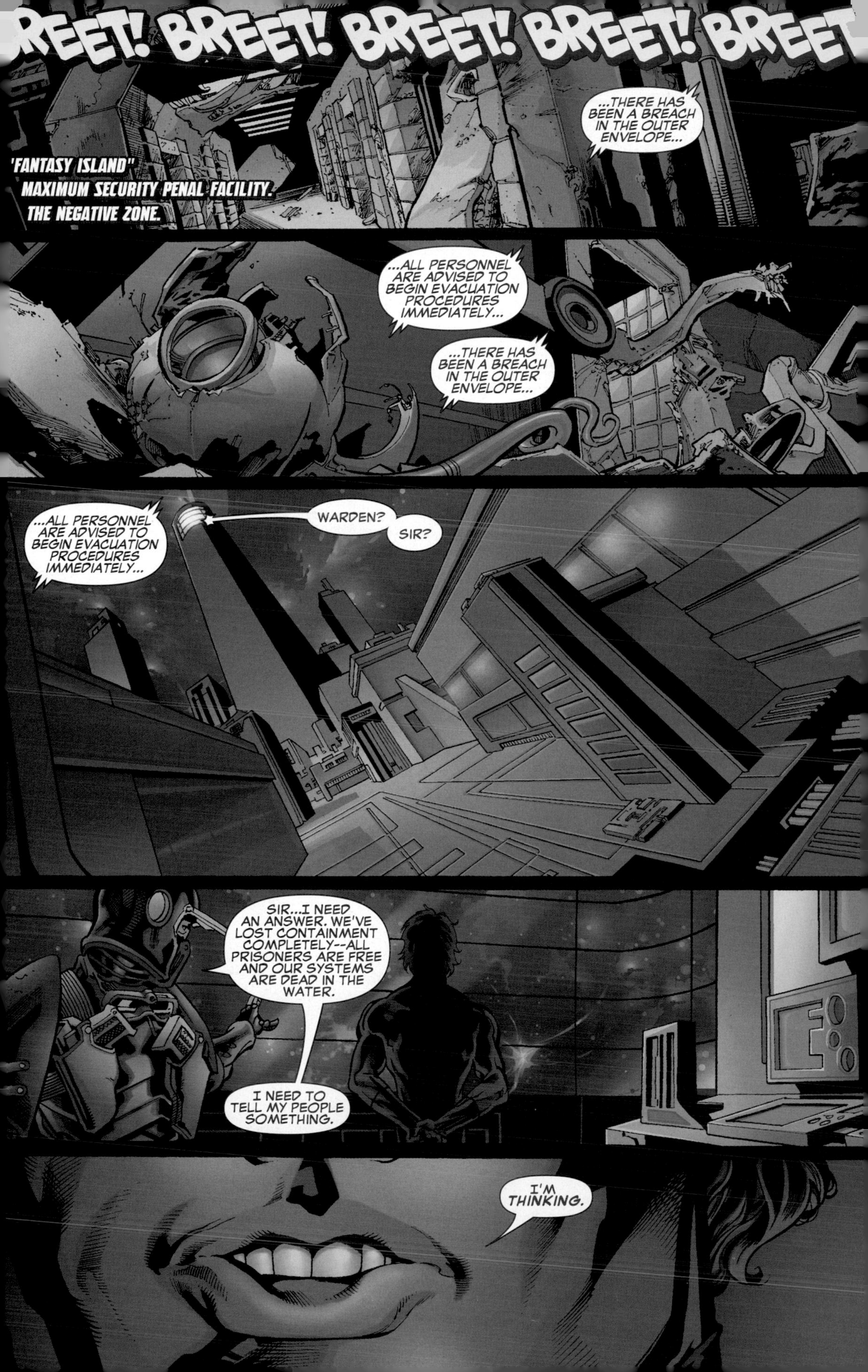
BREET! BREET! BREET! BREET! BREET
"FANTASY ISLAND" MAXIMUM SECURITY PENAL FACILITY. THE NEGATIVE ZONE.
...THERE HAS BEEN A BREACH IN THE OUTER ENVELOPE...
...ALL PERSONNEL ARE ADVISED TO BEGIN EVACUATION PROCEDURES IMMEDIATELY...
...THERE HAS BEEN A BREACH IN THE OUTER ENVELOPE...
...ALL PERSONNEL ARE ADVISED TO BEGIN EVACUATION PROCEDURES IMMEDIATELY...
WARDEN?
SIR?
SIR...I NEED AN ANSWER. WE'VE LOST CONTAINMENT COMPLETELY--ALL PRISONERS ARE FREE AND OUR SYSTEMS ARE DEAD IN THE WATER.
I NEED TO TELL MY PEOPLE SOMETHING.
I'M THINKING.

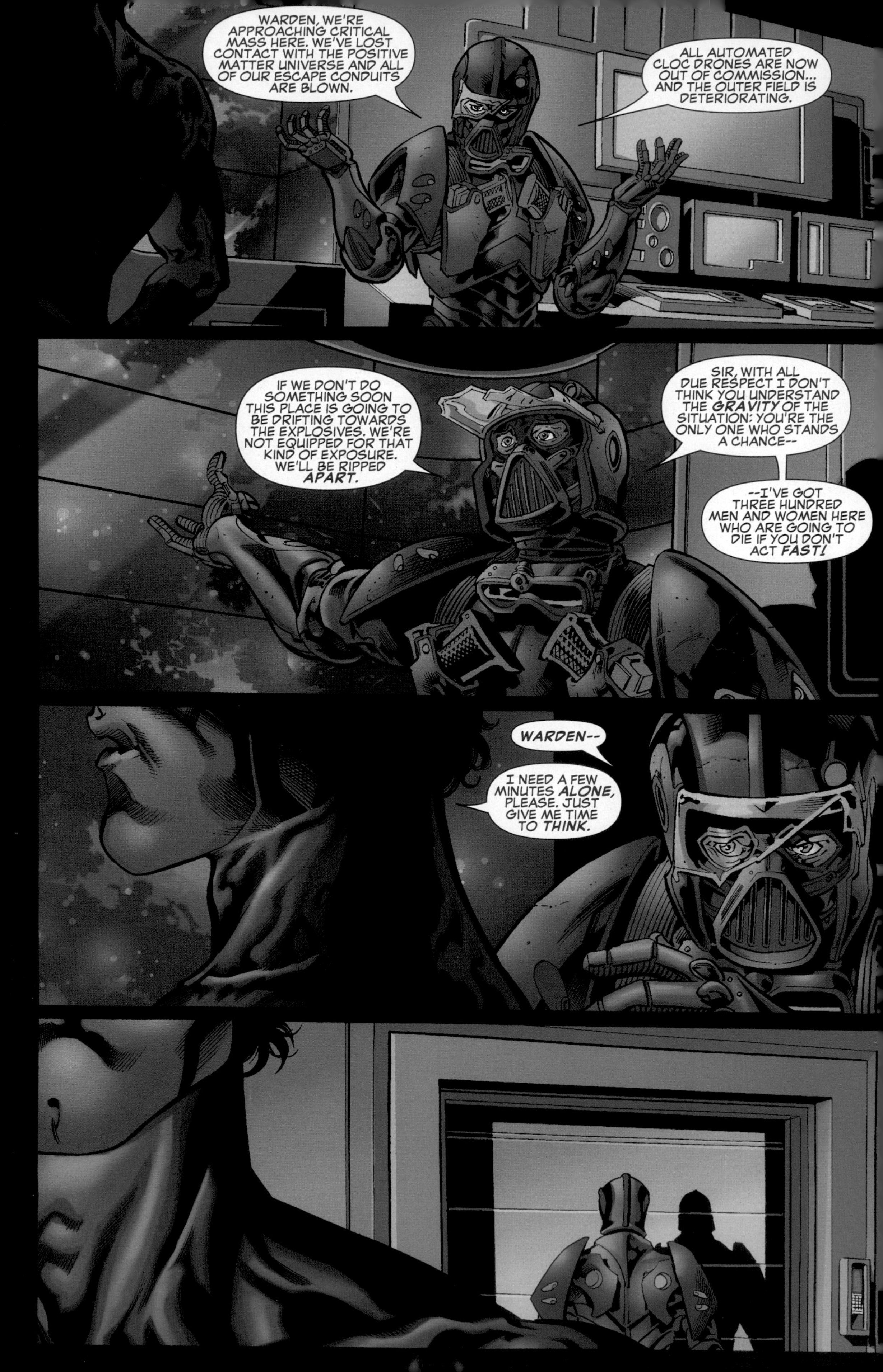
WARDEN, WE'RE APPROACHING CRITICAL MASS HERE. WE'VE LOST CONTACT WITH THE POSITIVE MATTER UNIVERSE AND ALL OF OUR ESCAPE CONDUITS ARE BLOWN.
ALL AUTOMATED CLOC DRONES ARE NOW OUT OF COMMISSION... AND THE OUTER FIELD IS DETERIORATING.
IF WE DON'T DO SOMETHING SOON THIS PLACE IS GOING TO BE DRIFTING TOWARDS THE EXPLOSIVES. WE'RE NOT EQUIPPED FOR THAT KIND OF EXPOSURE. WE'LL BE RIPPED APART.
SIR, WITH ALL DUE RESPECT I DON'T THINK YOU UNDERSTAND THE GRAVITY OF THE SITUATION: YOU'RE THE ONLY ONE WHO STANDS A CHANCE--
--I'VE GOT THREE HUNDRED MEN AND WOMEN HERE WHO ARE GOING TO DIE IF YOU DON'T ACT FAST!
WARDEN--
I NEED A FEW MINUTES ALONE, PLEASE. JUST GIVE ME TIME TO THINK.

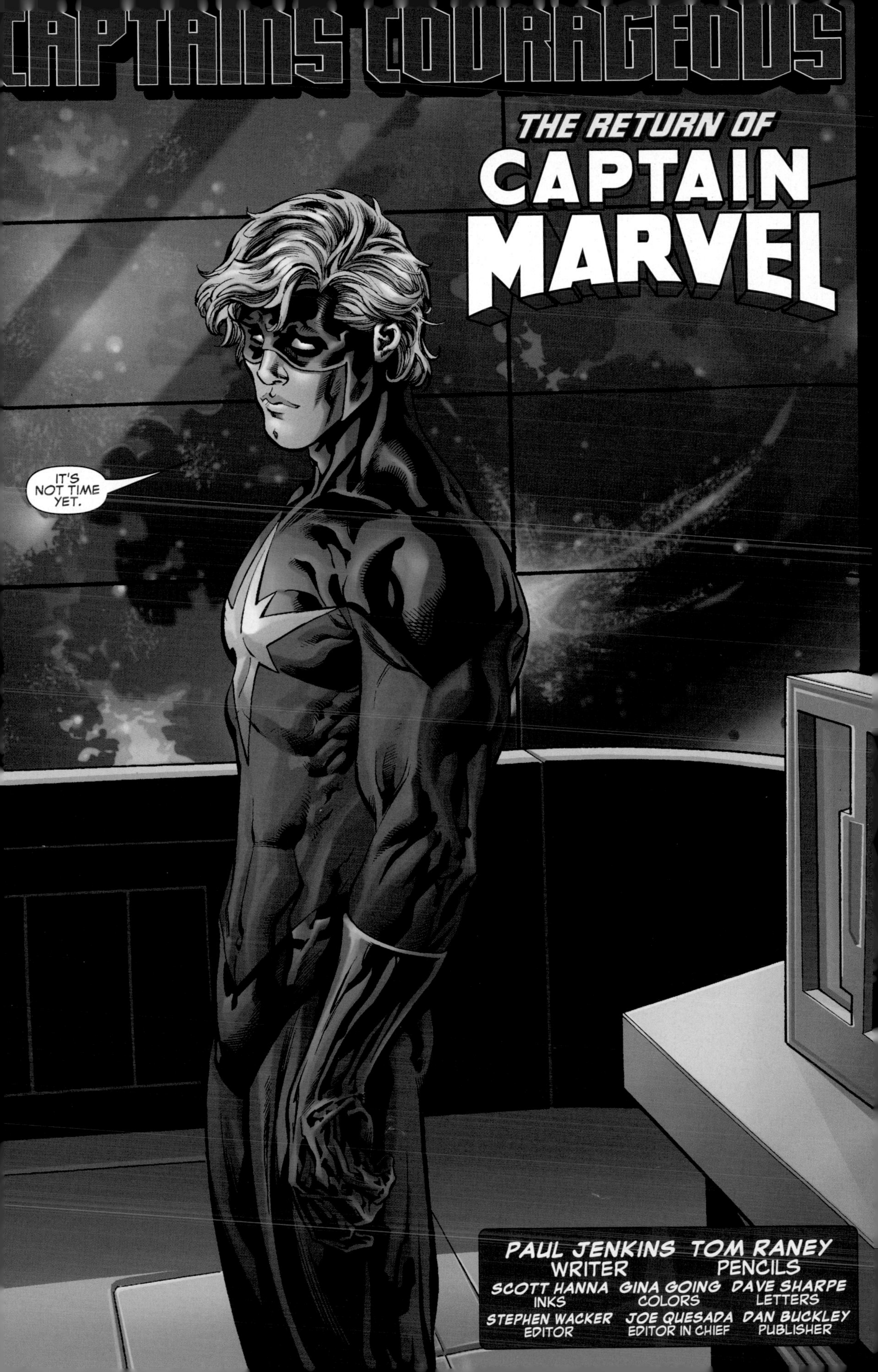
CAPTAINS COURAGEOUS
THE RETURN OF
CAPTAIN
MARVEL
IT'S NOT TIME YET.
PAUL JENKINS WRITER
TOM RANEY PENCILS
SCOTT HANNA INKS
GINA GOING COLORS
DAVE SHARPE LETTERS
STEPHEN WACKER EDITOR
JOE QUESADA EDITOR IN CHIEF
DAN BUCKLEY PUBLISHER

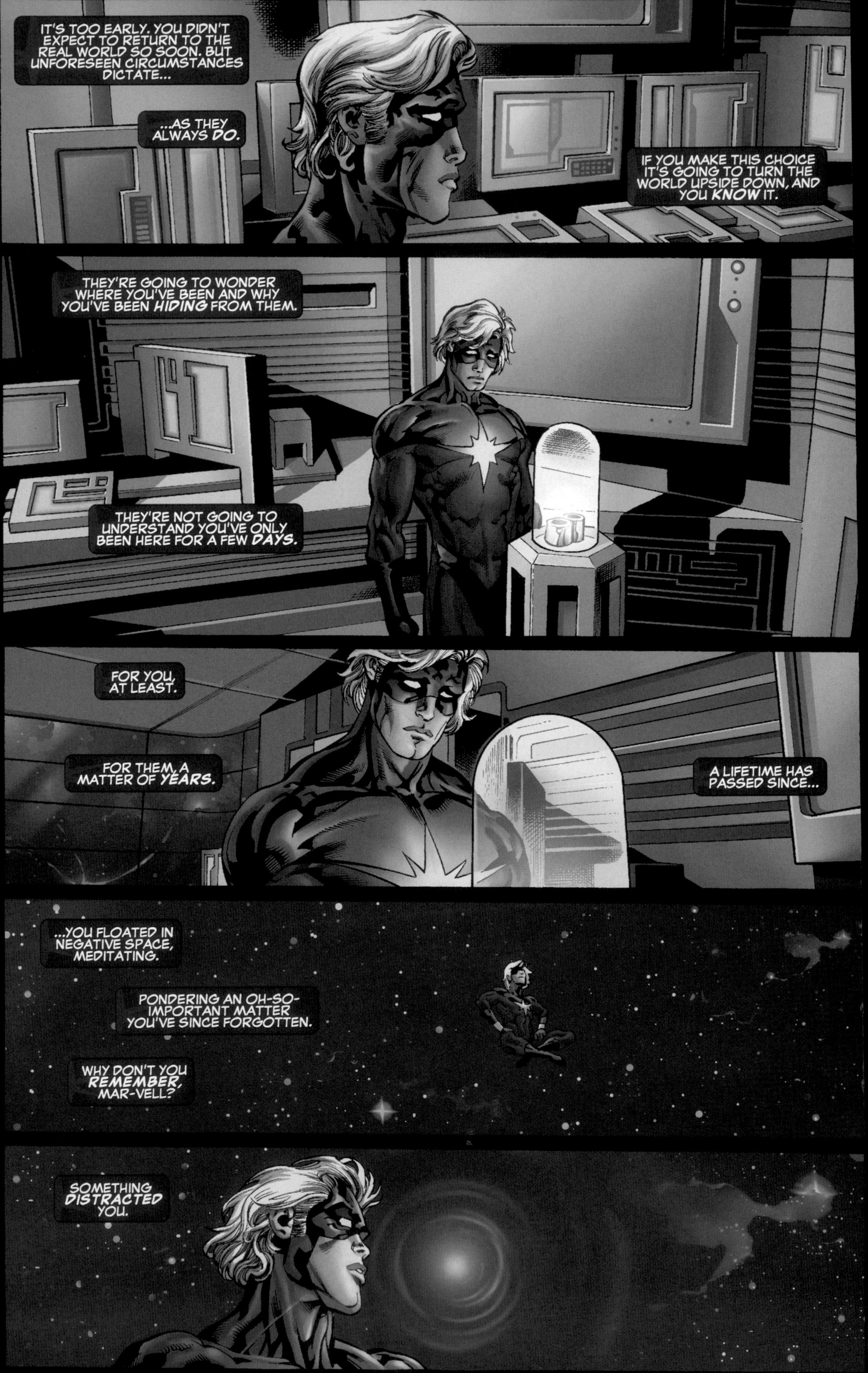
IT'S TOO EARLY. YOU DIDN'T EXPECT TO RETURN TO THE REAL WORLD SO SOON. BUT UNFORESEEN CIRCUMSTANCES DICTATE...
...AS THEY ALWAYS DO.
IF YOU MAKE THIS CHOICE IT'S GOING TO TURN THE WORLD UPSIDE DOWN, AND YOU KNOW IT.
THEY'RE GOING TO WONDER WHERE YOU'VE BEEN AND WHY YOU'VE BEEN HIDING FROM THEM.
THEY'RE NOT GOING TO UNDERSTAND YOU'VE ONLY BEEN HERE FOR A FEW DAYS.
FOR YOU, AT LEAST.
FOR THEM, A MATTER OF YEARS.
A LIFETIME HAS PASSED SINCE...
...YOU FLOATED IN NEGATIVE SPACE, MEDITATING.
PONDERING AN OH-SO-IMPORTANT MATTER YOU'VE SINCE FORGOTTEN.
WHY DON'T YOU REMEMBER, MAR-VELL?
SOMETHING DISTRACTED YOU.

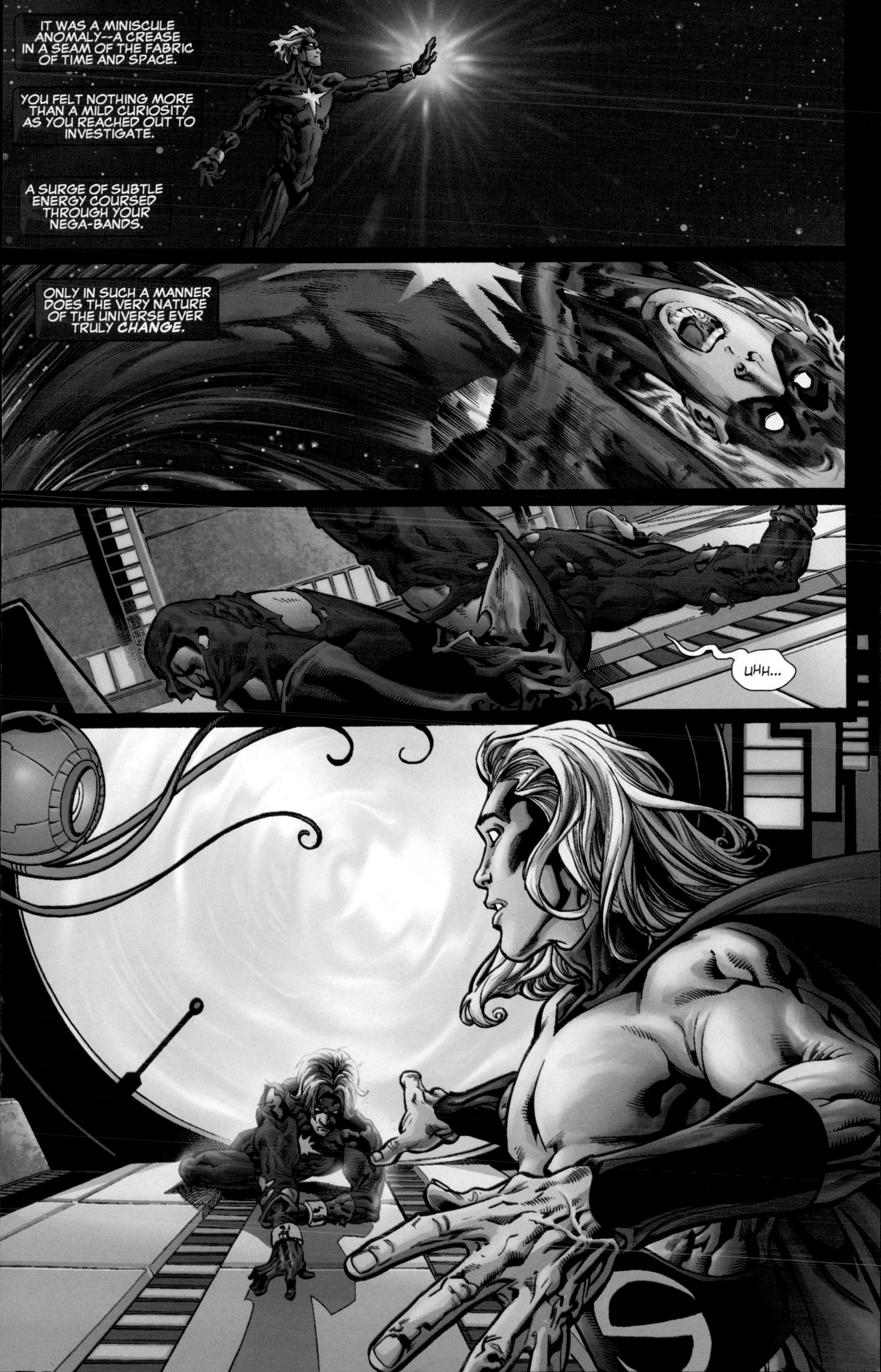
IT WAS A MINISCULE ANOMALY--A CREASE IN A SEAM OF THE FABRIC OF TIME AND SPACE.
YOU FELT NOTHING MORE THAN A MILD CURIOSITY AS YOU REACHED OUT TO INVESTIGATE.
A SURGE OF SUBTLE ENERGY COURSED THROUGH YOUR NEGA-BANDS.
ONLY IN SUCH A MANNER DOES THE VERY NATURE OF THE UNIVERSE EVER TRULY CHANGE.
UHH...

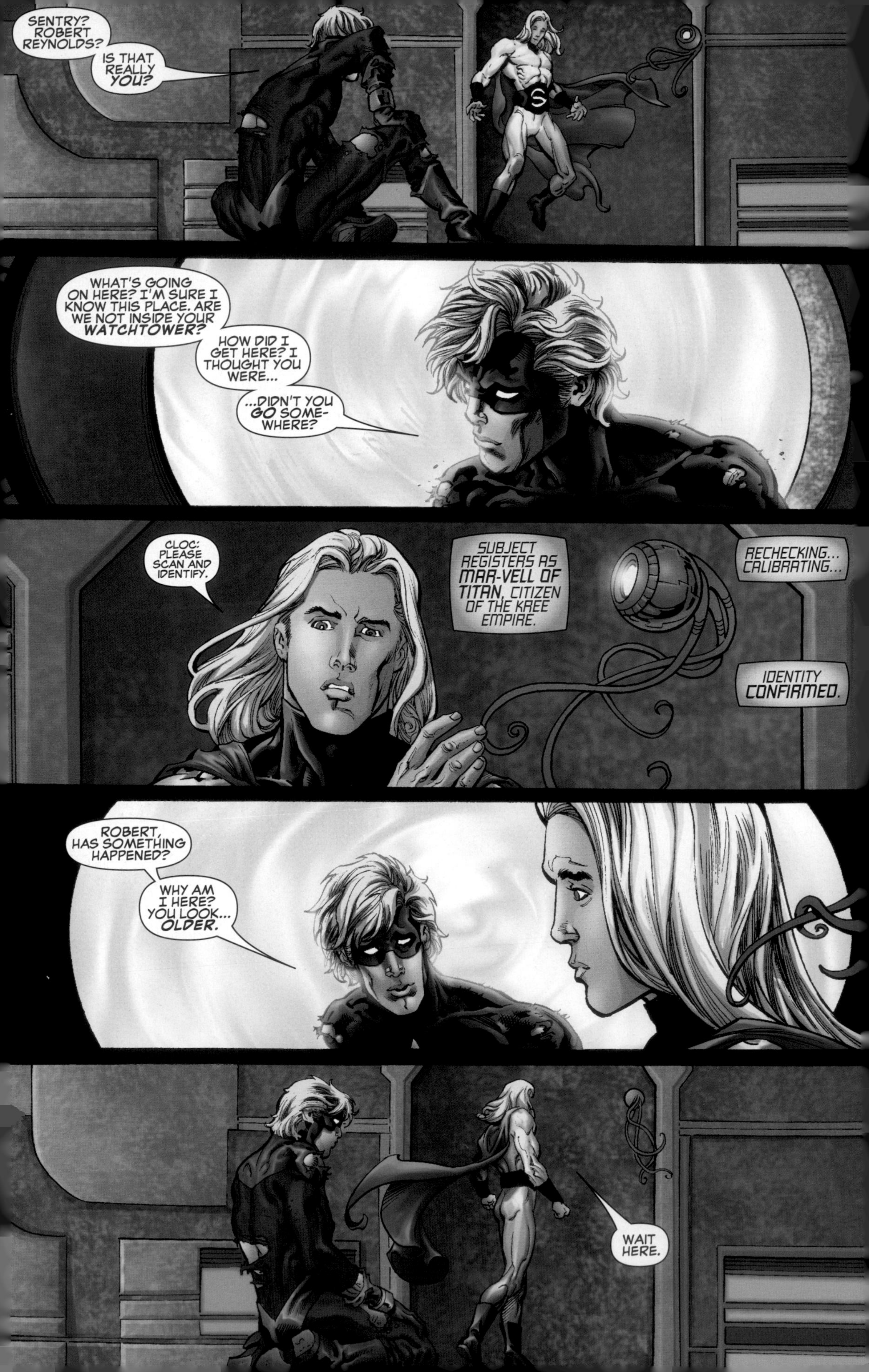

SENTRY? ROBERT REYNOLDS?
IS THAT REALLY YOU?
WHAT'S GOING ON HERE? I'M SURE I KNOW THIS PLACE. ARE WE NOT INSIDE YOUR WATCHTOWER?
HOW DID I GET HERE? I THOUGHT YOU WERE...
...DIDN'T YOU GO SOME-WHERE?
CLOC: PLEASE SCAN AND IDENTIFY.
SUBJECT REGISTERS AS MAR-VELL OF TITAN, CITIZEN OF THE KREE EMPIRE.
RECHECKING... CALIBRATING...
IDENTITY CONFIRMED.
ROBERT, HAS SOMETHING HAPPENED?
WHY AM I HERE? YOU LOOK... OLDER.
WAIT HERE.

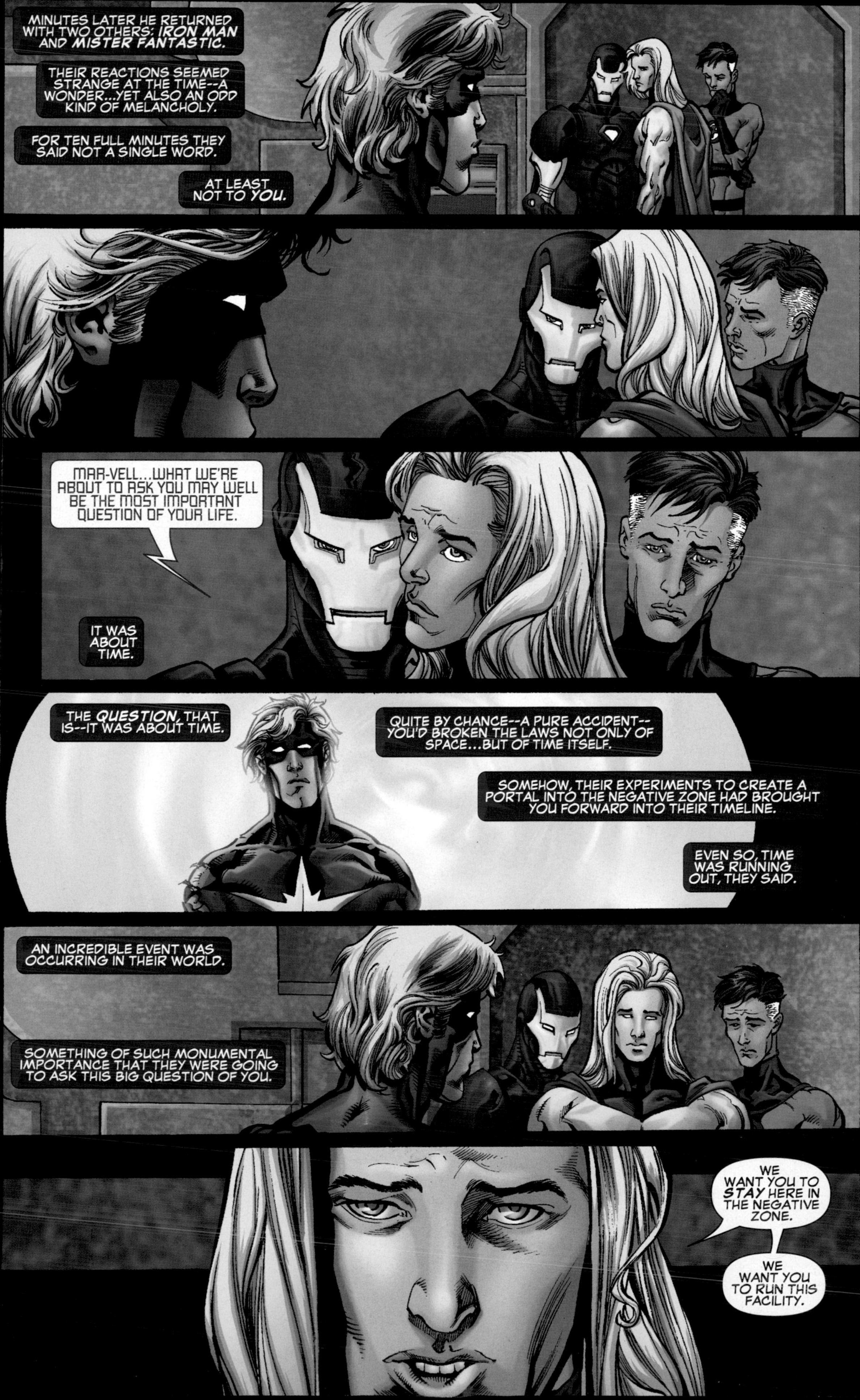

MINUTES LATER HE RETURNED WITH TWO OTHERS: IRON MAN AND MISTER FANTASTIC.
THEIR REACTIONS SEEMED STRANGE AT THE TIME--A WONDER...YET ALSO AN ODD KIND OF MELANCHOLY.
FOR TEN FULL MINUTES THEY SAID NOT A SINGLE WORD.
AT LEAST NOT TO YOU.
MAR-VELL...WHAT WE'RE ABOUT TO ASK YOU MAY WELL BE THE MOST IMPORTANT QUESTION OF YOUR LIFE.
IT WAS ABOUT TIME.
THE QUESTION, THAT IS--IT WAS ABOUT TIME.
QUITE BY CHANCE--A PURE ACCIDENT--YOU'D BROKEN THE LAWS NOT ONLY OF SPACE...BUT OF TIME ITSELF.
SOMEHOW, THEIR EXPERIMENTS TO CREATE A PORTAL INTO THE NEGATIVE ZONE HAD BROUGHT YOU FORWARD INTO THEIR TIMELINE.
EVEN SO, TIME WAS RUNNING OUT, THEY SAID.
AN INCREDIBLE EVENT WAS OCCURRING IN THEIR WORLD.
SOMETHING OF SUCH MONUMENTAL IMPORTANCE THAT THEY WERE GOING TO ASK THIS BIG QUESTION OF YOU.
WE WANT YOU TO STAY HERE IN THE NEGATIVE ZONE.
WE WANT YOU TO RUN THIS FACILITY.

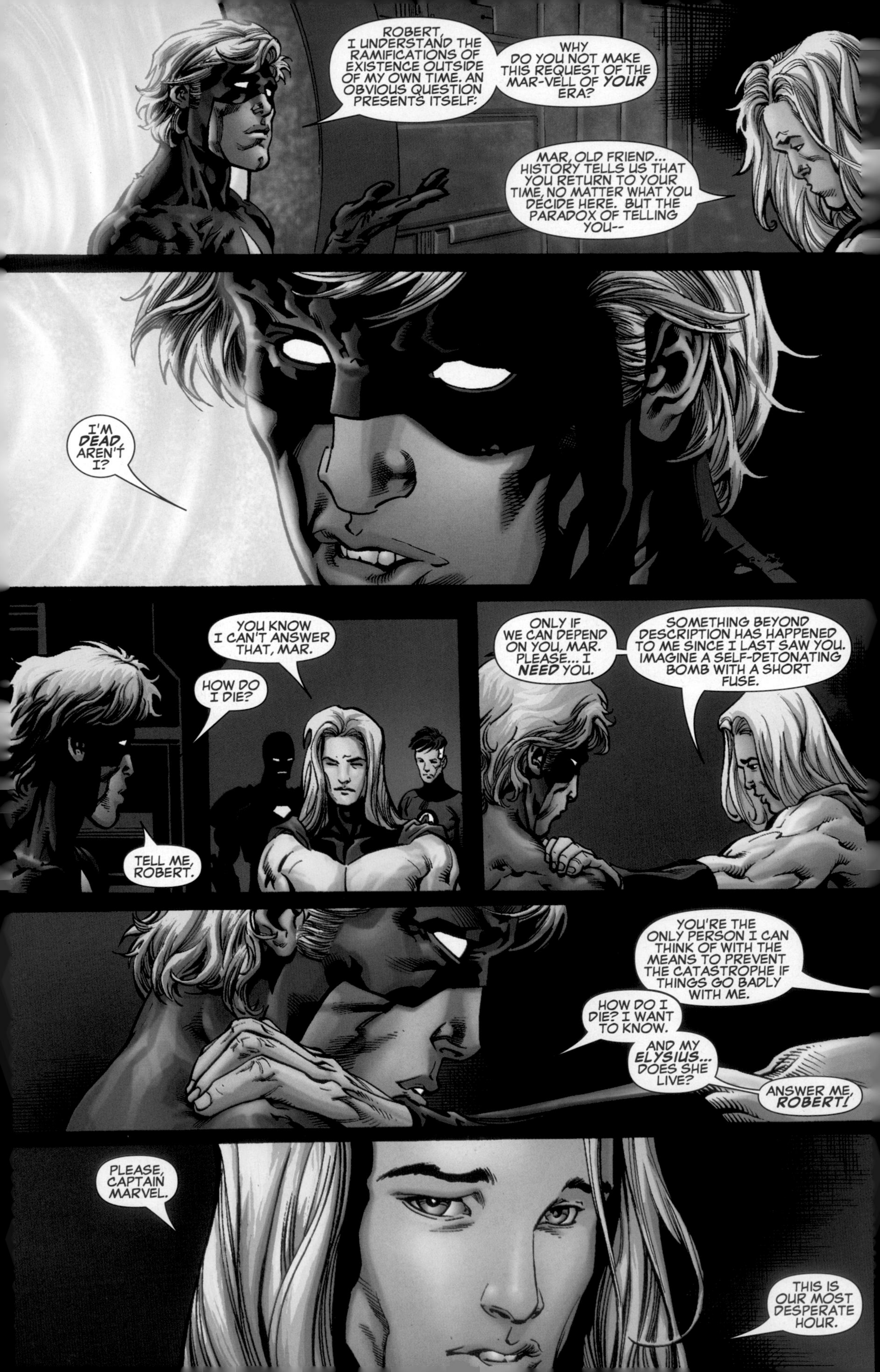
ROBERT, I UNDERSTAND THE RAMIFICATIONS OF EXISTENCE OUTSIDE OF MY OWN TIME. AN OBVIOUS QUESTION PRESENTS ITSELF:
WHY DO YOU NOT MAKE THIS REQUEST OF THE MAR-VELL OF YOUR ERA?
MAR, OLD FRIEND... HISTORY TELLS US THAT YOU RETURN TO YOUR TIME, NO MATTER WHAT YOU DECIDE HERE. BUT THE PARADOX OF TELLING YOU--
I'M DEAD, AREN'T I?
YOU KNOW I CAN'T ANSWER THAT, MAR.
HOW DO I DIE?
TELL ME, ROBERT.
ONLY IF WE CAN DEPEND ON YOU, MAR. PLEASE... I NEED YOU.
SOMETHING BEYOND DESCRIPTION HAS HAPPENED TO ME SINCE I LAST SAW YOU. IMAGINE A SELF-DETONATING BOMB WITH A SHORT FUSE.
YOU'RE THE ONLY PERSON I CAN THINK OF WITH THE MEANS TO PREVENT THE CATASTROPHE IF THINGS GO BADLY WITH ME.
HOW DO I DIE? I WANT TO KNOW.
AND MY ELYSIUS... DOES SHE LIVE?
ANSWER ME, ROBERT!
PLEASE, CAPTAIN MARVEL.
THIS IS OUR MOST DESPERATE HOUR.

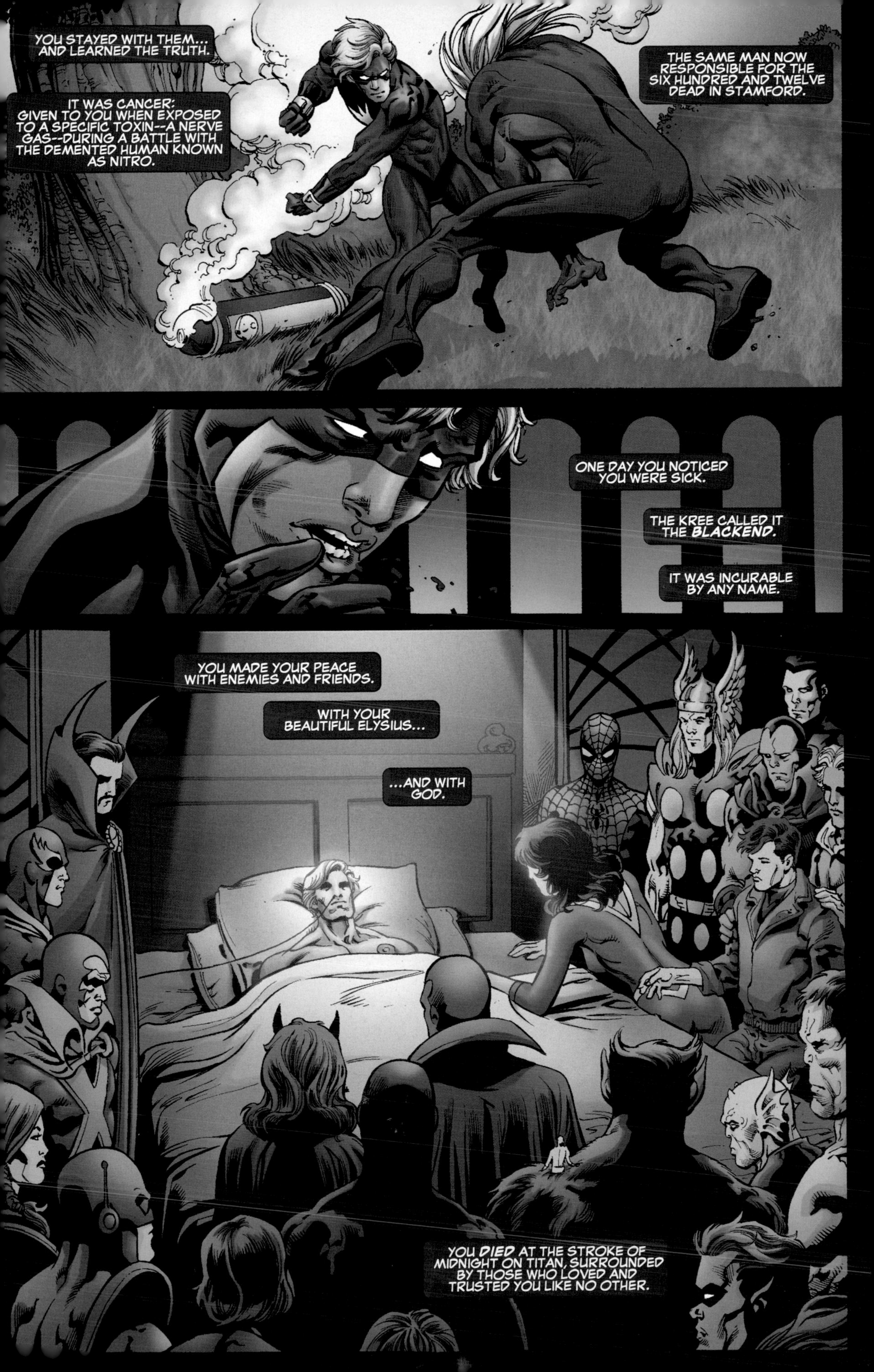
YOU STAYED WITH THEM... AND LEARNED THE TRUTH.
IT WAS CANCER: GIVEN TO YOU WHEN EXPOSED TO A SPECIFIC TOXIN--A NERVE GAS--DURING A BATTLE WITH THE DEMENTED HUMAN KNOWN AS NITRO.
THE SAME MAN NOW RESPONSIBLE FOR THE SIX HUNDRED AND TWELVE DEAD IN STAMFORD.
ONE DAY YOU NOTICED YOU WERE SICK.
THE KREE CALLED IT THE BLACKEND.
IT WAS INCURABLE BY ANY NAME.
YOU MADE YOUR PEACE WITH ENEMIES AND FRIENDS.
WITH YOUR BEAUTIFUL ELYSIUS...
...AND WITH GOD.
YOU DIED AT THE STROKE OF MIDNIGHT ON TITAN, SURROUNDED BY THOSE WHO LOVED AND TRUSTED YOU LIKE NO OTHER.

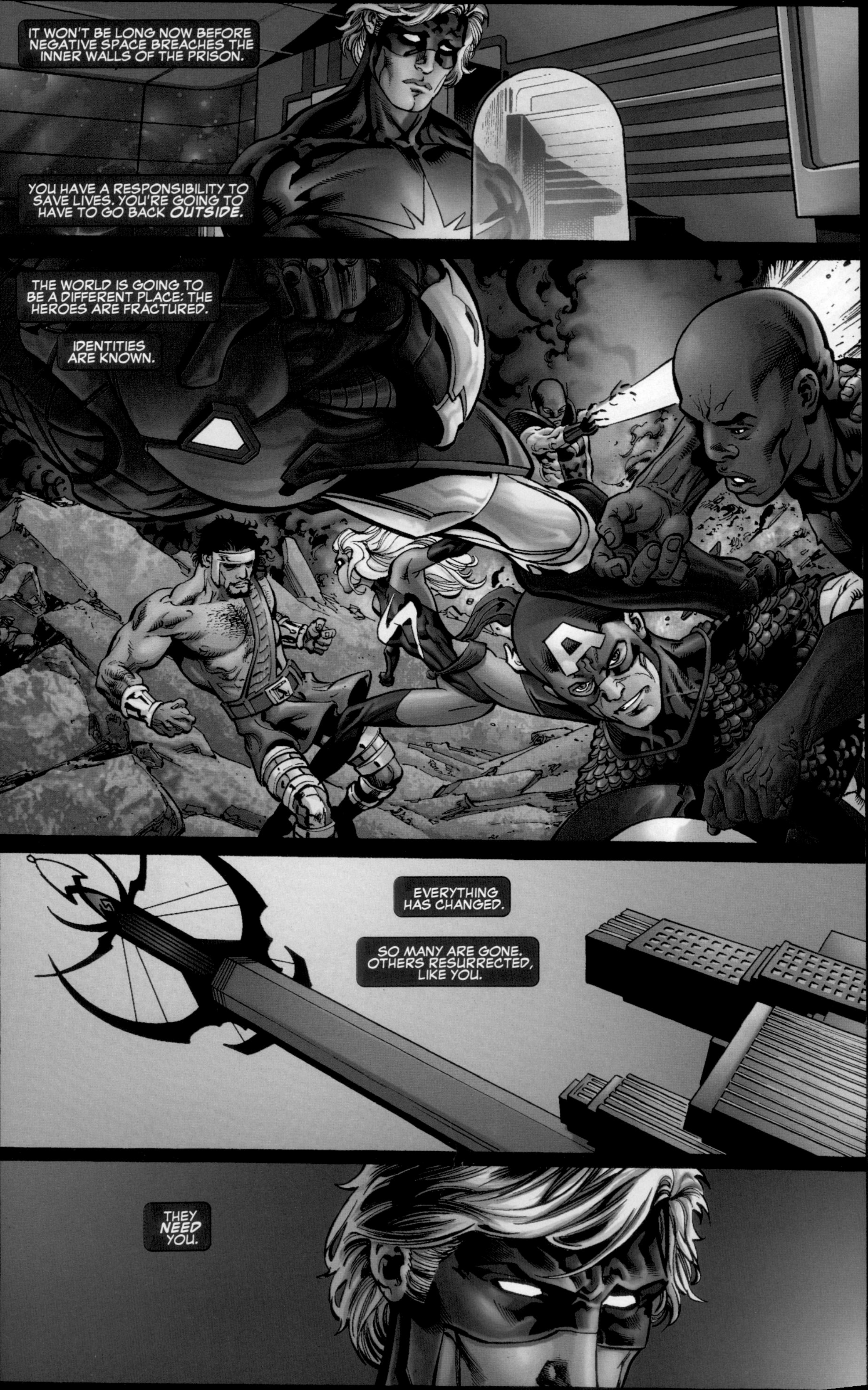
IT WON'T BE LONG NOW BEFORE NEGATIVE SPACE BREACHES THE INNER WALLS OF THE PRISON.
YOU HAVE A RESPONSIBILITY TO SAVE LIVES. YOU'RE GOING TO HAVE TO GO BACK *OUTSIDE*.
THE WORLD IS GOING TO BE A DIFFERENT PLACE: THE HEROES ARE FRACTURED.
IDENTITIES ARE KNOWN.
EVERYTHING HAS CHANGED.
SO MANY ARE GONE. OTHERS RESURRECTED, LIKE YOU.
THEY *NEED* YOU.

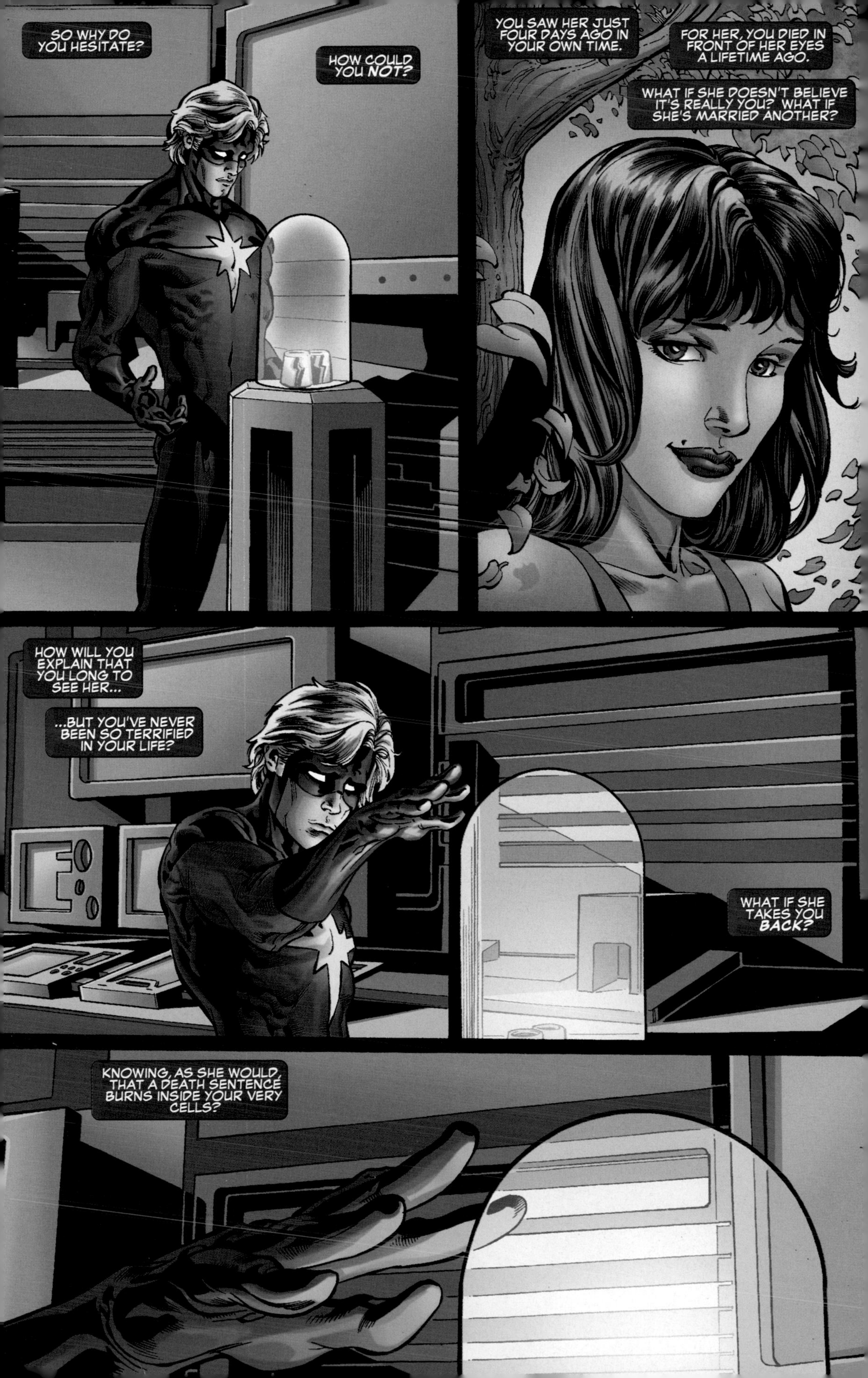
SO WHY DO YOU HESITATE?
HOW COULD YOU NOT?
YOU SAW HER JUST FOUR DAYS AGO IN YOUR OWN TIME.
FOR HER, YOU DIED IN FRONT OF HER EYES A LIFETIME AGO.
WHAT IF SHE DOESN'T BELIEVE IT'S REALLY YOU? WHAT IF SHE'S MARRIED ANOTHER?
HOW WILL YOU EXPLAIN THAT YOU LONG TO SEE HER...
...BUT YOU'VE NEVER BEEN SO TERRIFIED IN YOUR LIFE?
WHAT IF SHE TAKES YOU BACK?
KNOWING, AS SHE WOULD, THAT A DEATH SENTENCE BURNS INSIDE YOUR VERY CELLS?

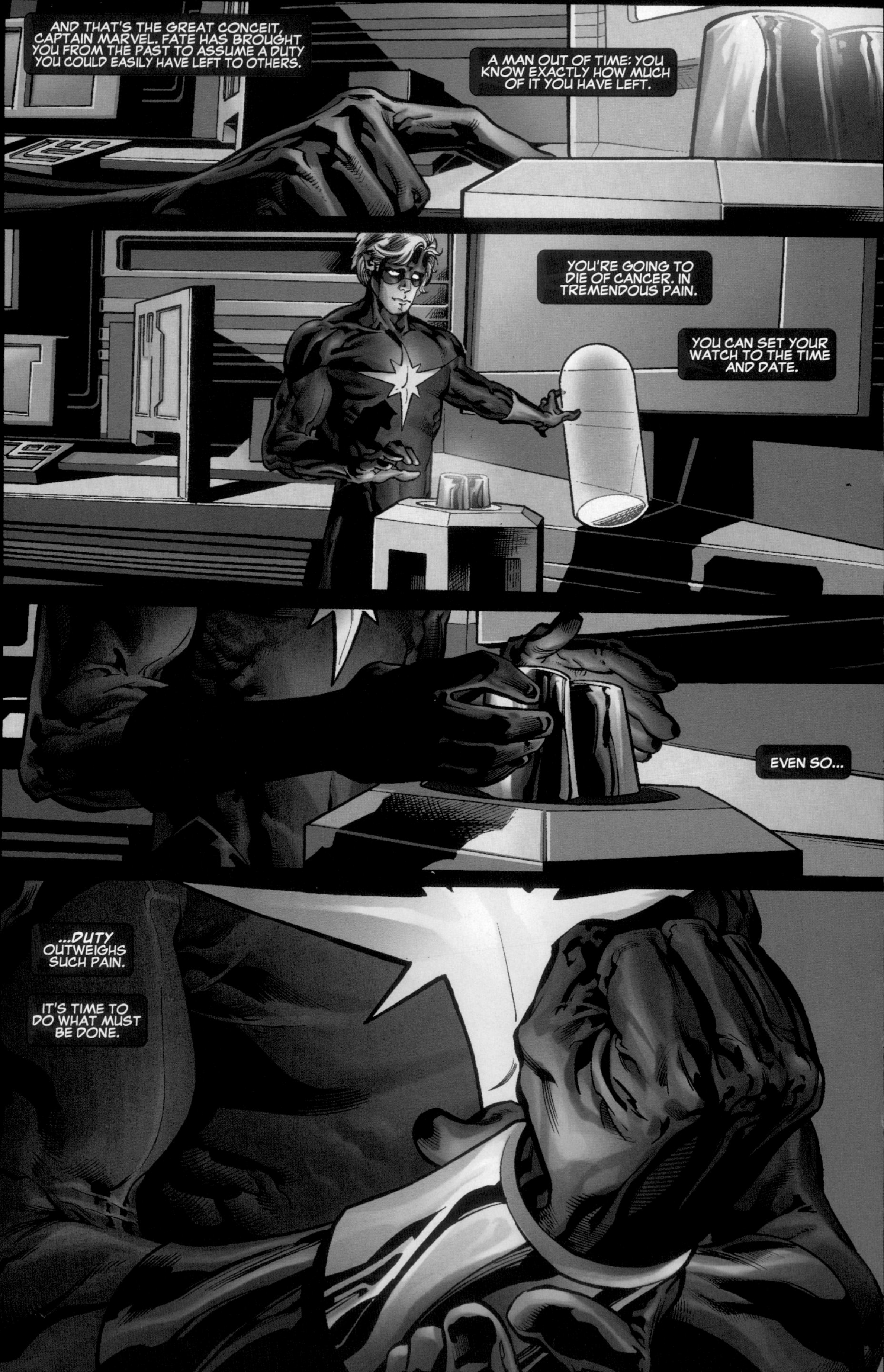
AND THAT'S THE GREAT CONCEIT, CAPTAIN MARVEL. FATE HAS BROUGHT YOU FROM THE PAST TO ASSUME A DUTY YOU COULD EASILY HAVE LEFT TO OTHERS.
A MAN OUT OF TIME: YOU KNOW EXACTLY HOW MUCH OF IT YOU HAVE LEFT.
YOU'RE GOING TO DIE OF CANCER. IN TREMENDOUS PAIN.
YOU CAN SET YOUR WATCH TO THE TIME AND DATE.
EVEN SO...
...DUTY OUTWEIGHS SUCH PAIN.
IT'S TIME TO DO WHAT MUST BE DONE.

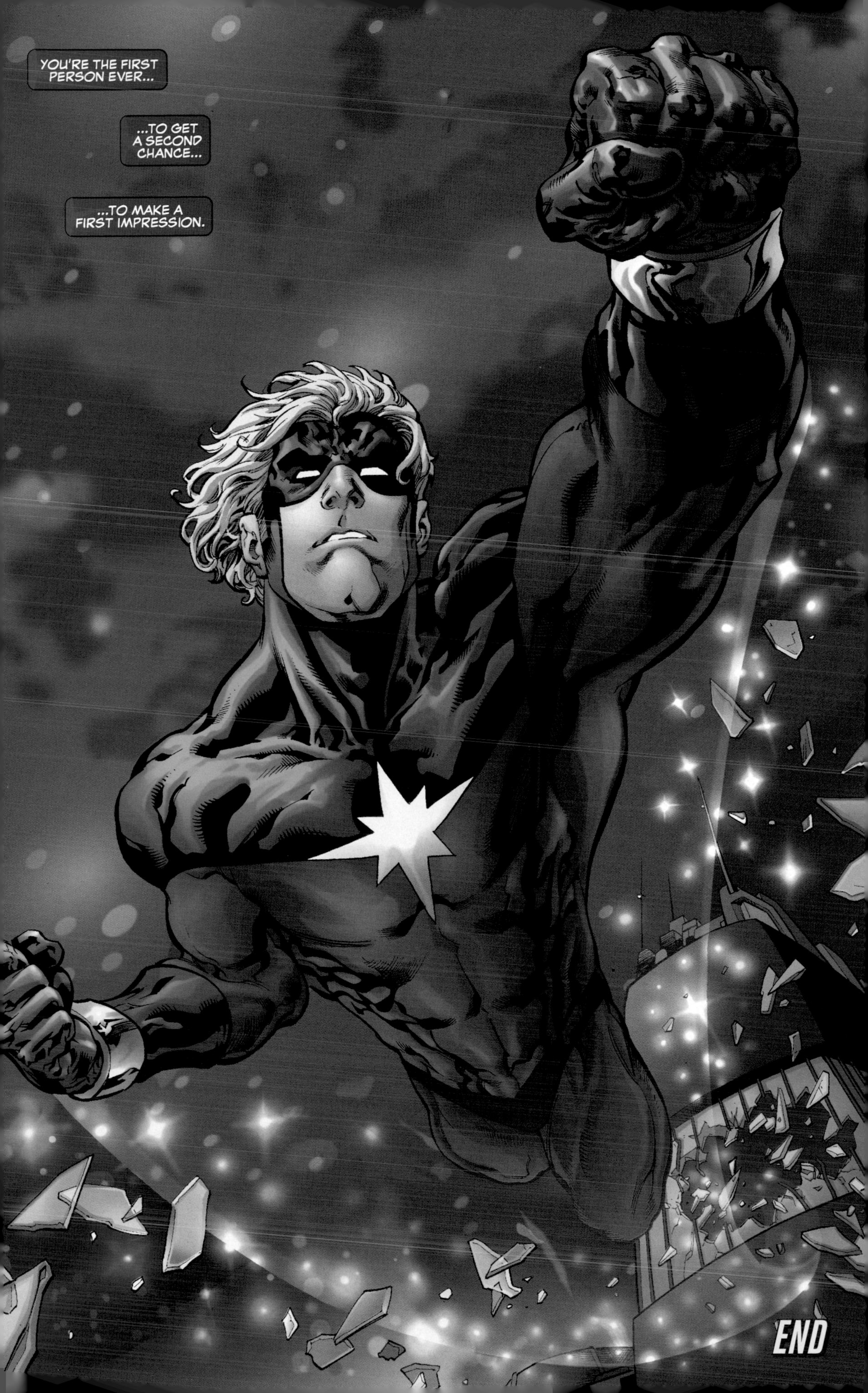
YOU'RE THE FIRST PERSON EVER...
...TO GET A SECOND CHANCE...
...TO MAKE A FIRST IMPRESSION.
END

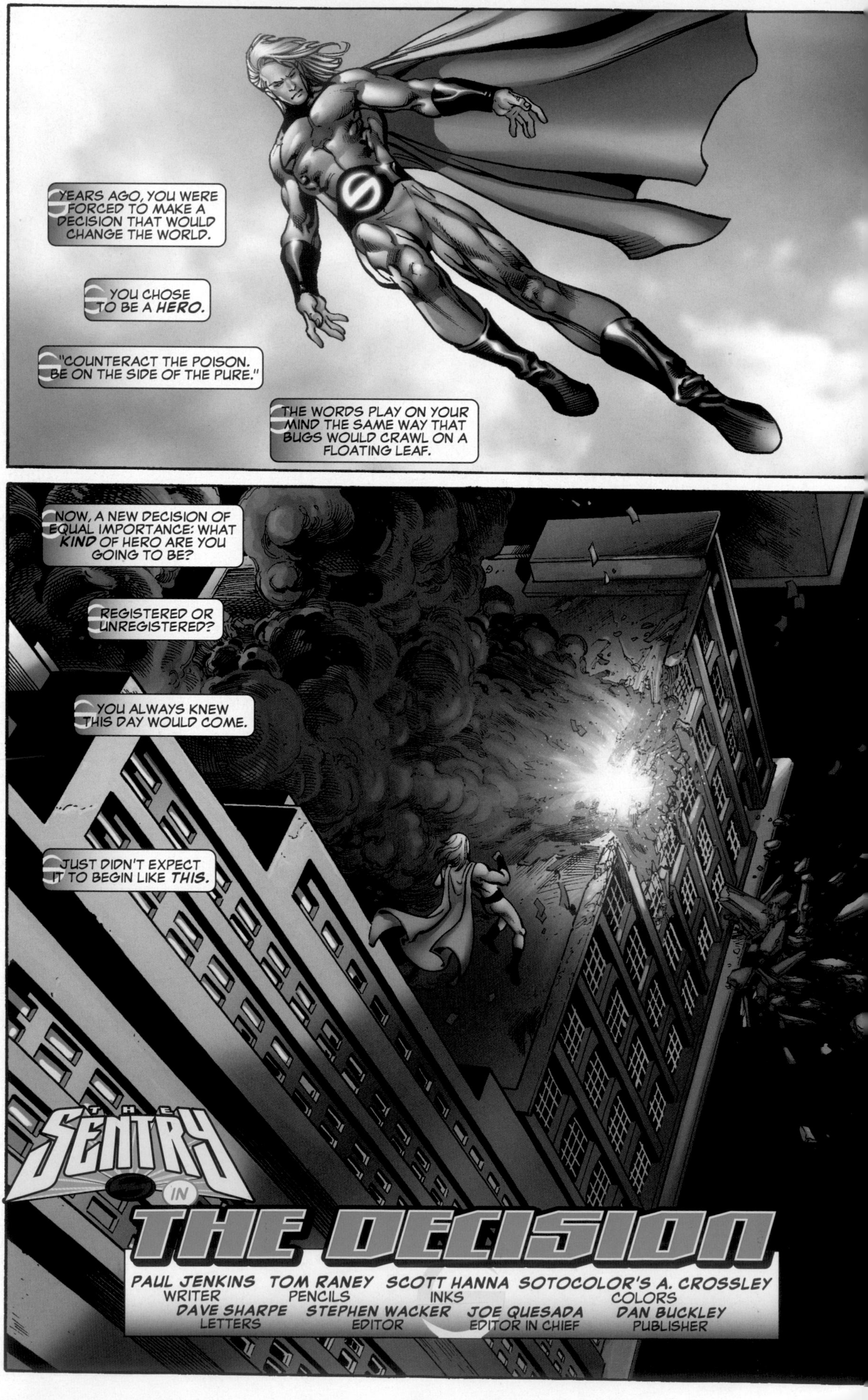
YEARS AGO, YOU WERE FORCED TO MAKE A DECISION THAT WOULD CHANGE THE WORLD.
YOU CHOSE TO BE A HERO.
"COUNTERACT THE POISON. BE ON THE SIDE OF THE PURE."
THE WORDS PLAY ON YOUR MIND THE SAME WAY THAT BUGS WOULD CRAWL ON A FLOATING LEAF.
NOW, A NEW DECISION OF EQUAL IMPORTANCE: WHAT KIND OF HERO ARE YOU GOING TO BE?
REGISTERED OR UNREGISTERED?
YOU ALWAYS KNEW THIS DAY WOULD COME.
JUST DIDN'T EXPECT IT TO BEGIN LIKE THIS.
THE SENTRY IN
THE DECISION
PAUL JENKINS WRITER
TOM RANEY PENCILS
SCOTT HANNA INKS
SOTOCOLOR'S A. CROSSLEY COLORS
DAVE SHARPE LETTERS
STEPHEN WACKER EDITOR
JOE QUESADA EDITOR IN CHIEF
DAN BUCKLEY PUBLISHER

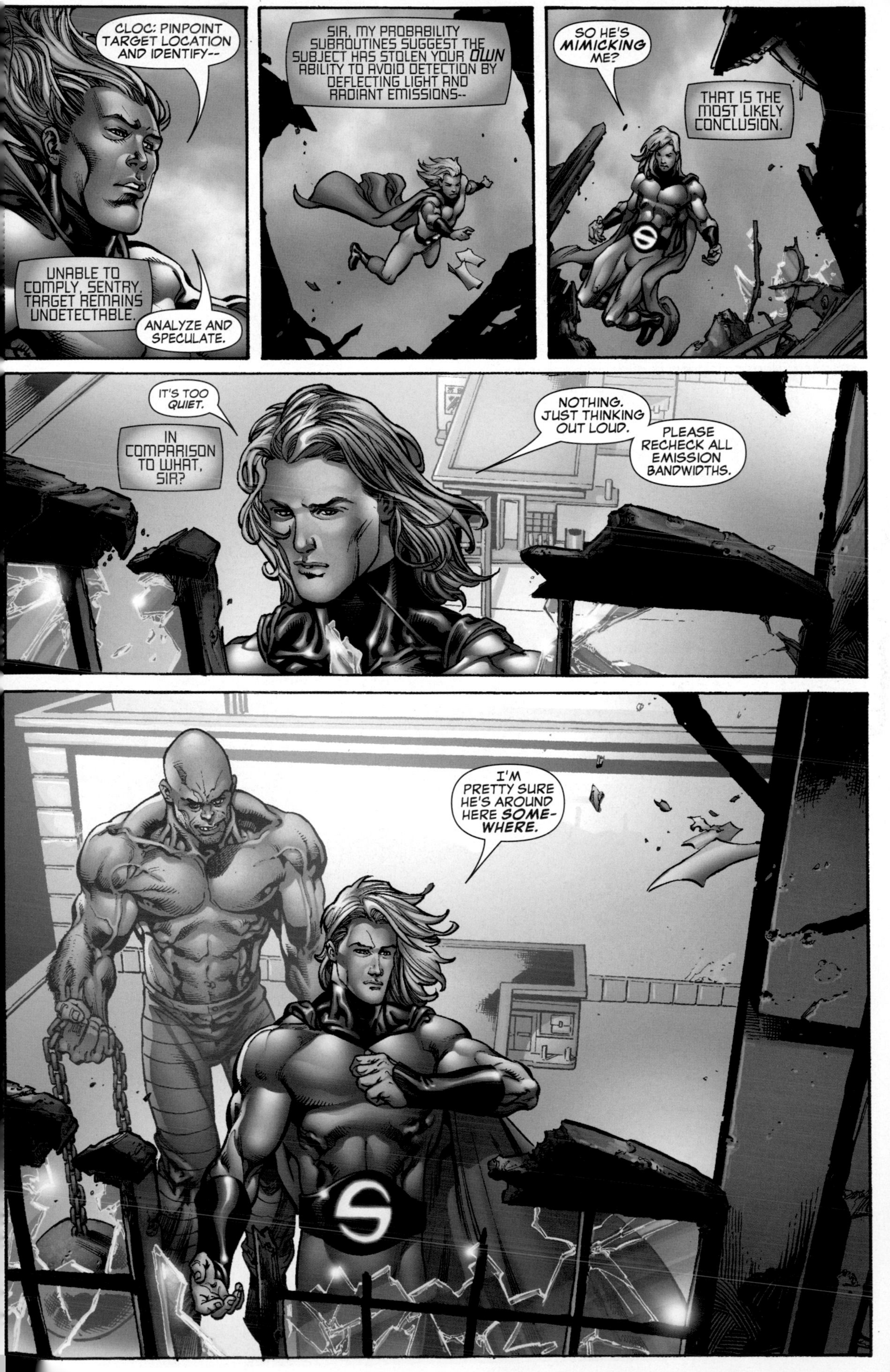
CLOC: PINPOINT TARGET LOCATION AND IDENTIFY--
UNABLE TO COMPLY, SENTRY. TARGET REMAINS UNDETECTABLE.
ANALYZE AND SPECULATE.
SIR, MY PROBABILITY SUBROUTINES SUGGEST THE SUBJECT HAS STOLEN YOUR OWN ABILITY TO AVOID DETECTION BY DEFLECTING LIGHT AND RADIANT EMISSIONS--
SO HE'S MIMICKING ME?
THAT IS THE MOST LIKELY CONCLUSION.
IT'S TOO QUIET.
IN COMPARISON TO WHAT, SIR?
NOTHING. JUST THINKING OUT LOUD.
PLEASE RECHECK ALL EMISSION BANDWIDTHS.
I'M PRETTY SURE HE'S AROUND HERE SOMEWHERE.

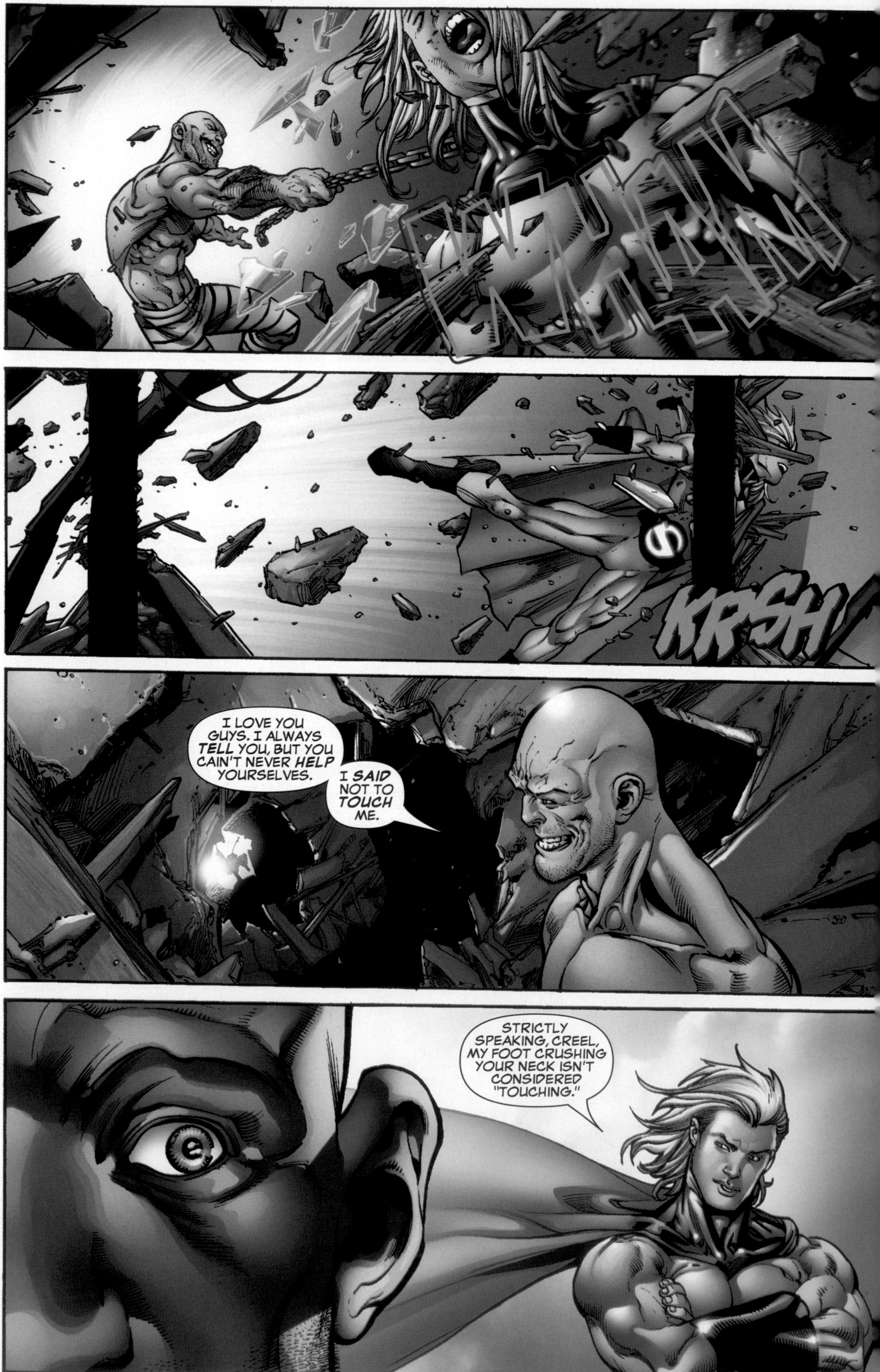
KRSH
I LOVE YOU GUYS. I ALWAYS TELL YOU, BUT YOU CAIN'T NEVER HELP YOURSELVES.
I SAID NOT TO TOUCH ME.
STRICTLY SPEAKING, CREEL, MY FOOT CRUSHING YOUR NECK ISN'T CONSIDERED "TOUCHING."

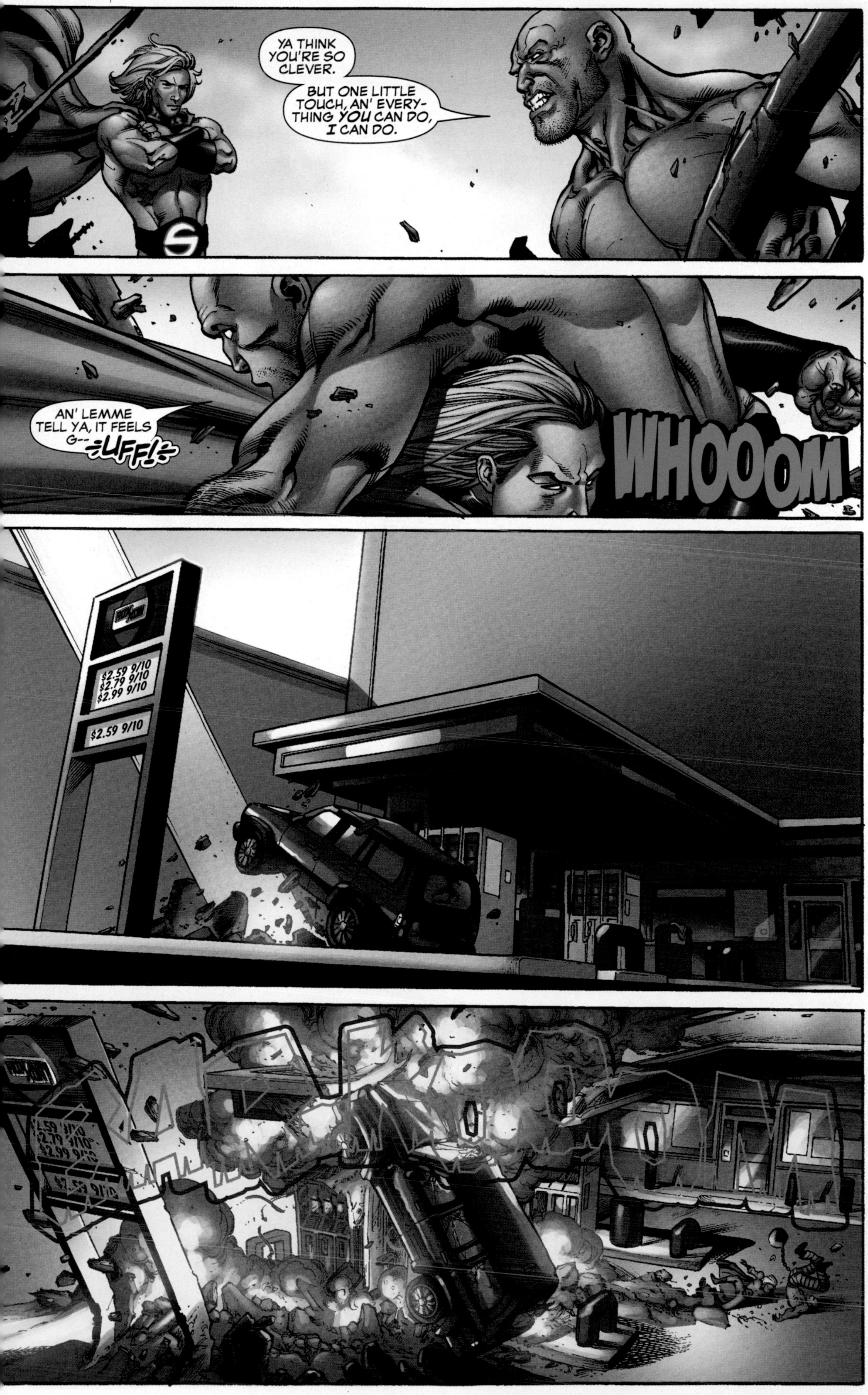
YA THINK YOU'RE SO CLEVER.
BUT ONE LITTLE TOUCH, AN' EVERYTHING YOU CAN DO, I CAN DO.
AN' LEMME TELL YA, IT FEELS G-- UFF!
WHOOOM
$2.59 9/10
$2.79 9/10
$2.99 9/10
$2.59 9/10

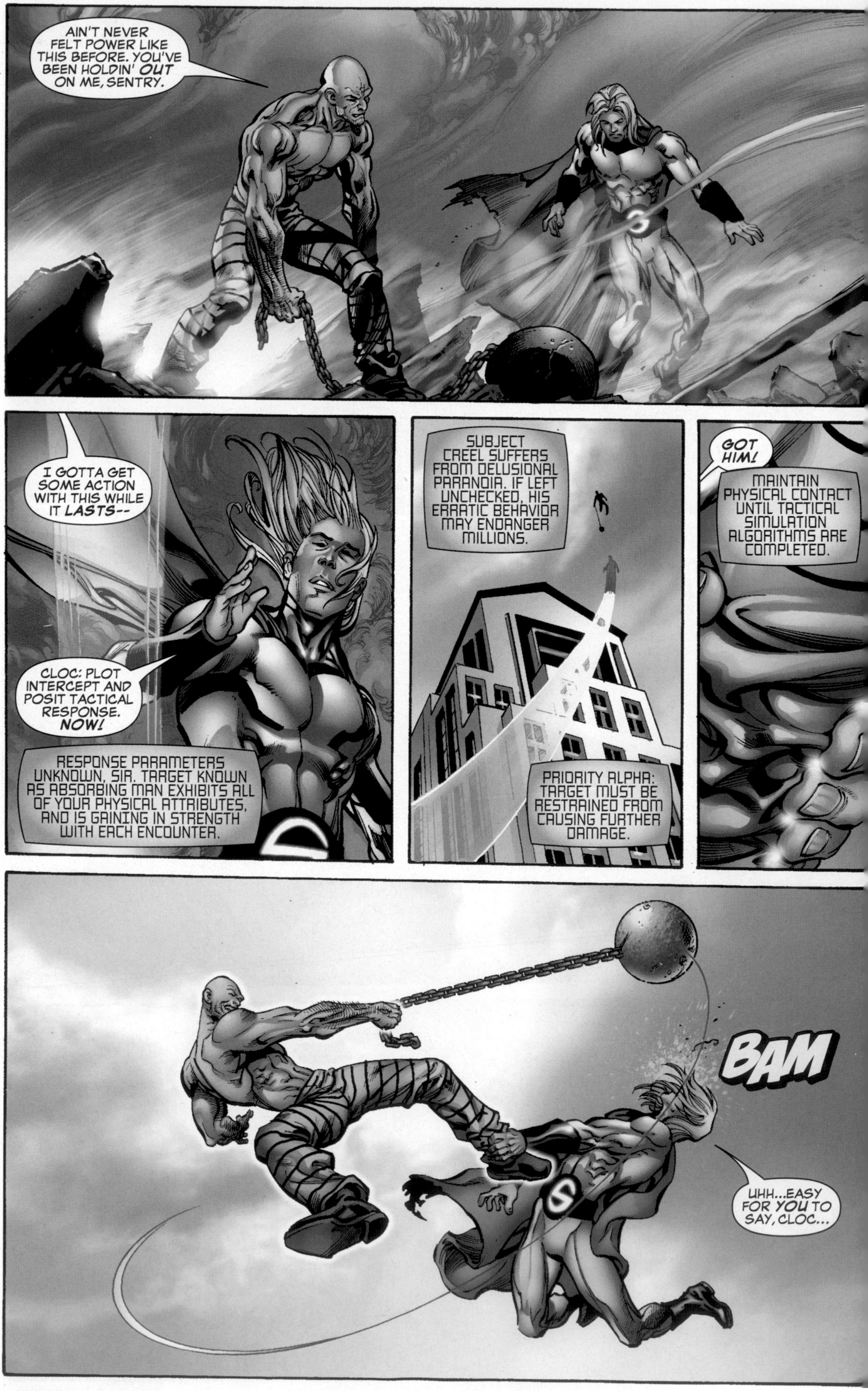
AIN'T NEVER FELT POWER LIKE THIS BEFORE. YOU'VE BEEN HOLDIN' OUT ON ME, SENTRY.
I GOTTA GET SOME ACTION WITH THIS WHILE IT LASTS--
CLOC: PLOT INTERCEPT AND POSIT TACTICAL RESPONSE. NOW!
RESPONSE PARAMETERS UNKNOWN, SIR. TARGET KNOWN AS ABSORBING MAN EXHIBITS ALL OF YOUR PHYSICAL ATTRIBUTES, AND IS GAINING IN STRENGTH WITH EACH ENCOUNTER.
SUBJECT CREEL SUFFERS FROM DELUSIONAL PARANOIA. IF LEFT UNCHECKED, HIS ERRATIC BEHAVIOR MAY ENDANGER MILLIONS.
PRIORITY ALPHA: TARGET MUST BE RESTRAINED FROM CAUSING FURTHER DAMAGE.
GOT HIM!
MAINTAIN PHYSICAL CONTACT UNTIL TACTICAL SIMULATION ALGORITHMS ARE COMPLETED.
BAM
UHH...EASY FOR YOU TO SAY, CLOC...

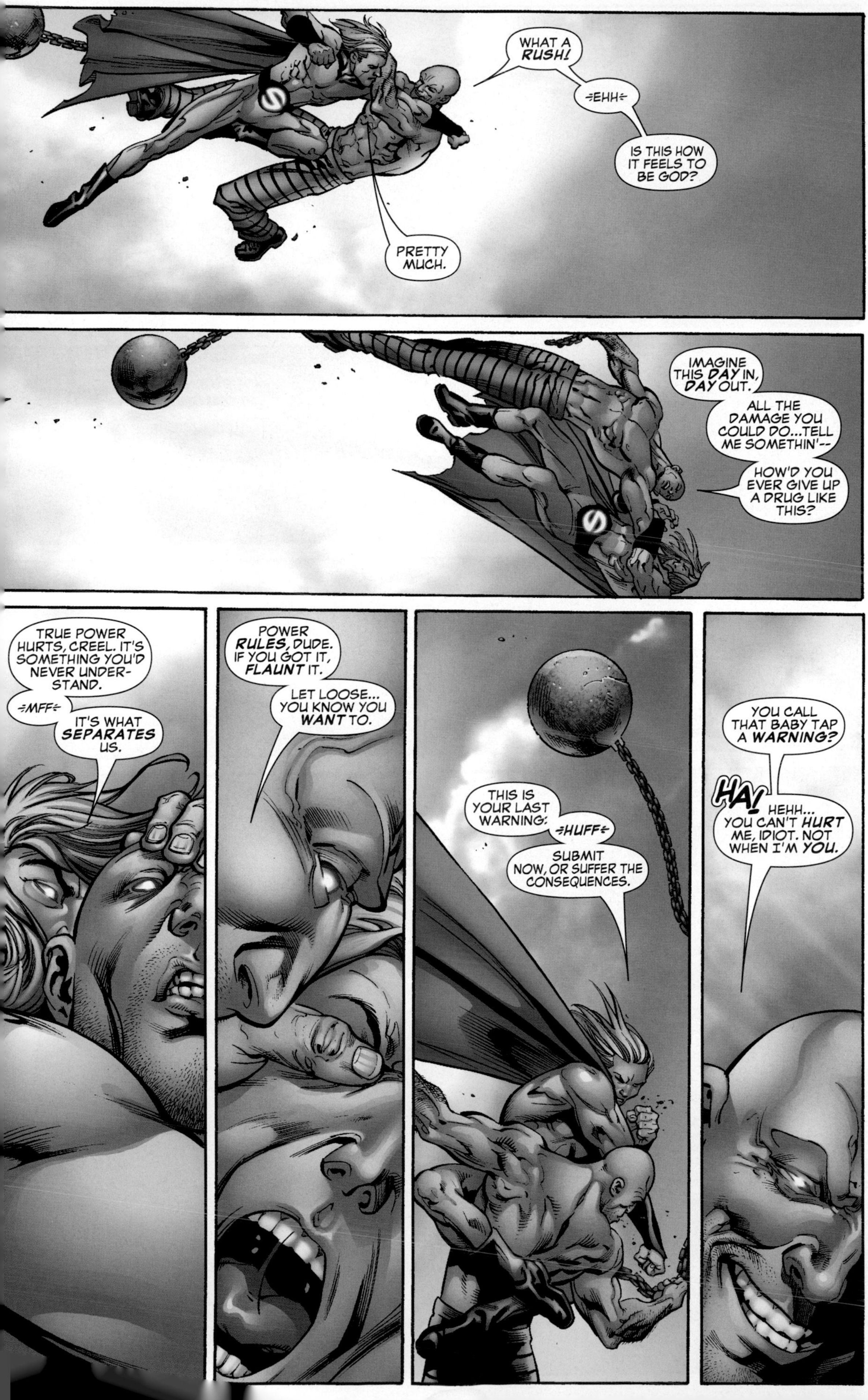
WHAT A RUSH!
=EHH=
IS THIS HOW IT FEELS TO BE GOD?
PRETTY MUCH.
IMAGINE THIS DAY IN, DAY OUT.
ALL THE DAMAGE YOU COULD DO...TELL ME SOMETHIN'--
HOW'D YOU EVER GIVE UP A DRUG LIKE THIS?
TRUE POWER HURTS, CREEL. IT'S SOMETHING YOU'D NEVER UNDER-STAND.
=MFF=
IT'S WHAT SEPARATES US.
POWER RULES, DUDE. IF YOU GOT IT, FLAUNT IT.
LET LOOSE... YOU KNOW YOU WANT TO.
THIS IS YOUR LAST WARNING:
=HUFF=
SUBMIT NOW, OR SUFFER THE CONSEQUENCES.
YOU CALL THAT BABY TAP A WARNING?
HA!
HEHH... YOU CAN'T HURT ME, IDIOT. NOT WHEN I'M YOU.

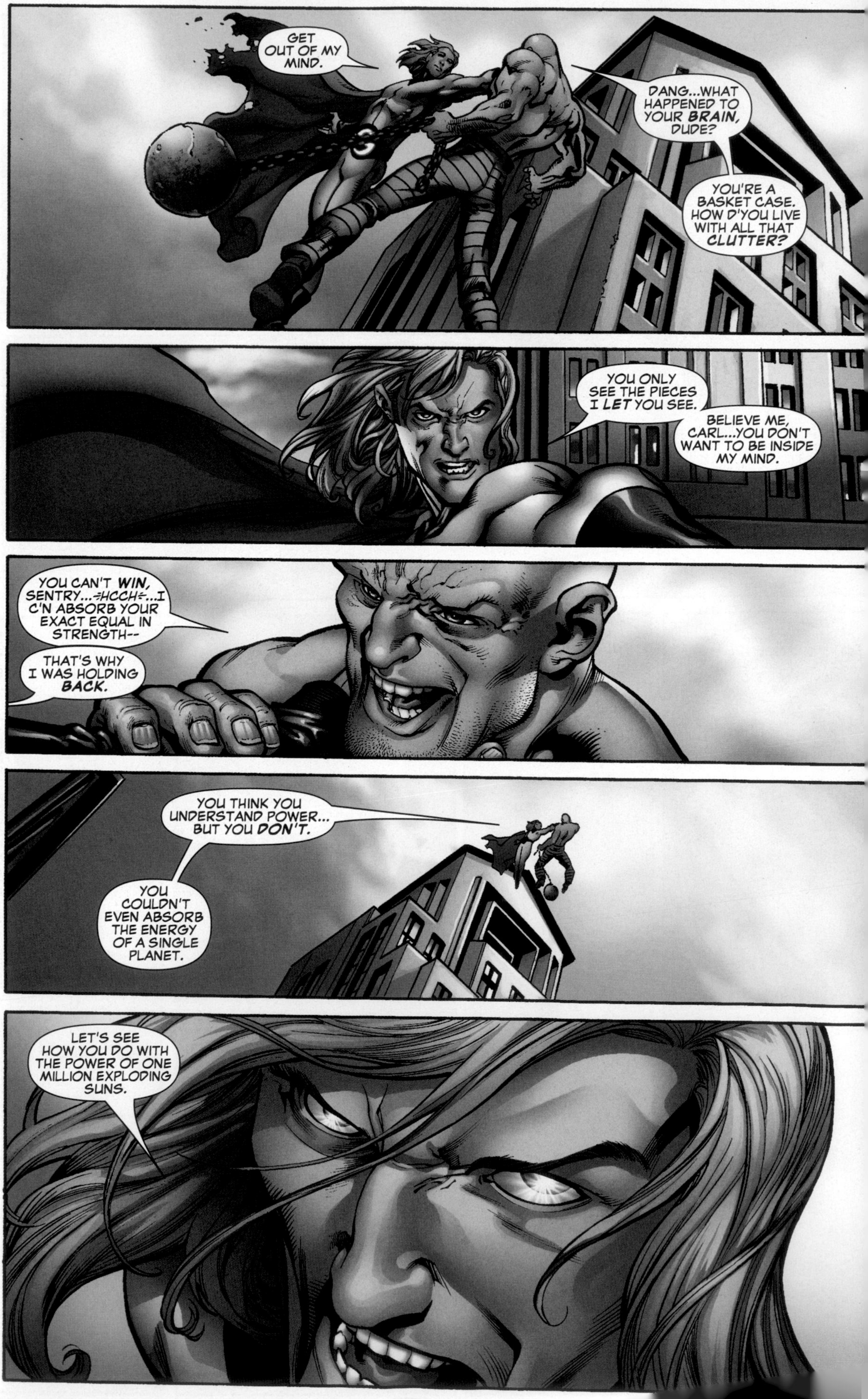
GET OUT OF MY MIND.
DANG...WHAT HAPPENED TO YOUR BRAIN, DUDE?
YOU'RE A BASKET CASE. HOW D'YOU LIVE WITH ALL THAT CLUTTER?
YOU ONLY SEE THE PIECES I LET YOU SEE.
BELIEVE ME, CARL...YOU DON'T WANT TO BE INSIDE MY MIND.
YOU CAN'T WIN, SENTRY...=HCCH=...I C'N ABSORB YOUR EXACT EQUAL IN STRENGTH--
THAT'S WHY I WAS HOLDING BACK.
YOU THINK YOU UNDERSTAND POWER... BUT YOU DON'T.
YOU COULDN'T EVEN ABSORB THE ENERGY OF A SINGLE PLANET.
LET'S SEE HOW YOU DO WITH THE POWER OF ONE MILLION EXPLODING SUNS.

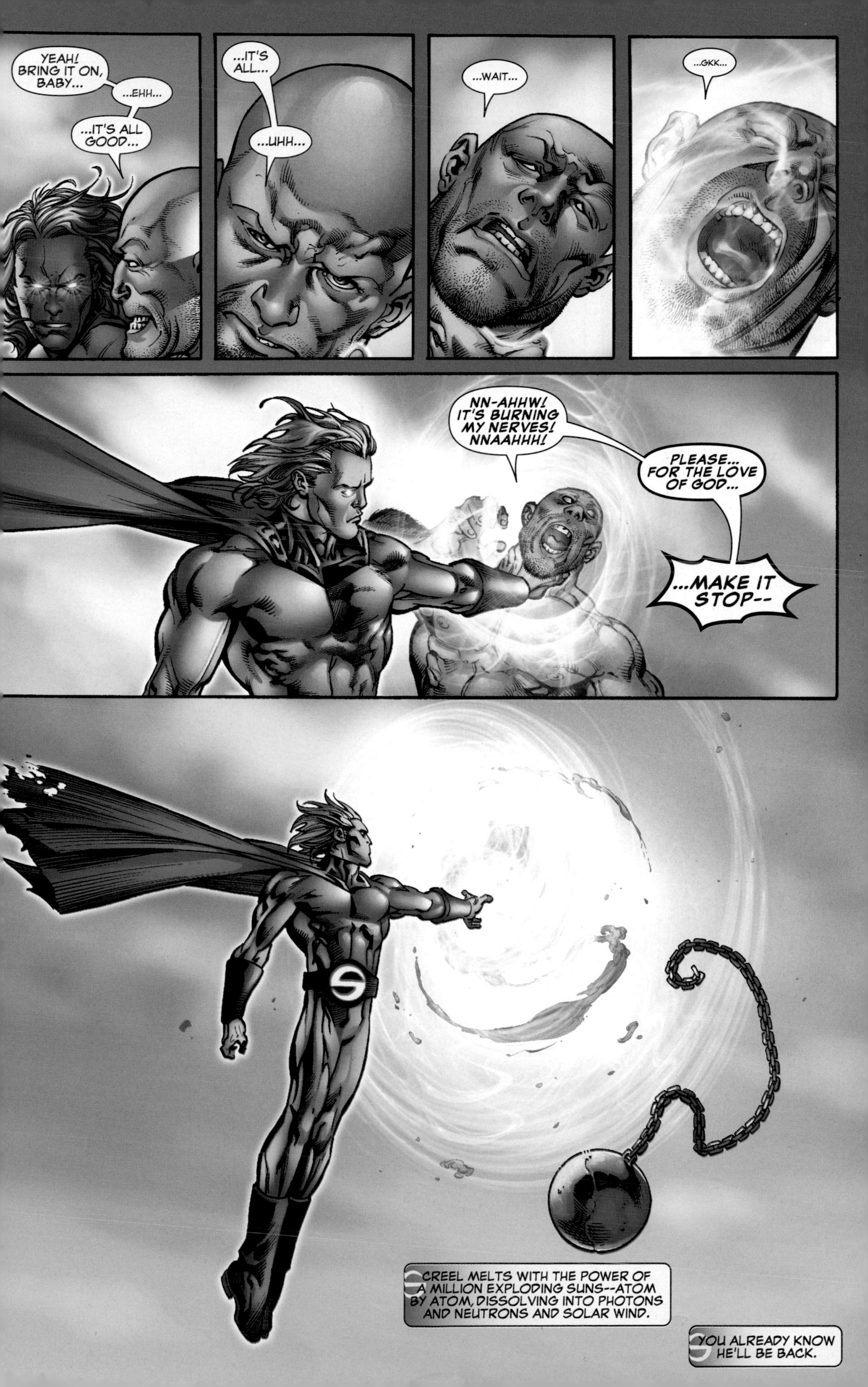

YEAH! BRING IT ON, BABY...
...EHH...
...IT'S ALL GOOD...
...IT'S ALL...
...UHH...
...WAIT...
...GKK...
NN-AHHW! IT'S BURNING MY NERVES! NNAAHHH!
PLEASE... FOR THE LOVE OF GOD...
...MAKE IT STOP--
CREEL MELTS WITH THE POWER OF A MILLION EXPLODING SUNS--ATOM BY ATOM, DISSOLVING INTO PHOTONS AND NEUTRONS AND SOLAR WIND.
YOU ALREADY KNOW HE'LL BE BACK.

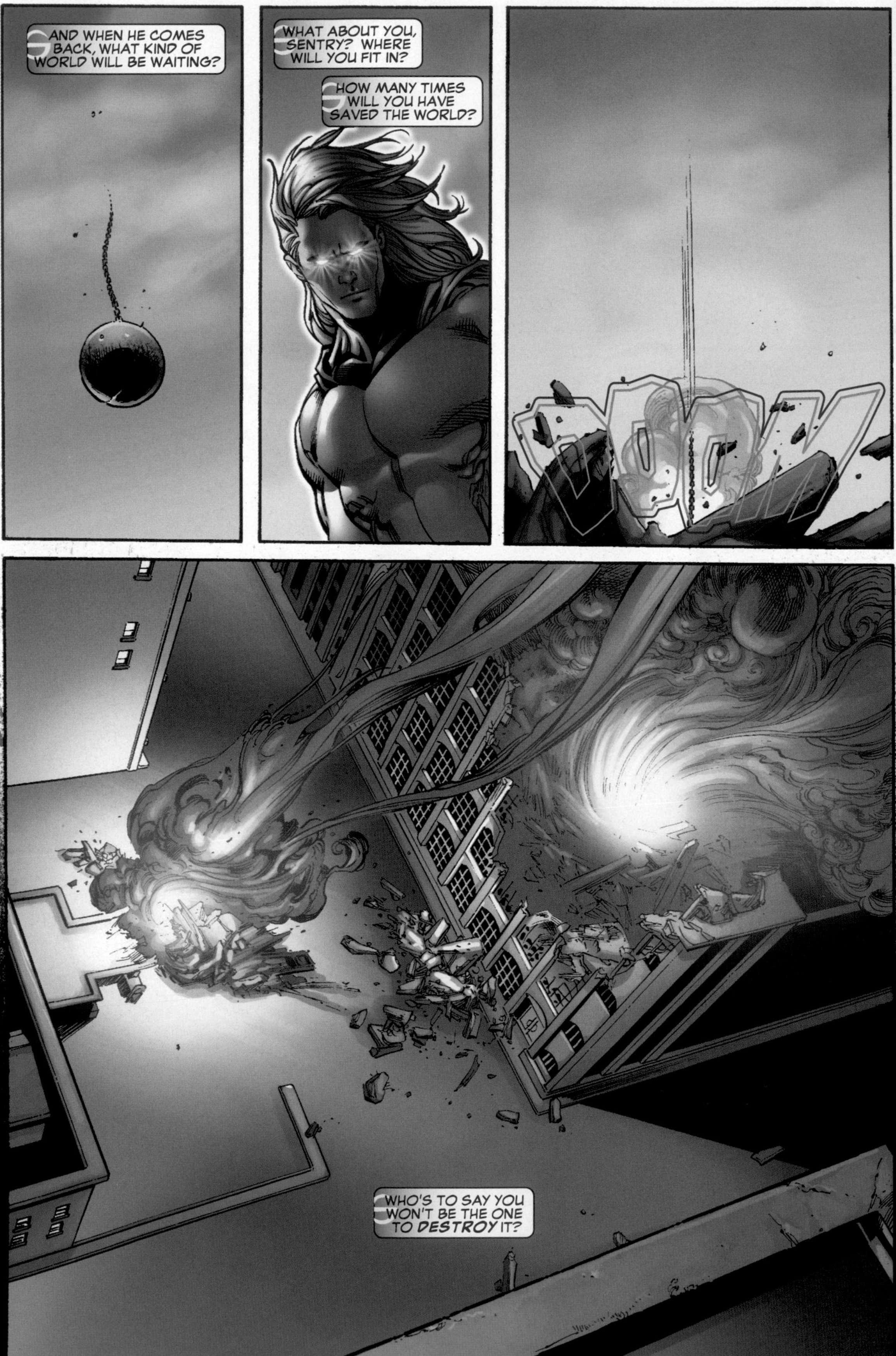
AND WHEN HE COMES BACK, WHAT KIND OF WORLD WILL BE WAITING?
WHAT ABOUT YOU, SENTRY? WHERE WILL YOU FIT IN?
HOW MANY TIMES WILL YOU HAVE SAVED THE WORLD?
WHO'S TO SAY YOU WON'T BE THE ONE TO DESTROY IT?

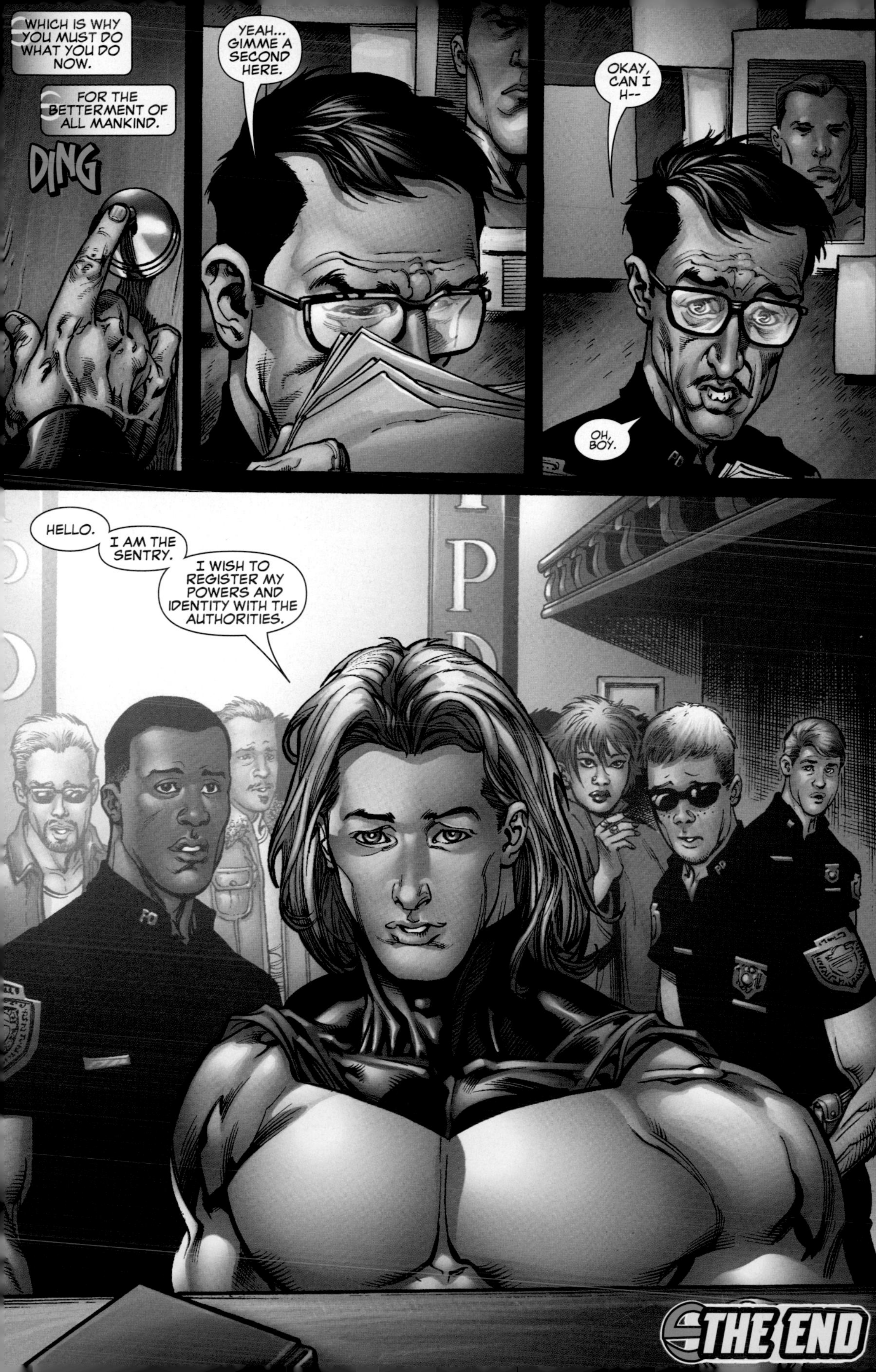
WHICH IS WHY YOU MUST DO WHAT YOU DO NOW.
FOR THE BETTERMENT OF ALL MANKIND.
DING
YEAH... GIMME A SECOND HERE.
OKAY, CAN I H--
OH, BOY.
HELLO.
I AM THE SENTRY.
I WISH TO REGISTER MY POWERS AND IDENTITY WITH THE AUTHORITIES.
THE END

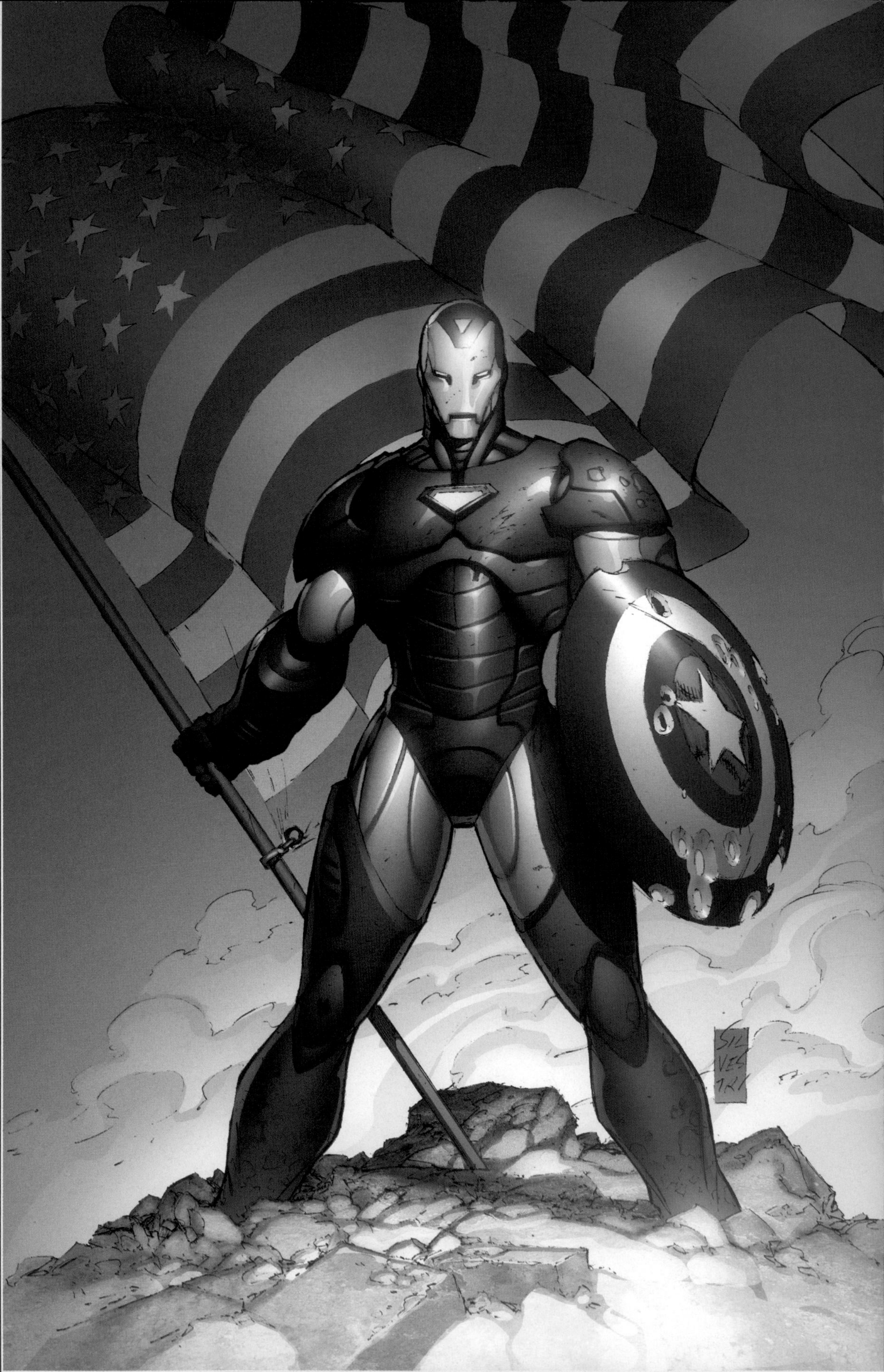

CIVIL WAR: THE INITIATIVE

CIVIL WAR
THE INITIATIVE

A Superhuman Registration Act has been passed, requiring all individuals possessing paranormal abilities to register their powers and identities with the government. Disagreement over the Act split the super hero community in two, with Tony Stark, Iron Man, as the figurehead of the pro-registration faction, and Steve Rogers, Captain America, leading the anti-registration rebellion. The conflict erupted into violence, only ending with the surrender and arrest— and eventual assassination—of Captain America.

Now, the Civil War is over, and Tony Stark has been named the Director of S.H.I.E.L.D., the international peacekeeping force. He has set into motion THE INITIATIVE, a plan for training and policing super heroes in this brave new world.

BRIAN BENDIS
(PAGES 1-12, 22-34)
WRITER

WARREN ELLIS
(PAGES 13-21)
WRITER

MARC SILVESTRI
PENCILS

TOP COW PRODUCTIONS
ART & LETTERS

**MICHAEL BROUSSARD &
ERIC BASALDUA**
BACKGROUND ARTISTS

**JOE WEEMS WITH MARCO GALLI
& RICK BASALDUA**
INKS

TROY PETERI
LETTERS

ROB LEVIN
FOR TOP COW

FRANK D'ARMATA
COLORS

RICH GINTER
PRODUCTION

MOLLY LAZER & AUBREY SITTERSON
ASSISTANT EDITORS

TOM BREVOORT
EDITOR

JOE QUESADA
EDITOR IN CHIEF

DAN BUCKLEY
PUBLISHER

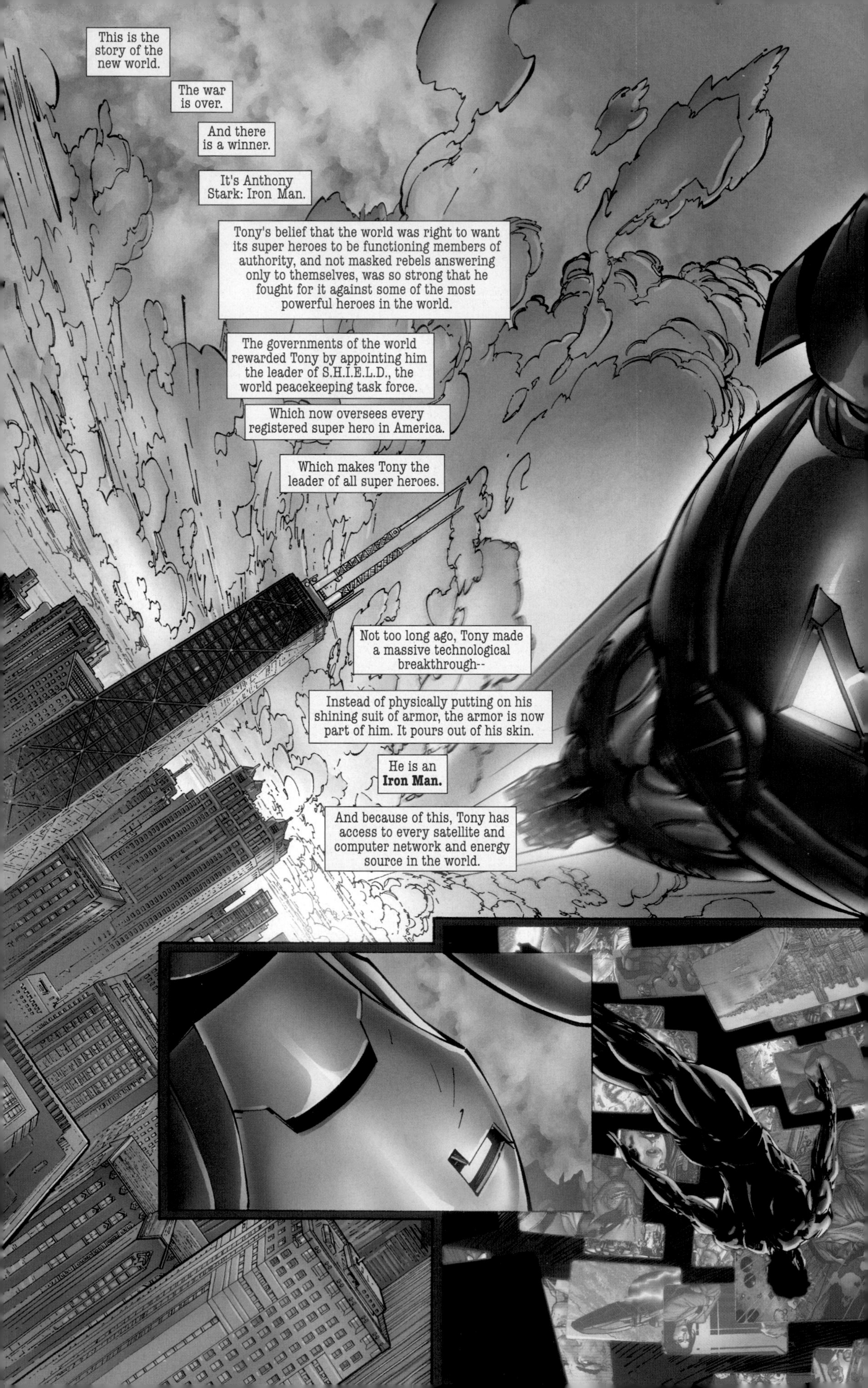
This is the story of the new world.
The war is over.
And there is a winner.
It's Anthony Stark: Iron Man.
Tony's belief that the world was right to want its super heroes to be functioning members of authority, and not masked rebels answering only to themselves, was so strong that he fought for it against some of the most powerful heroes in the world.
The governments of the world rewarded Tony by appointing him the leader of S.H.I.E.L.D., the world peacekeeping task force.
Which now oversees every registered super hero in America.
Which makes Tony the leader of all super heroes.
Not too long ago, Tony made a massive technological breakthrough--
Instead of physically putting on his shining suit of armor, the armor is now part of him. It pours out of his skin.
He is an **Iron Man.**
And because of this, Tony has access to every satellite and computer network and energy source in the world.

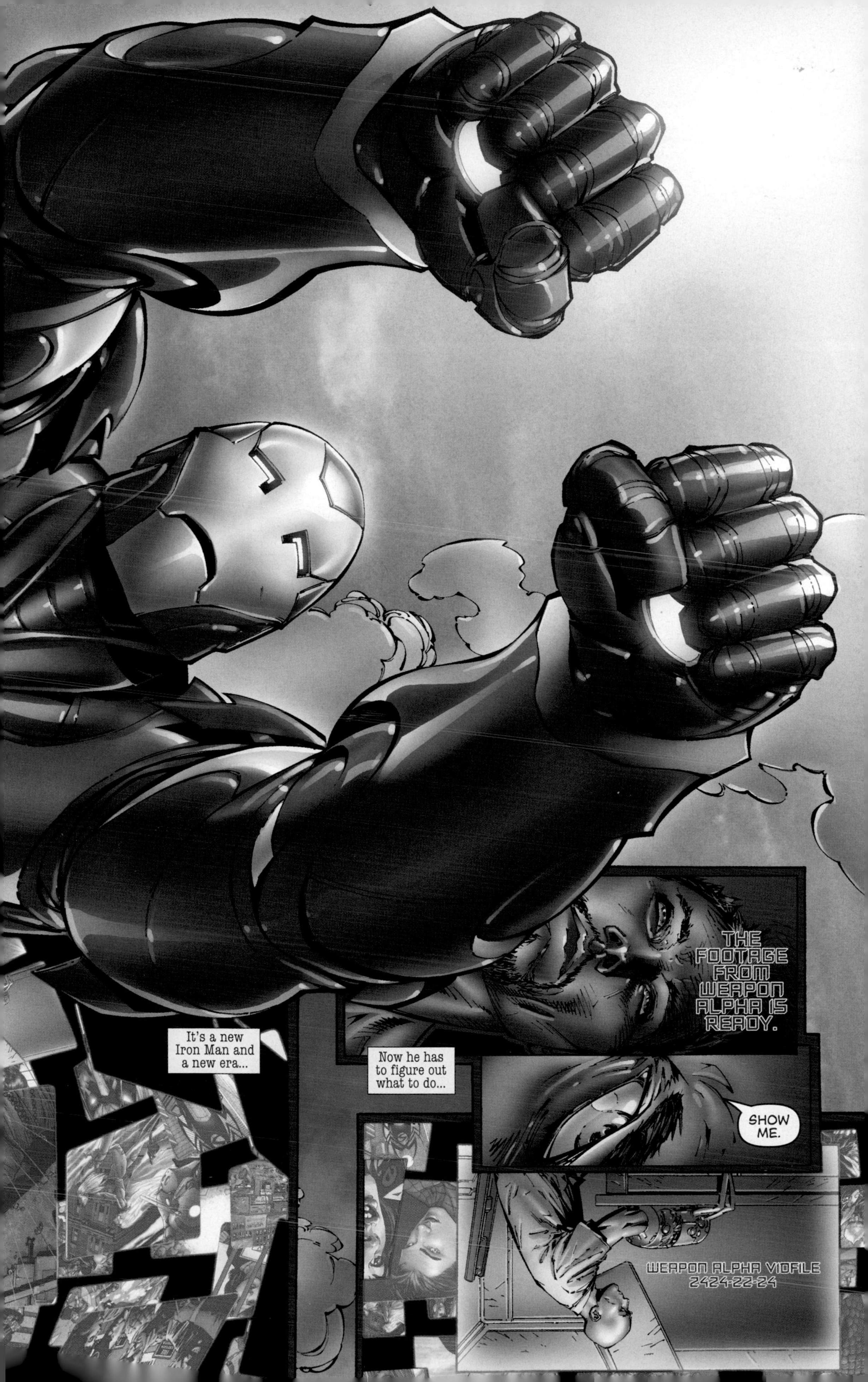
It's a new Iron Man and a new era...
Now he has to figure out what to do...
THE FOOTAGE FROM WEAPON ALPHA IS READY.
SHOW ME.
WEAPON ALPHA VIDFILE 2424-22-24

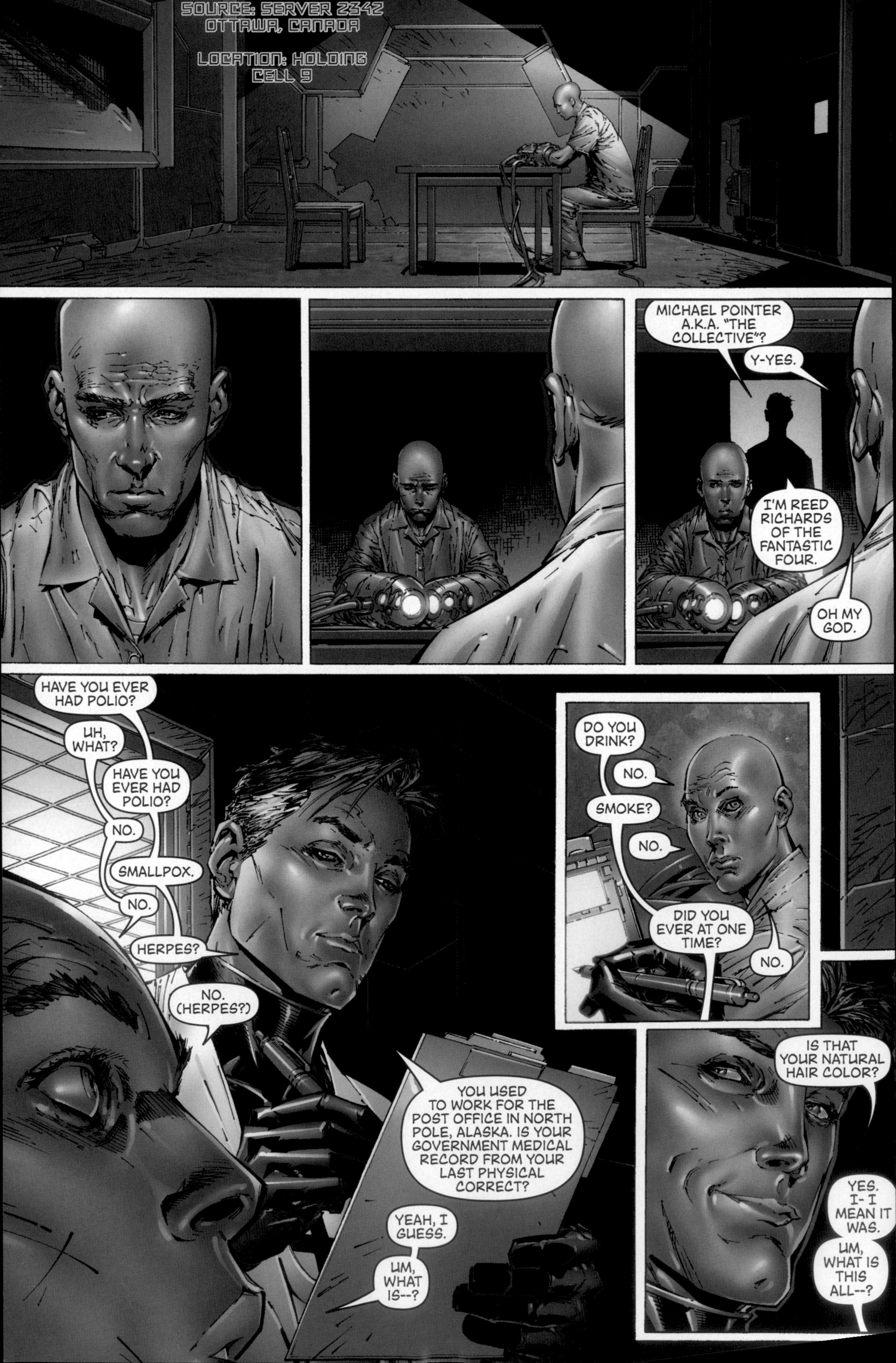
SOURCE: SERVER 2342
OTTAWA, CANADA
LOCATION: HOLDING
CELL 9
MICHAEL POINTER A.K.A. "THE COLLECTIVE"?
Y-YES.
I'M REED RICHARDS OF THE FANTASTIC FOUR.
OH MY GOD.
HAVE YOU EVER HAD POLIO?
UH, WHAT?
HAVE YOU EVER HAD POLIO?
NO.
SMALLPOX.
NO.
HERPES?
NO. (HERPES?)
DO YOU DRINK?
NO.
SMOKE?
NO.
DID YOU EVER AT ONE TIME?
NO.
YOU USED TO WORK FOR THE POST OFFICE IN NORTH POLE, ALASKA. IS YOUR GOVERNMENT MEDICAL RECORD FROM YOUR LAST PHYSICAL CORRECT?
YEAH, I GUESS.
UM, WHAT IS--?
IS THAT YOUR NATURAL HAIR COLOR?
YES. I- I MEAN IT WAS.
UM, WHAT IS THIS ALL--?

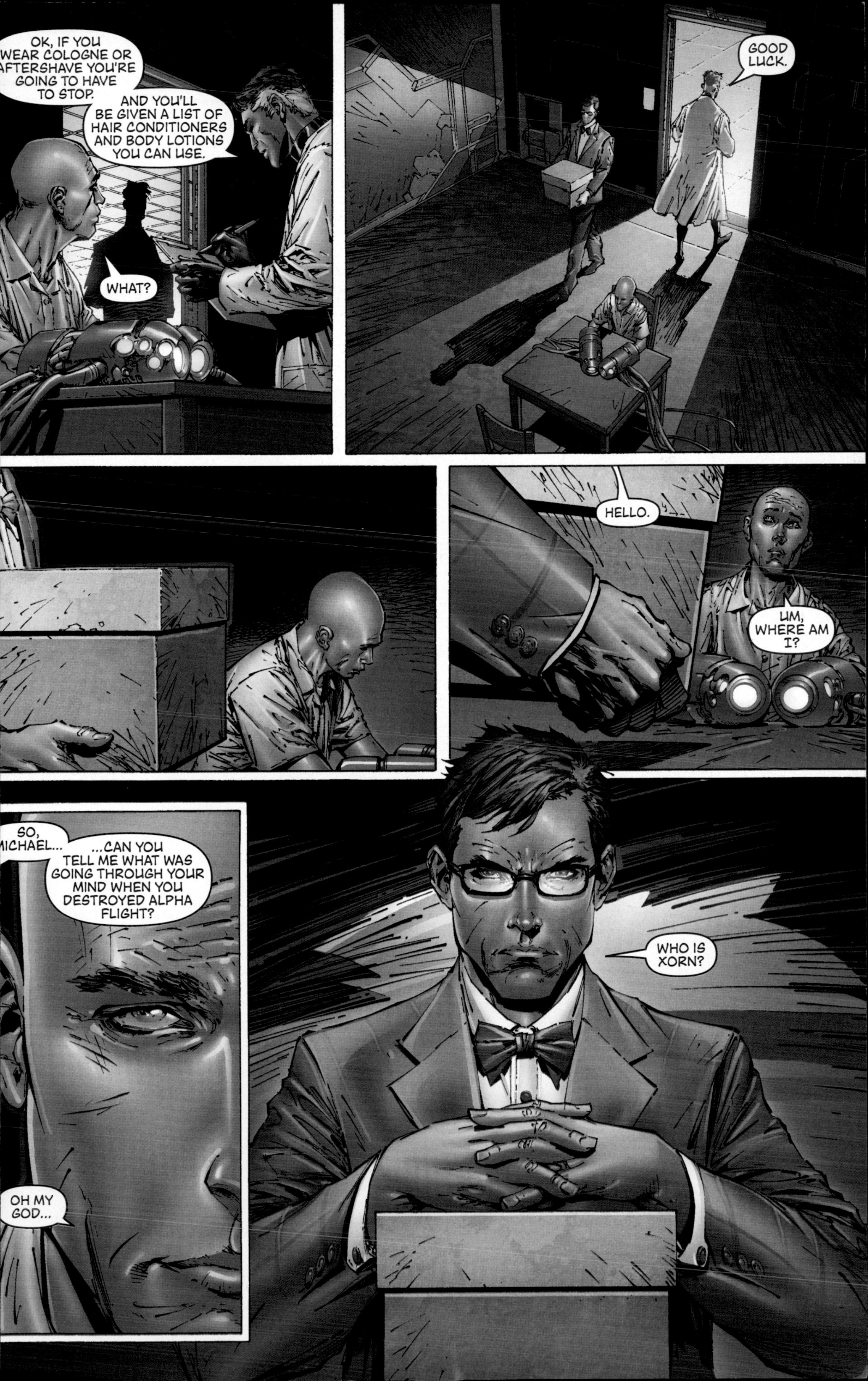
OK, IF YOU WEAR COLOGNE OR AFTERSHAVE YOU'RE GOING TO HAVE TO STOP.
AND YOU'LL BE GIVEN A LIST OF HAIR CONDITIONERS AND BODY LOTIONS YOU CAN USE.
WHAT?
GOOD LUCK.
HELLO.
UM, WHERE AM I?
SO, MICHAEL...
...CAN YOU TELL ME WHAT WAS GOING THROUGH YOUR MIND WHEN YOU DESTROYED ALPHA FLIGHT?
WHO IS XORN?
OH MY GOD...

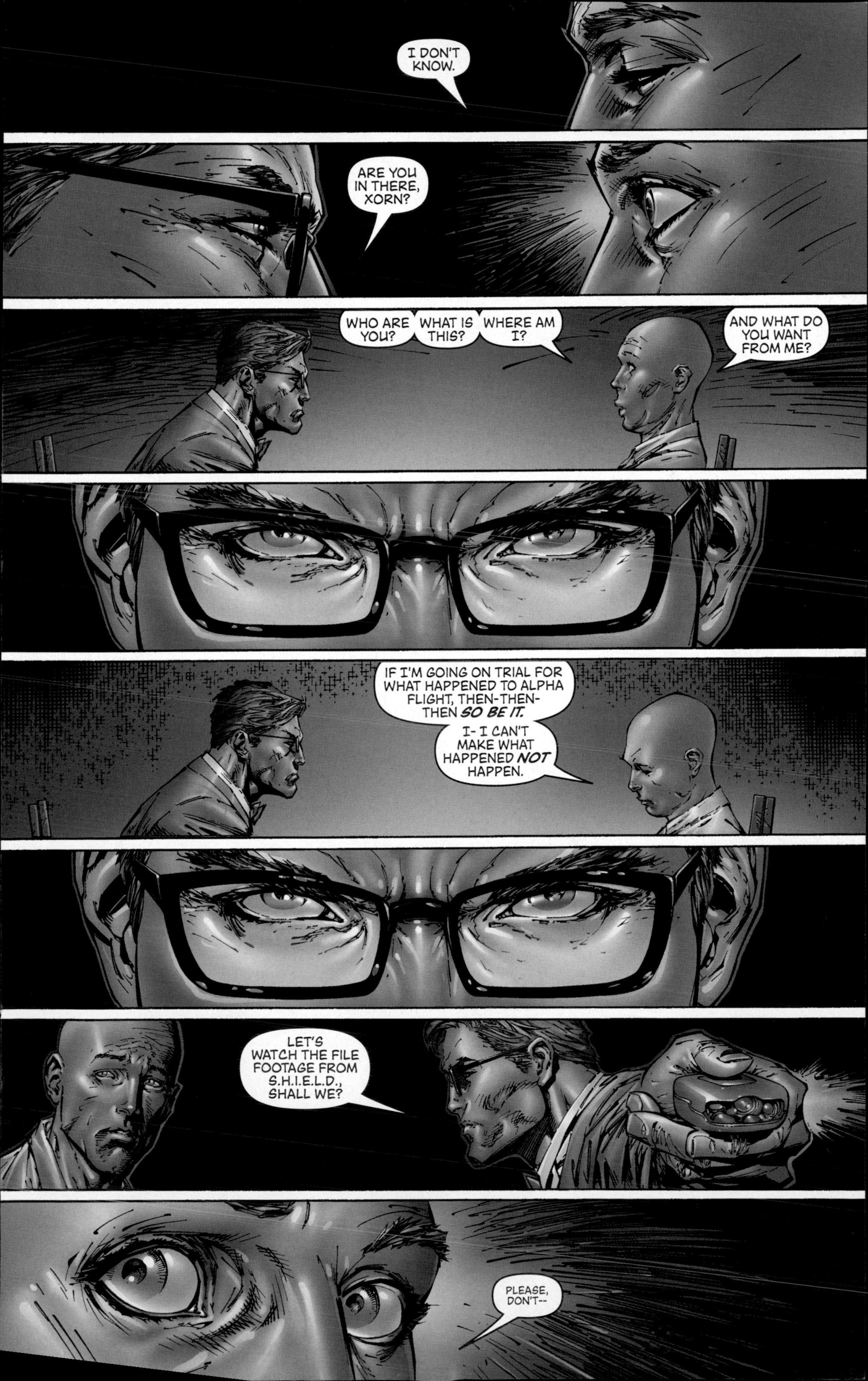
I DON'T KNOW.
ARE YOU IN THERE, XORN?
WHO ARE YOU?
WHAT IS THIS?
WHERE AM I?
AND WHAT DO YOU WANT FROM ME?
IF I'M GOING ON TRIAL FOR WHAT HAPPENED TO ALPHA FLIGHT, THEN-THEN-THEN *SO BE IT.*
I- I CAN'T MAKE WHAT HAPPENED ***NOT*** HAPPEN.
LET'S WATCH THE FILE FOOTAGE FROM S.H.I.E.L.D., SHALL WE?
PLEASE, DON'T--

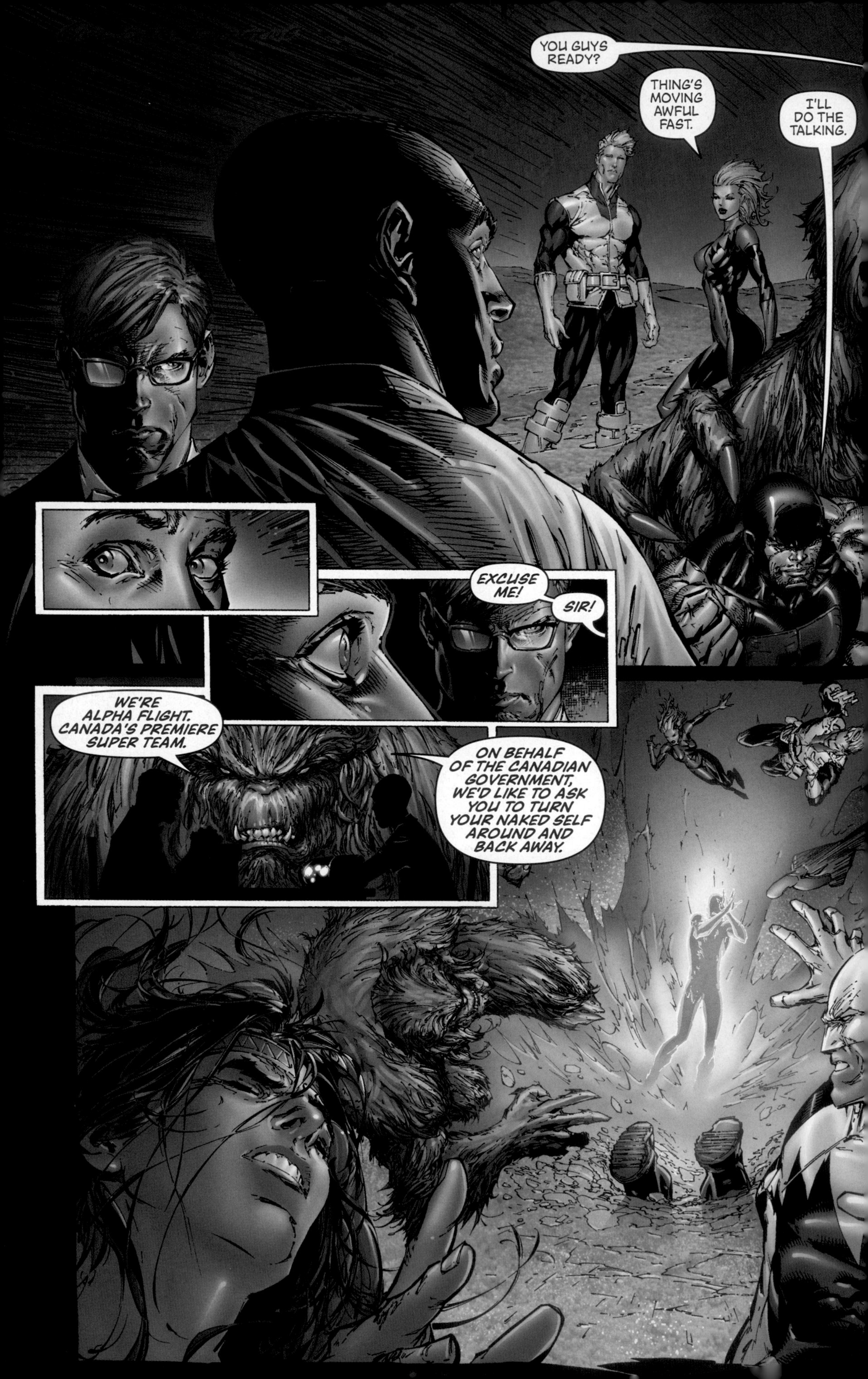
YOU GUYS READY?
THING'S MOVING AWFUL FAST.
I'LL DO THE TALKING.
EXCUSE ME!
SIR!
WE'RE ALPHA FLIGHT. CANADA'S PREMIERE SUPER TEAM.
ON BEHALF OF THE CANADIAN GOVERNMENT, WE'D LIKE TO ASK YOU TO TURN YOUR NAKED SELF AROUND AND BACK AWAY.

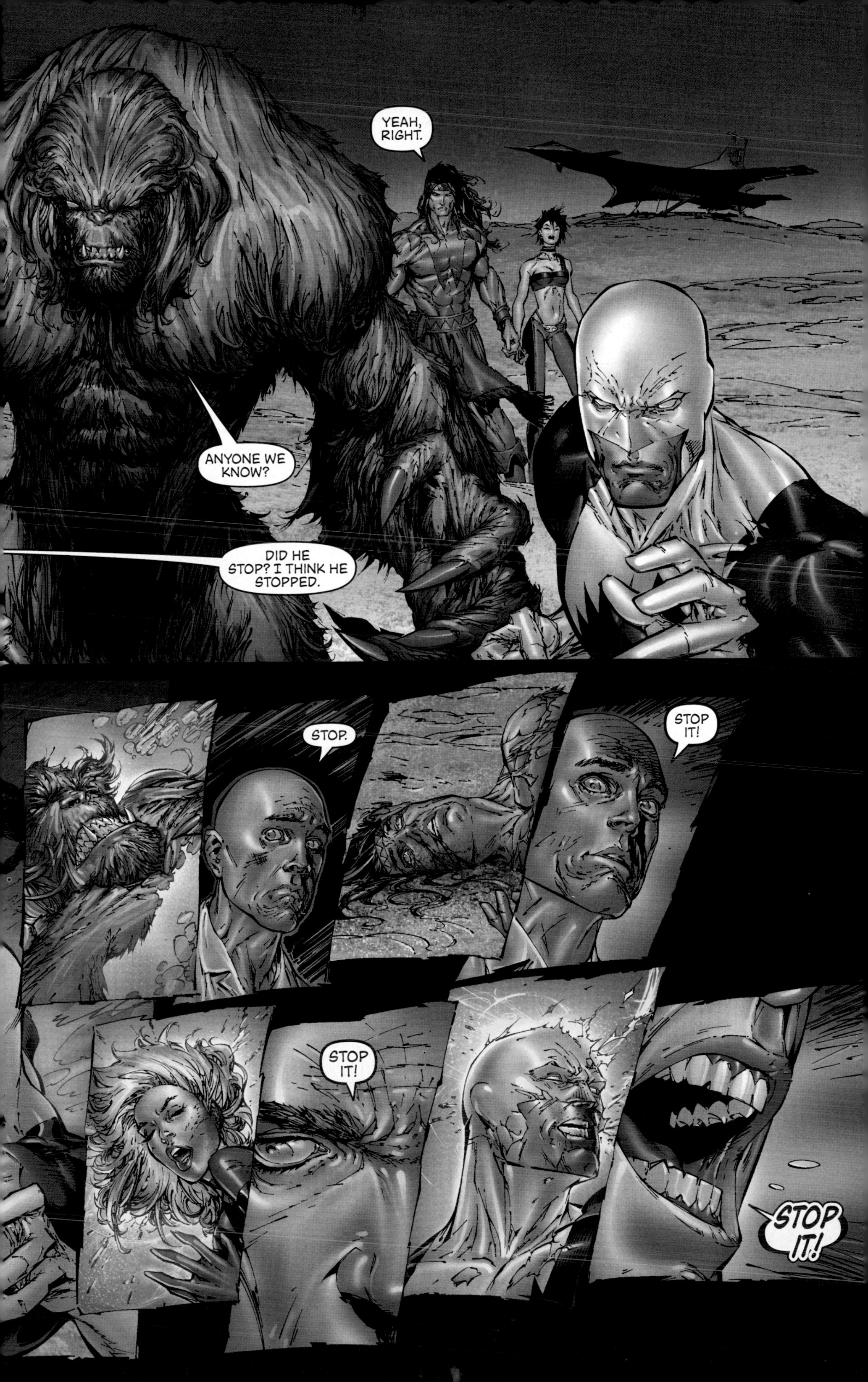
YEAH, RIGHT.
ANYONE WE KNOW?
DID HE STOP? I THINK HE STOPPED.
STOP.
STOP IT!
STOP IT!
STOP IT!

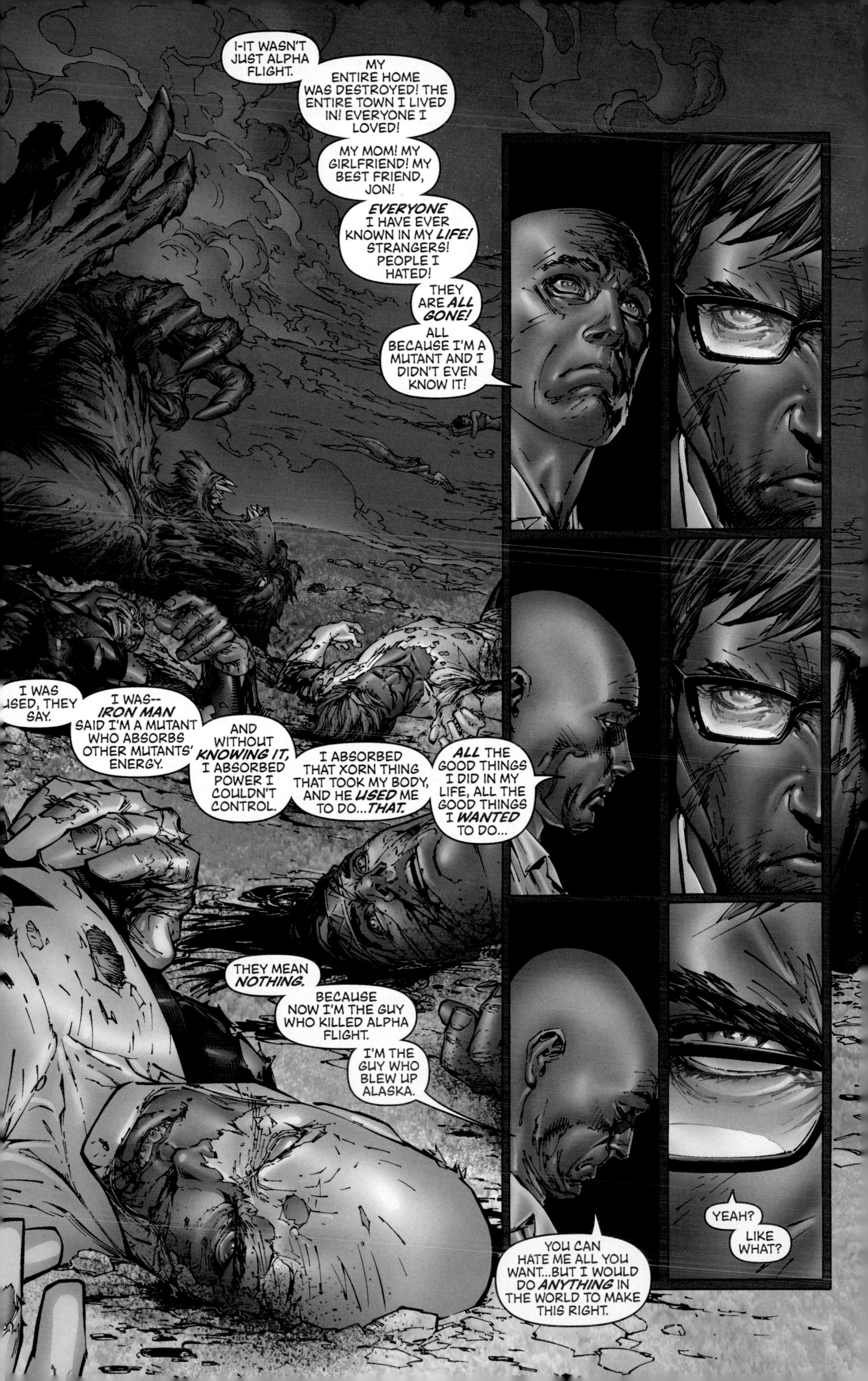
I-IT WASN'T JUST ALPHA FLIGHT.
MY ENTIRE HOME WAS DESTROYED! THE ENTIRE TOWN I LIVED IN! EVERYONE I LOVED!
MY MOM! MY GIRLFRIEND! MY BEST FRIEND, JON!
EVERYONE I HAVE EVER KNOWN IN MY LIFE! STRANGERS! PEOPLE I HATED!
THEY ARE ALL GONE!
ALL BECAUSE I'M A MUTANT AND I DIDN'T EVEN KNOW IT!
I WAS USED, THEY SAY.
I WAS-- IRON MAN SAID I'M A MUTANT WHO ABSORBS OTHER MUTANTS' ENERGY.
AND WITHOUT KNOWING IT, I ABSORBED POWER I COULDN'T CONTROL.
I ABSORBED THAT XORN THING THAT TOOK MY BODY, AND HE USED ME TO DO...THAT.
ALL THE GOOD THINGS I DID IN MY LIFE, ALL THE GOOD THINGS I WANTED TO DO...
THEY MEAN NOTHING.
BECAUSE NOW I'M THE GUY WHO KILLED ALPHA FLIGHT.
I'M THE GUY WHO BLEW UP ALASKA.
YOU CAN HATE ME ALL YOU WANT...BUT I WOULD DO ANYTHING IN THE WORLD TO MAKE THIS RIGHT.
YEAH? LIKE WHAT?

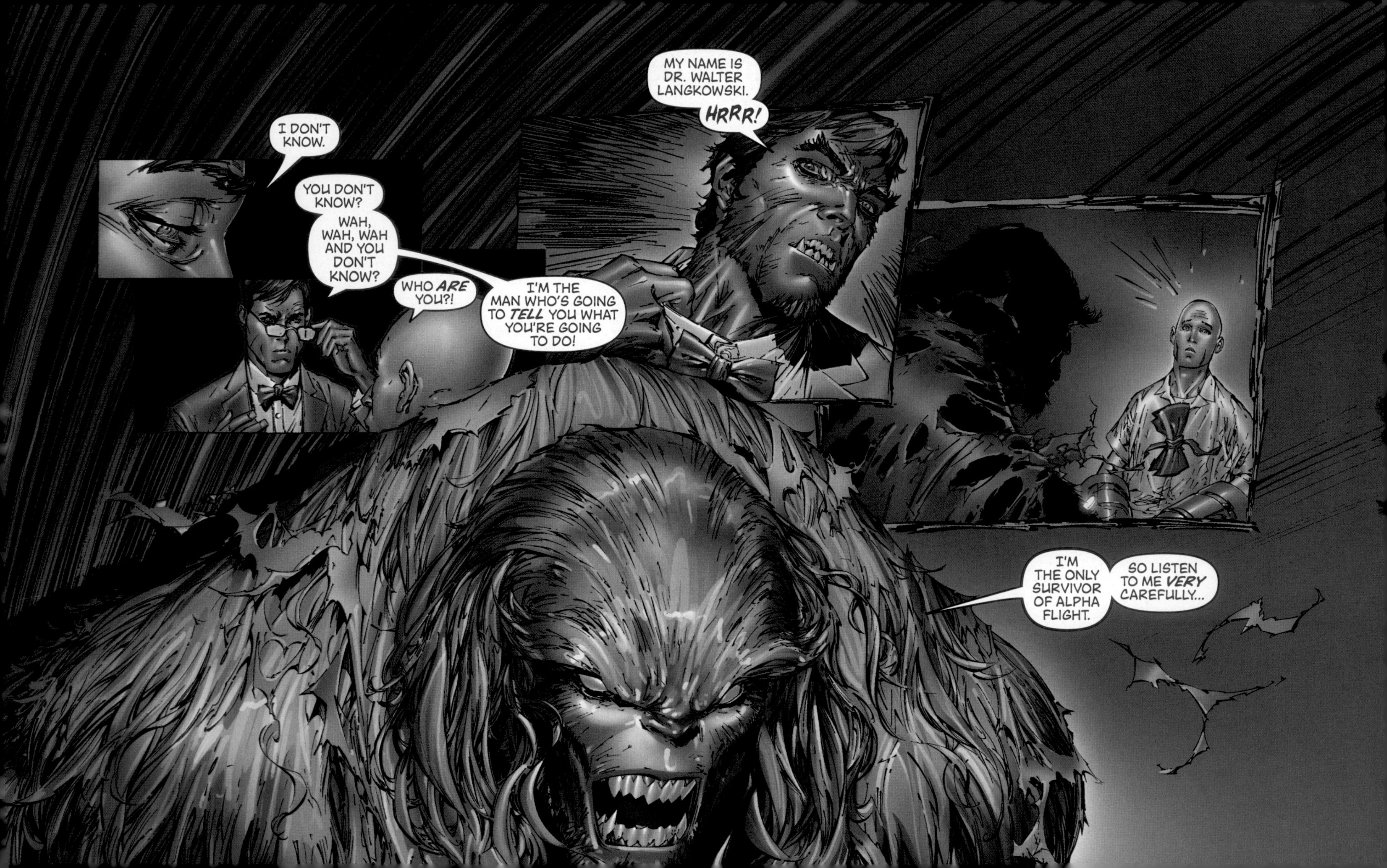
I DON'T KNOW.
YOU DON'T KNOW?
WAH, WAH, WAH AND YOU DON'T KNOW?
WHO *ARE* YOU?!
I'M THE MAN WHO'S GOING TO *TELL* YOU WHAT YOU'RE GOING TO DO!
MY NAME IS DR. WALTER LANGKOWSKI.
HRRR!
I'M THE ONLY SURVIVOR OF ALPHA FLIGHT.
SO LISTEN TO ME *VERY* CAREFULLY...

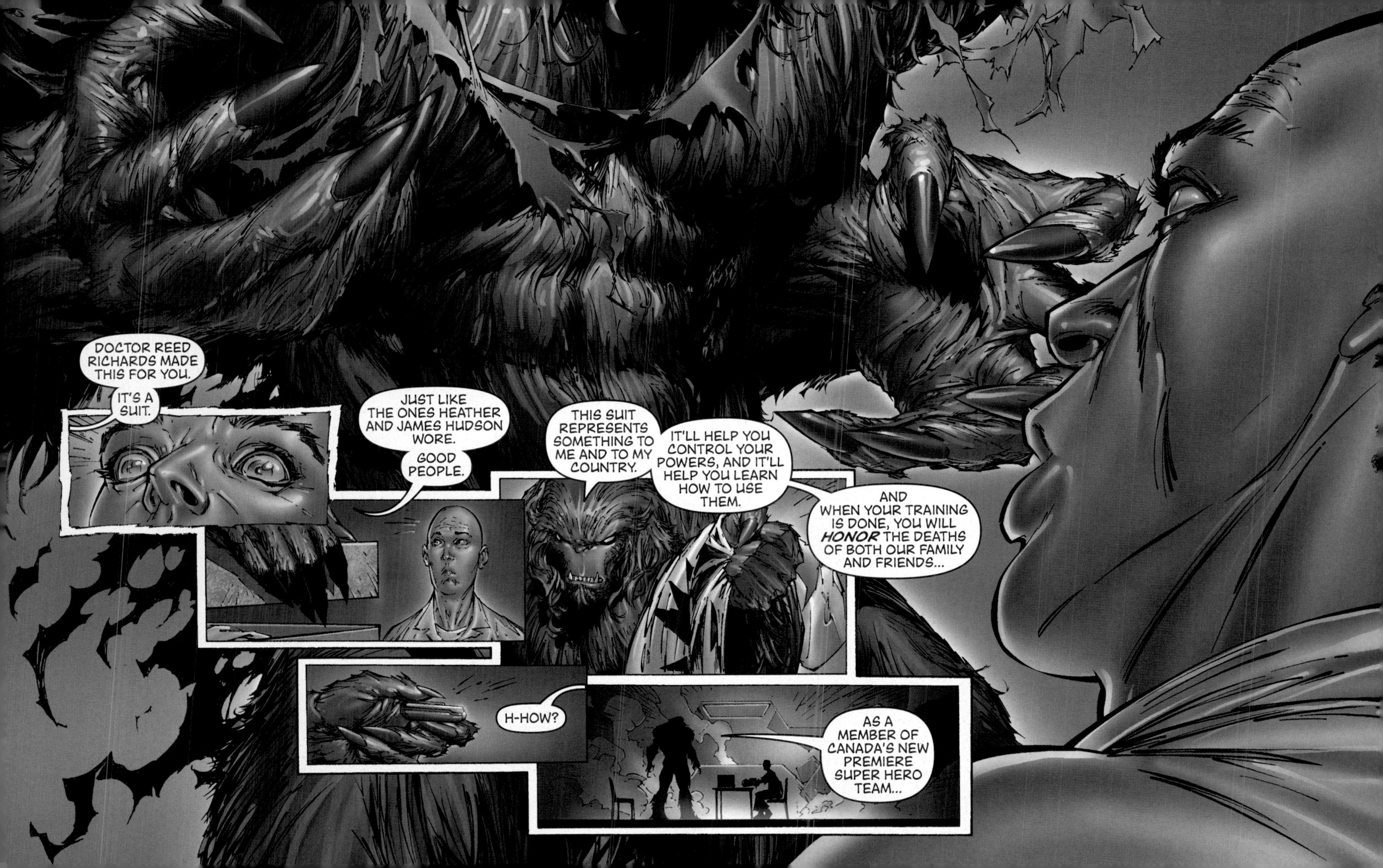
DOCTOR REED RICHARDS MADE THIS FOR YOU.
IT'S A SUIT.
JUST LIKE THE ONES HEATHER AND JAMES HUDSON WORE.
GOOD PEOPLE.
THIS SUIT REPRESENTS SOMETHING TO ME AND TO MY COUNTRY.
IT'LL HELP YOU CONTROL YOUR POWERS, AND IT'LL HELP YOU LEARN HOW TO USE THEM.
AND WHEN YOUR TRAINING IS DONE, YOU WILL *HONOR* THE DEATHS OF BOTH OUR FAMILY AND FRIENDS...
H-HOW?
AS A MEMBER OF CANADA'S NEW PREMIERE SUPER HERO TEAM...

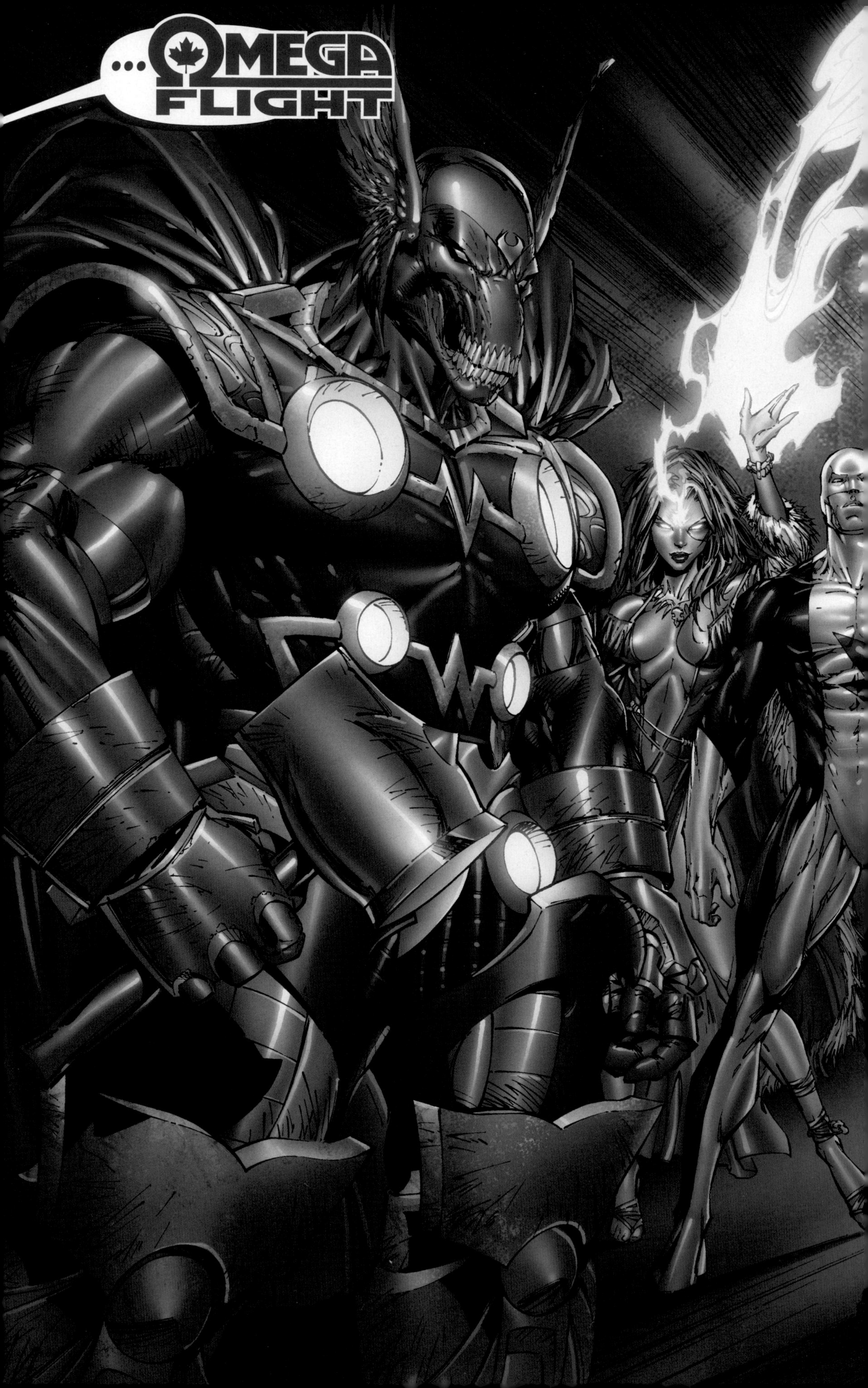
...OMEGA FLIGHT

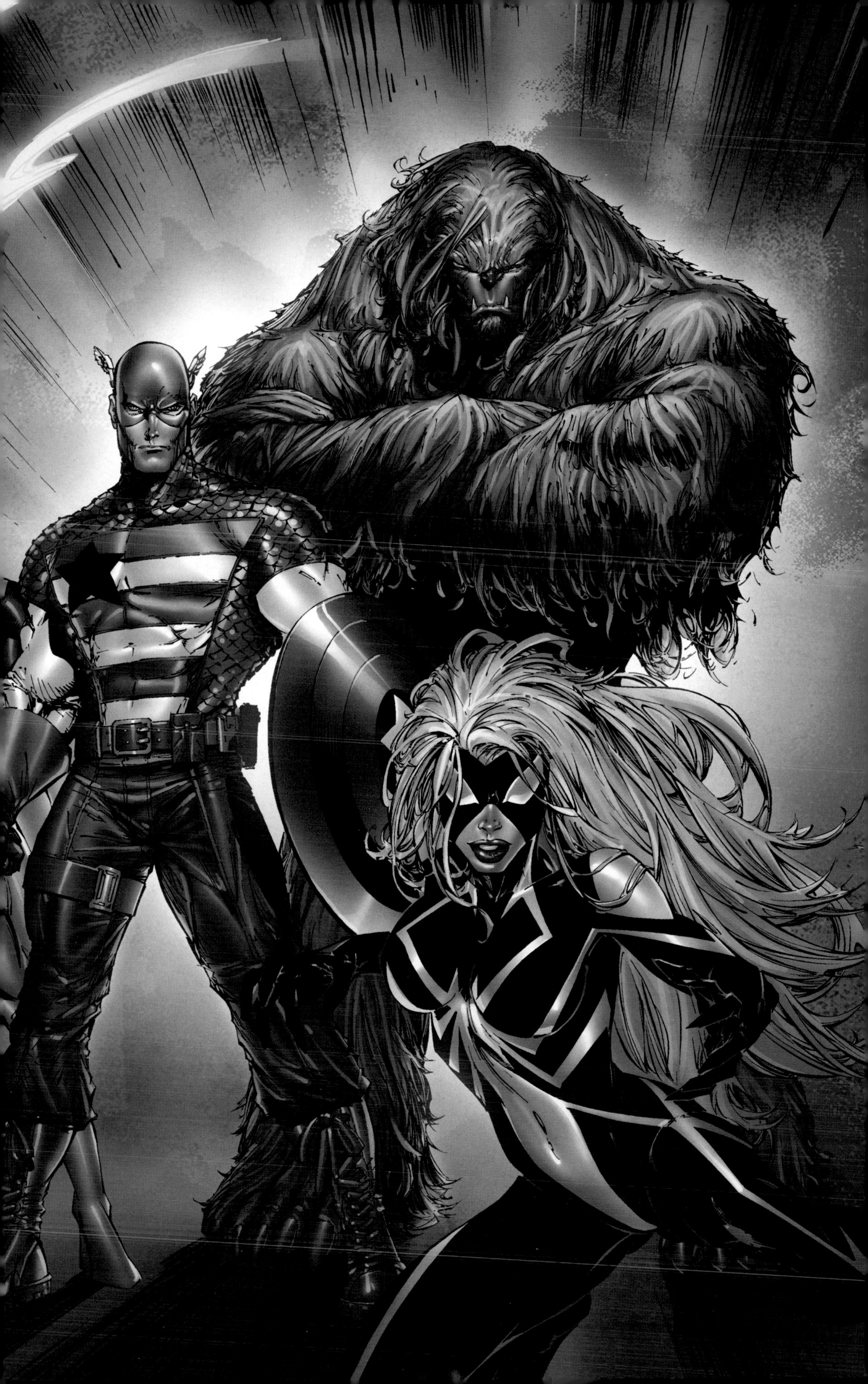

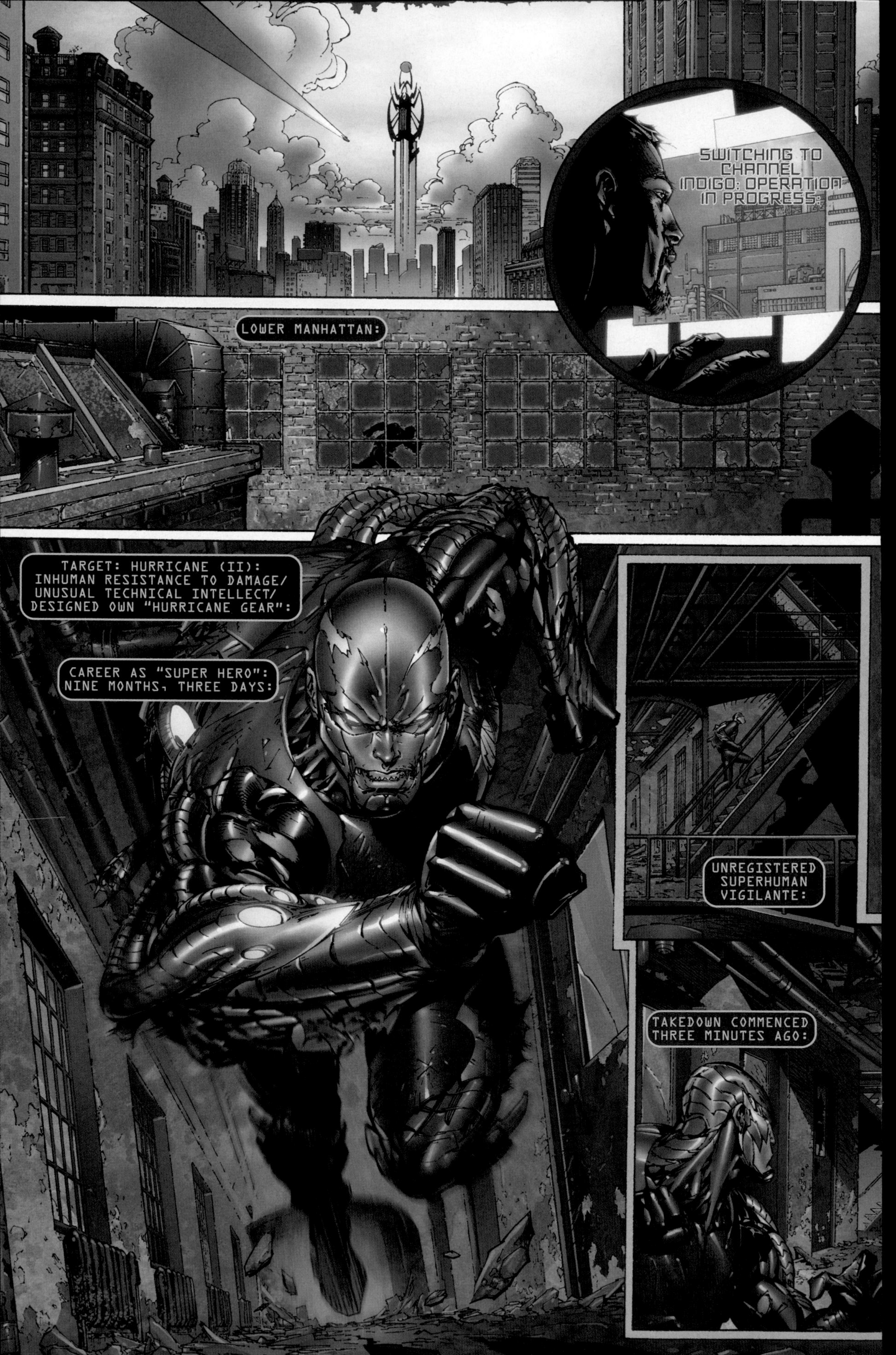

SWITCHING TO CHANNEL INDIGO: OPERATION IN PROGRESS:
LOWER MANHATTAN:
TARGET: HURRICANE (II): INHUMAN RESISTANCE TO DAMAGE/ UNUSUAL TECHNICAL INTELLECT/ DESIGNED OWN "HURRICANE GEAR":
CAREER AS "SUPER HERO": NINE MONTHS, THREE DAYS:
UNREGISTERED SUPERHUMAN VIGILANTE:
TAKEDOWN COMMENCED THREE MINUTES AGO:

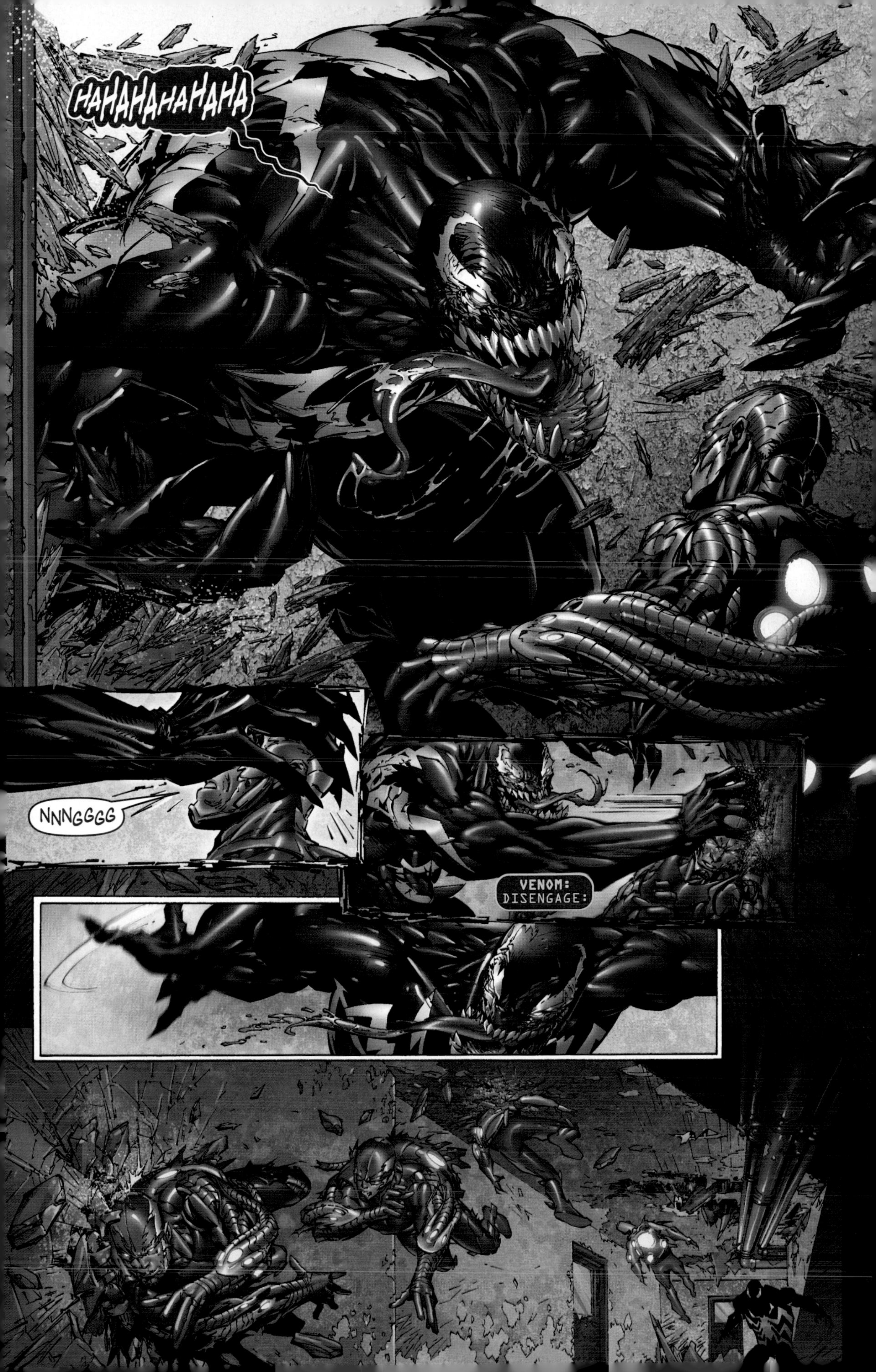
HAHAHAHAHAHA
NNNGGGG
VENOM:
DISENGAGE:

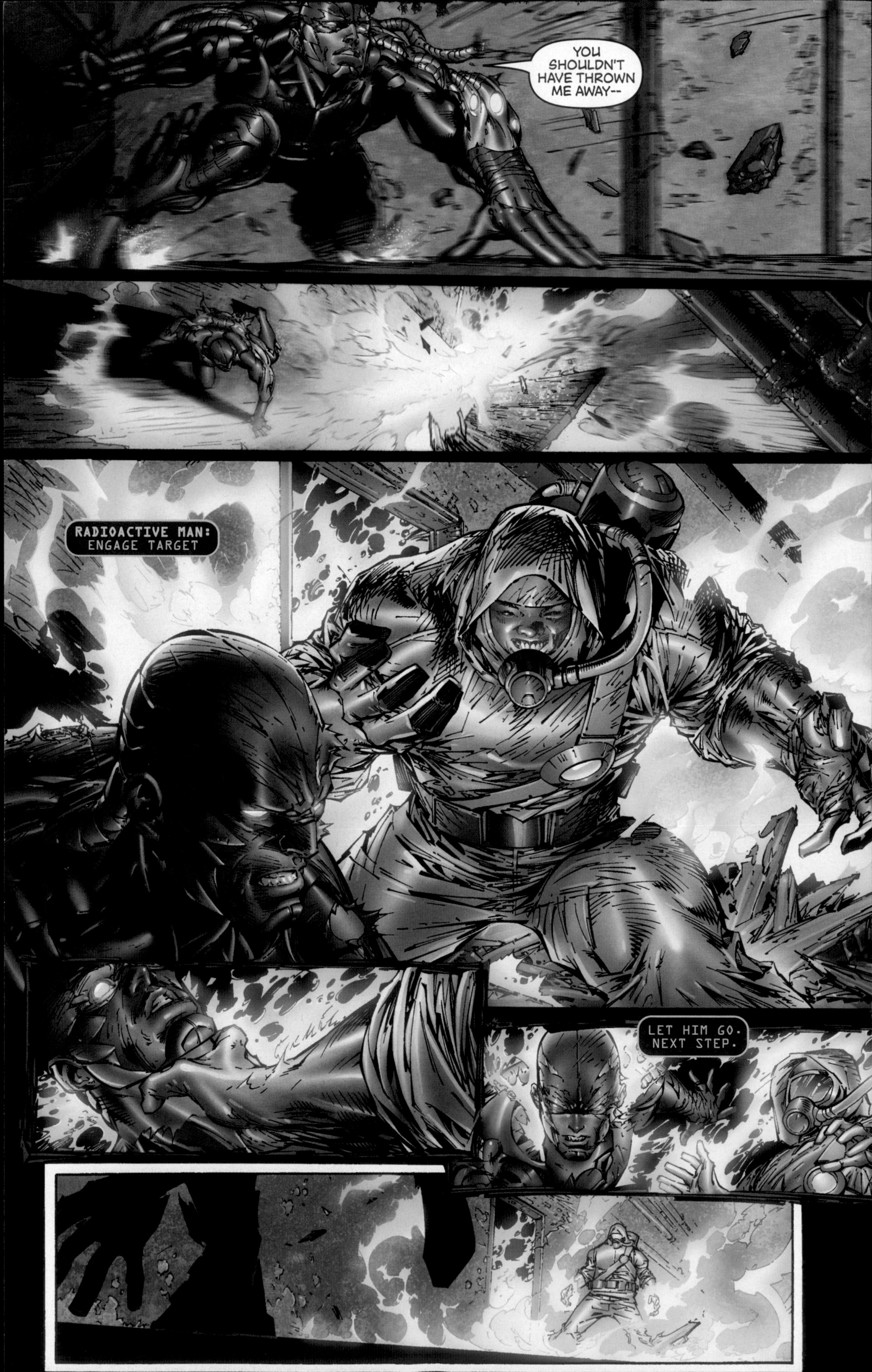
YOU SHOULDN'T HAVE THROWN ME AWAY--
RADIOACTIVE MAN:
ENGAGE TARGET
LET HIM GO.
NEXT STEP.

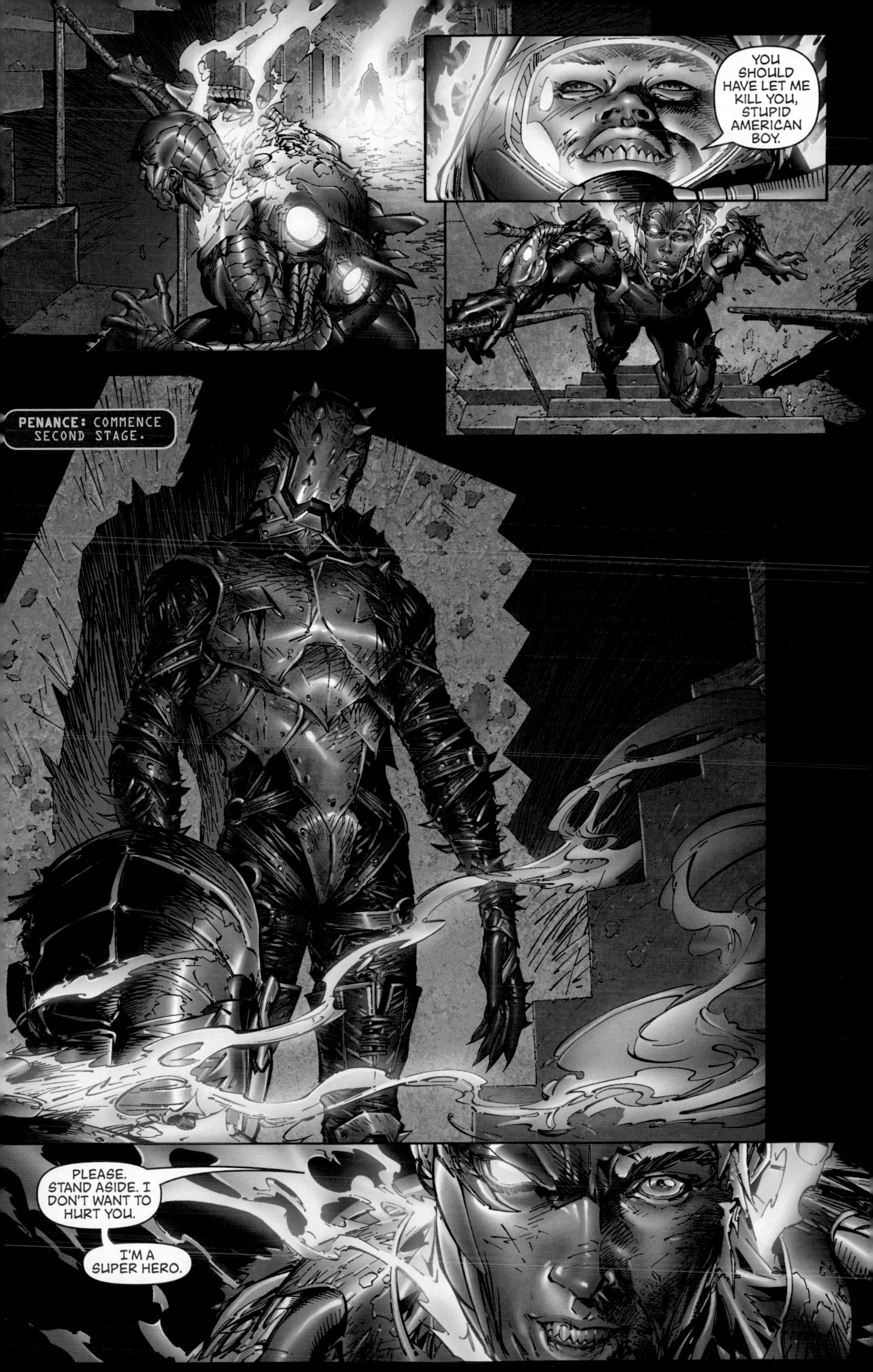
YOU SHOULD HAVE LET ME KILL YOU, STUPID AMERICAN BOY.
PENANCE: COMMENCE SECOND STAGE.
PLEASE. STAND ASIDE. I DON'T WANT TO HURT YOU.
I'M A SUPER HERO.

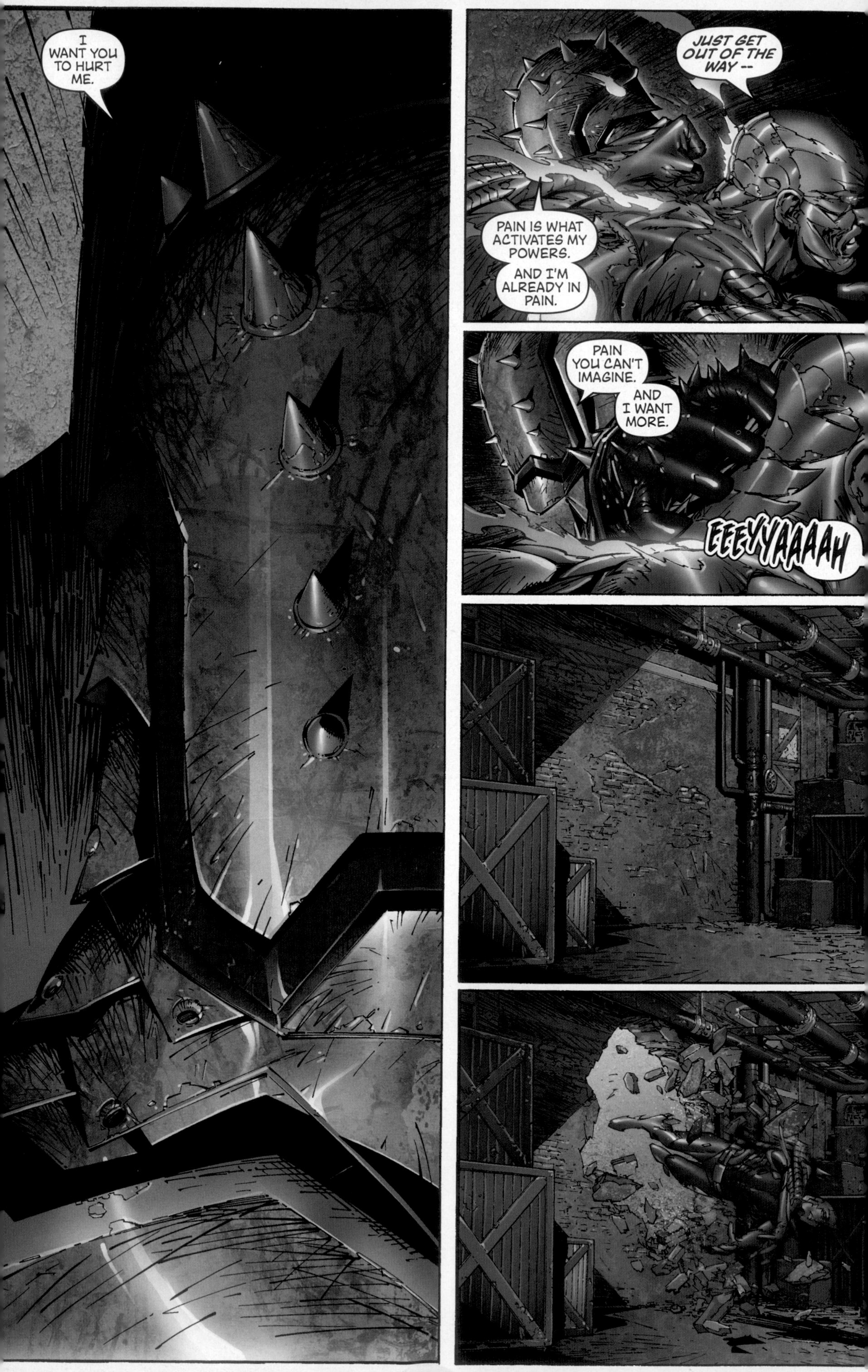
I WANT YOU TO HURT ME.
JUST GET OUT OF THE WAY --
PAIN IS WHAT ACTIVATES MY POWERS.
AND I'M ALREADY IN PAIN.
PAIN YOU CAN'T IMAGINE.
AND I WANT MORE.
EEEYYAAAAAH

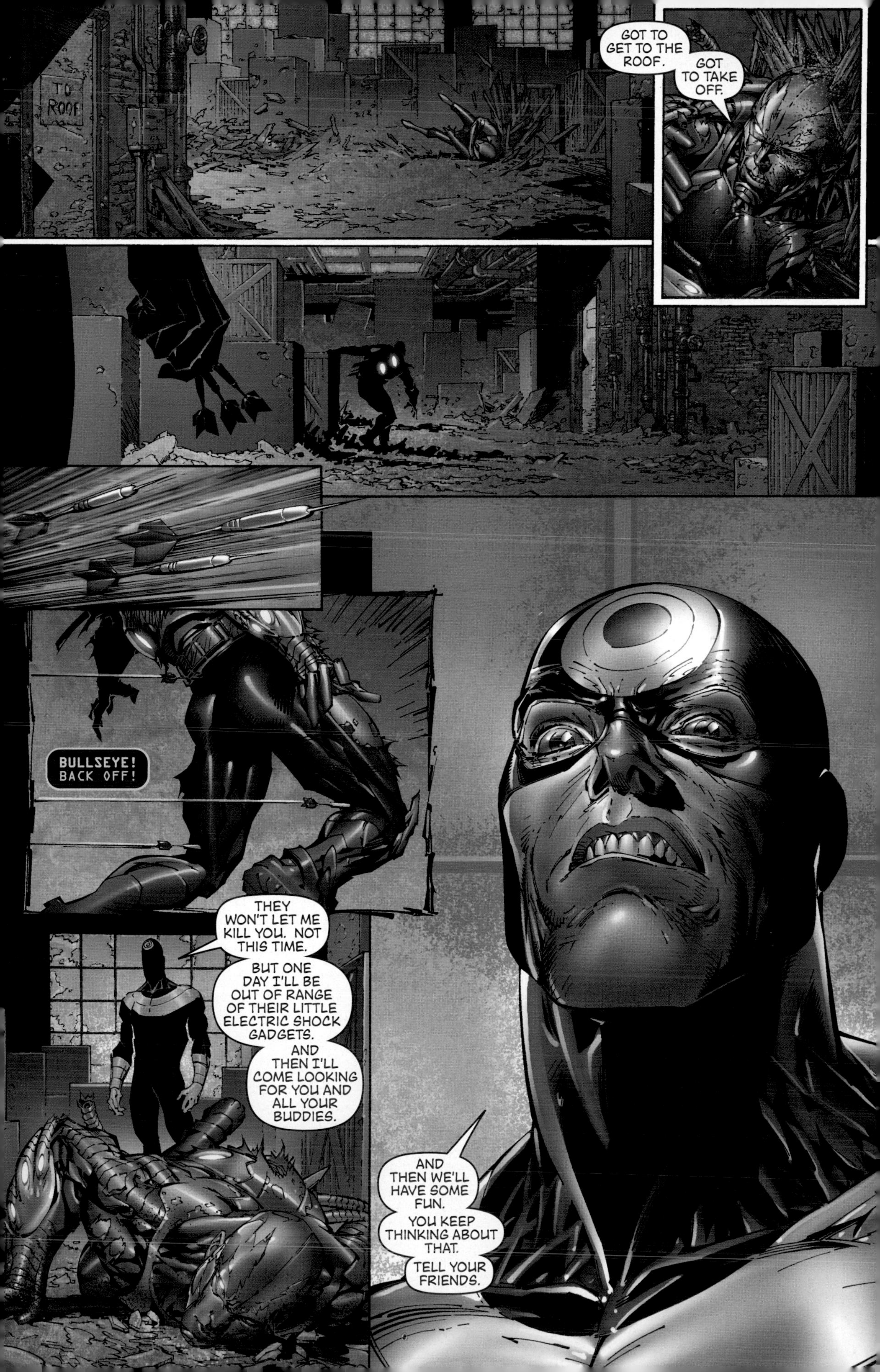

TO ROOF
GOT TO GET TO THE ROOF.
GOT TO TAKE OFF.
BULLSEYE! BACK OFF!
THEY WON'T LET ME KILL YOU. NOT THIS TIME.
BUT ONE DAY I'LL BE OUT OF RANGE OF THEIR LITTLE ELECTRIC SHOCK GADGETS.
AND THEN I'LL COME LOOKING FOR YOU AND ALL YOUR BUDDIES.
AND THEN WE'LL HAVE SOME FUN.
YOU KEEP THINKING ABOUT THAT.
TELL YOUR FRIENDS.

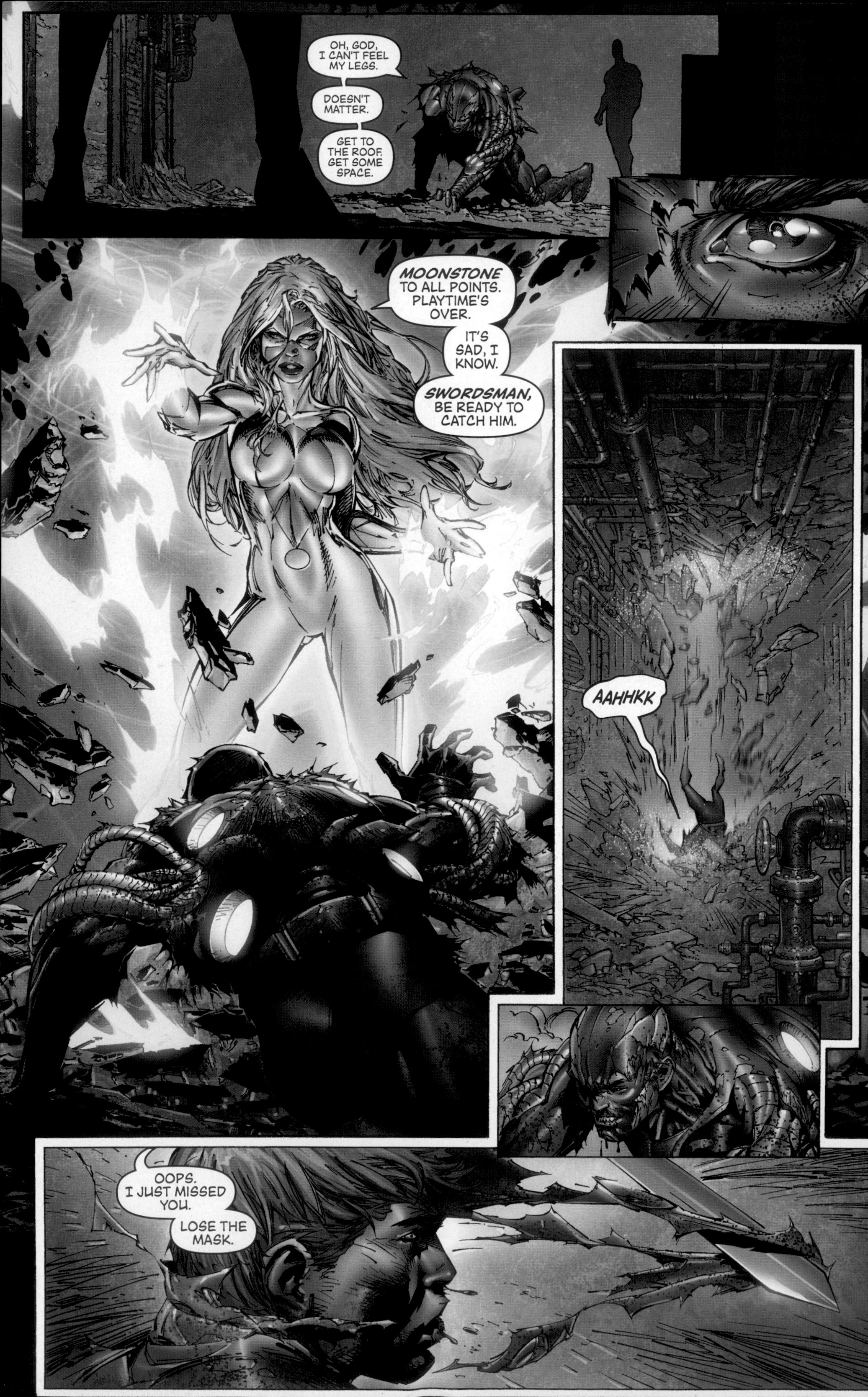
OH, GOD, I CAN'T FEEL MY LEGS.
DOESN'T MATTER.
GET TO THE ROOF. GET SOME SPACE.
MOONSTONE TO ALL POINTS. PLAYTIME'S OVER.
IT'S SAD, I KNOW.
SWORDSMAN, BE READY TO CATCH HIM.
AAHHKK
OOPS. I JUST MISSED YOU.
LOSE THE MASK.

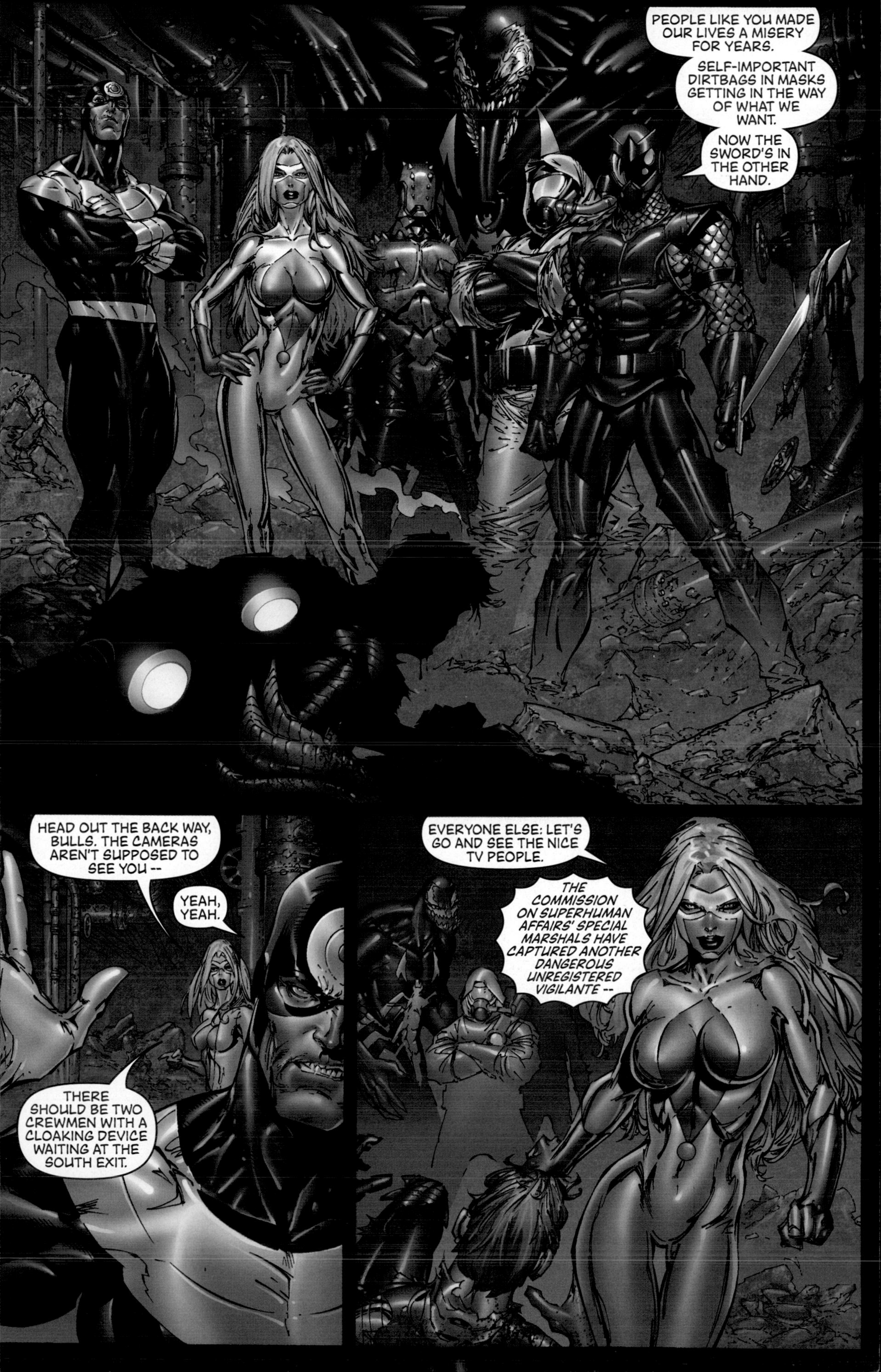
PEOPLE LIKE YOU MADE OUR LIVES A MISERY FOR YEARS.
SELF-IMPORTANT DIRTBAGS IN MASKS GETTING IN THE WAY OF WHAT WE WANT.
NOW THE SWORD'S IN THE OTHER HAND.
HEAD OUT THE BACK WAY, BULLS. THE CAMERAS AREN'T SUPPOSED TO SEE YOU --
YEAH, YEAH.
THERE SHOULD BE TWO CREWMEN WITH A CLOAKING DEVICE WAITING AT THE SOUTH EXIT.
EVERYONE ELSE: LET'S GO AND SEE THE NICE TV PEOPLE.
THE COMMISSION ON SUPERHUMAN AFFAIRS' SPECIAL MARSHALS HAVE CAPTURED ANOTHER DANGEROUS UNREGISTERED VIGILANTE --

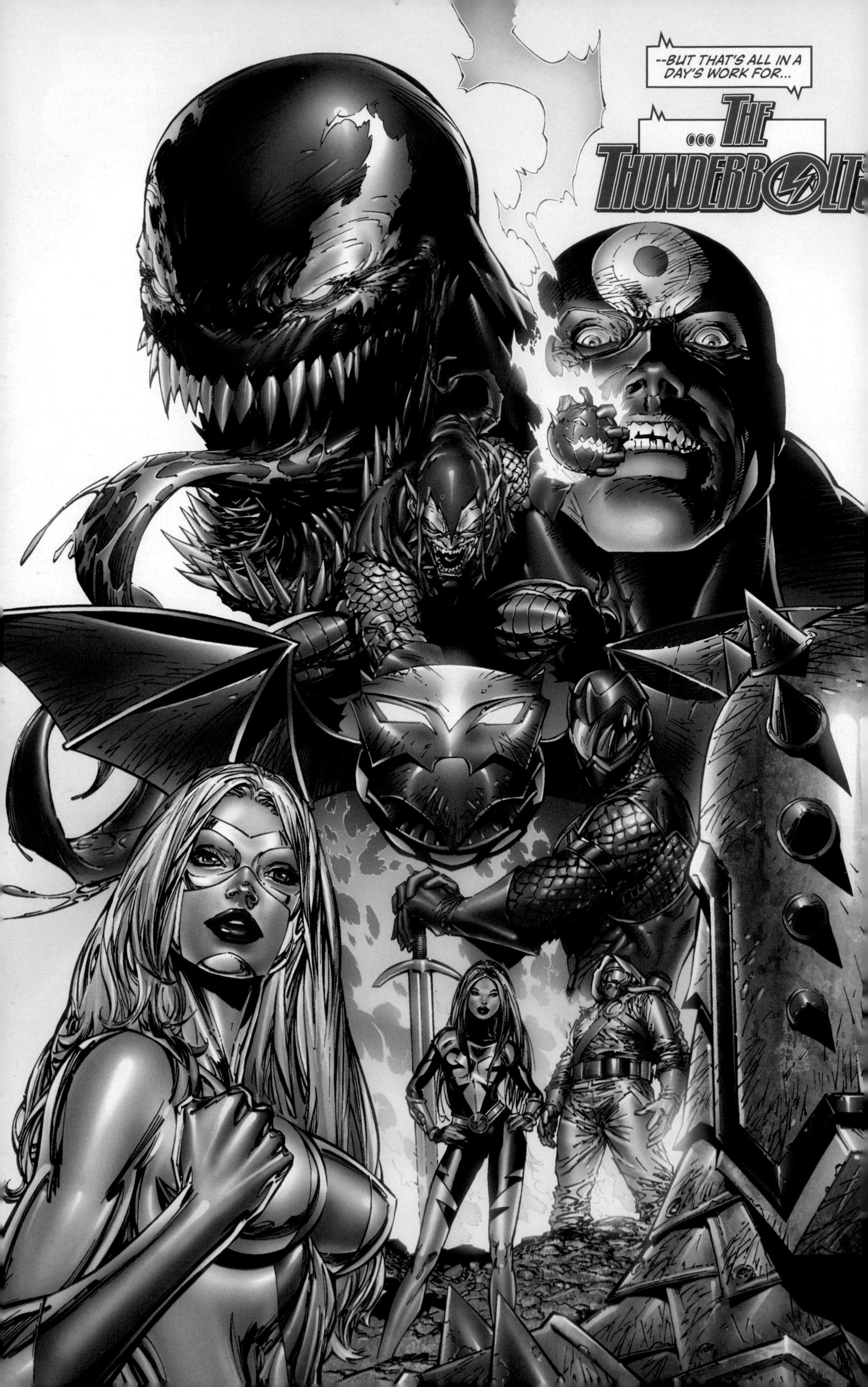
--BUT THAT'S ALL IN A DAY'S WORK FOR...
...THE THUNDERBOLTS

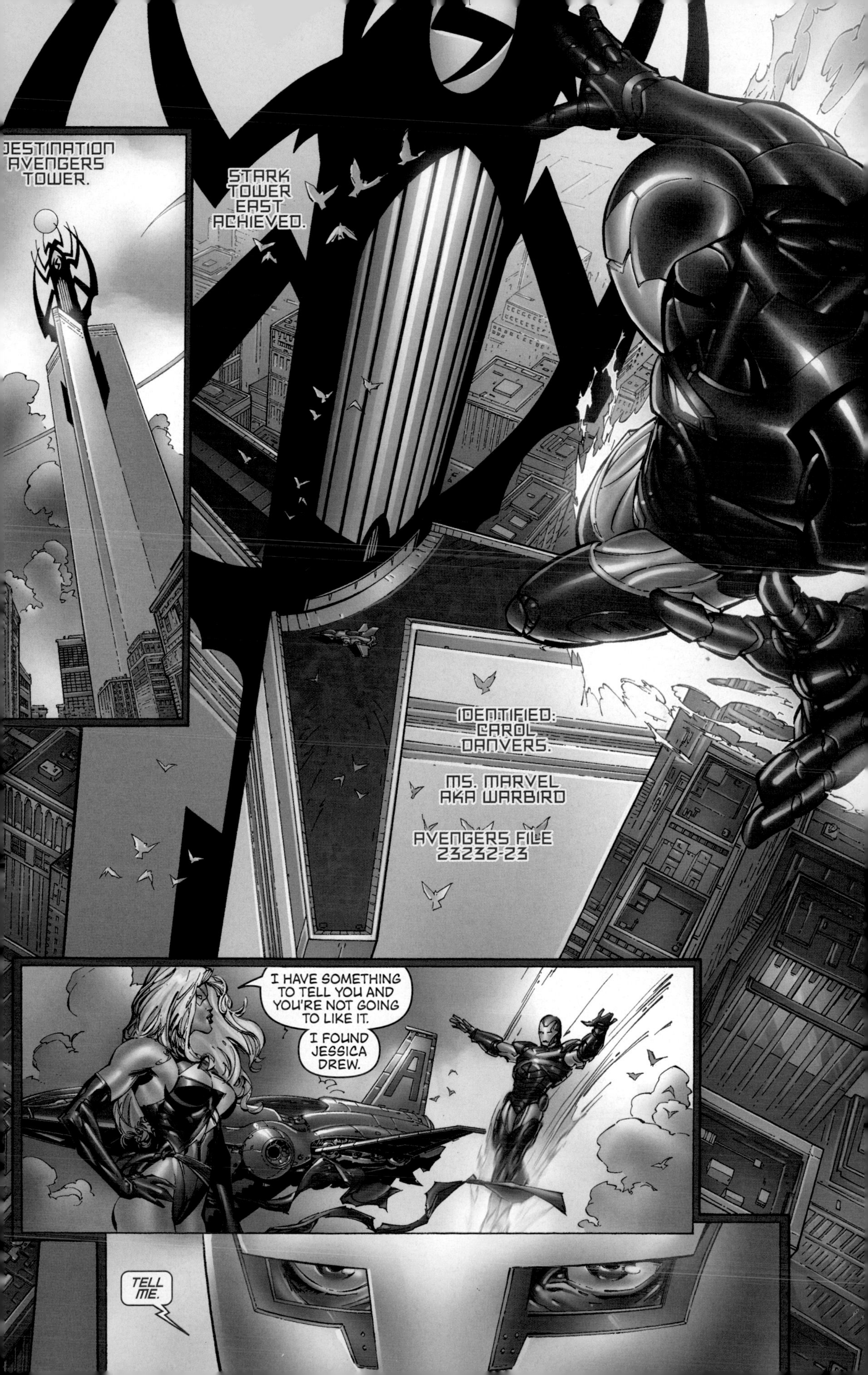
DESTINATION AVENGERS TOWER.
STARK TOWER EAST ACHIEVED.
IDENTIFIED: CAROL DANVERS.
MS. MARVEL AKA WARBIRD
AVENGERS FILE 23232-23
I HAVE SOMETHING TO TELL YOU AND YOU'RE NOT GOING TO LIKE IT.
I FOUND JESSICA DREW.
TELL ME.

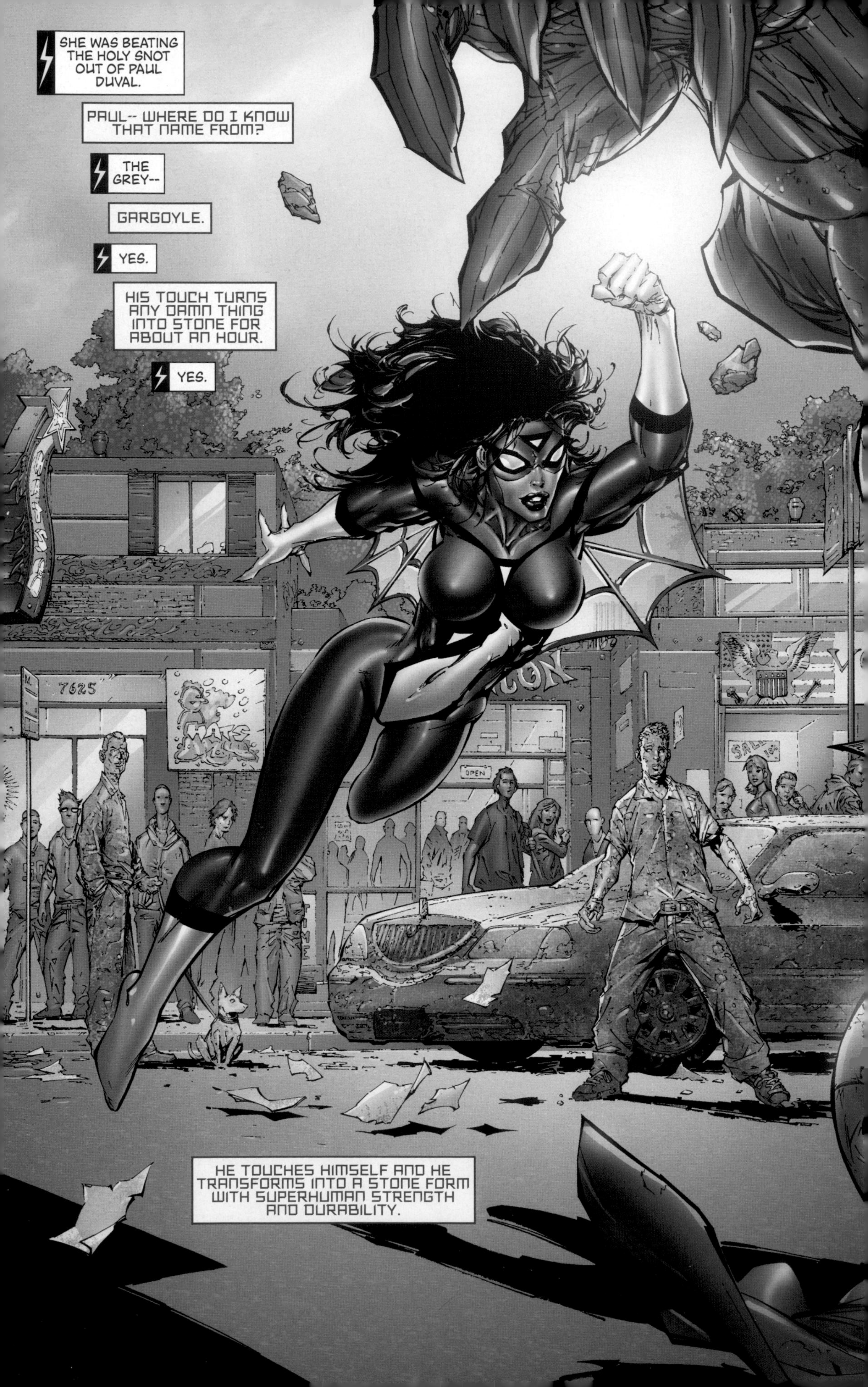
SHE WAS BEATING THE HOLY SNOT OUT OF PAUL DUVAL.
PAUL-- WHERE DO I KNOW THAT NAME FROM?
THE GREY--
GARGOYLE.
YES.
HIS TOUCH TURNS ANY DAMN THING INTO STONE FOR ABOUT AN HOUR.
YES.
7625
OPEN
HE TOUCHES HIMSELF AND HE TRANSFORMS INTO A STONE FORM WITH SUPERHUMAN STRENGTH AND DURABILITY.

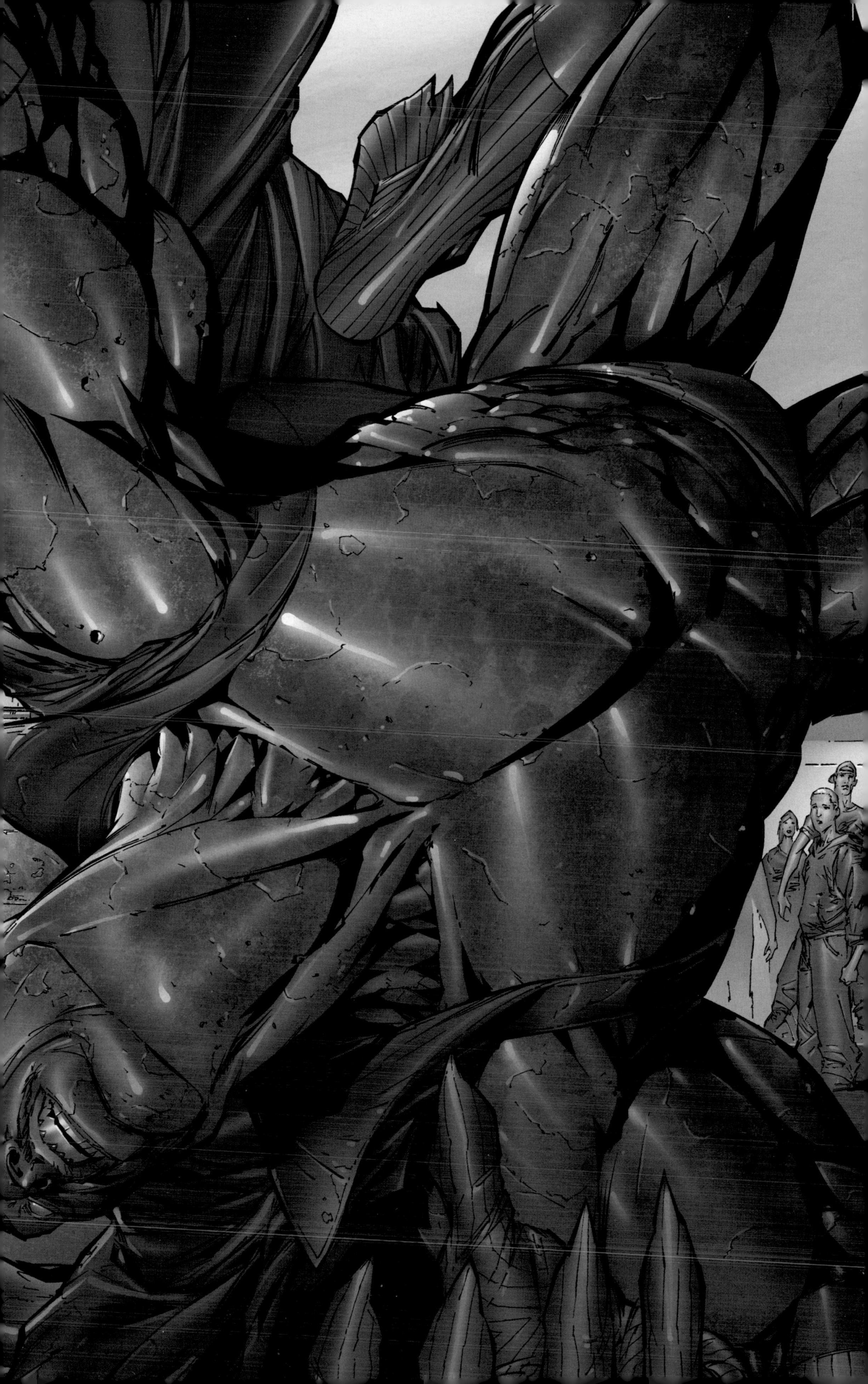

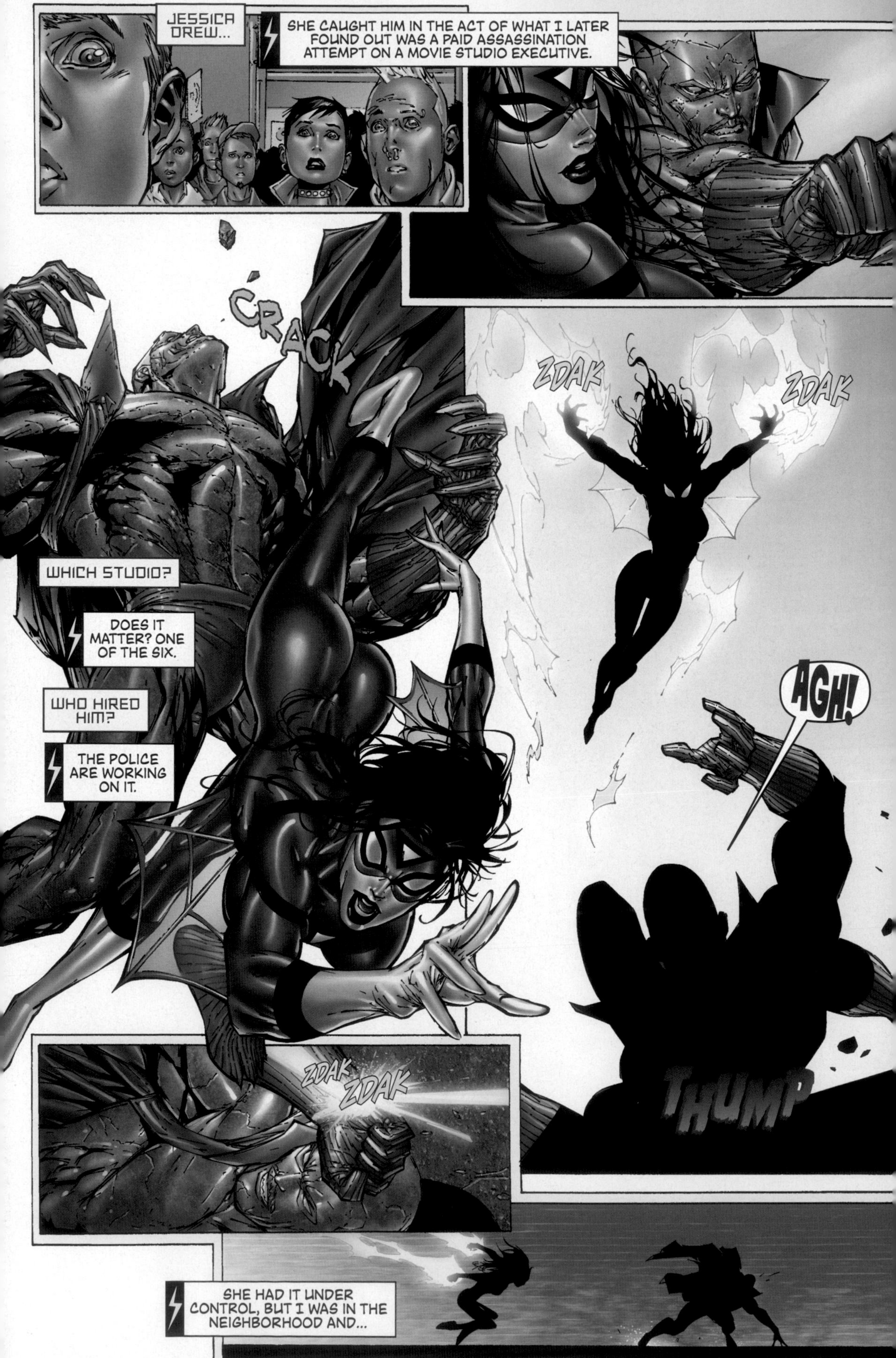
JESSICA DREW...
SHE CAUGHT HIM IN THE ACT OF WHAT I LATER FOUND OUT WAS A PAID ASSASSINATION ATTEMPT ON A MOVIE STUDIO EXECUTIVE.
CRACK
WHICH STUDIO?
DOES IT MATTER? ONE OF THE SIX.
WHO HIRED HIM?
THE POLICE ARE WORKING ON IT.
ZDAK
ZDAK
AGH!
THUMP
ZDAK
ZDAK
SHE HAD IT UNDER CONTROL, BUT I WAS IN THE NEIGHBORHOOD AND...

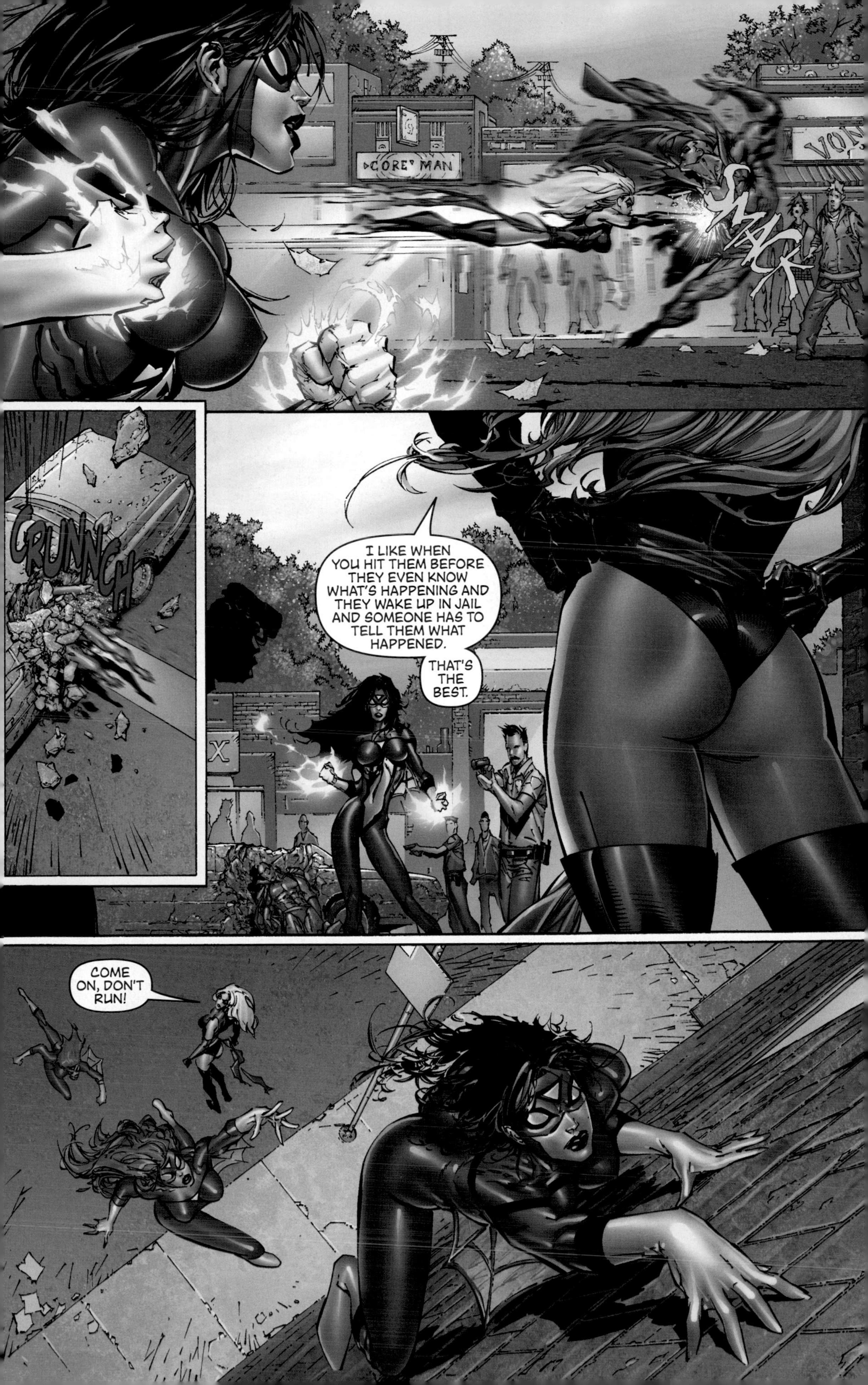

CORE' MAN
SMACK
CRUNNCH
I LIKE WHEN YOU HIT THEM BEFORE THEY EVEN KNOW WHAT'S HAPPENING AND THEY WAKE UP IN JAIL AND SOMEONE HAS TO TELL THEM WHAT HAPPENED.
THAT'S THE BEST.
COME ON, DON'T RUN!

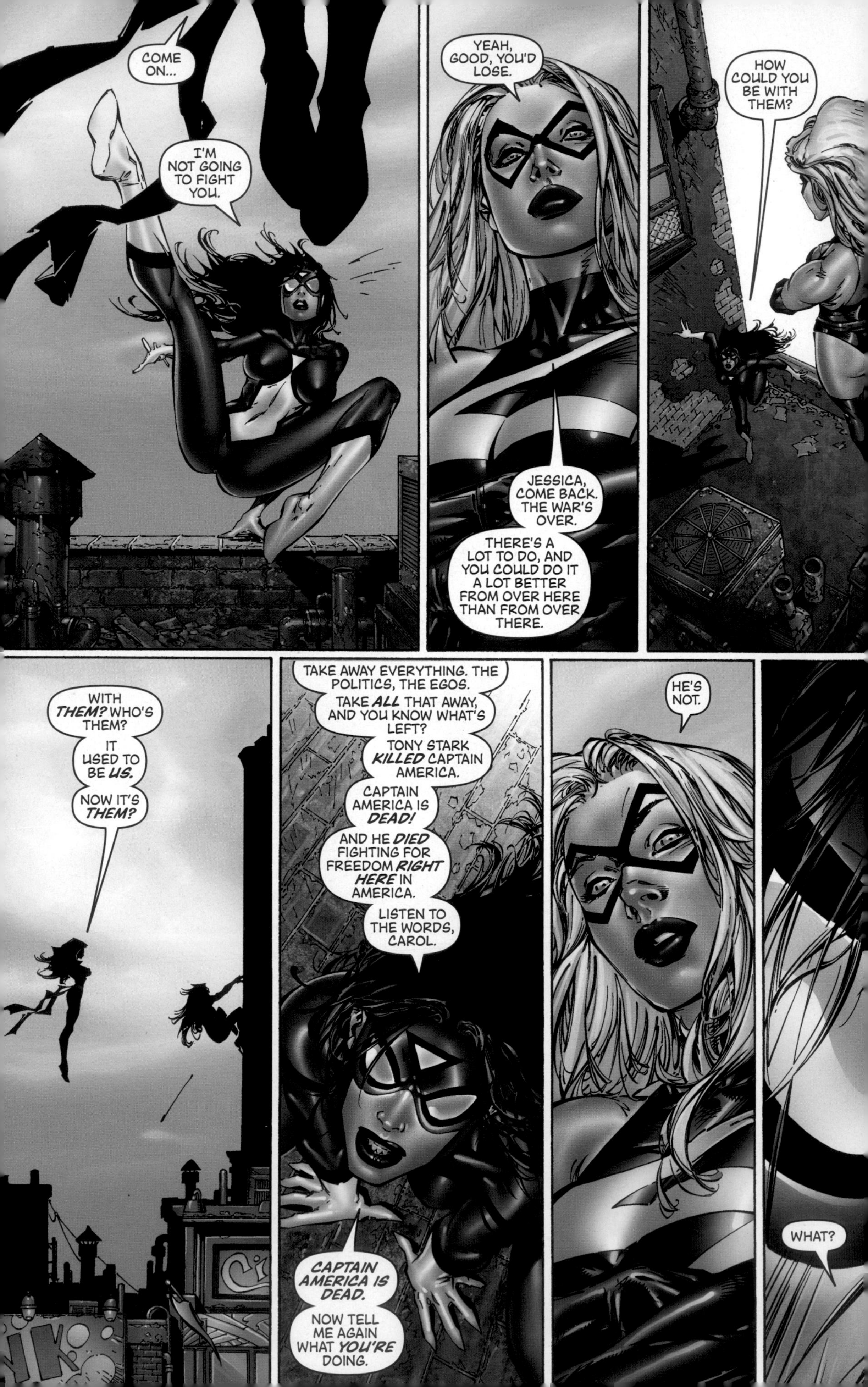
COME ON...
I'M NOT GOING TO FIGHT YOU.
YEAH, GOOD, YOU'D LOSE.
JESSICA, COME BACK. THE WAR'S OVER.
THERE'S A LOT TO DO, AND YOU COULD DO IT A LOT BETTER FROM OVER HERE THAN FROM OVER THERE.
HOW COULD YOU BE WITH THEM?
WITH *THEM?* WHO'S THEM?
IT USED TO BE *US.*
NOW IT'S *THEM?*
TAKE AWAY EVERYTHING. THE POLITICS, THE EGOS.
TAKE *ALL* THAT AWAY, AND YOU KNOW WHAT'S LEFT?
TONY STARK *KILLED* CAPTAIN AMERICA.
CAPTAIN AMERICA IS *DEAD!*
AND HE *DIED* FIGHTING FOR FREEDOM *RIGHT HERE* IN AMERICA.
LISTEN TO THE WORDS, CAROL.
CAPTAIN AMERICA IS DEAD.
NOW TELL ME AGAIN WHAT *YOU'RE* DOING.
HE'S NOT.
WHAT?

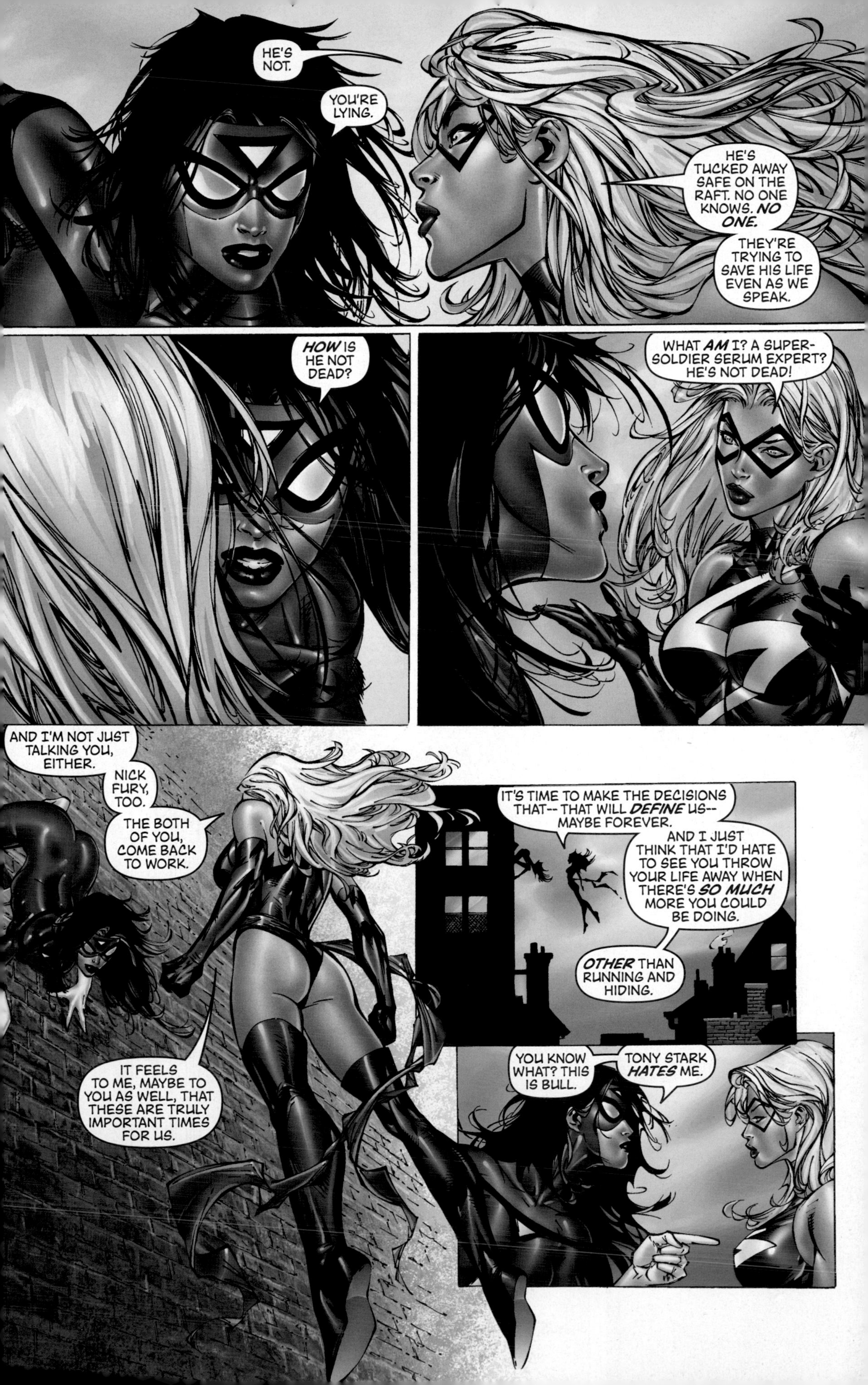
HE'S NOT.
YOU'RE LYING.
HE'S TUCKED AWAY SAFE ON THE RAFT. NO ONE KNOWS. NO ONE.
THEY'RE TRYING TO SAVE HIS LIFE EVEN AS WE SPEAK.
HOW IS HE NOT DEAD?
WHAT AM I? A SUPER-SOLDIER SERUM EXPERT? HE'S NOT DEAD!
AND I'M NOT JUST TALKING YOU, EITHER.
NICK FURY, TOO.
THE BOTH OF YOU, COME BACK TO WORK.
IT FEELS TO ME, MAYBE TO YOU AS WELL, THAT THESE ARE TRULY IMPORTANT TIMES FOR US.
IT'S TIME TO MAKE THE DECISIONS THAT-- THAT WILL DEFINE US-- MAYBE FOREVER.
AND I JUST THINK THAT I'D HATE TO SEE YOU THROW YOUR LIFE AWAY WHEN THERE'S SO MUCH MORE YOU COULD BE DOING.
OTHER THAN RUNNING AND HIDING.
YOU KNOW WHAT? THIS IS BULL.
TONY STARK HATES ME.

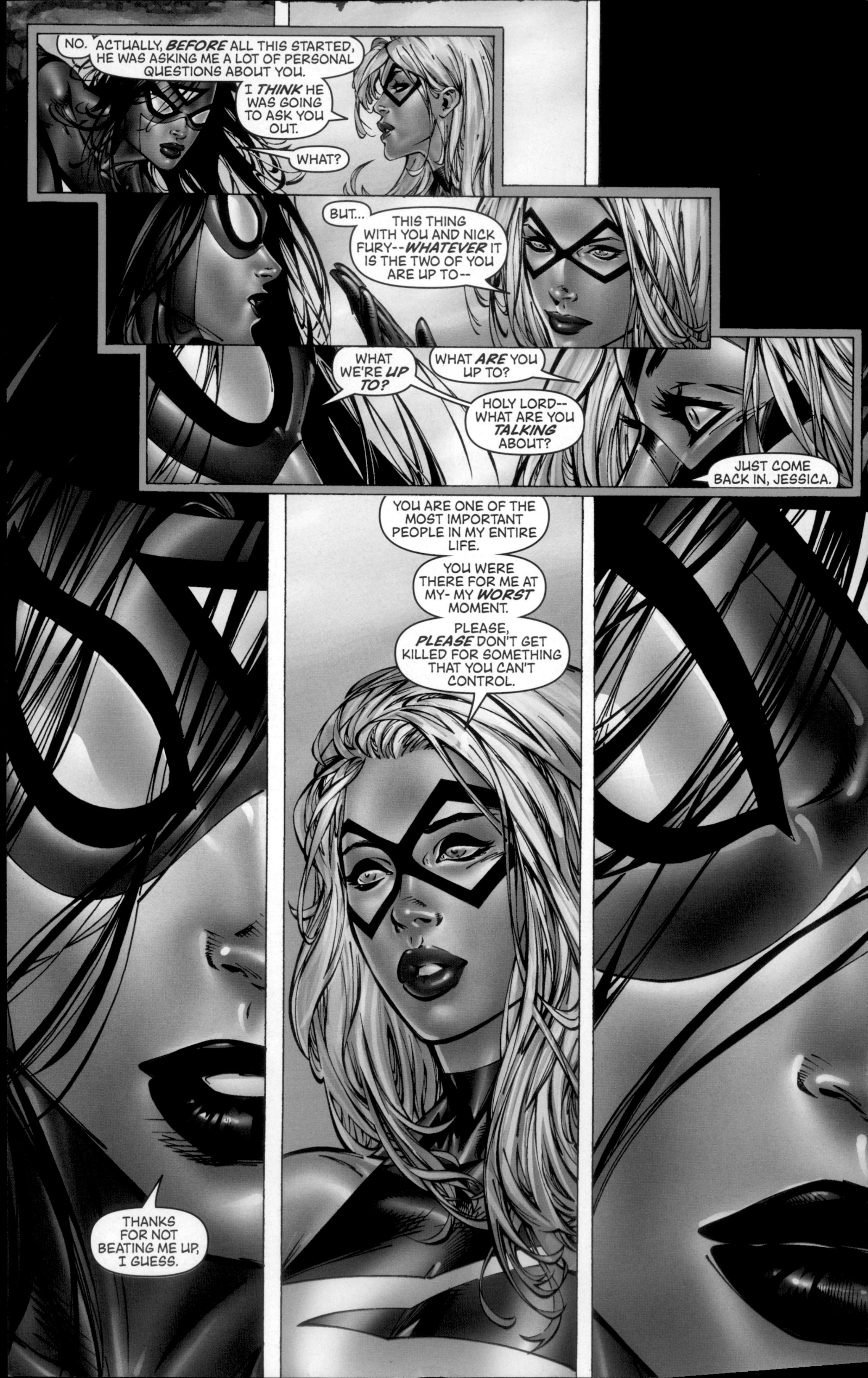

NO.
ACTUALLY, BEFORE ALL THIS STARTED, HE WAS ASKING ME A LOT OF PERSONAL QUESTIONS ABOUT YOU.
I THINK HE WAS GOING TO ASK YOU OUT.
WHAT?
BUT...
THIS THING WITH YOU AND NICK FURY--WHATEVER IT IS THE TWO OF YOU ARE UP TO--
WHAT WE'RE UP TO?
WHAT ARE YOU UP TO?
HOLY LORD-- WHAT ARE YOU TALKING ABOUT?
JUST COME BACK IN, JESSICA.
YOU ARE ONE OF THE MOST IMPORTANT PEOPLE IN MY ENTIRE LIFE.
YOU WERE THERE FOR ME AT MY- MY WORST MOMENT.
PLEASE, PLEASE DON'T GET KILLED FOR SOMETHING THAT YOU CAN'T CONTROL.
THANKS FOR NOT BEATING ME UP, I GUESS.

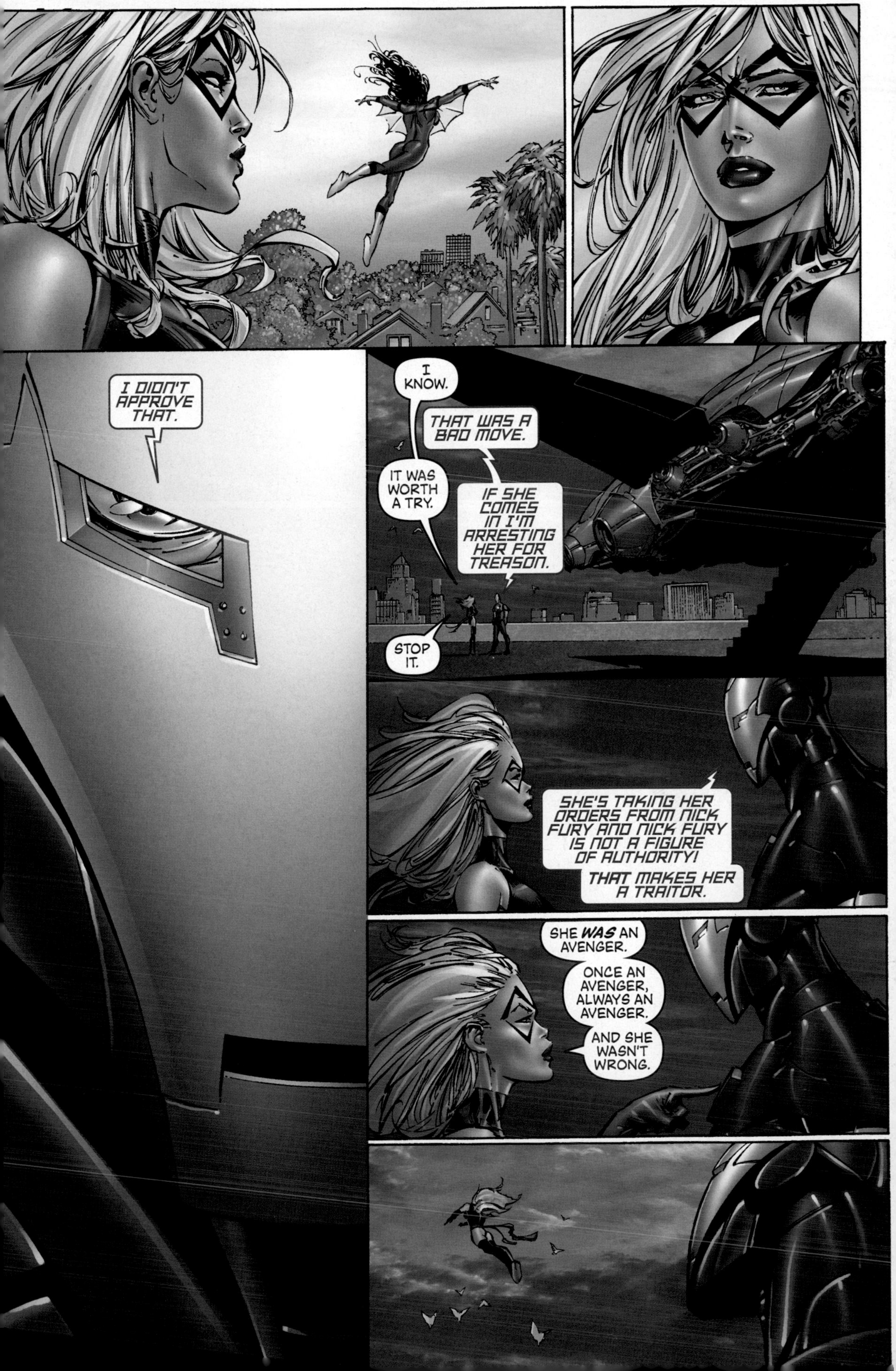
I DIDN'T APPROVE THAT.
I KNOW.
THAT WAS A BAD MOVE.
IT WAS WORTH A TRY.
IF SHE COMES IN I'M ARRESTING HER FOR TREASON.
STOP IT.
SHE'S TAKING HER ORDERS FROM NICK FURY AND NICK FURY IS NOT A FIGURE OF AUTHORITY!
THAT MAKES HER A TRAITOR.
SHE WAS AN AVENGER.
ONCE AN AVENGER, ALWAYS AN AVENGER.
AND SHE WASN'T WRONG.

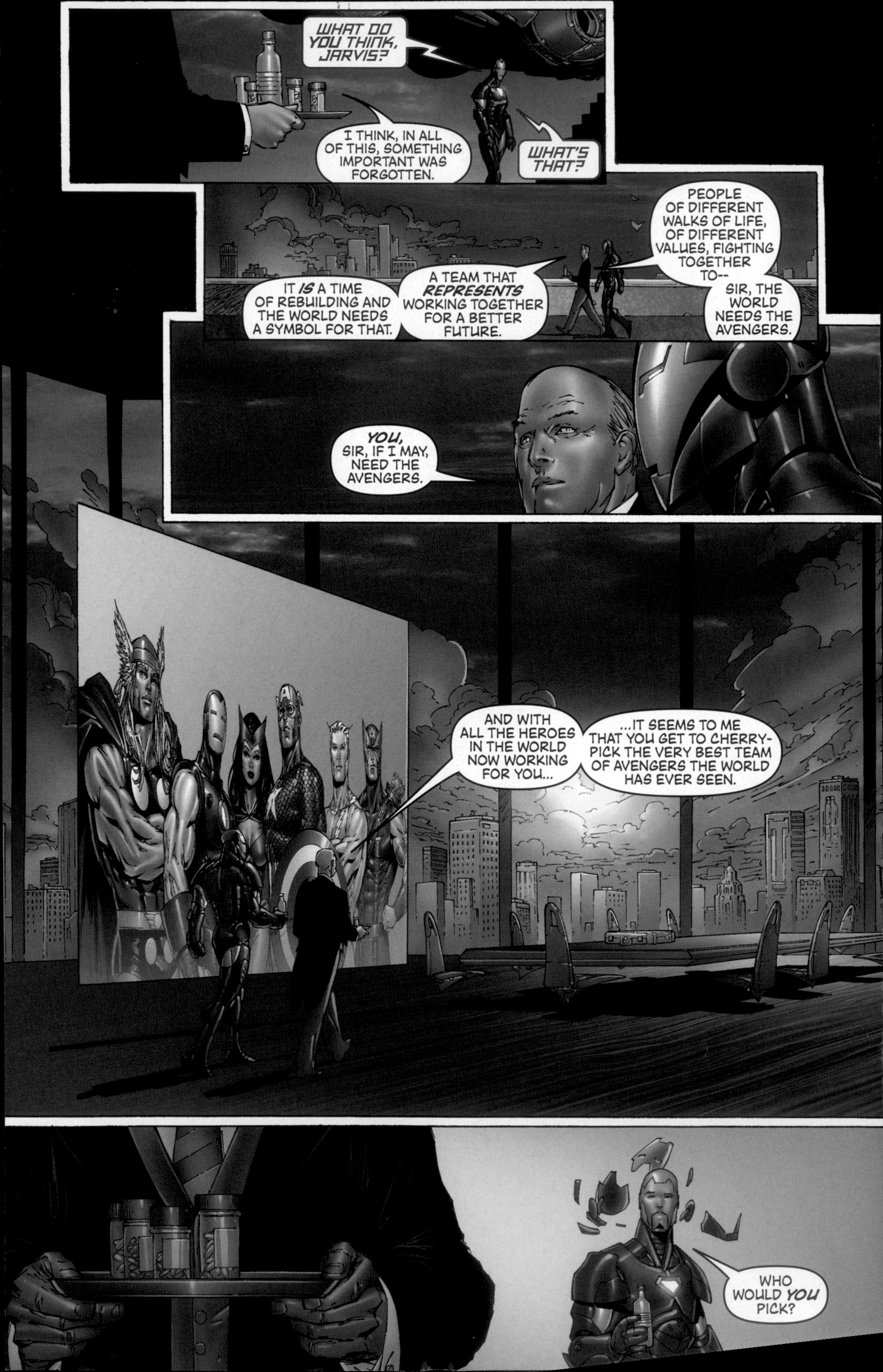
WHAT DO YOU THINK, JARVIS?
I THINK, IN ALL OF THIS, SOMETHING IMPORTANT WAS FORGOTTEN.
WHAT'S THAT?
IT *IS* A TIME OF REBUILDING AND THE WORLD NEEDS A SYMBOL FOR THAT.
A TEAM THAT *REPRESENTS* WORKING TOGETHER FOR A BETTER FUTURE.
PEOPLE OF DIFFERENT WALKS OF LIFE, OF DIFFERENT VALUES, FIGHTING TOGETHER TO--
SIR, THE WORLD NEEDS THE AVENGERS.
YOU, SIR, IF I MAY, NEED THE AVENGERS.
AND WITH ALL THE HEROES IN THE WORLD NOW WORKING FOR YOU...
...IT SEEMS TO ME THAT YOU GET TO CHERRY-PICK THE VERY BEST TEAM OF AVENGERS THE WORLD HAS EVER SEEN.
WHO WOULD *YOU* PICK?

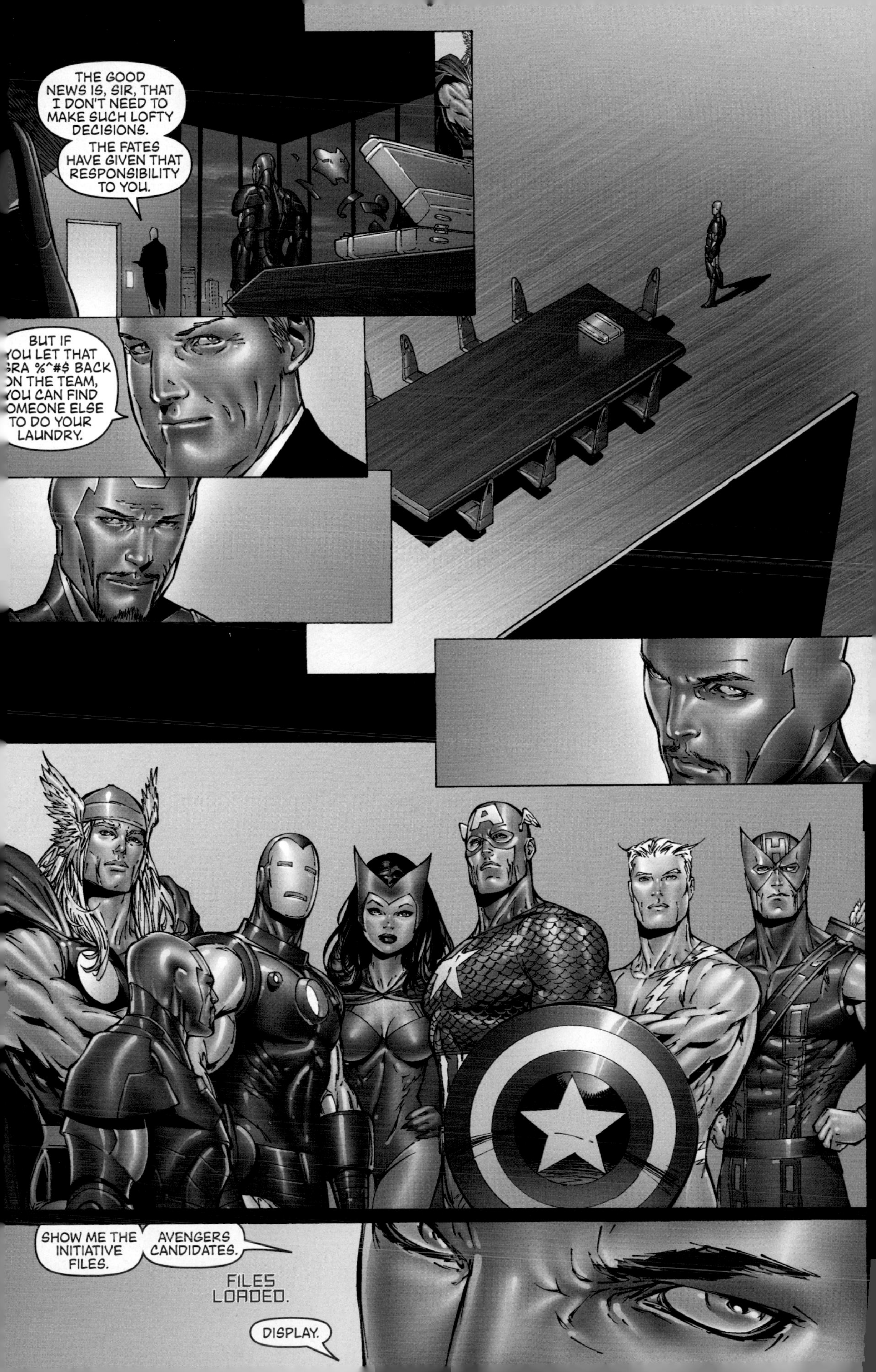
THE GOOD NEWS IS, SIR, THAT I DON'T NEED TO MAKE SUCH LOFTY DECISIONS.
THE FATES HAVE GIVEN THAT RESPONSIBILITY TO YOU.
BUT IF YOU LET THAT GRA %^#$ BACK ON THE TEAM, YOU CAN FIND SOMEONE ELSE TO DO YOUR LAUNDRY.
SHOW ME THE INITIATIVE FILES.
AVENGERS CANDIDATES.
FILES LOADED.
DISPLAY.

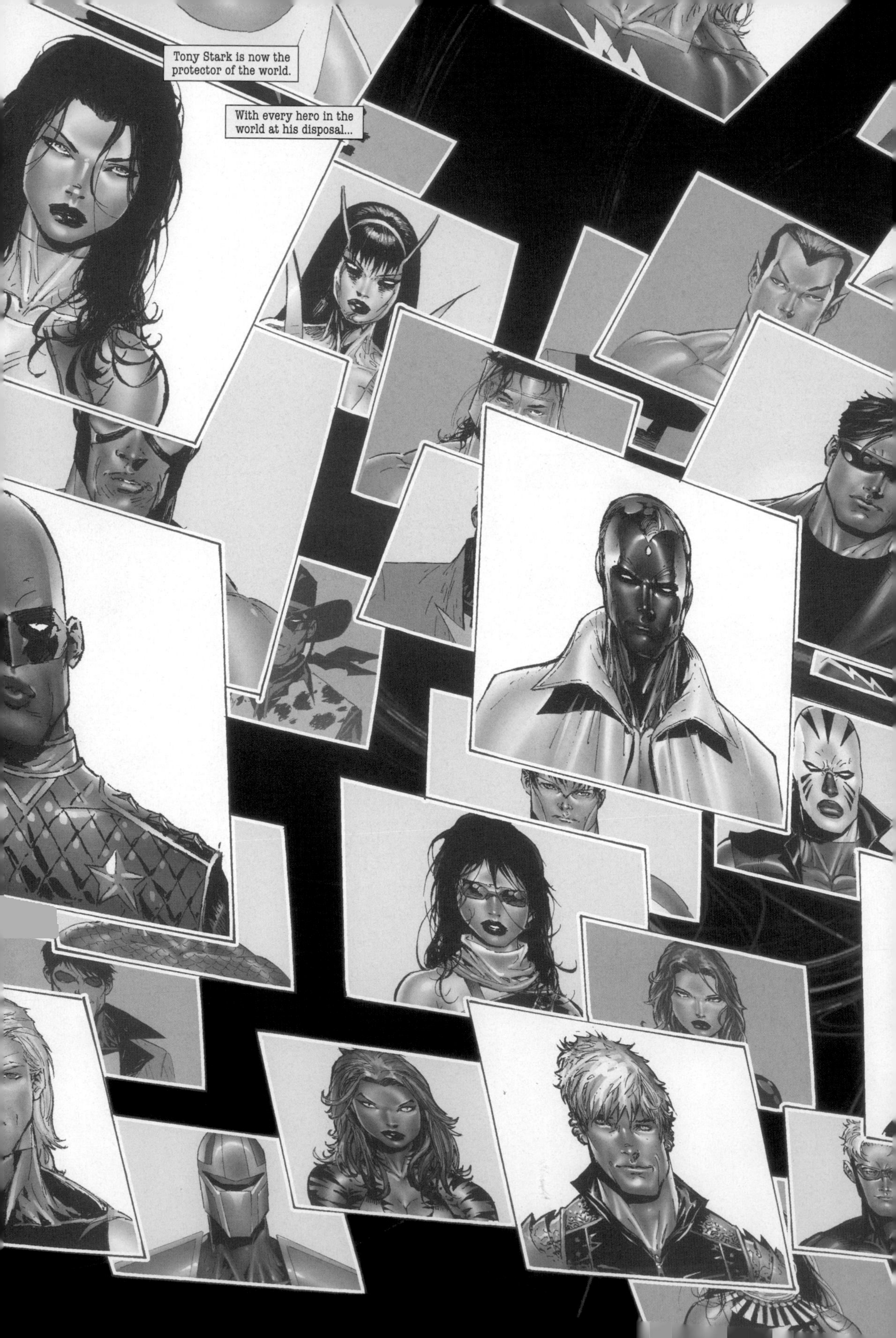
Tony Stark is now the protector of the world.
With every hero in the world at his disposal...

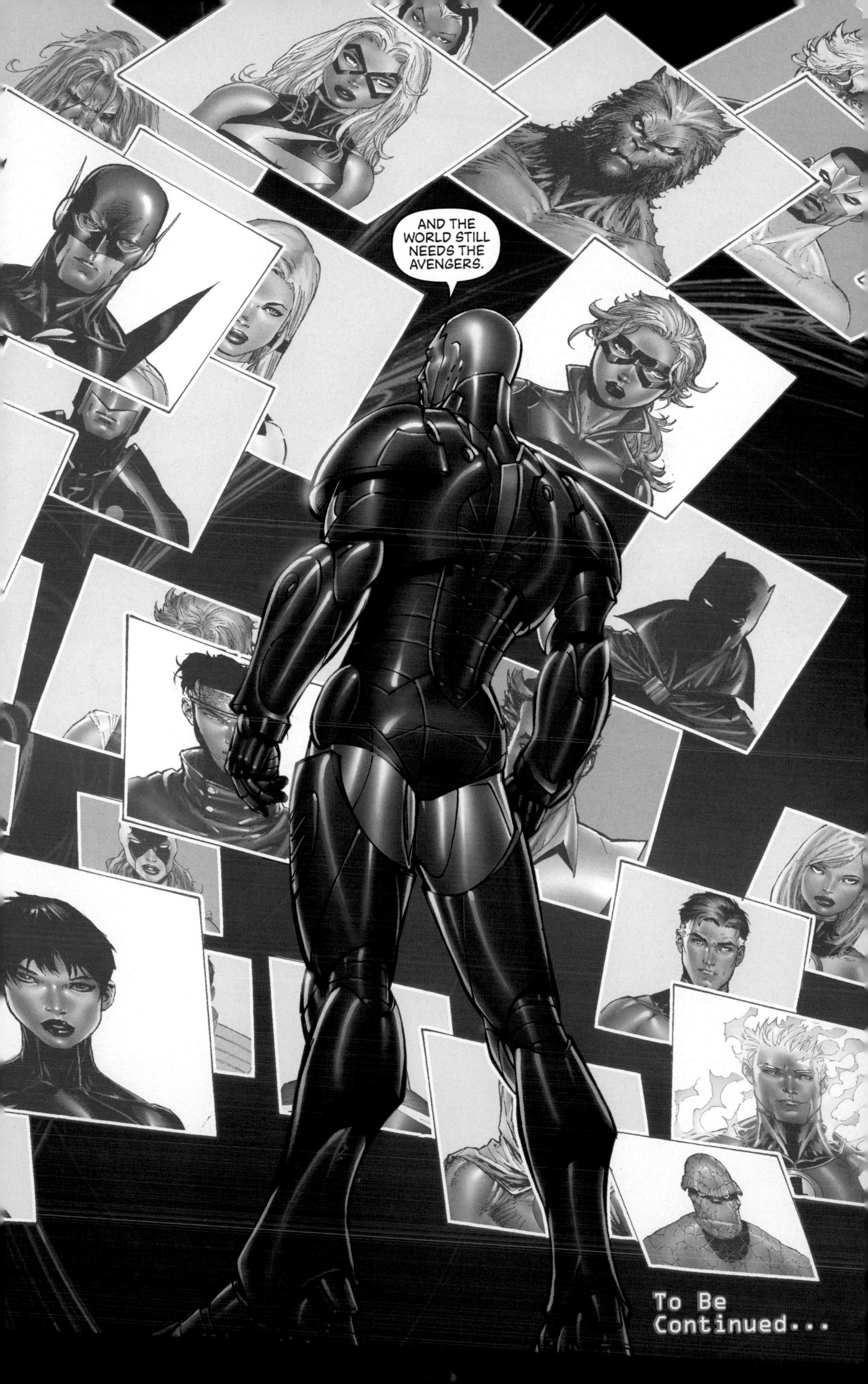
AND THE WORLD STILL NEEDS THE AVENGERS.
To Be Continued...

WHOSE SIDE...
...ARE YOU ON?

THAT WAS THE QUESTION THAT
SPLIT THE NATION'S HEROES DOWN
THE MIDDLE, FOR REGISTRATION OR
AGAINST. IRON MAN AND CAPTAIN
AMERICA LED OPPOSING SIDES ON
THE ISSUE UNTIL CAP'S SURRENDER
AND SUBSEQUENT ASSASSINATION.
BUT WITNESS TWO NEW QUESTIONS:
"WHAT IF CAPTAIN AMERICA
LED ALL THE HEROES AGAINST
REGISTRATION?" AND "WHAT IF IRON
MAN LOST THE SUPER HERO CIVIL
WAR?" TWO DIVERSE DIRECTIONS
THAT NOT ONLY CHANGE THE LIVES
OF OUR HEROES BUT ALSO THE
COUNTRY THEY SWORE TO DEFEND!

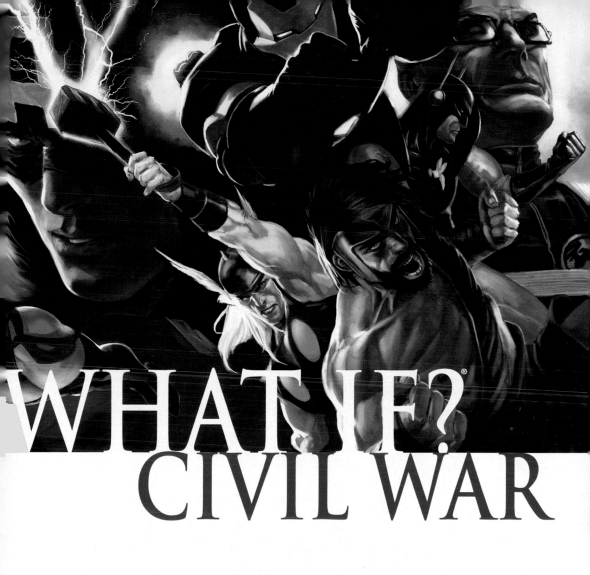

WHAT IF?®
CIVIL WAR

There exist parallel worlds beyond our own. Within these worlds, each living being faces turning points in their existence, and a choice must be made at every one of these points—choices that will affect their own destinies, and perhaps that of their world or even the universe itself. Call it the "road not taken"—the chance missed, the decision deferred... of what might have been, what could have happened—but for the invisible workings of an incomprehensible fate. Call it...

WHAT IF...

WHAT HAPPENED IN

CIVIL WAR

Stamford, Connecticut is destroyed during a televised fight between the New Warriors and a group of villains. Public Sentiment turns against super heroes and advocates call out for reform. A proposed Superhuman Registration Act is soon passed which requires all individuals possessing paranormal abilities to register with the government.

Some heroes, such as Iron Man, see this as a natural evolution of the role of superhumans in society. Captain America was asked to spearhead the new initiative and help bring in heroes who refused to comply. Rather than hunt down his friends and allies, Cap went underground and formed a resistance movement to fight back against the law.

When Cap realized the scope of the damage that the warring heroes were causing, he surrendered to Iron Man's pro-registration forces and ended the superhuman civil war. Cap was determined to fight the law from within the system until an assassin's bullet changed all that. Now Cap is dead and Iron Man is left grieving for his fallen friend...

THE STRANGER
Written by – Ed Brubaker
Illustrated by – Marko Djurdjevic

With acknowledgement to the works of Frank Miller.

WHAT IF CAPTAIN AMERICA LED ALL THE HEROES AGAINST REGISTRATION?
Written by – Kevin Grevioux
Penciled by – Gustavo
Inked by – Sandu Florea (Pgs. 3-18, 23),
Victor Olazaba (Pg. 19-20, 22),
Scott Koblish (Pg.21, 24-25, 27) &
Gustavo (Pg. 26)
Colored by – GuruEFX

WHAT IF IRON MAN LOST THE CIVIL WAR?
Written by – Christos Gage
Illustrated by – Harvey Tolibao
Colored by – Avalon's Ed Tadeo (Pgs. 29-40) &
Jay David Ramos (Pgs. 41-46)

Letters – Virtual Caligraphy's Joe Caramagna
Production – The Bullpen's Rich Ginter
Special Thanks to Scott "Pond Scum" Elmer

Wraparound Cover – Marko Djurdejevic
Single Cover – Marc Silvestri & Jelena Kevic-Djurdjevic
Frontispiece Art by – Jelena Kevic-Djurdjevic

Editorial Assistance – Michael Horwitz
Assistant Editors – Chris Allo & Nathan Cosby
Consulting Editors – Tom Brevoort & Mark Paniccia

Editor – Justin F. Gabrie
Editor-In-Chief – Joe Quesada
Publisher – Dan Buckley

Dedicated to Roy Thomas – The first to ask the question...

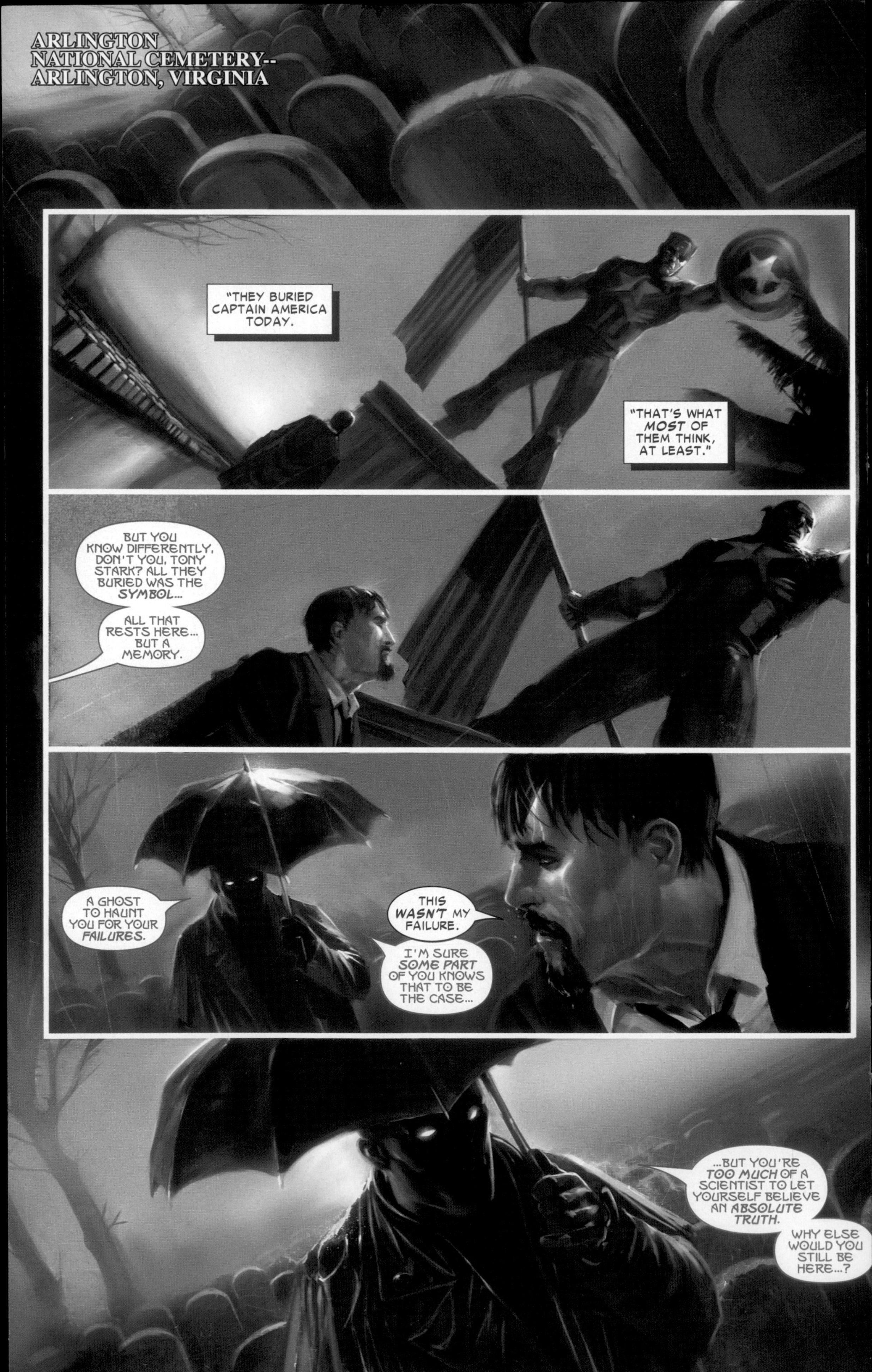
ARLINGTON NATIONAL CEMETERY-- ARLINGTON, VIRGINIA
"THEY BURIED CAPTAIN AMERICA TODAY.
"THAT'S WHAT MOST OF THEM THINK, AT LEAST."
BUT YOU KNOW DIFFERENTLY, DON'T YOU, TONY STARK? ALL THEY BURIED WAS THE SYMBOL...
ALL THAT RESTS HERE... BUT A MEMORY.
A GHOST TO HAUNT YOU FOR YOUR FAILURES.
THIS WASN'T MY FAILURE.
I'M SURE SOME PART OF YOU KNOWS THAT TO BE THE CASE...
...BUT YOU'RE TOO MUCH OF A SCIENTIST TO LET YOURSELF BELIEVE AN ABSOLUTE TRUTH.
WHY ELSE WOULD YOU STILL BE HERE...?

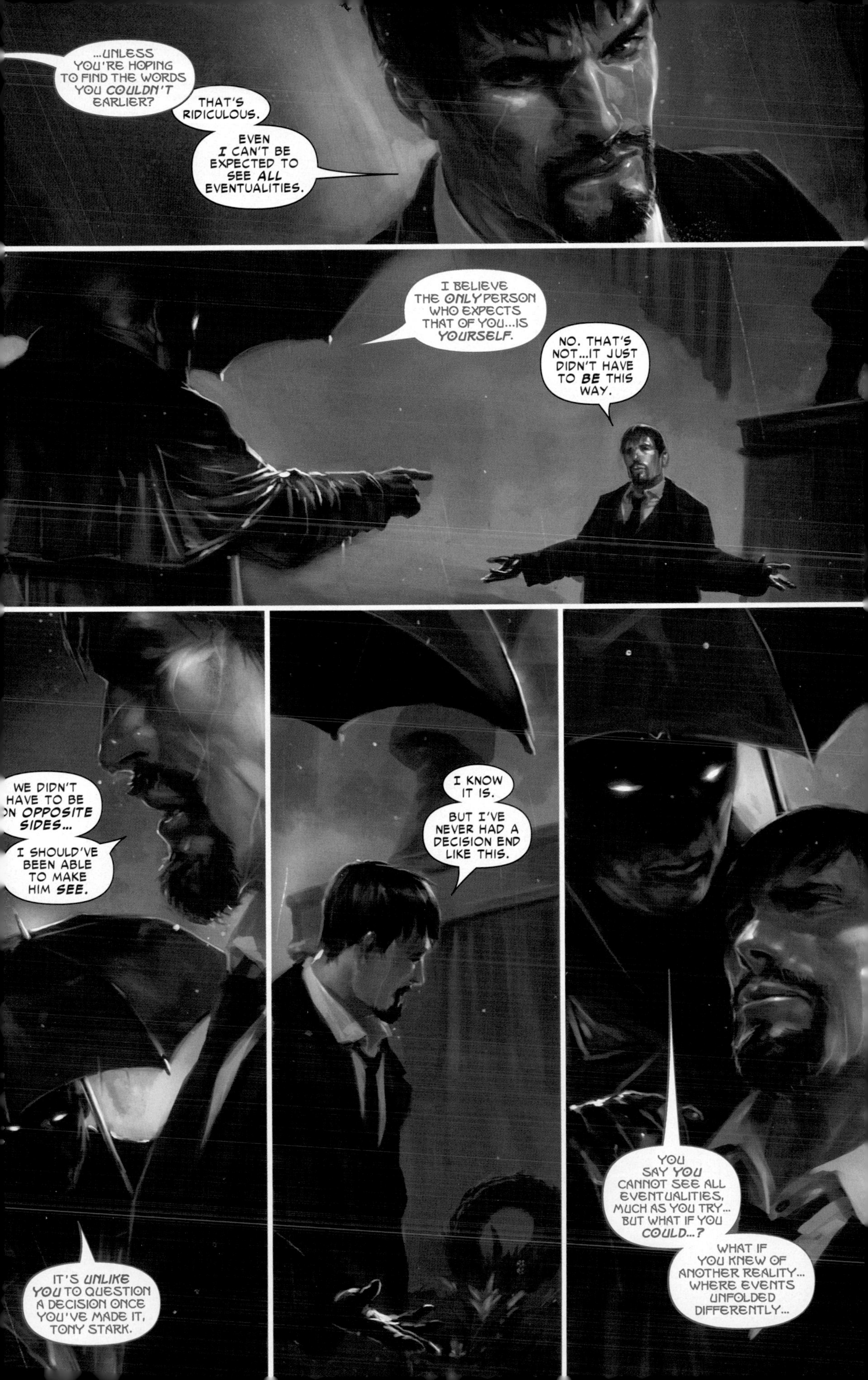
...UNLESS YOU'RE HOPING TO FIND THE WORDS YOU COULDN'T EARLIER?
THAT'S RIDICULOUS.
EVEN I CAN'T BE EXPECTED TO SEE ALL EVENTUALITIES.
I BELIEVE THE ONLY PERSON WHO EXPECTS THAT OF YOU...IS YOURSELF.
NO. THAT'S NOT...IT JUST DIDN'T HAVE TO BE THIS WAY.
WE DIDN'T HAVE TO BE ON OPPOSITE SIDES...
I SHOULD'VE BEEN ABLE TO MAKE HIM SEE.
IT'S UNLIKE YOU TO QUESTION A DECISION ONCE YOU'VE MADE IT, TONY STARK.
I KNOW IT IS.
BUT I'VE NEVER HAD A DECISION END LIKE THIS.
YOU SAY YOU CANNOT SEE ALL EVENTUALITIES, MUCH AS YOU TRY... BUT WHAT IF YOU COULD...?
WHAT IF YOU KNEW OF ANOTHER REALITY... WHERE EVENTS UNFOLDED DIFFERENTLY...

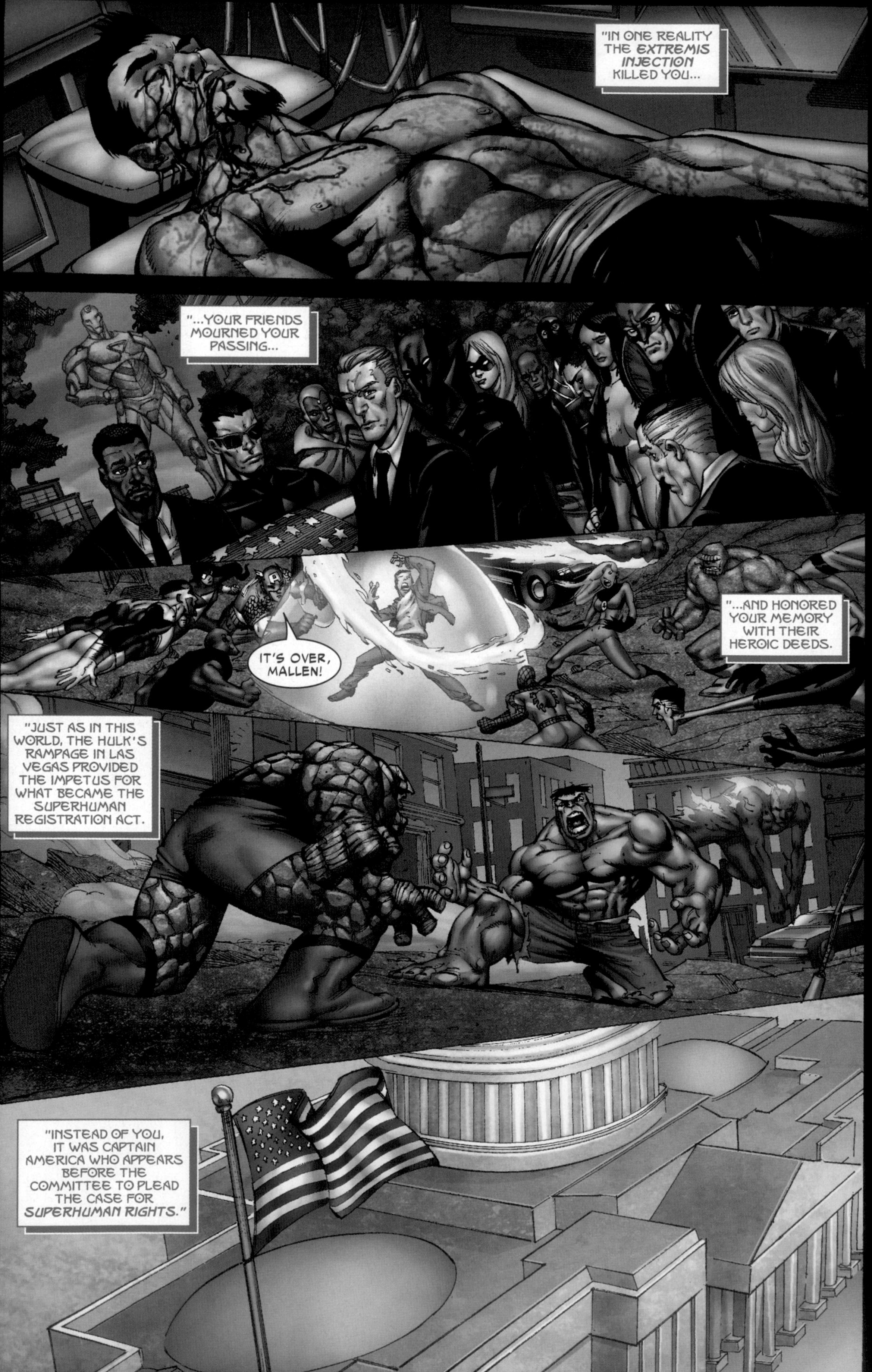
"IN ONE REALITY THE EXTREMIS INJECTION KILLED YOU...
"...YOUR FRIENDS MOURNED YOUR PASSING...
IT'S OVER, MALLEN!
"...AND HONORED YOUR MEMORY WITH THEIR HEROIC DEEDS.
"JUST AS IN THIS WORLD, THE HULK'S RAMPAGE IN LAS VEGAS PROVIDED THE IMPETUS FOR WHAT BECAME THE SUPERHUMAN REGISTRATION ACT.
"INSTEAD OF YOU, IT WAS CAPTAIN AMERICA WHO APPEARS BEFORE THE COMMITTEE TO PLEAD THE CASE FOR SUPERHUMAN RIGHTS."

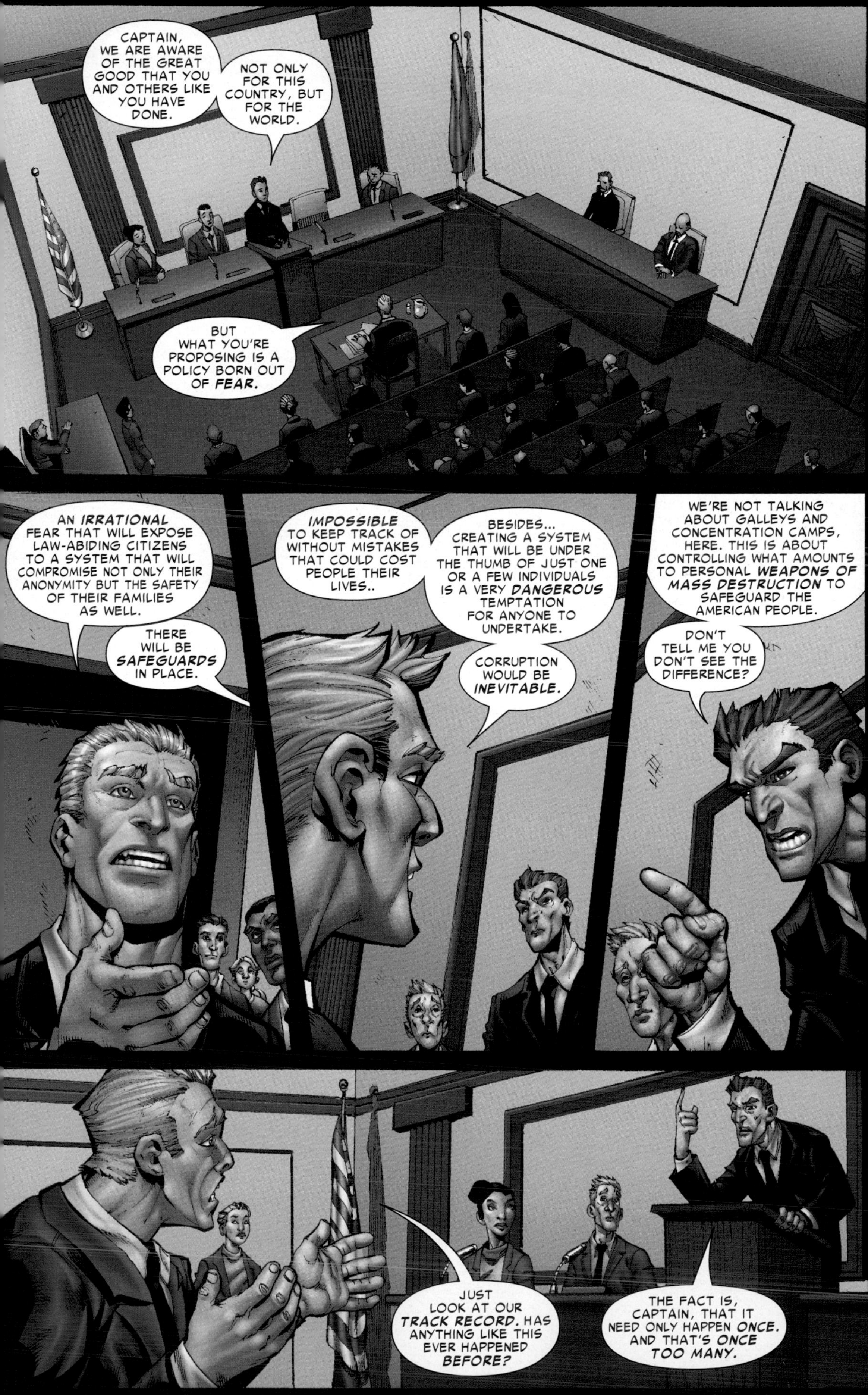
CAPTAIN, WE ARE AWARE OF THE GREAT GOOD THAT YOU AND OTHERS LIKE YOU HAVE DONE.
NOT ONLY FOR THIS COUNTRY, BUT FOR THE WORLD.
BUT WHAT YOU'RE PROPOSING IS A POLICY BORN OUT OF ***FEAR.***
AN *IRRATIONAL* FEAR THAT WILL EXPOSE LAW-ABIDING CITIZENS TO A SYSTEM THAT WILL COMPROMISE NOT ONLY THEIR ANONYMITY BUT THE SAFETY OF THEIR FAMILIES AS WELL.
THERE WILL BE ***SAFEGUARDS*** IN PLACE.
IMPOSSIBLE TO KEEP TRACK OF WITHOUT MISTAKES THAT COULD COST PEOPLE THEIR LIVES..
BESIDES... CREATING A SYSTEM THAT WILL BE UNDER THE THUMB OF JUST ONE OR A FEW INDIVIDUALS IS A VERY ***DANGEROUS*** TEMPTATION FOR ANYONE TO UNDERTAKE.
CORRUPTION WOULD BE ***INEVITABLE.***
WE'RE NOT TALKING ABOUT GALLEYS AND CONCENTRATION CAMPS, HERE. THIS IS ABOUT CONTROLLING WHAT AMOUNTS TO PERSONAL ***WEAPONS OF MASS DESTRUCTION*** TO SAFEGUARD THE AMERICAN PEOPLE.
DON'T TELL ME YOU DON'T SEE THE DIFFERENCE?
JUST LOOK AT OUR ***TRACK RECORD.*** HAS ANYTHING LIKE THIS EVER HAPPENED *BEFORE?*
THE FACT IS, CAPTAIN, THAT IT NEED ONLY HAPPEN *ONCE.* AND THAT'S ***ONCE TOO MANY.***

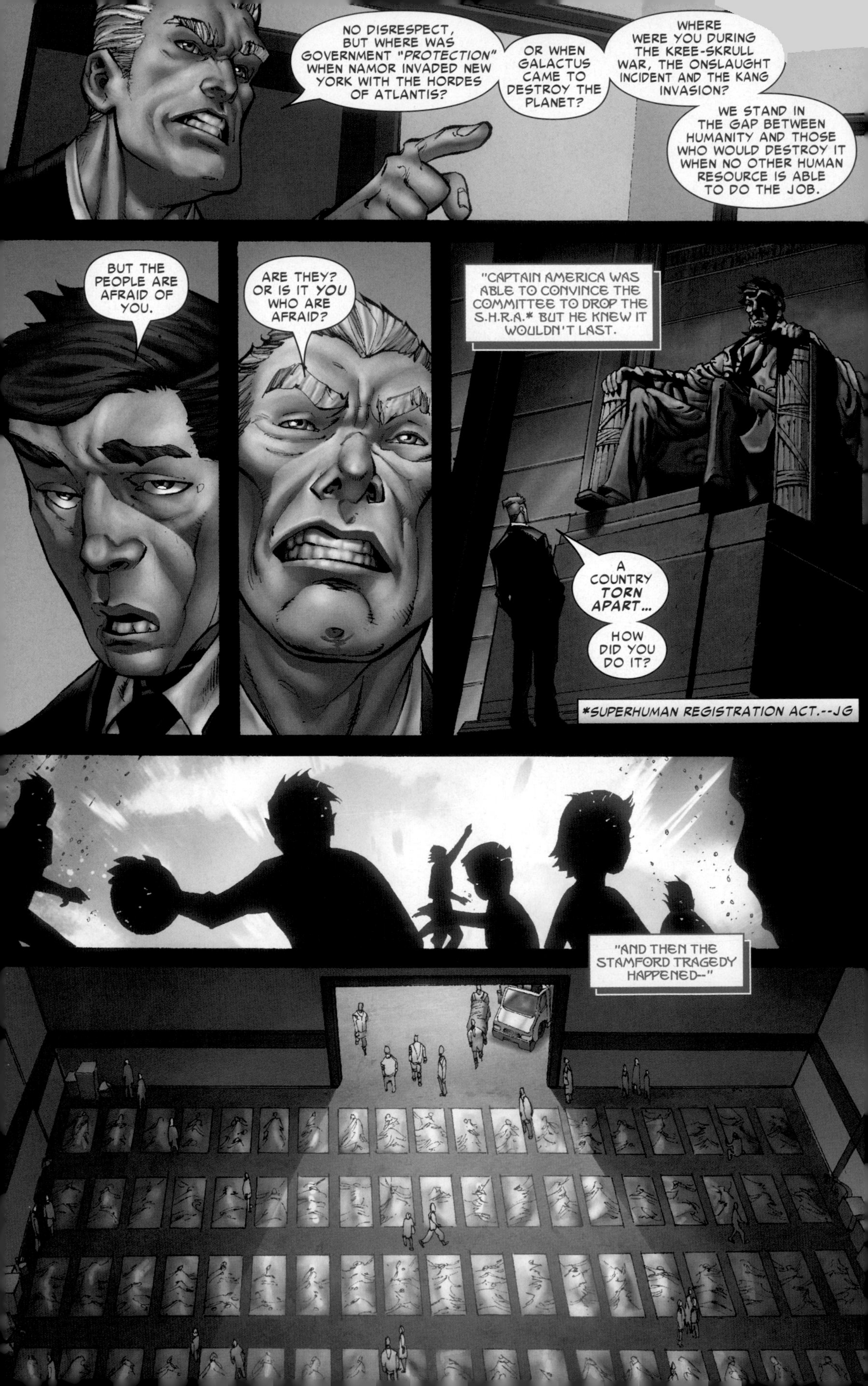
NO DISRESPECT, BUT WHERE WAS GOVERNMENT "PROTECTION" WHEN NAMOR INVADED NEW YORK WITH THE HORDES OF ATLANTIS?
OR WHEN GALACTUS CAME TO DESTROY THE PLANET?
WHERE WERE YOU DURING THE KREE-SKRULL WAR, THE ONSLAUGHT INCIDENT AND THE KANG INVASION?
WE STAND IN THE GAP BETWEEN HUMANITY AND THOSE WHO WOULD DESTROY IT WHEN NO OTHER HUMAN RESOURCE IS ABLE TO DO THE JOB.
BUT THE PEOPLE ARE AFRAID OF YOU.
ARE THEY? OR IS IT YOU WHO ARE AFRAID?
"CAPTAIN AMERICA WAS ABLE TO CONVINCE THE COMMITTEE TO DROP THE S.H.R.A.* BUT HE KNEW IT WOULDN'T LAST.
A COUNTRY TORN APART...
HOW DID YOU DO IT?
*SUPERHUMAN REGISTRATION ACT.--JG
"AND THEN THE STAMFORD TRAGEDY HAPPENED--"

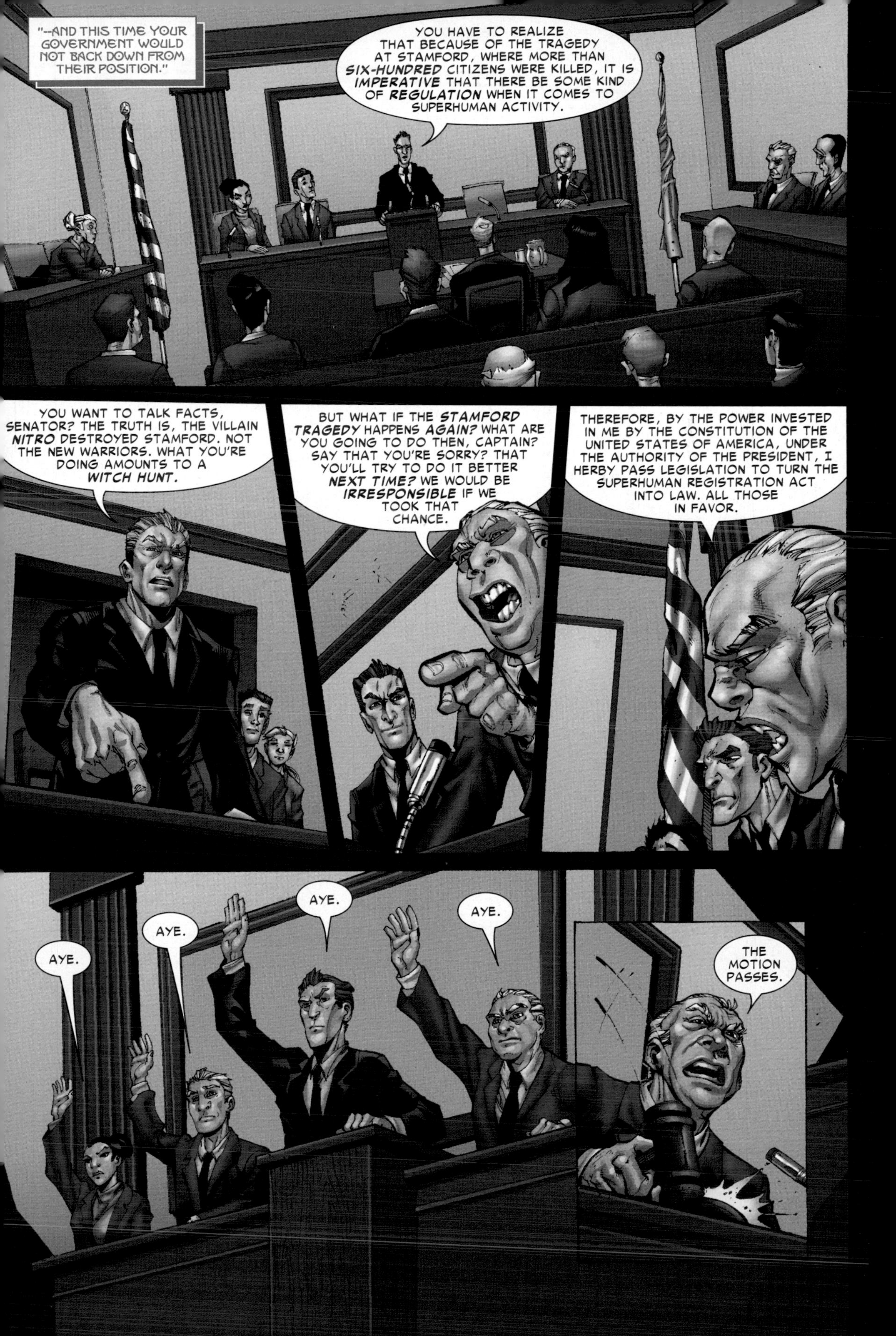
"--AND THIS TIME YOUR GOVERNMENT WOULD NOT BACK DOWN FROM THEIR POSITION."
YOU HAVE TO REALIZE THAT BECAUSE OF THE TRAGEDY AT STAMFORD, WHERE MORE THAN SIX-HUNDRED CITIZENS WERE KILLED, IT IS IMPERATIVE THAT THERE BE SOME KIND OF REGULATION WHEN IT COMES TO SUPERHUMAN ACTIVITY.
YOU WANT TO TALK FACTS, SENATOR? THE TRUTH IS, THE VILLAIN NITRO DESTROYED STAMFORD. NOT THE NEW WARRIORS. WHAT YOU'RE DOING AMOUNTS TO A WITCH HUNT.
BUT WHAT IF THE STAMFORD TRAGEDY HAPPENS AGAIN? WHAT ARE YOU GOING TO DO THEN, CAPTAIN? SAY THAT YOU'RE SORRY? THAT YOU'LL TRY TO DO IT BETTER NEXT TIME? WE WOULD BE IRRESPONSIBLE IF WE TOOK THAT CHANCE.
THEREFORE, BY THE POWER INVESTED IN ME BY THE CONSTITUTION OF THE UNITED STATES OF AMERICA, UNDER THE AUTHORITY OF THE PRESIDENT, I HERBY PASS LEGISLATION TO TURN THE SUPERHUMAN REGISTRATION ACT INTO LAW. ALL THOSE IN FAVOR.
AYE.
AYE.
AYE.
AYE.
THE MOTION PASSES.

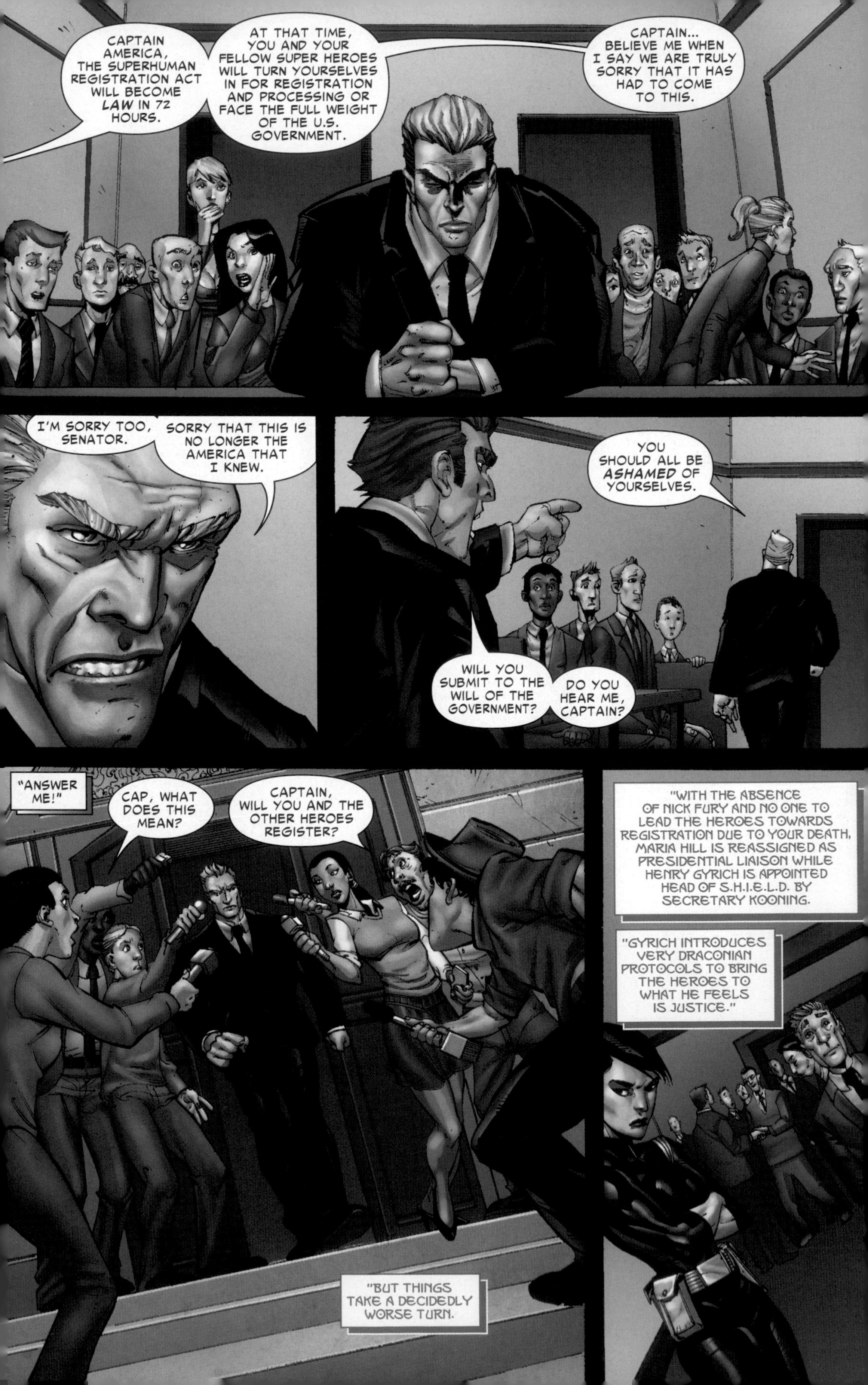
CAPTAIN AMERICA, THE SUPERHUMAN REGISTRATION ACT WILL BECOME LAW IN 72 HOURS.
AT THAT TIME, YOU AND YOUR FELLOW SUPER HEROES WILL TURN YOURSELVES IN FOR REGISTRATION AND PROCESSING OR FACE THE FULL WEIGHT OF THE U.S. GOVERNMENT.
CAPTAIN... BELIEVE ME WHEN I SAY WE ARE TRULY SORRY THAT IT HAS HAD TO COME TO THIS.
I'M SORRY TOO, SENATOR.
SORRY THAT THIS IS NO LONGER THE AMERICA THAT I KNEW.
YOU SHOULD ALL BE ASHAMED OF YOURSELVES.
WILL YOU SUBMIT TO THE WILL OF THE GOVERNMENT?
DO YOU HEAR ME, CAPTAIN?
"ANSWER ME!"
CAP, WHAT DOES THIS MEAN?
CAPTAIN, WILL YOU AND THE OTHER HEROES REGISTER?
"BUT THINGS TAKE A DECIDEDLY WORSE TURN.
"WITH THE ABSENCE OF NICK FURY AND NO ONE TO LEAD THE HEROES TOWARDS REGISTRATION DUE TO YOUR DEATH, MARIA HILL IS REASSIGNED AS PRESIDENTIAL LIAISON WHILE HENRY GYRICH IS APPOINTED HEAD OF S.H.I.E.L.D. BY SECRETARY KOONING.
"GYRICH INTRODUCES VERY DRACONIAN PROTOCOLS TO BRING THE HEROES TO WHAT HE FEELS IS JUSTICE."

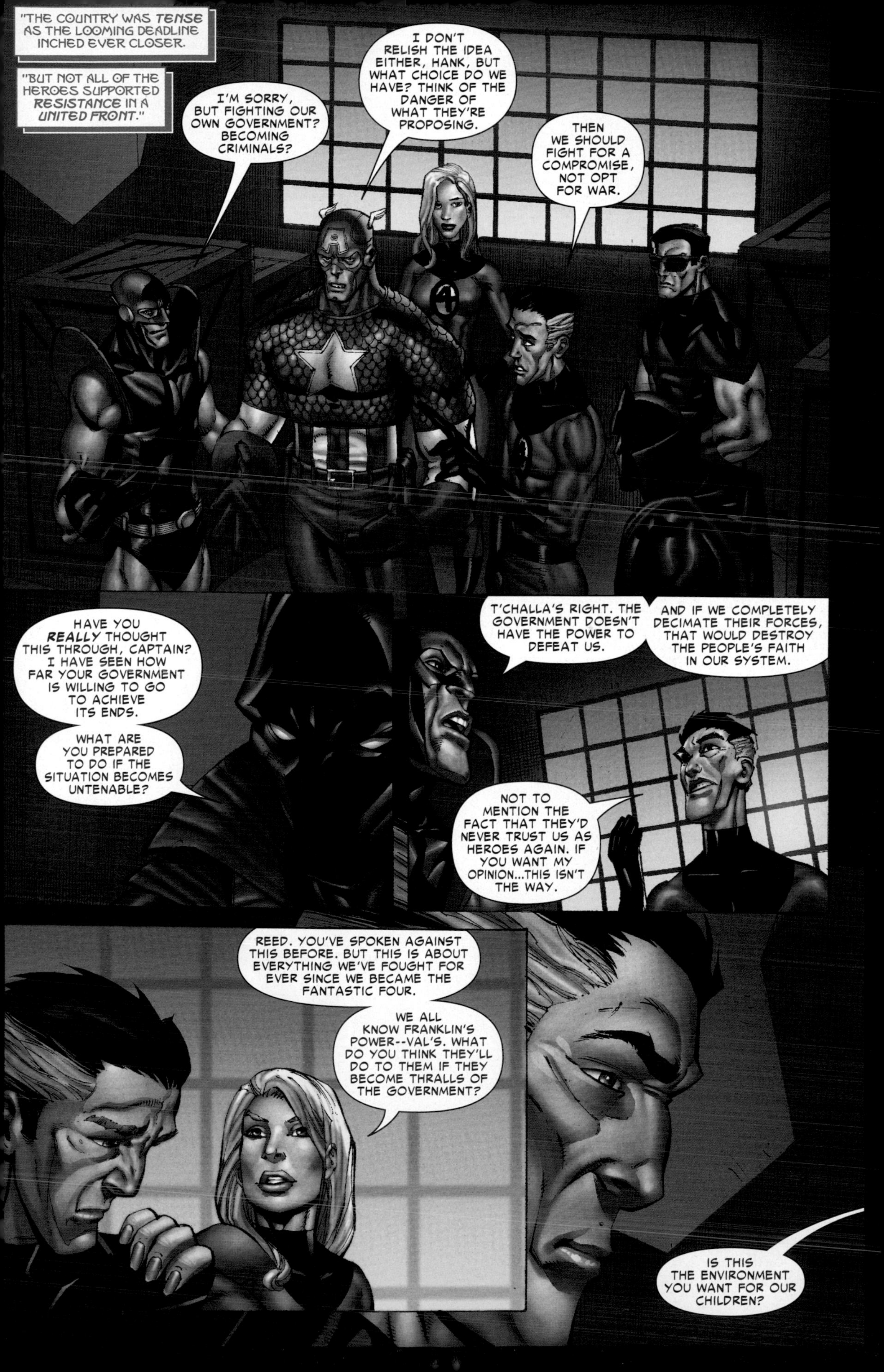
"THE COUNTRY WAS TENSE AS THE LOOMING DEADLINE INCHED EVER CLOSER.
"BUT NOT ALL OF THE HEROES SUPPORTED RESISTANCE IN A UNITED FRONT."
I'M SORRY, BUT FIGHTING OUR OWN GOVERNMENT? BECOMING CRIMINALS?
I DON'T RELISH THE IDEA EITHER, HANK, BUT WHAT CHOICE DO WE HAVE? THINK OF THE DANGER OF WHAT THEY'RE PROPOSING.
THEN WE SHOULD FIGHT FOR A COMPROMISE, NOT OPT FOR WAR.
HAVE YOU REALLY THOUGHT THIS THROUGH, CAPTAIN? I HAVE SEEN HOW FAR YOUR GOVERNMENT IS WILLING TO GO TO ACHIEVE ITS ENDS.
WHAT ARE YOU PREPARED TO DO IF THE SITUATION BECOMES UNTENABLE?
T'CHALLA'S RIGHT. THE GOVERNMENT DOESN'T HAVE THE POWER TO DEFEAT US.
AND IF WE COMPLETELY DECIMATE THEIR FORCES, THAT WOULD DESTROY THE PEOPLE'S FAITH IN OUR SYSTEM.
NOT TO MENTION THE FACT THAT THEY'D NEVER TRUST US AS HEROES AGAIN. IF YOU WANT MY OPINION...THIS ISN'T THE WAY.
REED. YOU'VE SPOKEN AGAINST THIS BEFORE. BUT THIS IS ABOUT EVERYTHING WE'VE FOUGHT FOR EVER SINCE WE BECAME THE FANTASTIC FOUR.
WE ALL KNOW FRANKLIN'S POWER--VAL'S. WHAT DO YOU THINK THEY'LL DO TO THEM IF THEY BECOME THRALLS OF THE GOVERNMENT?
IS THIS THE ENVIRONMENT YOU WANT FOR OUR CHILDREN?

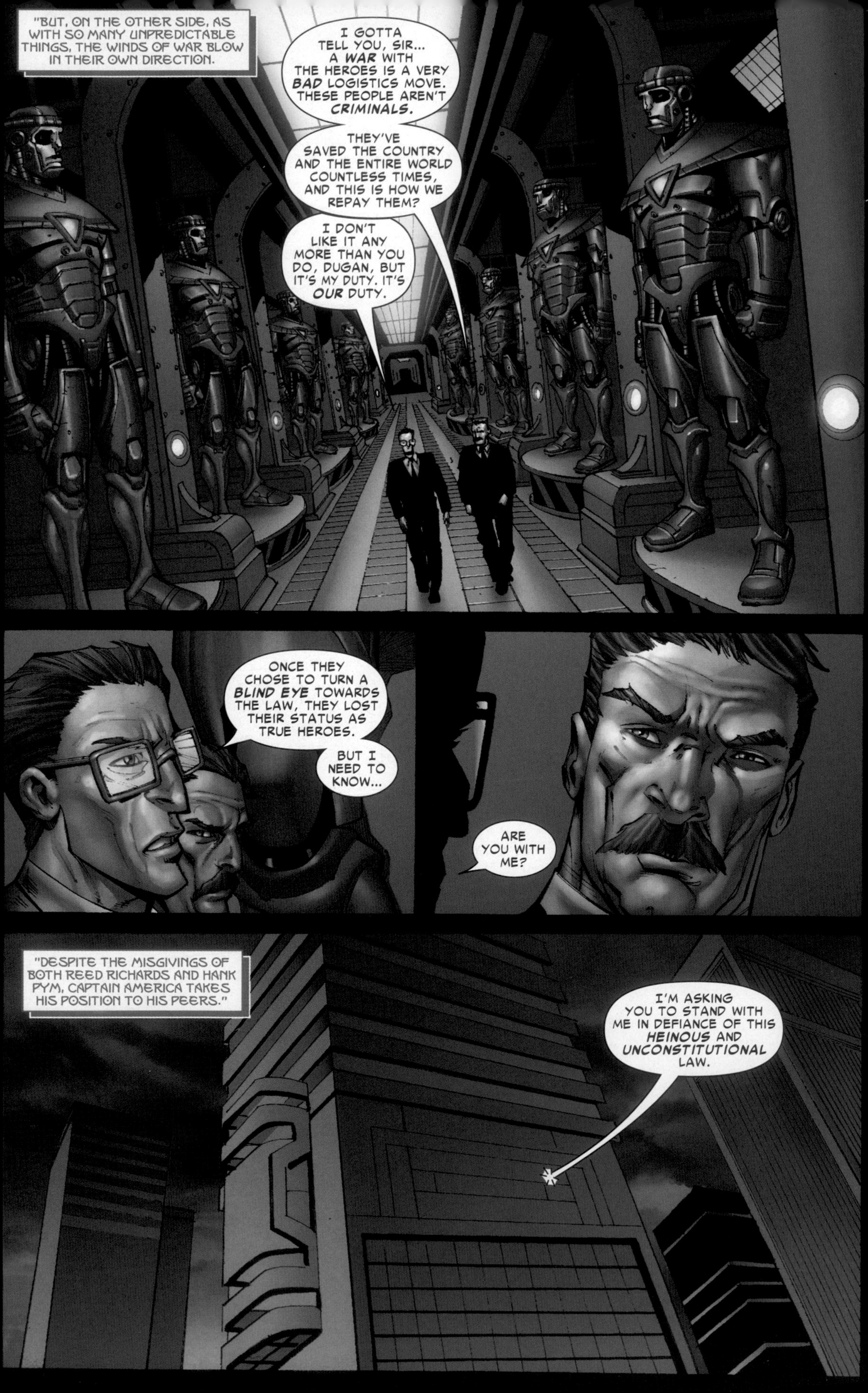
"BUT, ON THE OTHER SIDE, AS WITH SO MANY UNPREDICTABLE THINGS, THE WINDS OF WAR BLOW IN THEIR OWN DIRECTION.
I GOTTA TELL YOU, SIR... A WAR WITH THE HEROES IS A VERY BAD LOGISTICS MOVE. THESE PEOPLE AREN'T CRIMINALS.
THEY'VE SAVED THE COUNTRY AND THE ENTIRE WORLD COUNTLESS TIMES, AND THIS IS HOW WE REPAY THEM?
I DON'T LIKE IT ANY MORE THAN YOU DO, DUGAN, BUT IT'S MY DUTY. IT'S OUR DUTY.
ONCE THEY CHOSE TO TURN A BLIND EYE TOWARDS THE LAW, THEY LOST THEIR STATUS AS TRUE HEROES.
BUT I NEED TO KNOW...
ARE YOU WITH ME?
"DESPITE THE MISGIVINGS OF BOTH REED RICHARDS AND HANK PYM, CAPTAIN AMERICA TAKES HIS POSITION TO HIS PEERS."
I'M ASKING YOU TO STAND WITH ME IN DEFIANCE OF THIS HEINOUS AND UNCONSTITUTIONAL LAW.

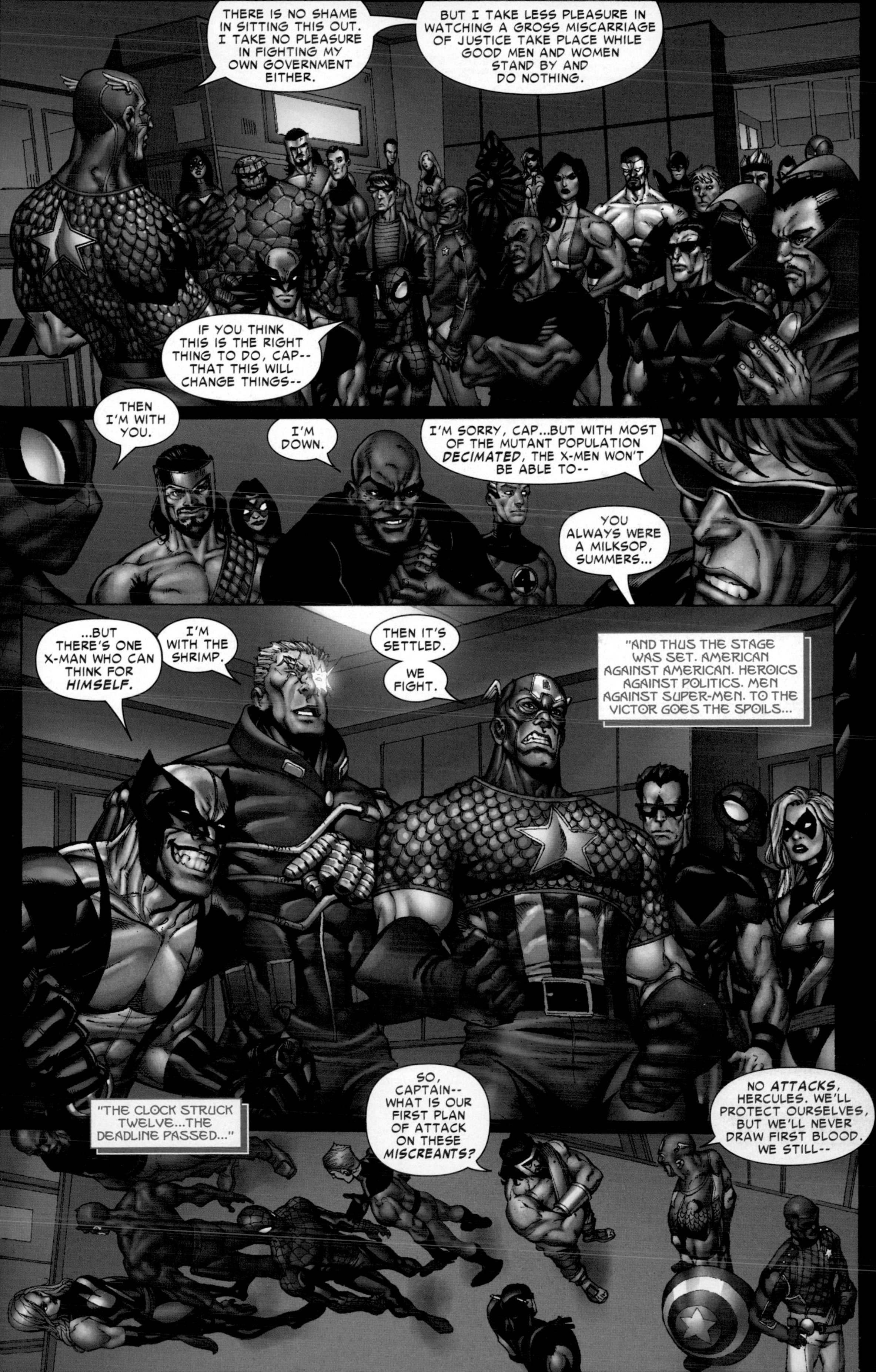
THERE IS NO SHAME IN SITTING THIS OUT. I TAKE NO PLEASURE IN FIGHTING MY OWN GOVERNMENT EITHER.
BUT I TAKE LESS PLEASURE IN WATCHING A GROSS MISCARRIAGE OF JUSTICE TAKE PLACE WHILE GOOD MEN AND WOMEN STAND BY AND DO NOTHING.
IF YOU THINK THIS IS THE RIGHT THING TO DO, CAP-- THAT THIS WILL CHANGE THINGS--
THEN I'M WITH YOU.
I'M DOWN.
I'M SORRY, CAP...BUT WITH MOST OF THE MUTANT POPULATION *DECIMATED*, THE X-MEN WON'T BE ABLE TO--
YOU ALWAYS WERE A MILKSOP, SUMMERS...
...BUT THERE'S ONE X-MAN WHO CAN THINK FOR *HIMSELF.*
I'M WITH THE SHRIMP.
THEN IT'S SETTLED.
WE FIGHT.
"AND THUS THE STAGE WAS SET. AMERICAN AGAINST AMERICAN. HEROICS AGAINST POLITICS. MEN AGAINST SUPER-MEN. TO THE VICTOR GOES THE SPOILS...
"THE CLOCK STRUCK TWELVE...THE DEADLINE PASSED..."
SO, CAPTAIN-- WHAT IS OUR FIRST PLAN OF ATTACK ON THESE *MISCREANTS?*
NO *ATTACKS*, HERCULES. WE'LL PROTECT OURSELVES, BUT WE'LL NEVER DRAW FIRST BLOOD. WE STILL--

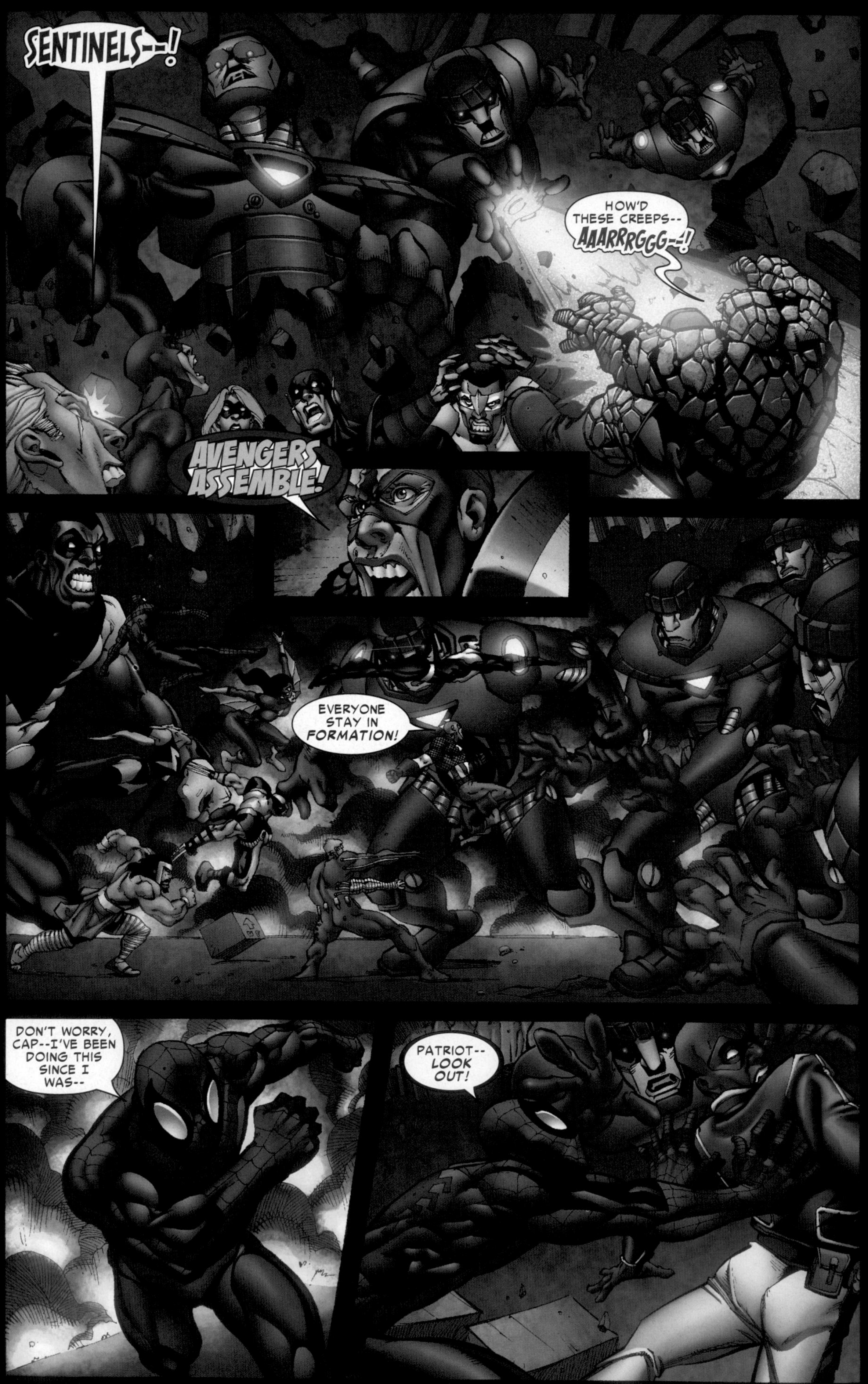
SENTINELS--!
HOW'D THESE CREEPS--
AAARRRGGG--!
AVENGERS ASSEMBLE!
EVERYONE STAY IN FORMATION!
DON'T WORRY, CAP--I'VE BEEN DOING THIS SINCE I WAS--
PATRIOT-- LOOK OUT!

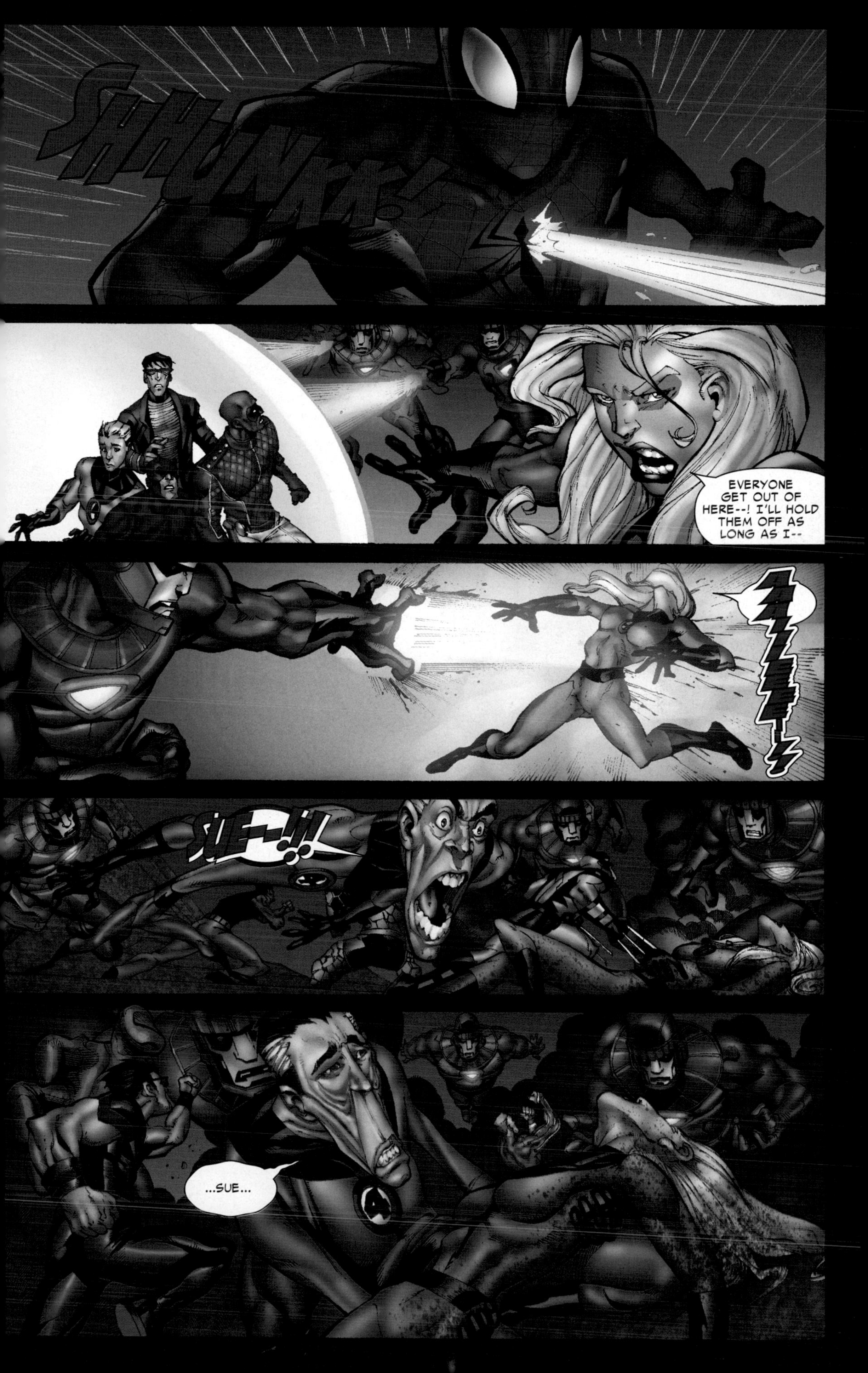
SHHUNK!
EVERYONE GET OUT OF HERE--! I'LL HOLD THEM OFF AS LONG AS I--
SUE--!!!
...SUE...

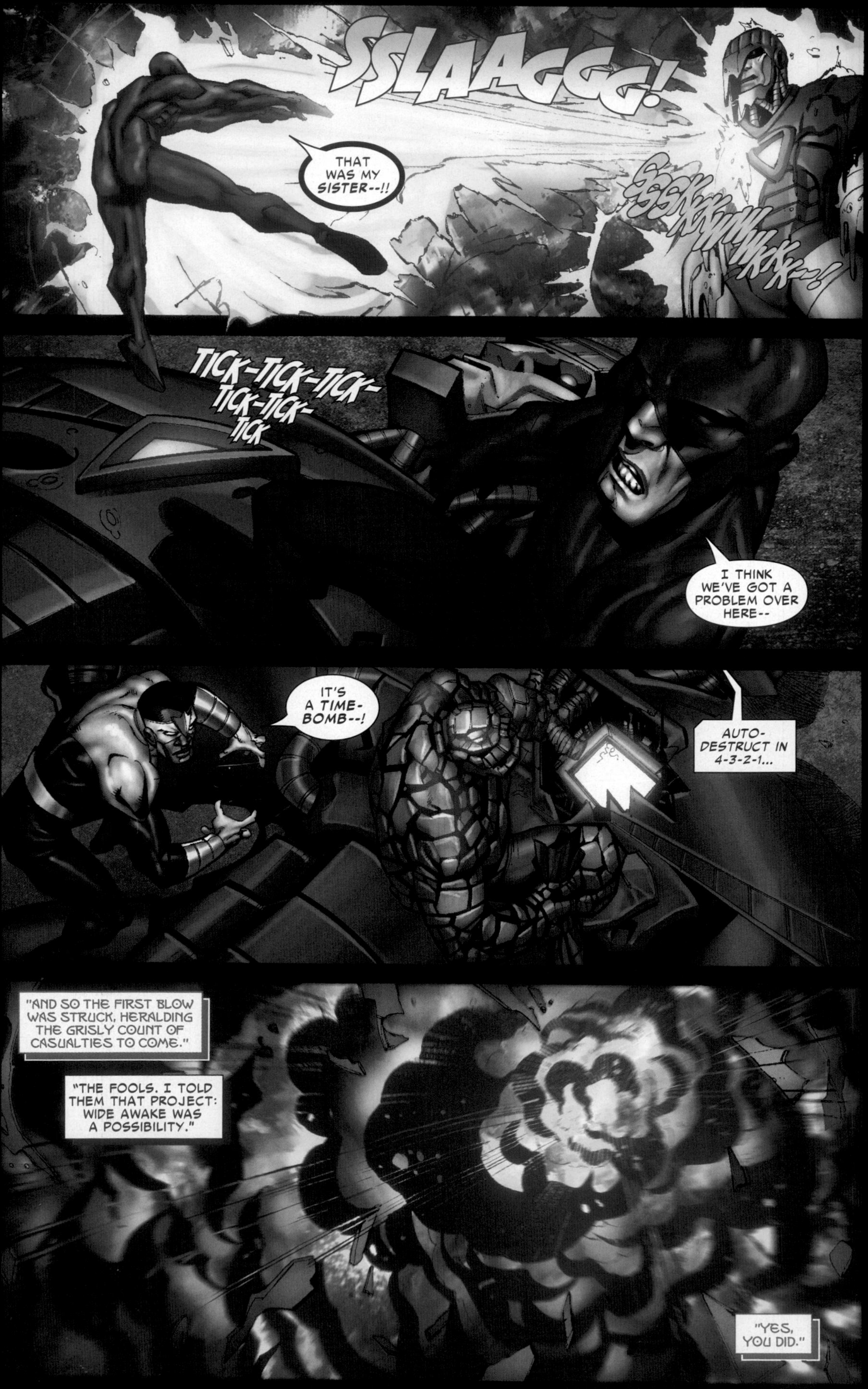
SSLAAGGG!
THAT WAS MY SISTER--!!
SSSKKKWWKKK--!
TICK-TICK-TICK-TICK-TICK-TICK
I THINK WE'VE GOT A PROBLEM OVER HERE--
IT'S A TIME-BOMB--!
AUTO-DESTRUCT IN 4-3-2-1...
"AND SO THE FIRST BLOW WAS STRUCK, HERALDING THE GRISLY COUNT OF CASUALTIES TO COME."
"THE FOOLS. I TOLD THEM THAT PROJECT: WIDE AWAKE WAS A POSSIBILITY."
"YES, YOU DID."

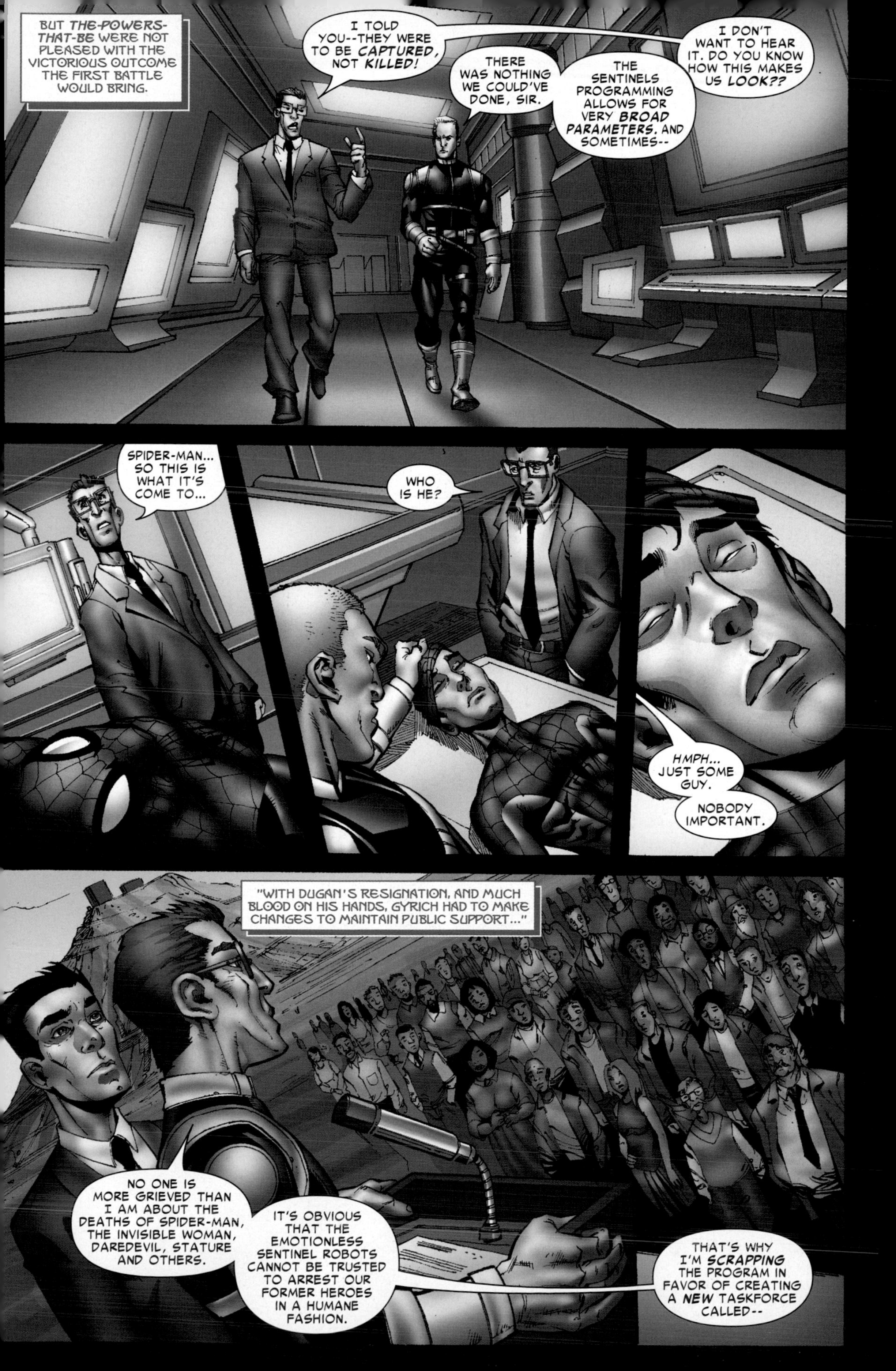
BUT THE-POWERS-THAT-BE WERE NOT PLEASED WITH THE VICTORIOUS OUTCOME THE FIRST BATTLE WOULD BRING.
I TOLD YOU--THEY WERE TO BE CAPTURED, NOT KILLED!
THERE WAS NOTHING WE COULD'VE DONE, SIR.
THE SENTINELS PROGRAMMING ALLOWS FOR VERY BROAD PARAMETERS. AND SOMETIMES--
I DON'T WANT TO HEAR IT. DO YOU KNOW HOW THIS MAKES US LOOK??
SPIDER-MAN... SO THIS IS WHAT IT'S COME TO...
WHO IS HE?
HMPH... JUST SOME GUY.
NOBODY IMPORTANT.
"WITH DUGAN'S RESIGNATION, AND MUCH BLOOD ON HIS HANDS, GYRICH HAD TO MAKE CHANGES TO MAINTAIN PUBLIC SUPPORT..."
NO ONE IS MORE GRIEVED THAN I AM ABOUT THE DEATHS OF SPIDER-MAN, THE INVISIBLE WOMAN, DAREDEVIL, STATURE AND OTHERS.
IT'S OBVIOUS THAT THE EMOTIONLESS SENTINEL ROBOTS CANNOT BE TRUSTED TO ARREST OUR FORMER HEROES IN A HUMANE FASHION.
THAT'S WHY I'M SCRAPPING THE PROGRAM IN FAVOR OF CREATING A NEW TASKFORCE CALLED--

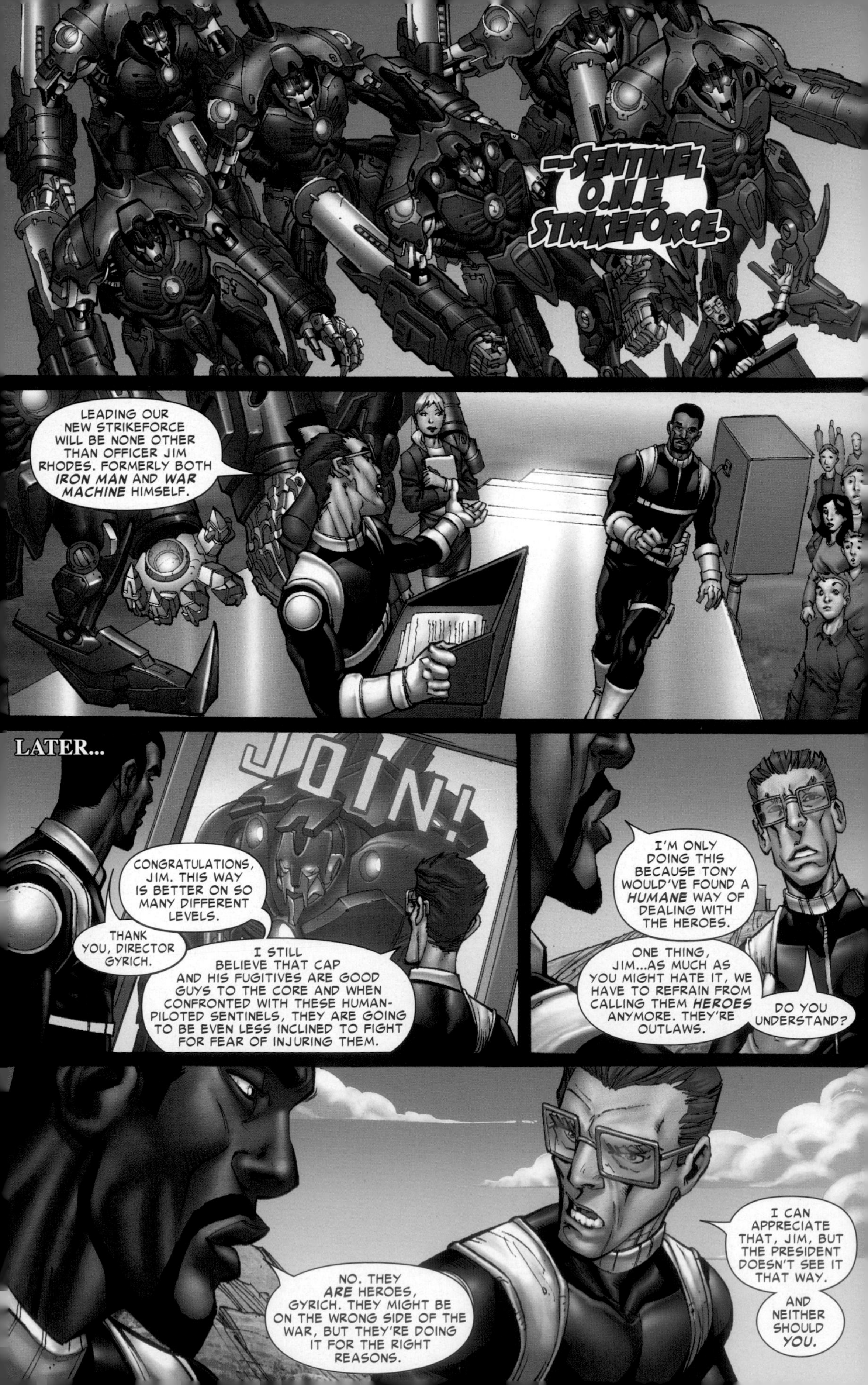
--SENTINEL O.N.E. STRIKEFORCE.
LEADING OUR NEW STRIKEFORCE WILL BE NONE OTHER THAN OFFICER JIM RHODES. FORMERLY BOTH *IRON MAN* AND *WAR MACHINE* HIMSELF.
LATER...
CONGRATULATIONS, JIM. THIS WAY IS BETTER ON SO MANY DIFFERENT LEVELS.
THANK YOU, DIRECTOR GYRICH.
I STILL BELIEVE THAT CAP AND HIS FUGITIVES ARE GOOD GUYS TO THE CORE AND WHEN CONFRONTED WITH THESE HUMAN-PILOTED SENTINELS, THEY ARE GOING TO BE EVEN LESS INCLINED TO FIGHT FOR FEAR OF INJURING THEM.
I'M ONLY DOING THIS BECAUSE TONY WOULD'VE FOUND A *HUMANE* WAY OF DEALING WITH THE HEROES.
ONE THING, JIM...AS MUCH AS YOU MIGHT HATE IT, WE HAVE TO REFRAIN FROM CALLING THEM *HEROES* ANYMORE. THEY'RE OUTLAWS.
DO YOU UNDERSTAND?
NO. THEY *ARE* HEROES, GYRICH. THEY MIGHT BE ON THE WRONG SIDE OF THE WAR, BUT THEY'RE DOING IT FOR THE RIGHT REASONS.
I CAN APPRECIATE THAT, JIM, BUT THE PRESIDENT DOESN'T SEE IT THAT WAY.
AND NEITHER SHOULD *YOU*.

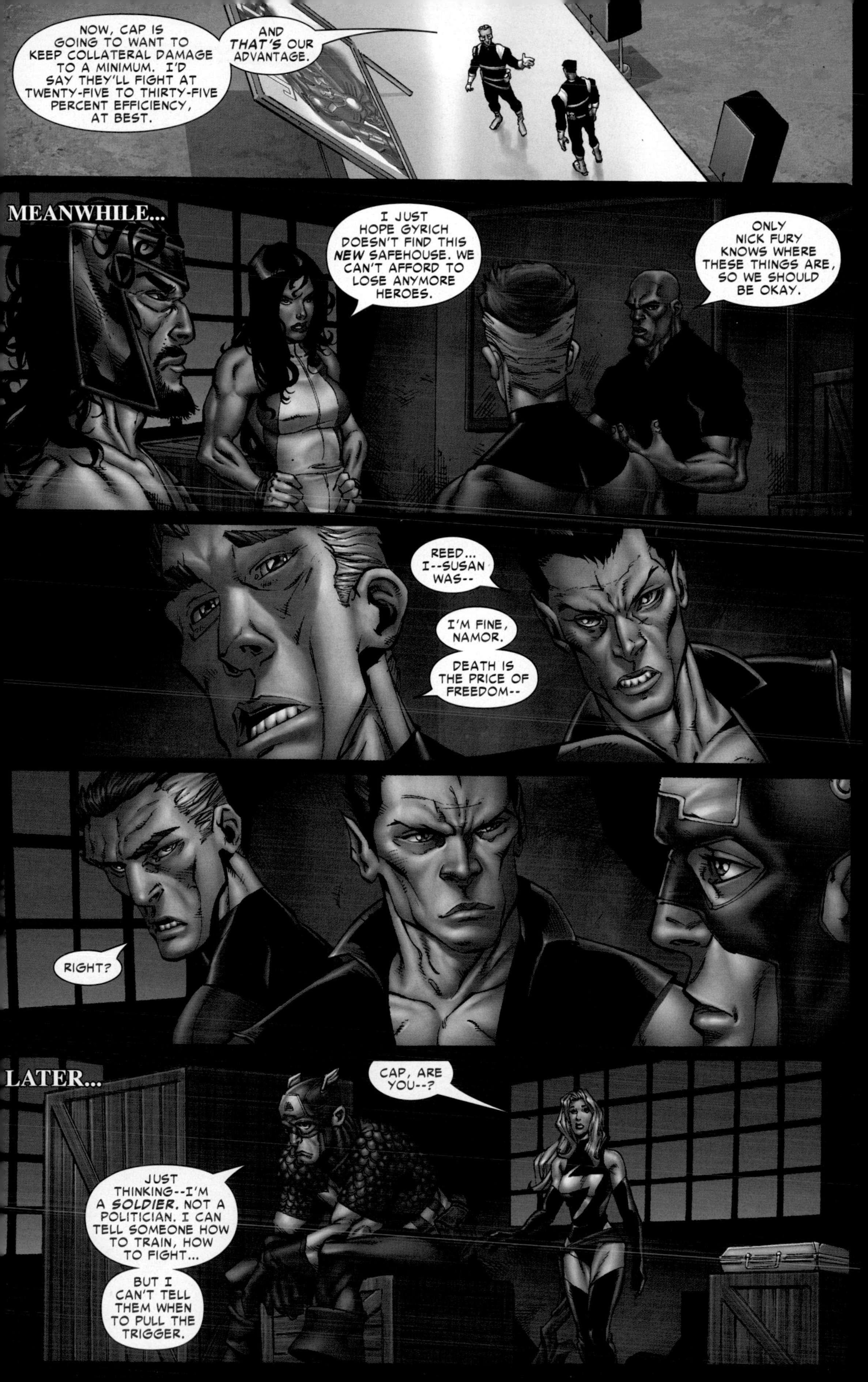
NOW, CAP IS GOING TO WANT TO KEEP COLLATERAL DAMAGE TO A MINIMUM. I'D SAY THEY'LL FIGHT AT TWENTY-FIVE TO THIRTY-FIVE PERCENT EFFICIENCY, AT BEST.
AND *THAT'S* OUR ADVANTAGE.
MEANWHILE...
I JUST HOPE GYRICH DOESN'T FIND THIS *NEW* SAFEHOUSE. WE CAN'T AFFORD TO LOSE ANYMORE HEROES.
ONLY NICK FURY KNOWS WHERE THESE THINGS ARE, SO WE SHOULD BE OKAY.
REED... I--SUSAN WAS--
I'M FINE, NAMOR.
DEATH IS THE PRICE OF FREEDOM--
RIGHT?
LATER...
CAP, ARE YOU--?
JUST THINKING--I'M A *SOLDIER*. NOT A POLITICIAN. I CAN TELL SOMEONE HOW TO TRAIN, HOW TO FIGHT...
BUT I CAN'T TELL THEM WHEN TO PULL THE TRIGGER.

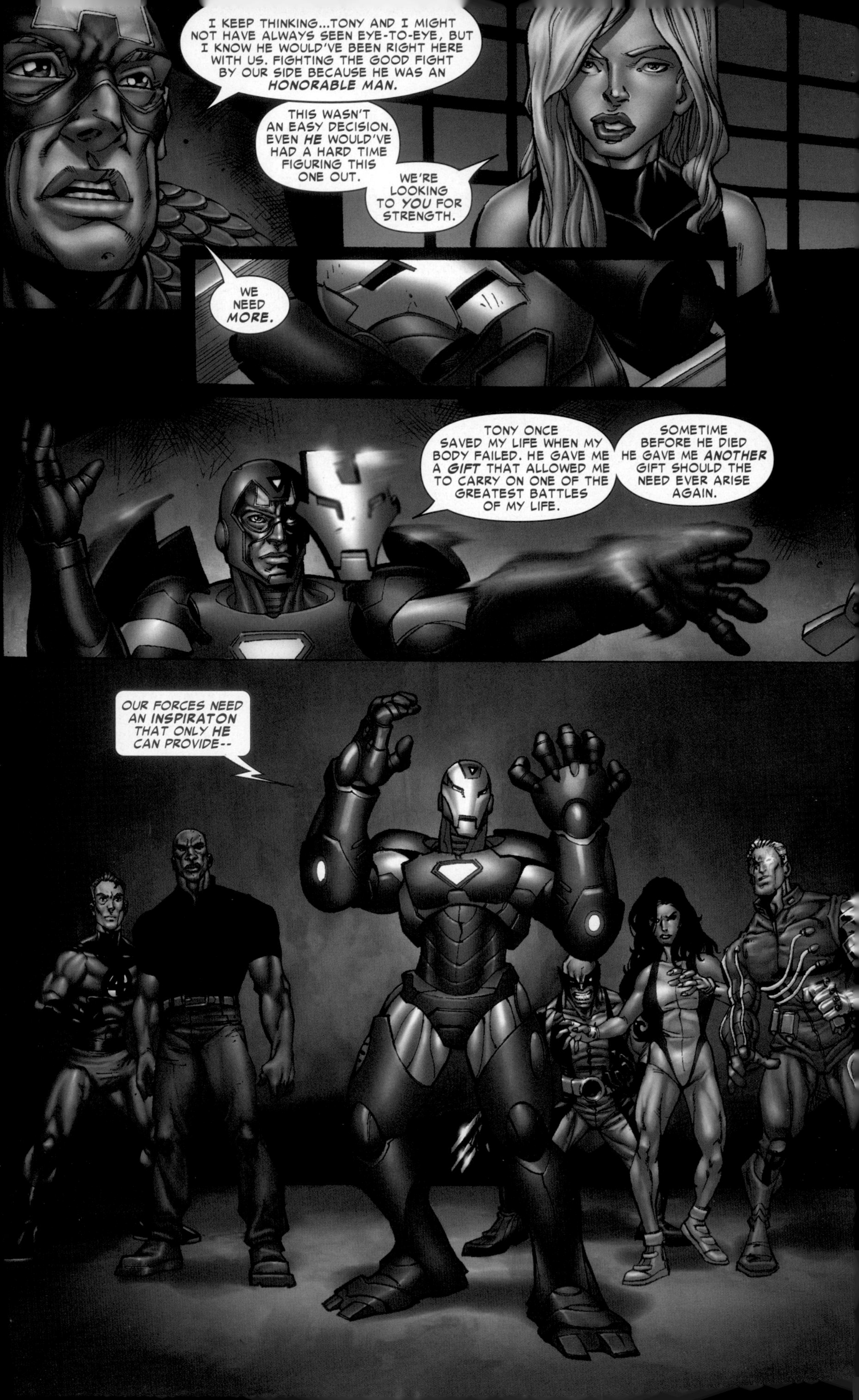
I KEEP THINKING...TONY AND I MIGHT NOT HAVE ALWAYS SEEN EYE-TO-EYE, BUT I KNOW HE WOULD'VE BEEN RIGHT HERE WITH US. FIGHTING THE GOOD FIGHT BY OUR SIDE BECAUSE HE WAS AN HONORABLE MAN.
THIS WASN'T AN EASY DECISION. EVEN HE WOULD'VE HAD A HARD TIME FIGURING THIS ONE OUT.
WE'RE LOOKING TO YOU FOR STRENGTH.
WE NEED MORE.
TONY ONCE SAVED MY LIFE WHEN MY BODY FAILED. HE GAVE ME A GIFT THAT ALLOWED ME TO CARRY ON ONE OF THE GREATEST BATTLES OF MY LIFE.
SOMETIME BEFORE HE DIED HE GAVE ME ANOTHER GIFT SHOULD THE NEED EVER ARISE AGAIN.
OUR FORCES NEED AN INSPIRATON THAT ONLY HE CAN PROVIDE--

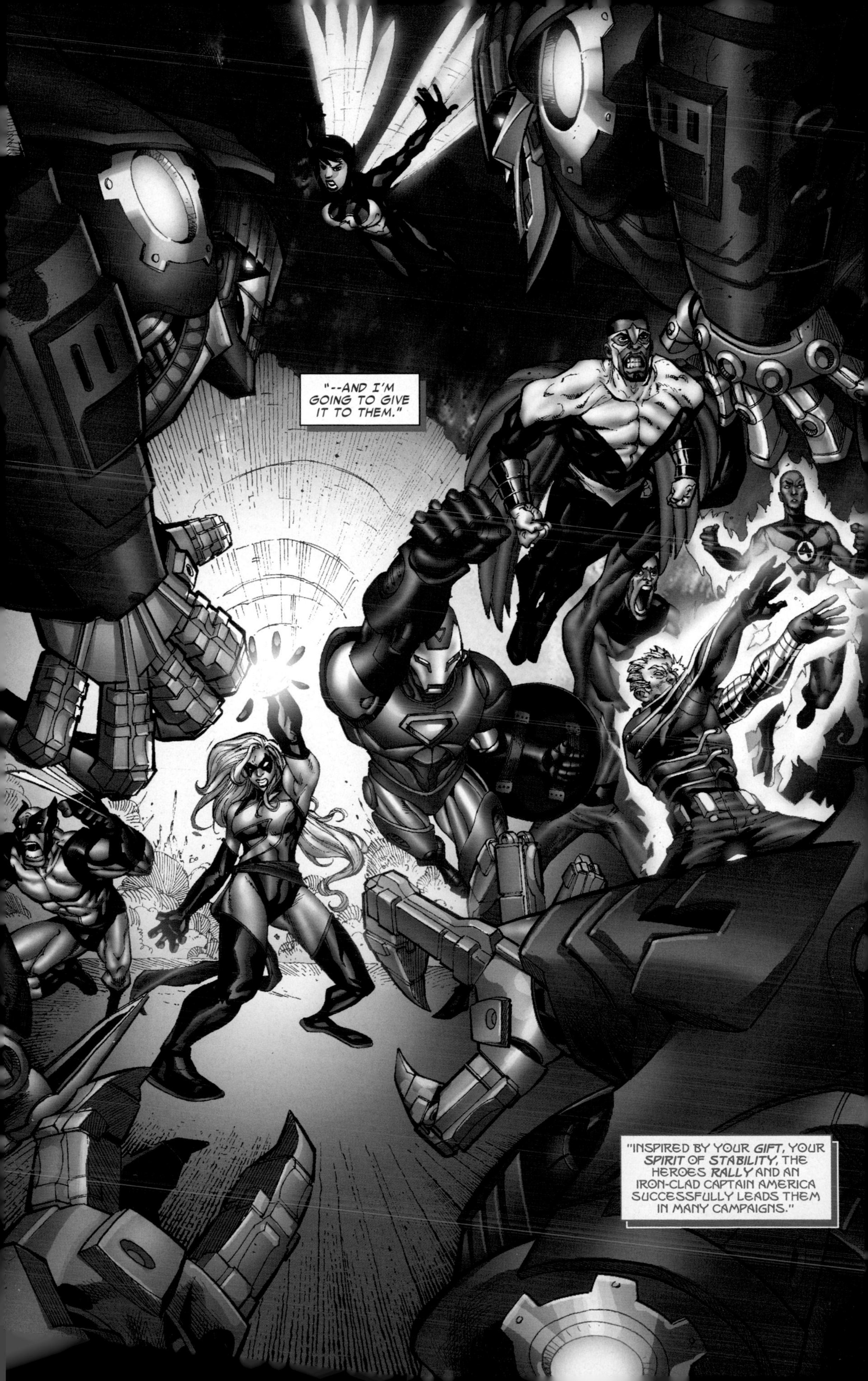
"--AND I'M GOING TO GIVE IT TO THEM."
"INSPIRED BY YOUR GIFT, YOUR SPIRIT OF STABILITY, THE HEROES RALLY AND AN IRON-CLAD CAPTAIN AMERICA SUCCESSFULLY LEADS THEM IN MANY CAMPAIGNS."

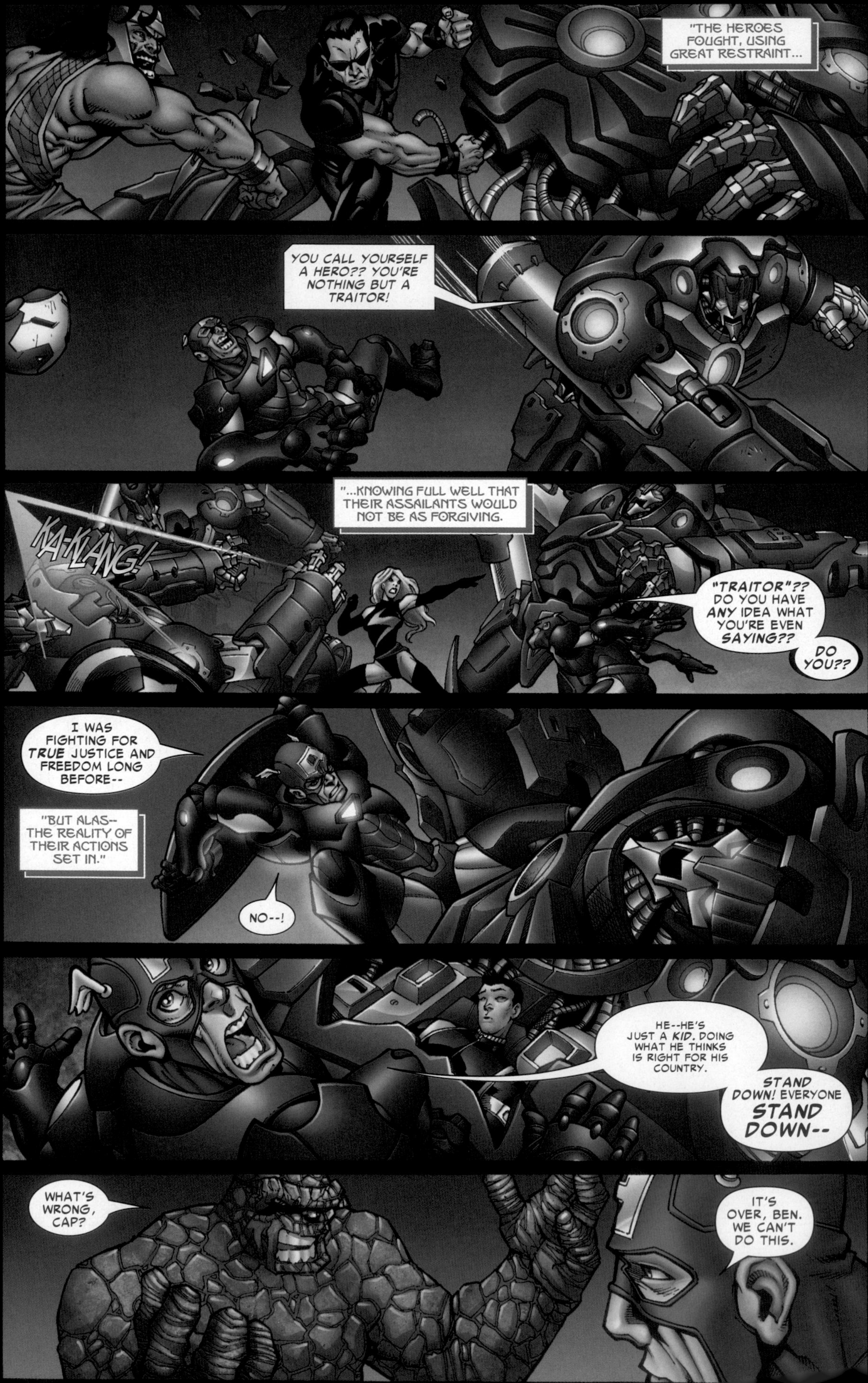
"THE HEROES FOUGHT, USING GREAT RESTRAINT...
YOU CALL YOURSELF A HERO?? YOU'RE NOTHING BUT A TRAITOR!
"...KNOWING FULL WELL THAT THEIR ASSAILANTS WOULD NOT BE AS FORGIVING.
KA-KLANG!
"TRAITOR"?? DO YOU HAVE ANY IDEA WHAT YOU'RE EVEN SAYING??
DO YOU??
I WAS FIGHTING FOR TRUE JUSTICE AND FREEDOM LONG BEFORE--
"BUT ALAS-- THE REALITY OF THEIR ACTIONS SET IN."
NO--!
HE--HE'S JUST A KID. DOING WHAT HE THINKS IS RIGHT FOR HIS COUNTRY.
STAND DOWN! EVERYONE STAND DOWN--
WHAT'S WRONG, CAP?
IT'S OVER, BEN. WE CAN'T DO THIS.

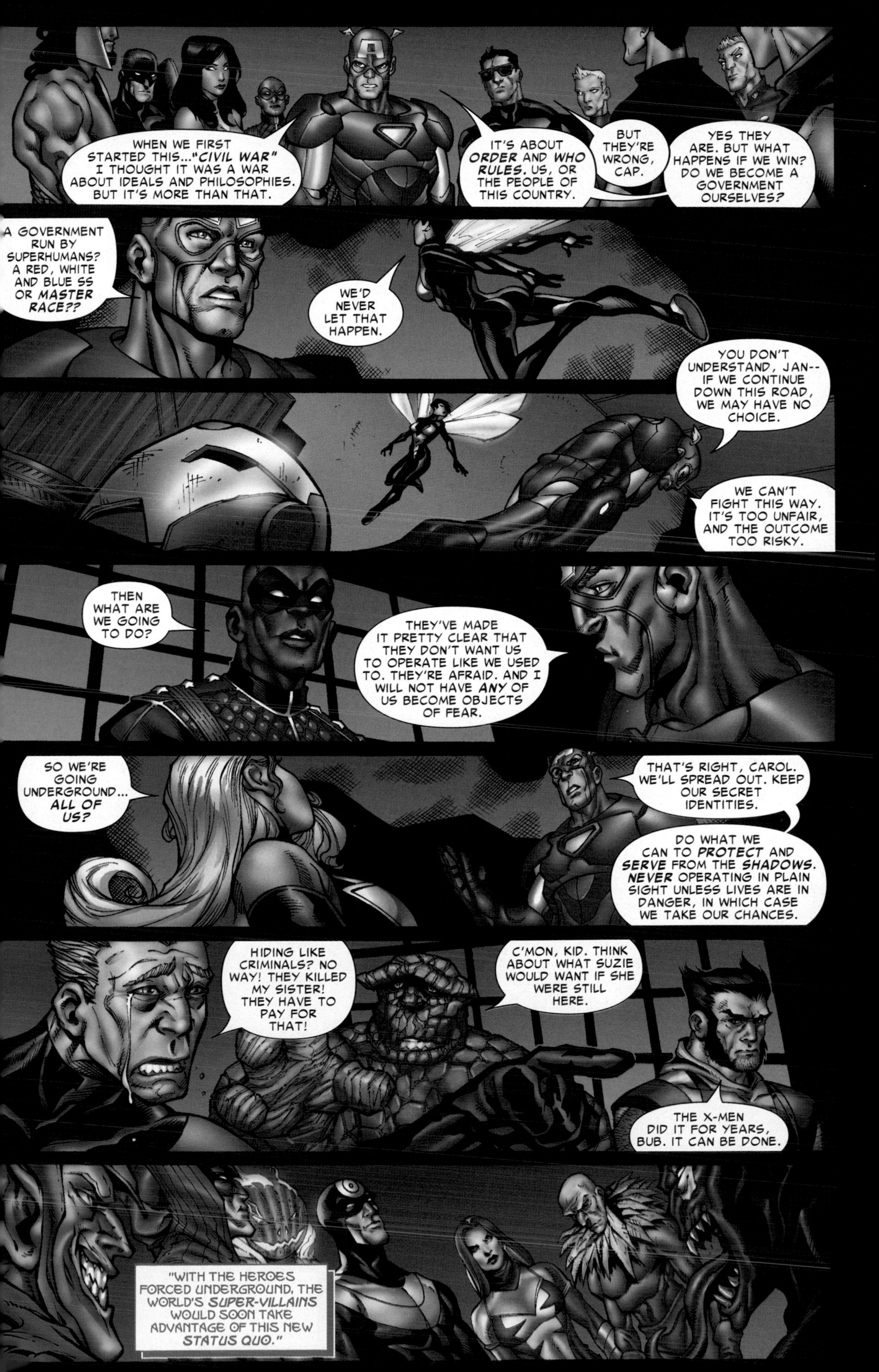
WHEN WE FIRST STARTED THIS..."CIVIL WAR" I THOUGHT IT WAS A WAR ABOUT IDEALS AND PHILOSOPHIES. BUT IT'S MORE THAN THAT.
IT'S ABOUT ORDER AND WHO RULES. US, OR THE PEOPLE OF THIS COUNTRY.
BUT THEY'RE WRONG, CAP.
YES THEY ARE. BUT WHAT HAPPENS IF WE WIN? DO WE BECOME A GOVERNMENT OURSELVES?
A GOVERNMENT RUN BY SUPERHUMANS? A RED, WHITE AND BLUE SS OR MASTER RACE??
WE'D NEVER LET THAT HAPPEN.
YOU DON'T UNDERSTAND, JAN-- IF WE CONTINUE DOWN THIS ROAD, WE MAY HAVE NO CHOICE.
WE CAN'T FIGHT THIS WAY. IT'S TOO UNFAIR, AND THE OUTCOME TOO RISKY.
THEN WHAT ARE WE GOING TO DO?
THEY'VE MADE IT PRETTY CLEAR THAT THEY DON'T WANT US TO OPERATE LIKE WE USED TO. THEY'RE AFRAID. AND I WILL NOT HAVE ANY OF US BECOME OBJECTS OF FEAR.
SO WE'RE GOING UNDERGROUND... ALL OF US?
THAT'S RIGHT, CAROL. WE'LL SPREAD OUT. KEEP OUR SECRET IDENTITIES.
DO WHAT WE CAN TO PROTECT AND SERVE FROM THE SHADOWS. NEVER OPERATING IN PLAIN SIGHT UNLESS LIVES ARE IN DANGER, IN WHICH CASE WE TAKE OUR CHANCES.
HIDING LIKE CRIMINALS? NO WAY! THEY KILLED MY SISTER! THEY HAVE TO PAY FOR THAT!
C'MON, KID. THINK ABOUT WHAT SUZIE WOULD WANT IF SHE WERE STILL HERE.
THE X-MEN DID IT FOR YEARS, BUB. IT CAN BE DONE.
"WITH THE HEROES FORCED UNDERGROUND, THE WORLD'S SUPER-VILLAINS WOULD SOON TAKE ADVANTAGE OF THIS NEW STATUS QUO."

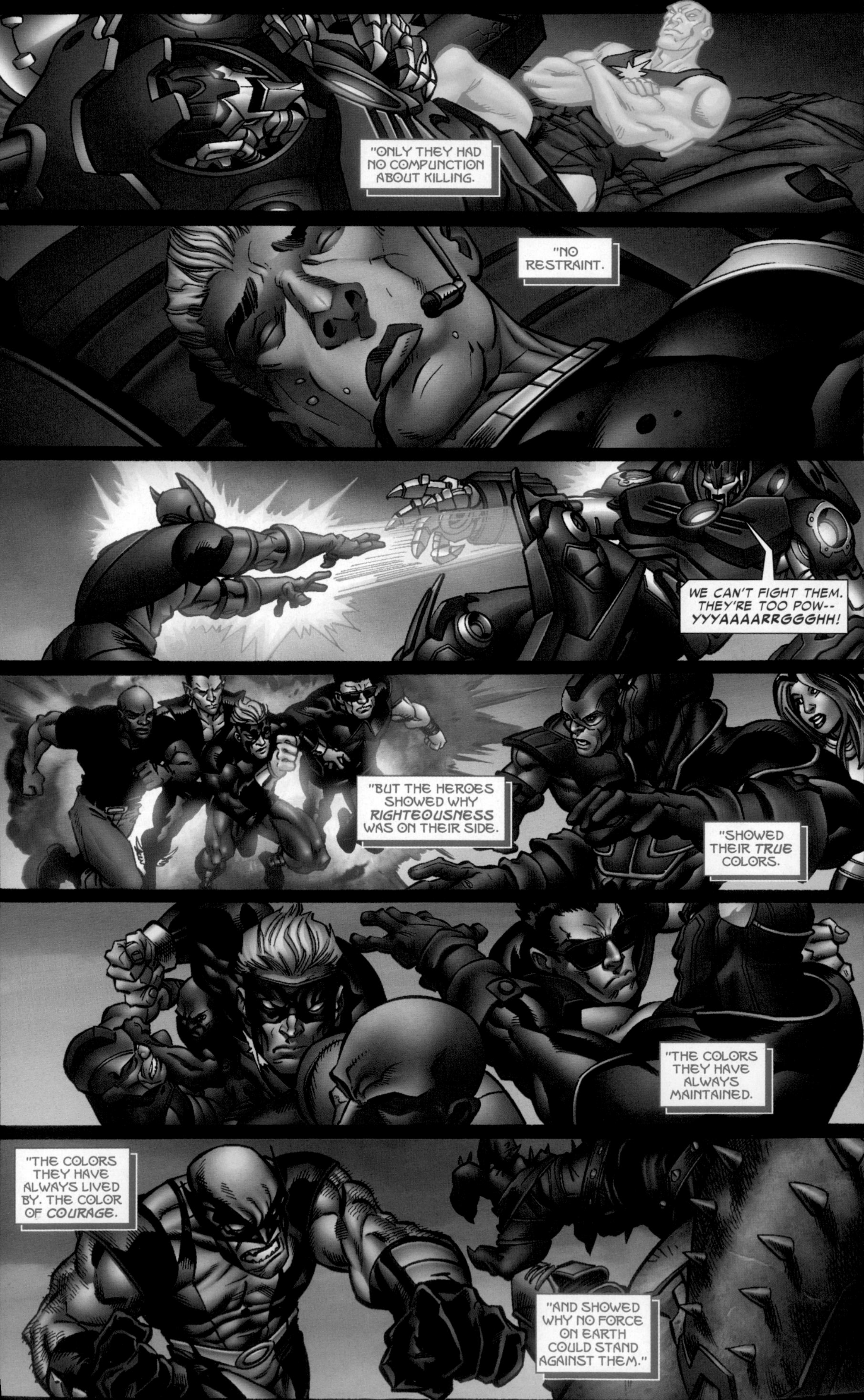
"ONLY THEY HAD NO COMPUNCTION ABOUT KILLING.
"NO RESTRAINT.
WE CAN'T FIGHT THEM. THEY'RE TOO POW-- YYYAAAARRGGGHH!
"BUT THE HEROES SHOWED WHY RIGHTEOUSNESS WAS ON THEIR SIDE.
"SHOWED THEIR TRUE COLORS.
"THE COLORS THEY HAVE ALWAYS MAINTAINED.
"THE COLORS THEY HAVE ALWAYS LIVED BY. THE COLOR OF COURAGE.
"AND SHOWED WHY NO FORCE ON EARTH COULD STAND AGAINST THEM."

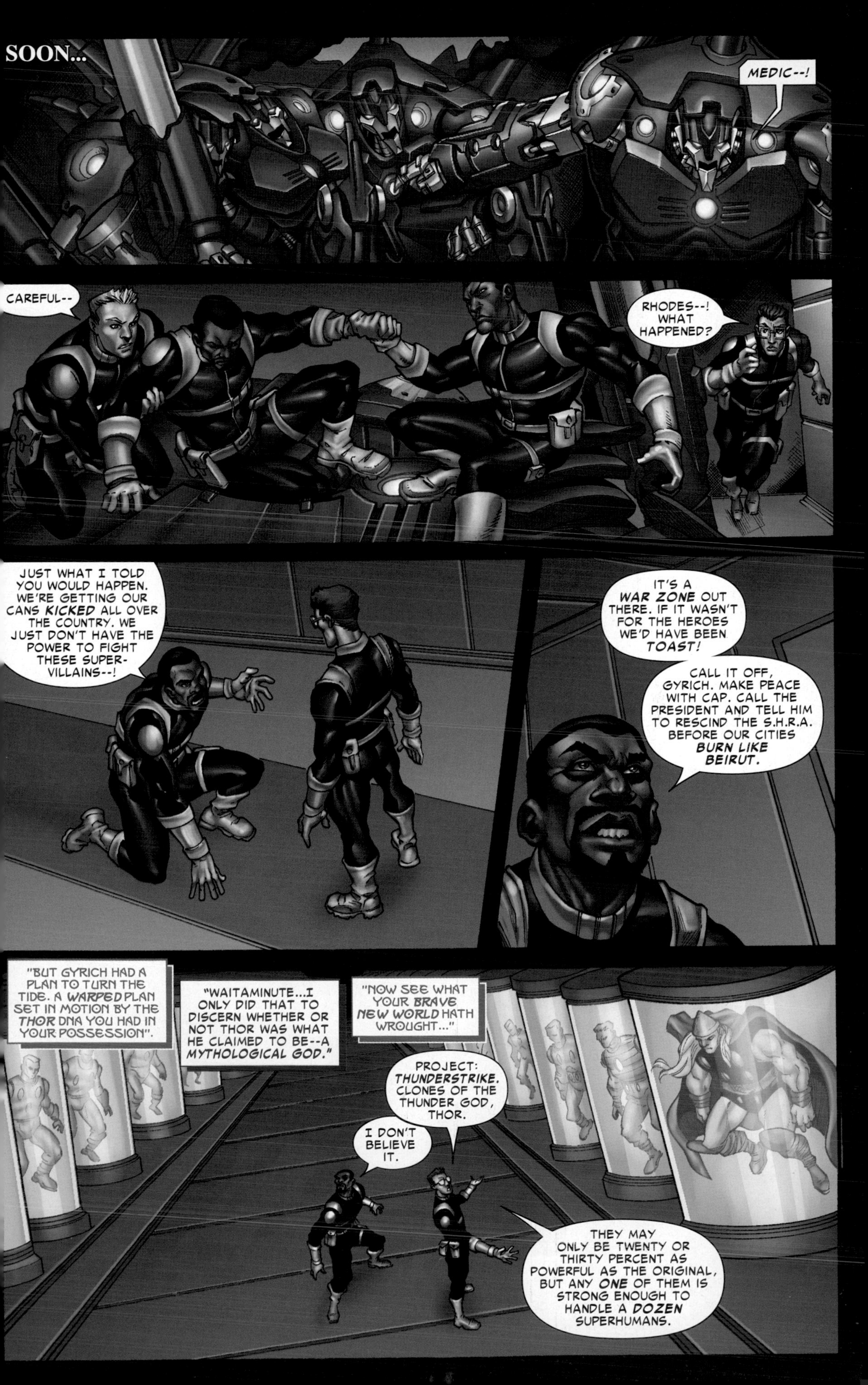
SOON...
MEDIC--!
CAREFUL--
RHODES--! WHAT HAPPENED?
JUST WHAT I TOLD YOU WOULD HAPPEN. WE'RE GETTING OUR CANS KICKED ALL OVER THE COUNTRY. WE JUST DON'T HAVE THE POWER TO FIGHT THESE SUPER-VILLAINS--!
IT'S A WAR ZONE OUT THERE. IF IT WASN'T FOR THE HEROES WE'D HAVE BEEN TOAST!
CALL IT OFF, GYRICH. MAKE PEACE WITH CAP. CALL THE PRESIDENT AND TELL HIM TO RESCIND THE S.H.R.A. BEFORE OUR CITIES BURN LIKE BEIRUT.
"BUT GYRICH HAD A PLAN TO TURN THE TIDE. A WARPED PLAN SET IN MOTION BY THE THOR DNA YOU HAD IN YOUR POSSESSION".
"WAITAMINUTE...I ONLY DID THAT TO DISCERN WHETHER OR NOT THOR WAS WHAT HE CLAIMED TO BE--A MYTHOLOGICAL GOD."
"NOW SEE WHAT YOUR BRAVE NEW WORLD HATH WROUGHT..."
PROJECT: THUNDERSTRIKE. CLONES OF THE THUNDER GOD, THOR.
I DON'T BELIEVE IT.
THEY MAY ONLY BE TWENTY OR THIRTY PERCENT AS POWERFUL AS THE ORIGINAL, BUT ANY ONE OF THEM IS STRONG ENOUGH TO HANDLE A DOZEN SUPERHUMANS.

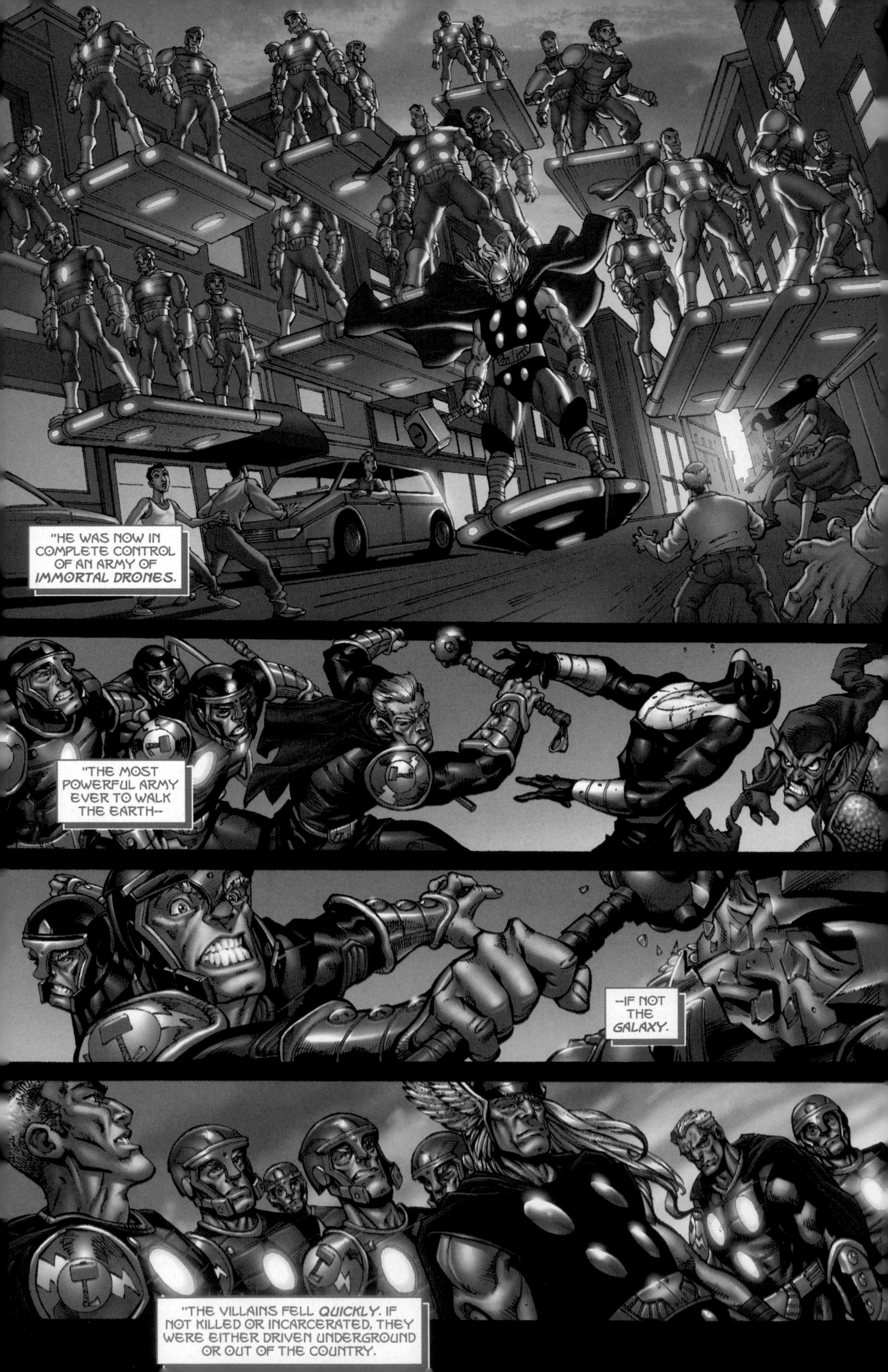
"HE WAS NOW IN COMPLETE CONTROL OF AN ARMY OF IMMORTAL DRONES.
"THE MOST POWERFUL ARMY EVER TO WALK THE EARTH--
--IF NOT THE GALAXY.
"THE VILLAINS FELL QUICKLY. IF NOT KILLED OR INCARCERATED, THEY WERE EITHER DRIVEN UNDERGROUND OR OUT OF THE COUNTRY.

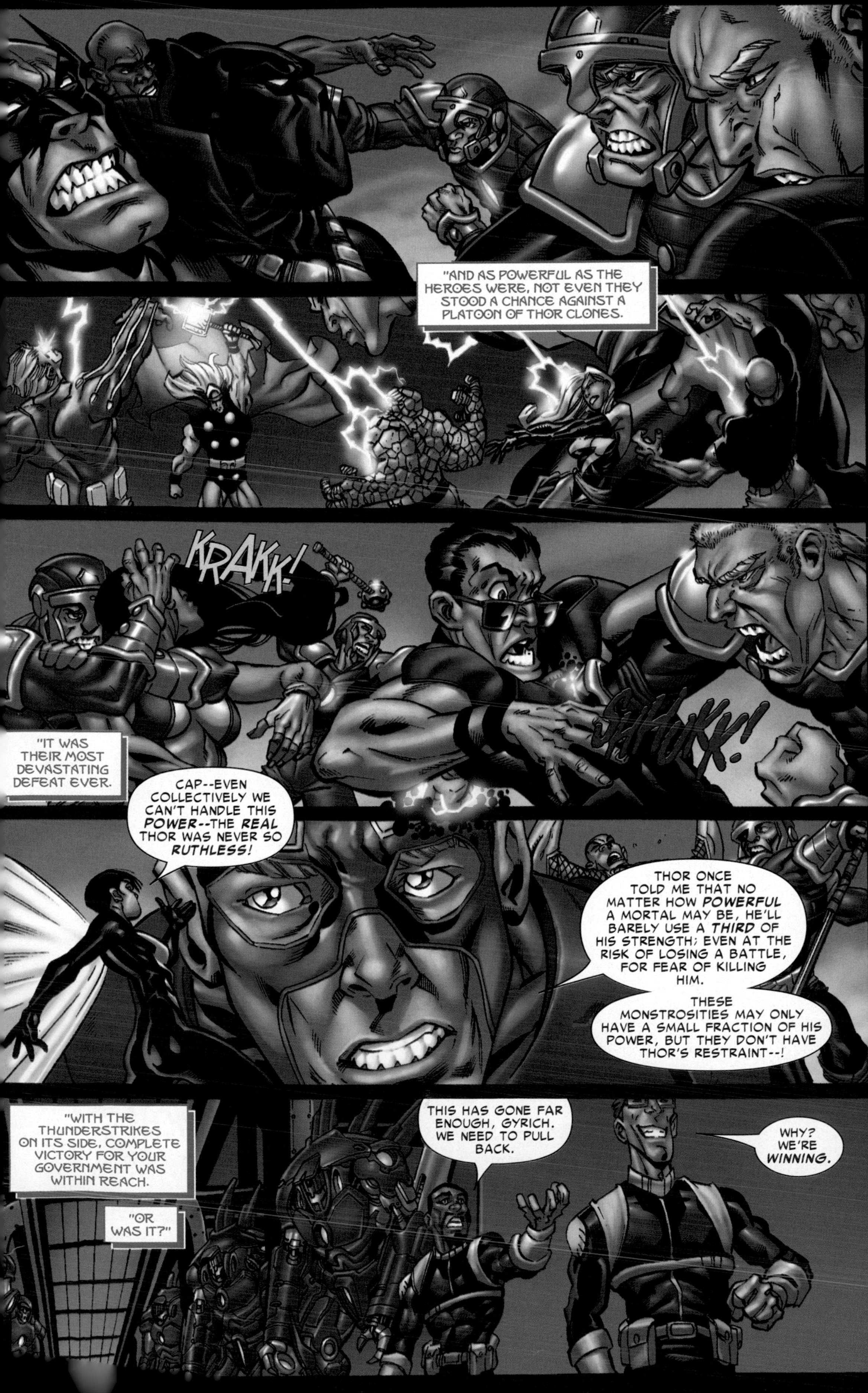
"AND AS POWERFUL AS THE HEROES WERE, NOT EVEN THEY STOOD A CHANCE AGAINST A PLATOON OF THOR CLONES.
KRAKK!
SHUKK!
"IT WAS THEIR MOST DEVASTATING DEFEAT EVER.
CAP--EVEN COLLECTIVELY WE CAN'T HANDLE THIS POWER--THE REAL THOR WAS NEVER SO RUTHLESS!
THOR ONCE TOLD ME THAT NO MATTER HOW POWERFUL A MORTAL MAY BE, HE'LL BARELY USE A THIRD OF HIS STRENGTH; EVEN AT THE RISK OF LOSING A BATTLE, FOR FEAR OF KILLING HIM.
THESE MONSTROSITIES MAY ONLY HAVE A SMALL FRACTION OF HIS POWER, BUT THEY DON'T HAVE THOR'S RESTRAINT--!
"WITH THE THUNDERSTRIKES ON ITS SIDE, COMPLETE VICTORY FOR YOUR GOVERNMENT WAS WITHIN REACH.
"OR WAS IT?"
THIS HAS GONE FAR ENOUGH, GYRICH. WE NEED TO PULL BACK.
WHY? WE'RE WINNING.

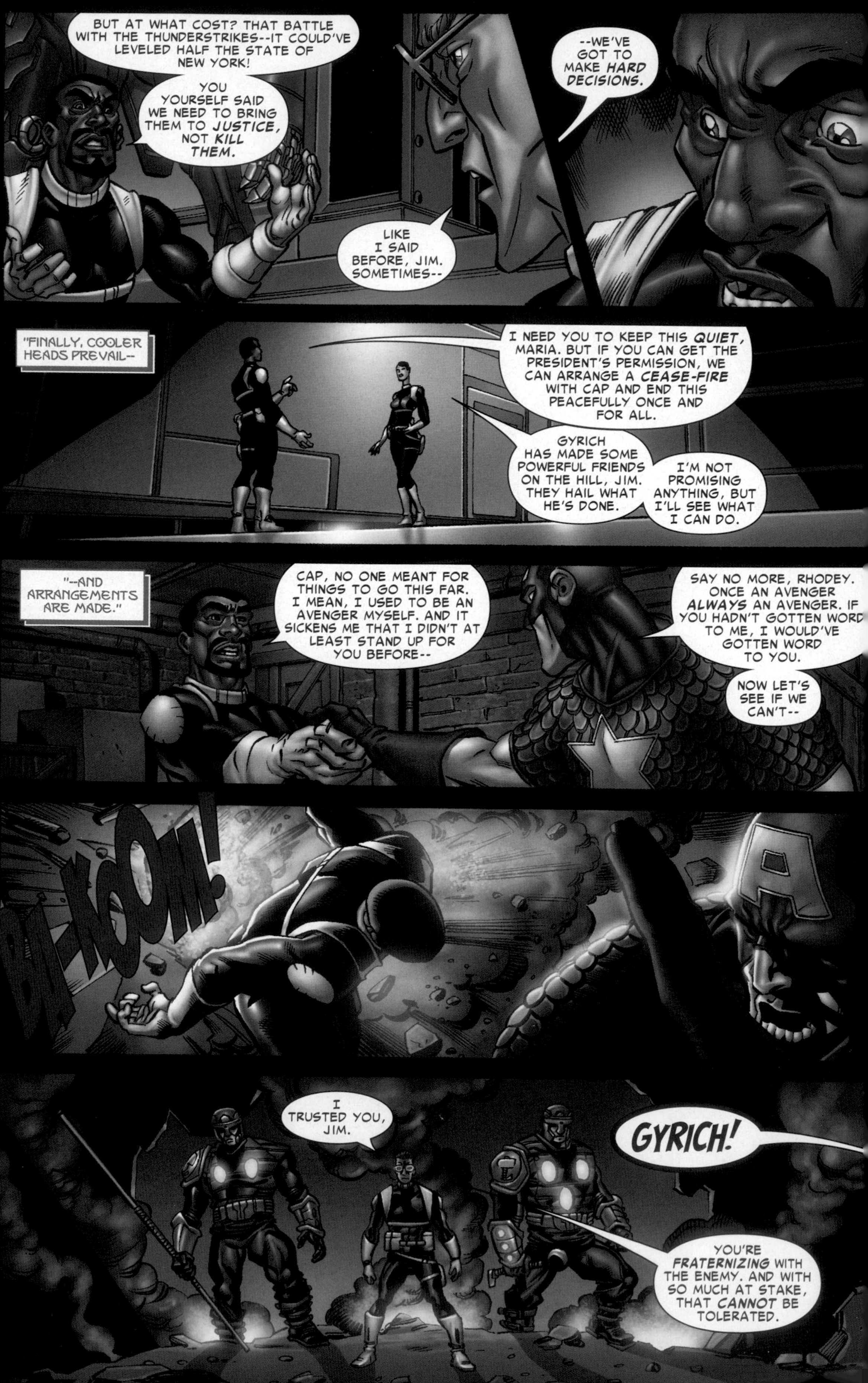
BUT AT WHAT COST? THAT BATTLE WITH THE THUNDERSTRIKES--IT COULD'VE LEVELED HALF THE STATE OF NEW YORK!
YOU YOURSELF SAID WE NEED TO BRING THEM TO JUSTICE, NOT KILL THEM.
LIKE I SAID BEFORE, JIM. SOMETIMES--
--WE'VE GOT TO MAKE HARD DECISIONS.
"FINALLY, COOLER HEADS PREVAIL--
I NEED YOU TO KEEP THIS QUIET, MARIA. BUT IF YOU CAN GET THE PRESIDENT'S PERMISSION, WE CAN ARRANGE A CEASE-FIRE WITH CAP AND END THIS PEACEFULLY ONCE AND FOR ALL.
GYRICH HAS MADE SOME POWERFUL FRIENDS ON THE HILL, JIM. THEY HAIL WHAT HE'S DONE.
I'M NOT PROMISING ANYTHING, BUT I'LL SEE WHAT I CAN DO.
"--AND ARRANGEMENTS ARE MADE."
CAP, NO ONE MEANT FOR THINGS TO GO THIS FAR. I MEAN, I USED TO BE AN AVENGER MYSELF. AND IT SICKENS ME THAT I DIDN'T AT LEAST STAND UP FOR YOU BEFORE--
SAY NO MORE, RHODEY. ONCE AN AVENGER ALWAYS AN AVENGER. IF YOU HADN'T GOTTEN WORD TO ME, I WOULD'VE GOTTEN WORD TO YOU.
NOW LET'S SEE IF WE CAN'T--
BA-KOOM!
I TRUSTED YOU, JIM.
GYRICH!
YOU'RE FRATERNIZING WITH THE ENEMY. AND WITH SO MUCH AT STAKE, THAT CANNOT BE TOLERATED.

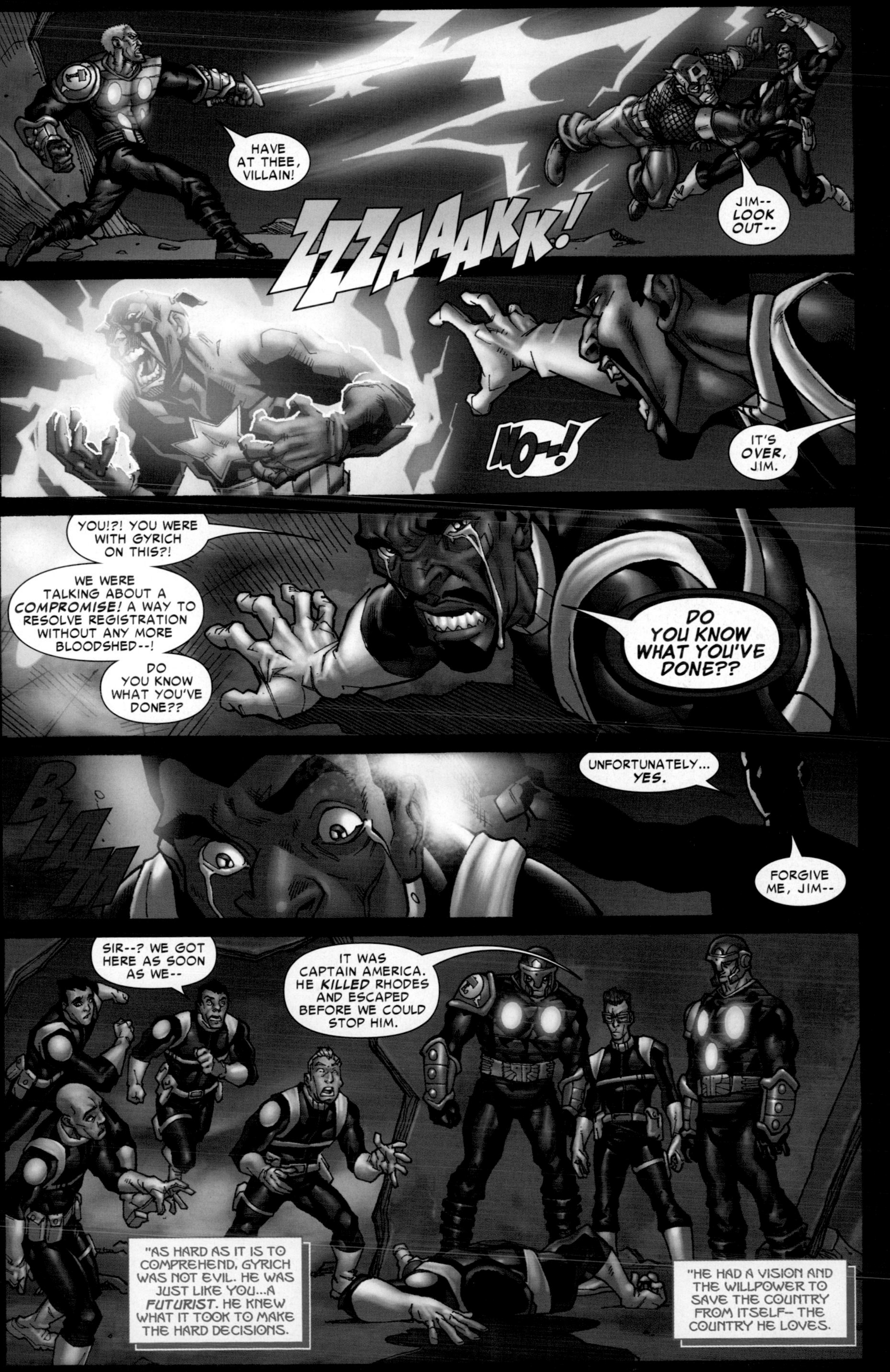

HAVE AT THEE, VILLAIN!
JIM-- LOOK OUT--
ZZZAAAKK!
NO--!
IT'S OVER, JIM.
YOU!?! YOU WERE WITH GYRICH ON THIS?!
WE WERE TALKING ABOUT A COMPROMISE! A WAY TO RESOLVE REGISTRATION WITHOUT ANY MORE BLOODSHED--!
DO YOU KNOW WHAT YOU'VE DONE??
DO YOU KNOW WHAT YOU'VE DONE??
UNFORTUNATELY... YES.
FORGIVE ME, JIM--
SIR--? WE GOT HERE AS SOON AS WE--
IT WAS CAPTAIN AMERICA. HE KILLED RHODES AND ESCAPED BEFORE WE COULD STOP HIM.
"AS HARD AS IT IS TO COMPREHEND, GYRICH WAS NOT EVIL. HE WAS JUST LIKE YOU...A FUTURIST. HE KNEW WHAT IT TOOK TO MAKE THE HARD DECISIONS.
"HE HAD A VISION AND THE WILLPOWER TO SAVE THE COUNTRY FROM ITSELF-- THE COUNTRY HE LOVES.

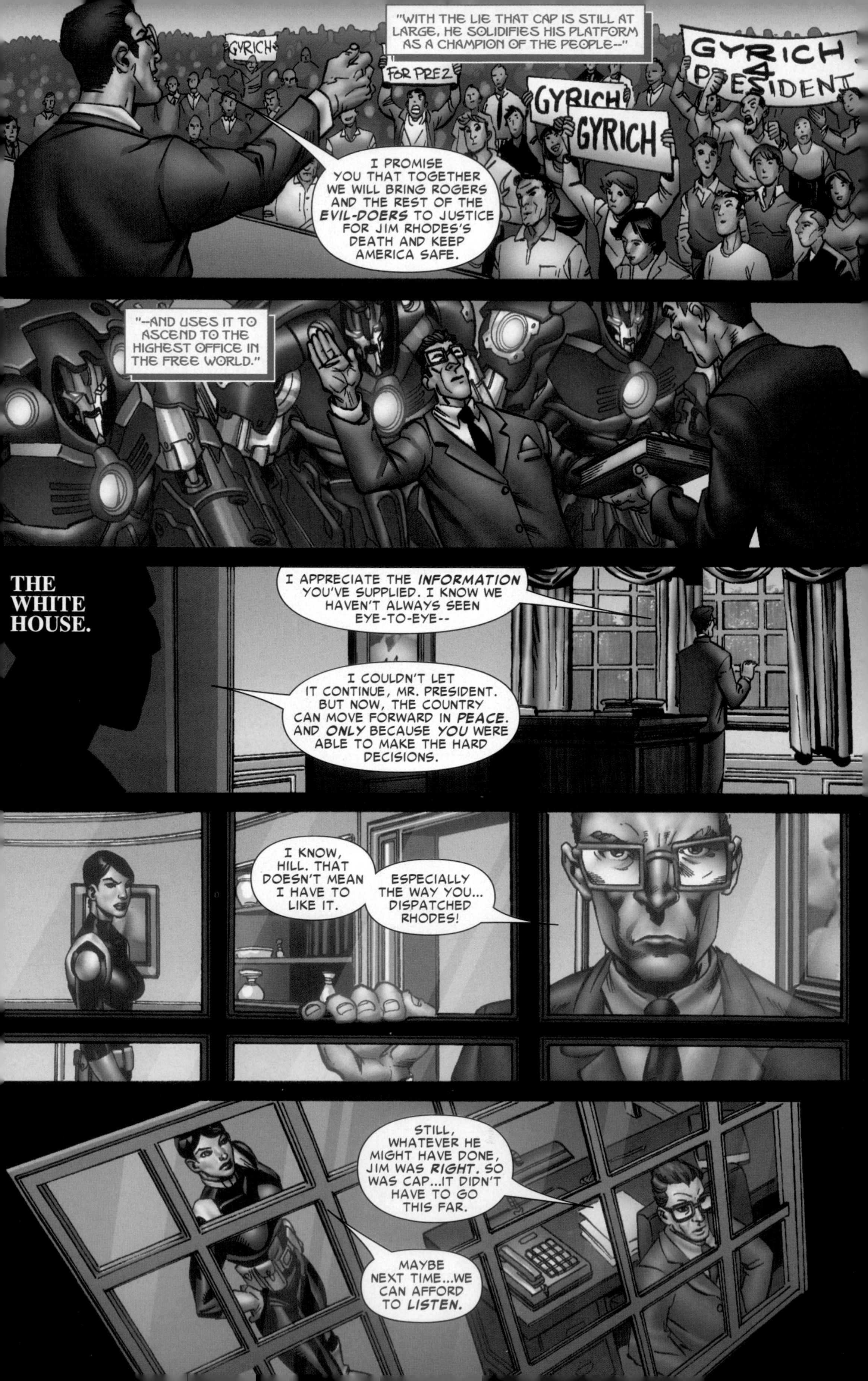
"WITH THE LIE THAT CAP IS STILL AT LARGE, HE SOLIDIFIES HIS PLATFORM AS A CHAMPION OF THE PEOPLE--"
GYRICH
FOR PREZ
GYRICH
GYRICH
GYRICH 4 PRESIDENT
I PROMISE YOU THAT TOGETHER WE WILL BRING ROGERS AND THE REST OF THE EVIL-DOERS TO JUSTICE FOR JIM RHODES'S DEATH AND KEEP AMERICA SAFE.
"--AND USES IT TO ASCEND TO THE HIGHEST OFFICE IN THE FREE WORLD."
THE WHITE HOUSE.
I APPRECIATE THE INFORMATION YOU'VE SUPPLIED. I KNOW WE HAVEN'T ALWAYS SEEN EYE-TO-EYE--
I COULDN'T LET IT CONTINUE, MR. PRESIDENT. BUT NOW, THE COUNTRY CAN MOVE FORWARD IN PEACE. AND ONLY BECAUSE YOU WERE ABLE TO MAKE THE HARD DECISIONS.
I KNOW, HILL. THAT DOESN'T MEAN I HAVE TO LIKE IT.
ESPECIALLY THE WAY YOU... DISPATCHED RHODES!
STILL, WHATEVER HE MIGHT HAVE DONE, JIM WAS RIGHT. SO WAS CAP...IT DIDN'T HAVE TO GO THIS FAR.
MAYBE NEXT TIME...WE CAN AFFORD TO LISTEN.

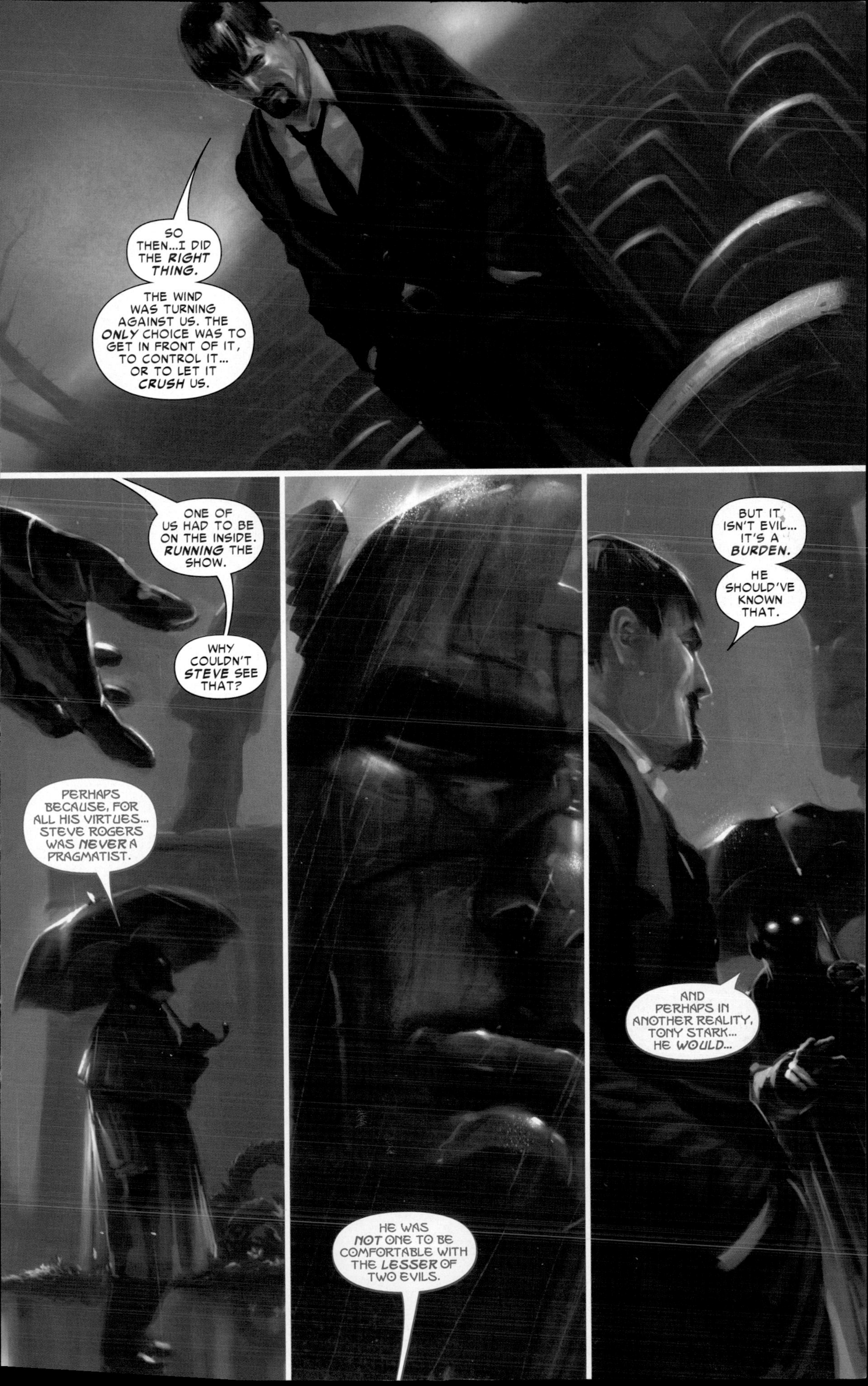
SO THEN...I DID THE RIGHT THING.
THE WIND WAS TURNING AGAINST US. THE ONLY CHOICE WAS TO GET IN FRONT OF IT, TO CONTROL IT... OR TO LET IT CRUSH US.
ONE OF US HAD TO BE ON THE INSIDE. RUNNING THE SHOW.
WHY COULDN'T STEVE SEE THAT?
PERHAPS BECAUSE, FOR ALL HIS VIRTUES... STEVE ROGERS WAS NEVER A PRAGMATIST.
HE WAS NOT ONE TO BE COMFORTABLE WITH THE LESSER OF TWO EVILS.
BUT IT ISN'T EVIL... IT'S A BURDEN.
HE SHOULD'VE KNOWN THAT.
AND PERHAPS IN ANOTHER REALITY, TONY STARK... HE WOULD...

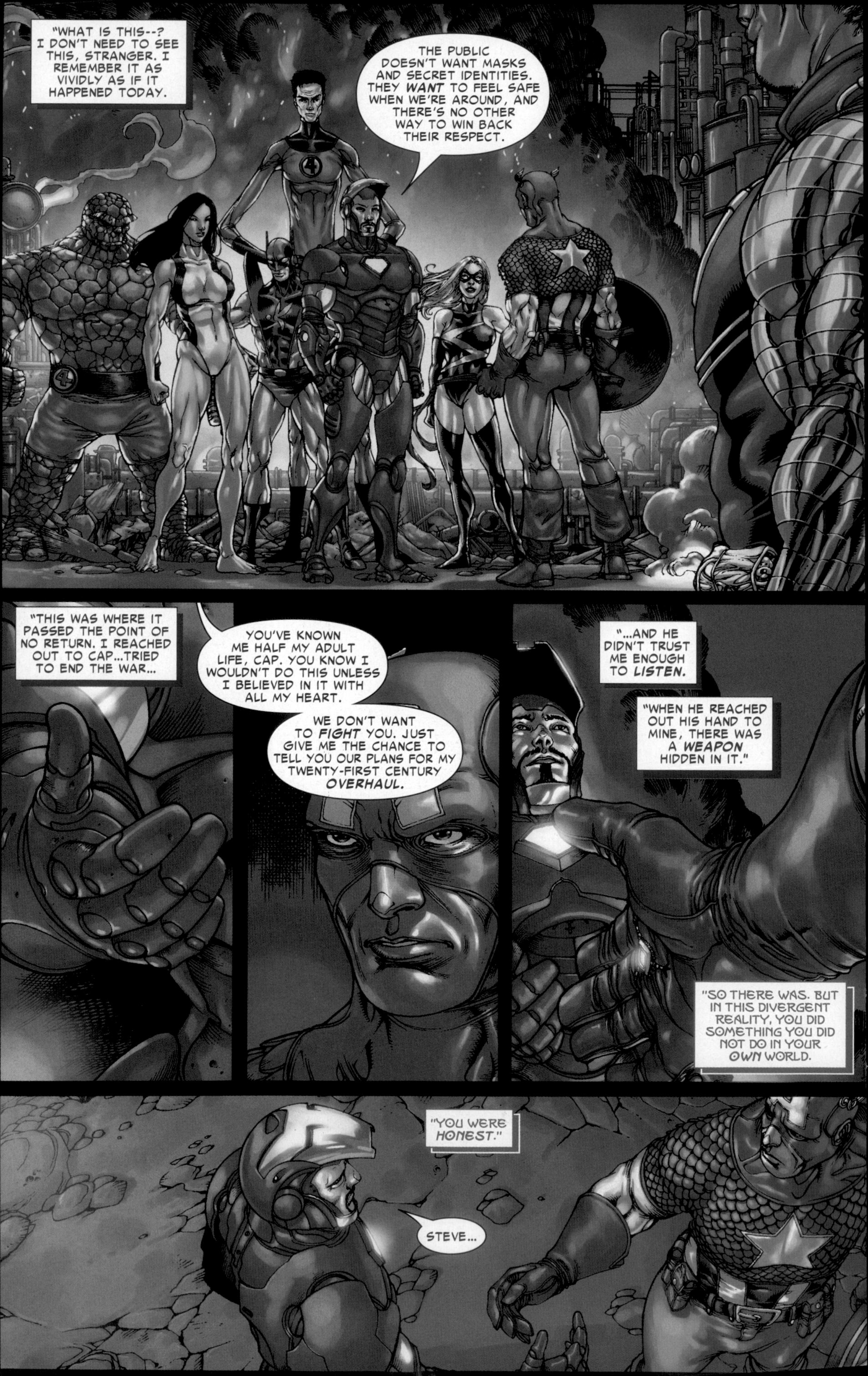
"WHAT IS THIS--? I DON'T NEED TO SEE THIS, STRANGER. I REMEMBER IT AS VIVIDLY AS IF IT HAPPENED TODAY.
THE PUBLIC DOESN'T WANT MASKS AND SECRET IDENTITIES. THEY WANT TO FEEL SAFE WHEN WE'RE AROUND, AND THERE'S NO OTHER WAY TO WIN BACK THEIR RESPECT.
"THIS WAS WHERE IT PASSED THE POINT OF NO RETURN. I REACHED OUT TO CAP...TRIED TO END THE WAR...
YOU'VE KNOWN ME HALF MY ADULT LIFE, CAP. YOU KNOW I WOULDN'T DO THIS UNLESS I BELIEVED IN IT WITH ALL MY HEART.
WE DON'T WANT TO FIGHT YOU. JUST GIVE ME THE CHANCE TO TELL YOU OUR PLANS FOR MY TWENTY-FIRST CENTURY OVERHAUL.
"...AND HE DIDN'T TRUST ME ENOUGH TO LISTEN.
"WHEN HE REACHED OUT HIS HAND TO MINE, THERE WAS A WEAPON HIDDEN IN IT."
"SO THERE WAS. BUT IN THIS DIVERGENT REALITY, YOU DID SOMETHING YOU DID NOT DO IN YOUR OWN WORLD.
"YOU WERE HONEST."
STEVE...

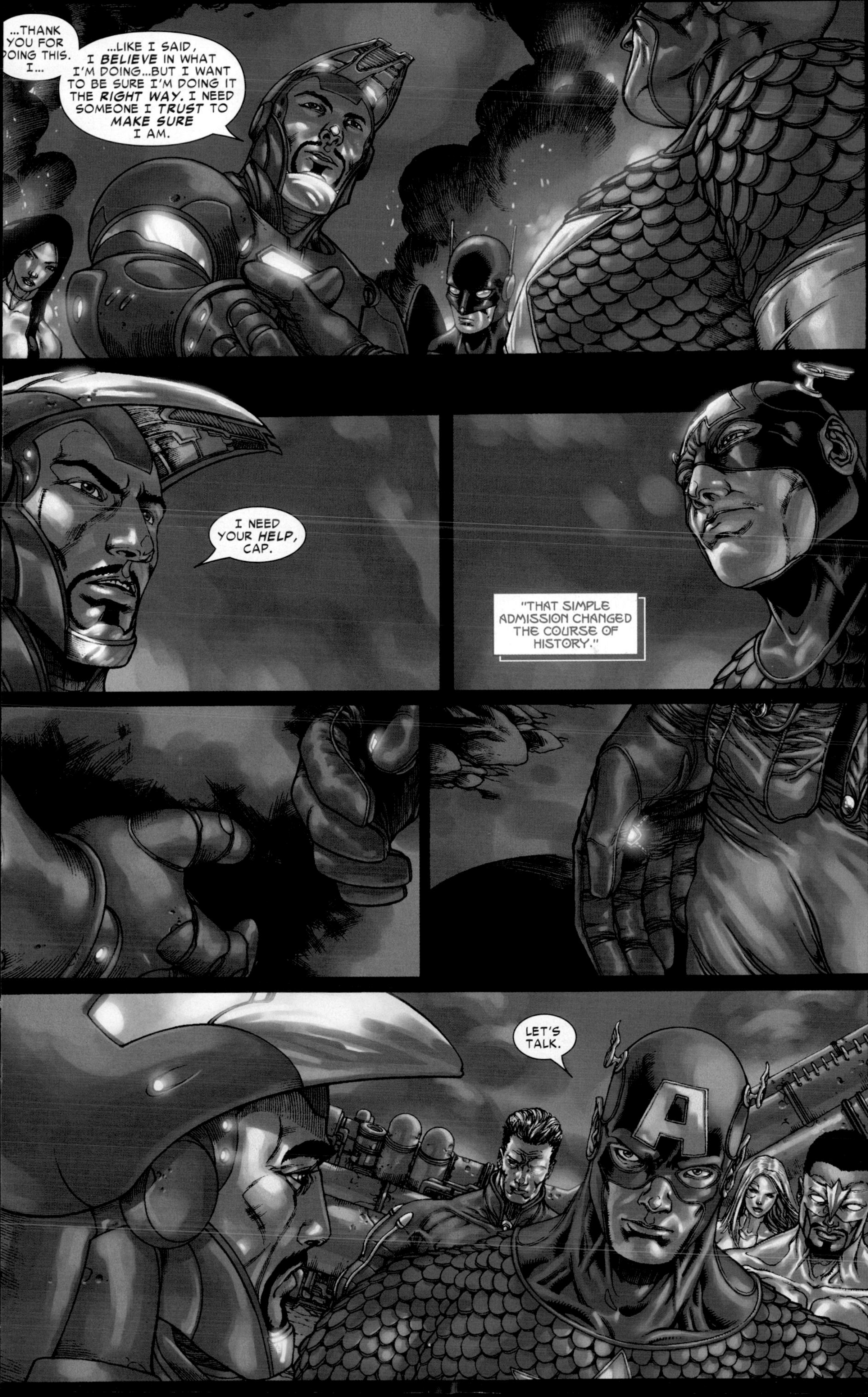
...THANK YOU FOR DOING THIS. I...
...LIKE I SAID, I BELIEVE IN WHAT I'M DOING...BUT I WANT TO BE SURE I'M DOING IT THE RIGHT WAY. I NEED SOMEONE I TRUST TO MAKE SURE I AM.
I NEED YOUR HELP, CAP.
"THAT SIMPLE ADMISSION CHANGED THE COURSE OF HISTORY."
LET'S TALK.

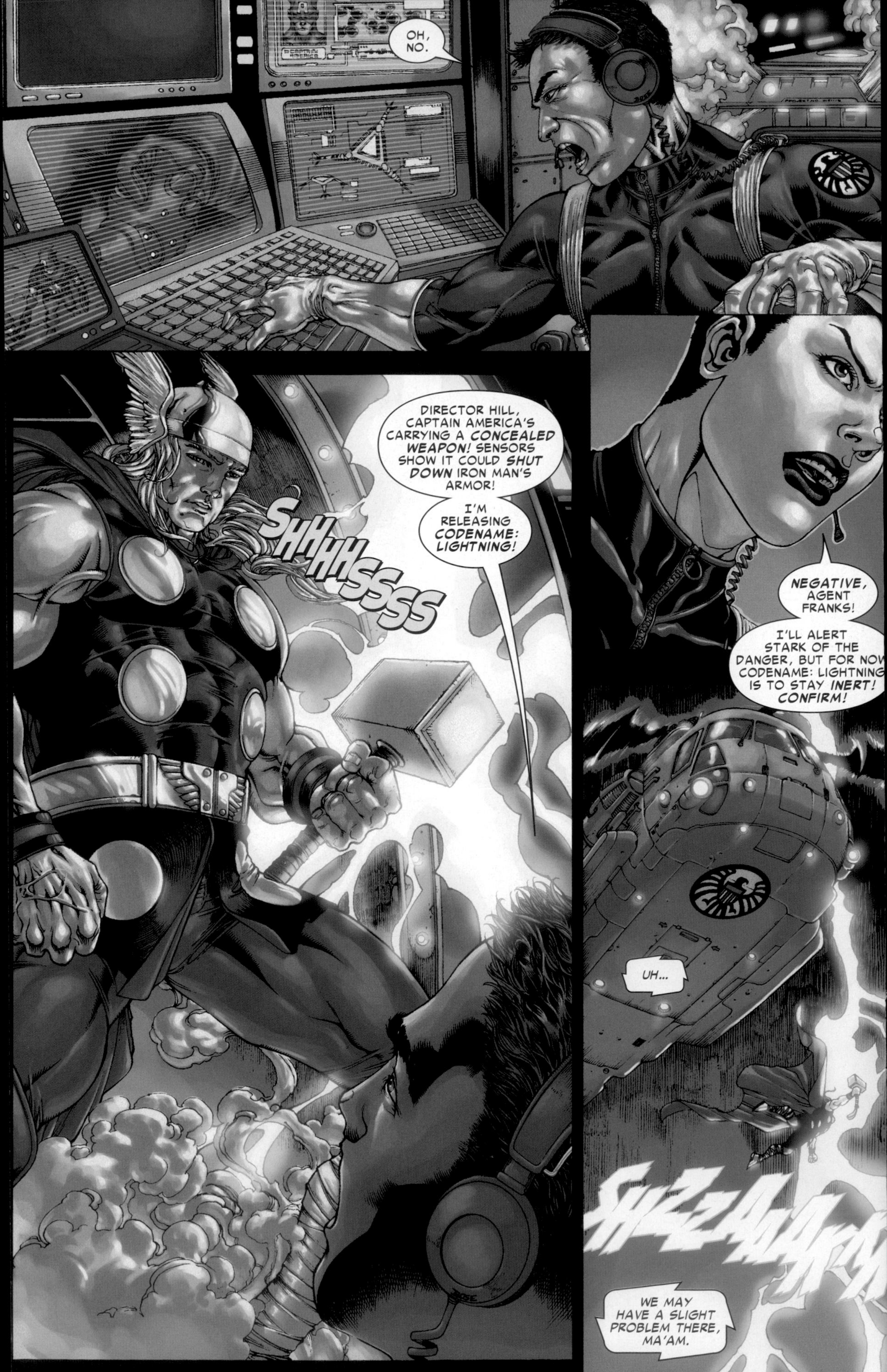
OH, NO.
DIRECTOR HILL, CAPTAIN AMERICA'S CARRYING A *CONCEALED WEAPON!* SENSORS SHOW IT COULD *SHUT DOWN* IRON MAN'S ARMOR!
I'M RELEASING *CODENAME: LIGHTNING!*
SHHHHSSSSS
NEGATIVE, AGENT FRANKS!
I'LL ALERT STARK OF THE DANGER, BUT FOR NOW CODENAME: LIGHTNING IS TO STAY *INERT! CONFIRM!*
UH...
WE MAY HAVE A SLIGHT PROBLEM THERE, MA'AM.

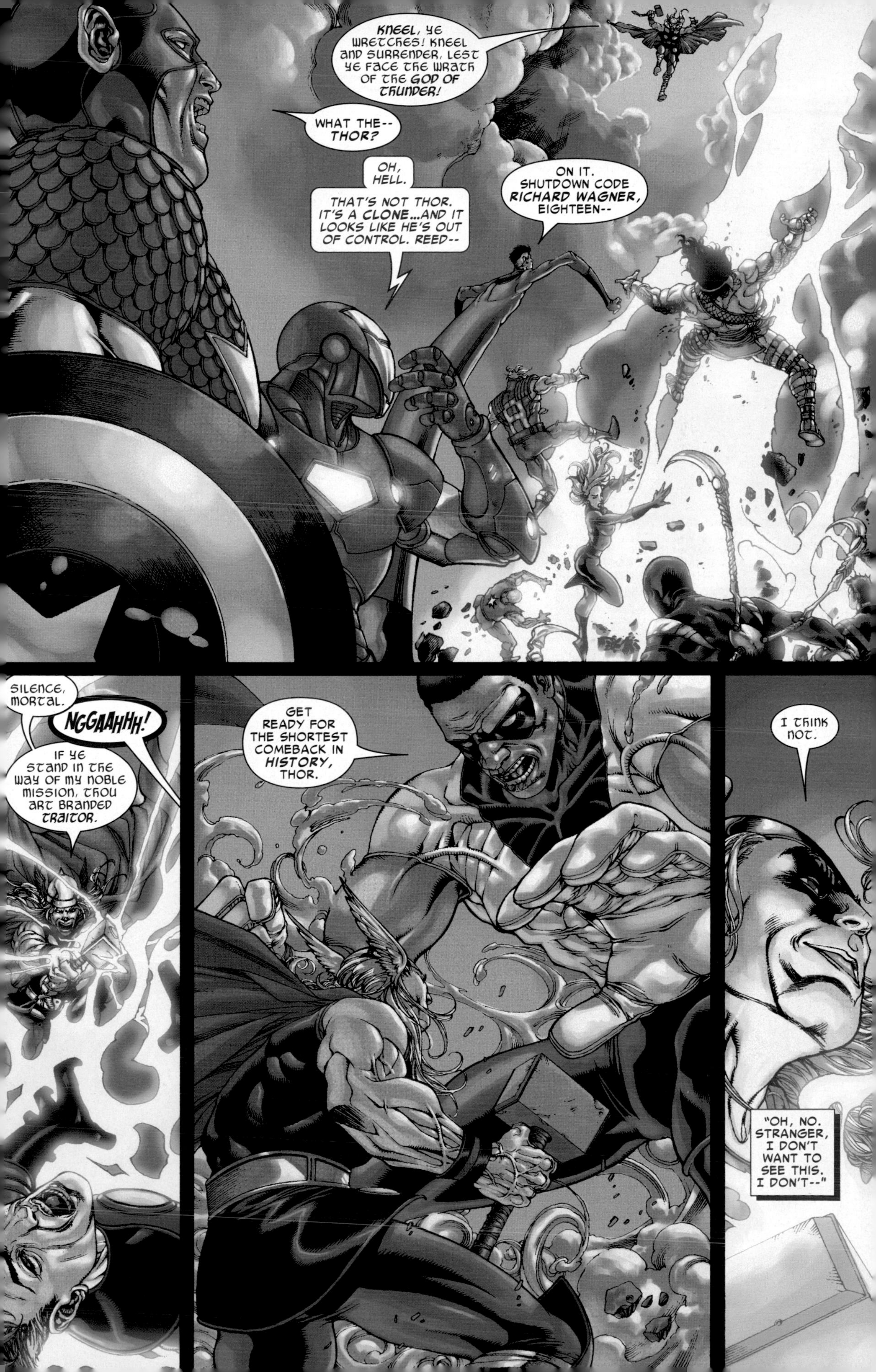
KNEEL, YE WRETCHES! KNEEL AND SURRENDER, LEST YE FACE THE WRATH OF THE GOD OF THUNDER!
WHAT THE-- THOR?
OH, HELL.
THAT'S NOT THOR. IT'S A CLONE...AND IT LOOKS LIKE HE'S OUT OF CONTROL. REED--
ON IT. SHUTDOWN CODE RICHARD WAGNER, EIGHTEEN--
SILENCE, MORTAL.
NGGAAHHH!
IF YE STAND IN THE WAY OF MY NOBLE MISSION, THOU ART BRANDED TRAITOR.
GET READY FOR THE SHORTEST COMEBACK IN HISTORY, THOR.
I THINK NOT.
"OH, NO. STRANGER, I DON'T WANT TO SEE THIS. I DON'T--"

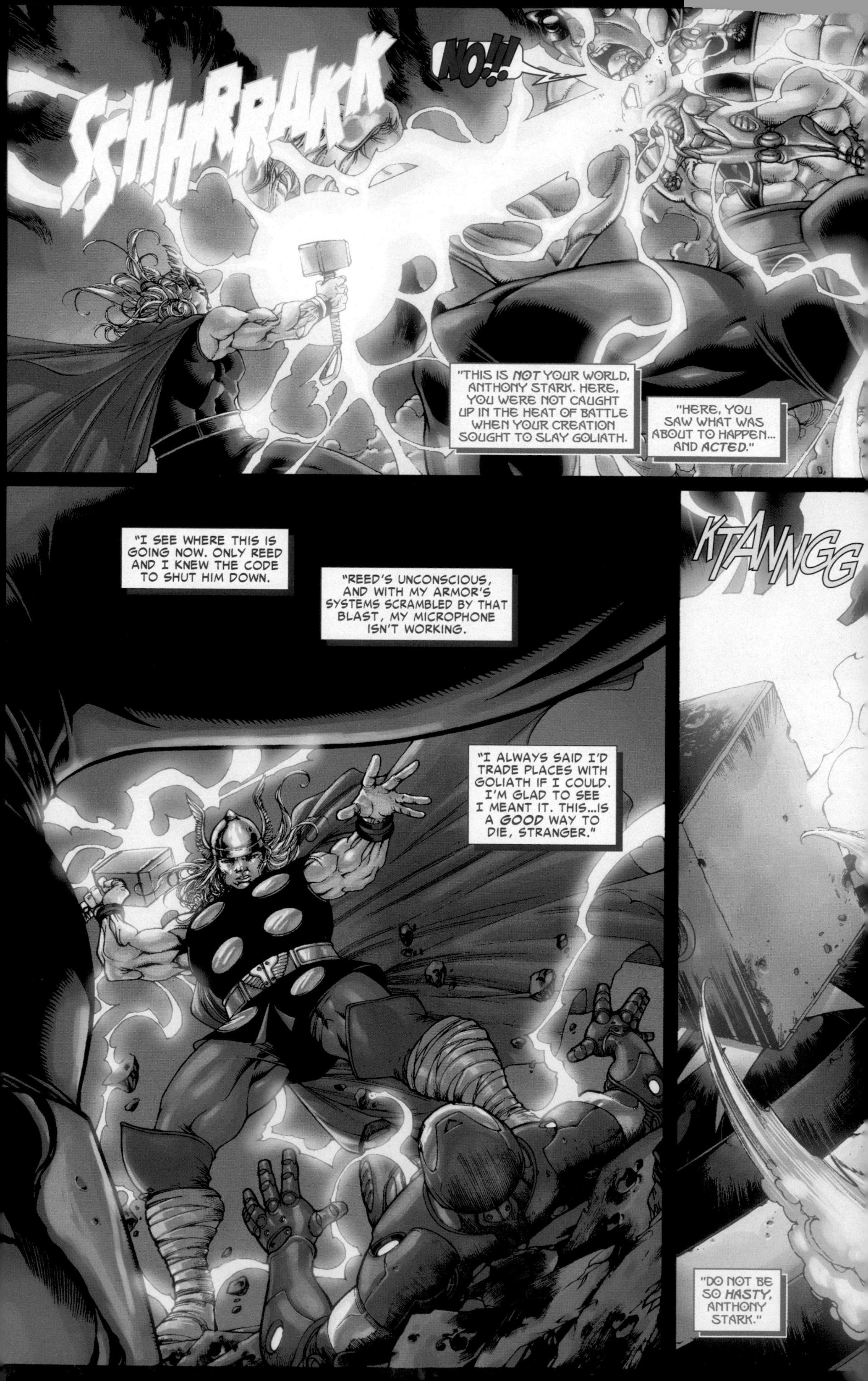
SHHRRAKK
NO!!!
"THIS IS *NOT* YOUR WORLD, ANTHONY STARK. HERE, YOU WERE NOT CAUGHT UP IN THE HEAT OF BATTLE WHEN YOUR CREATION SOUGHT TO SLAY GOLIATH.
"HERE, YOU SAW WHAT WAS ABOUT TO HAPPEN... AND *ACTED.*"
"I SEE WHERE THIS IS GOING NOW. ONLY REED AND I KNEW THE CODE TO SHUT HIM DOWN.
"REED'S UNCONSCIOUS, AND WITH MY ARMOR'S SYSTEMS SCRAMBLED BY THAT BLAST, MY MICROPHONE ISN'T WORKING.
"I ALWAYS SAID I'D TRADE PLACES WITH GOLIATH IF I COULD. I'M GLAD TO SEE I MEANT IT. THIS...IS A *GOOD* WAY TO DIE, STRANGER."
KTANNGG
"DO NOT BE SO *HASTY,* ANTHONY STARK."

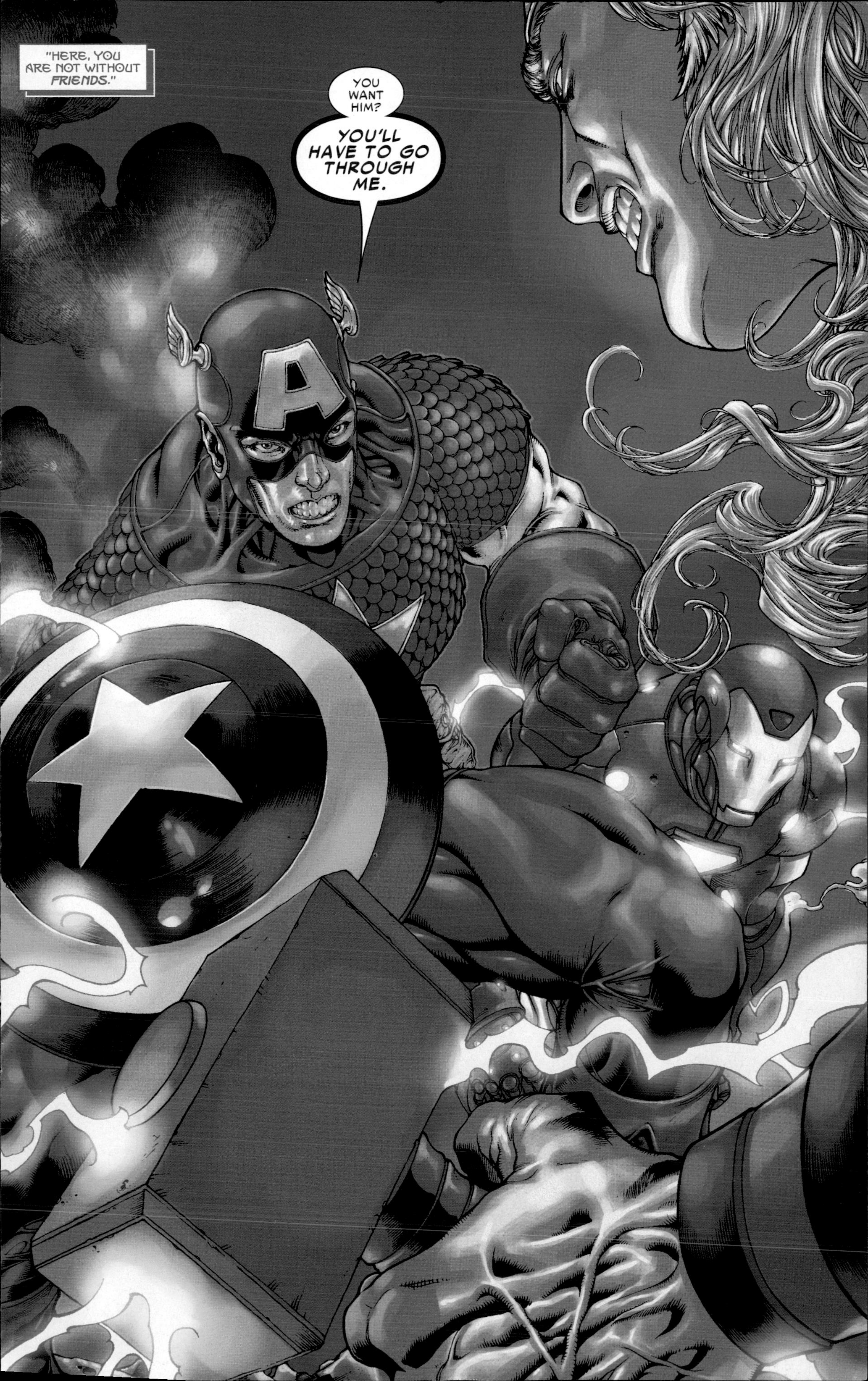
"HERE, YOU ARE NOT WITHOUT *FRIENDS*."
YOU WANT HIM?
YOU'LL HAVE TO GO THROUGH ME.

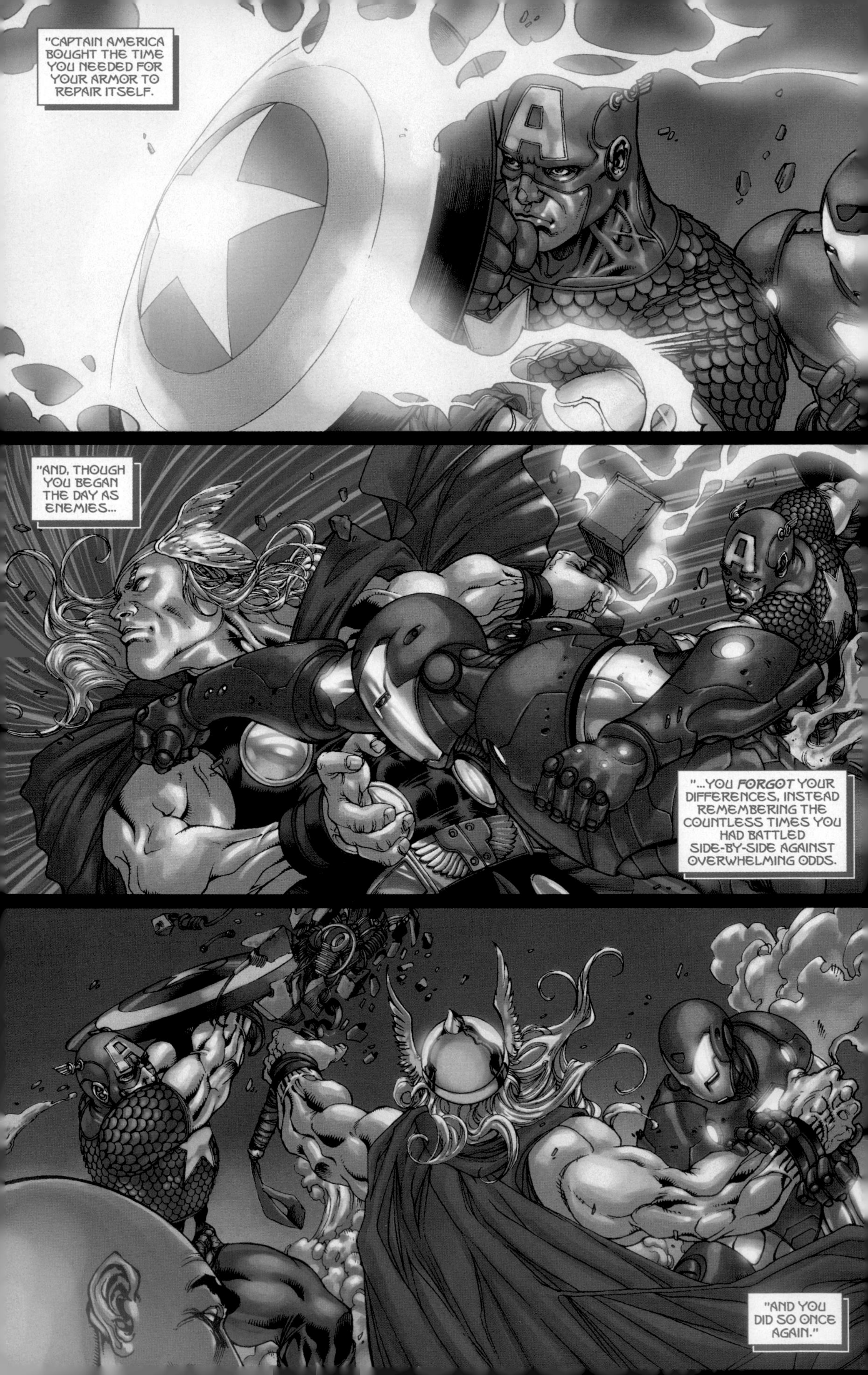
"CAPTAIN AMERICA BOUGHT THE TIME YOU NEEDED FOR YOUR ARMOR TO REPAIR ITSELF.
"AND, THOUGH YOU BEGAN THE DAY AS ENEMIES...
"...YOU FORGOT YOUR DIFFERENCES, INSTEAD REMEMBERING THE COUNTLESS TIMES YOU HAD BATTLED SIDE-BY-SIDE AGAINST OVERWHELMING ODDS.
"AND YOU DID SO ONCE AGAIN."

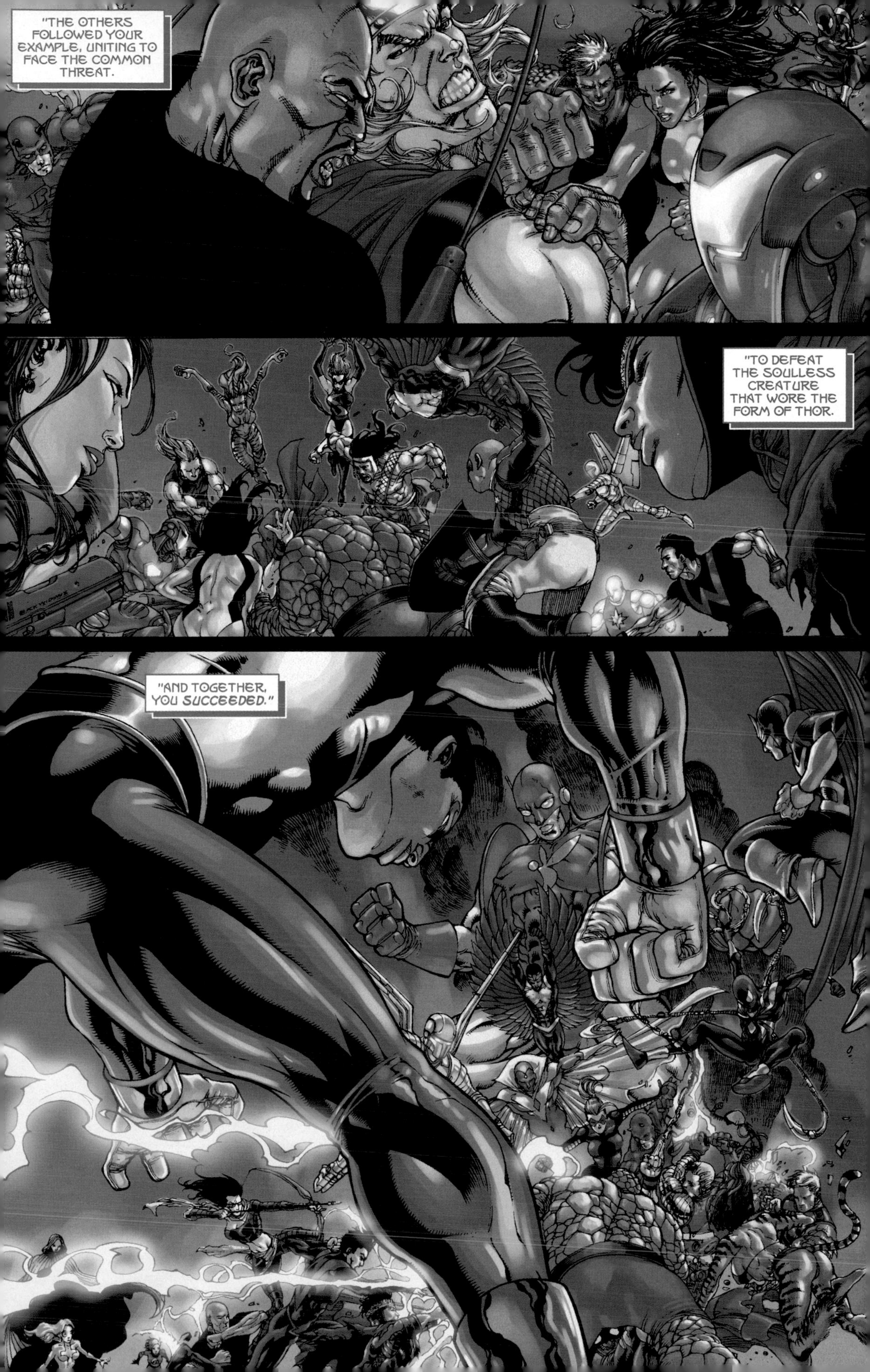
"THE OTHERS FOLLOWED YOUR EXAMPLE, UNITING TO FACE THE COMMON THREAT.
"TO DEFEAT THE SOULLESS CREATURE THAT WORE THE FORM OF THOR.
"AND TOGETHER, YOU SUCCEEDED."

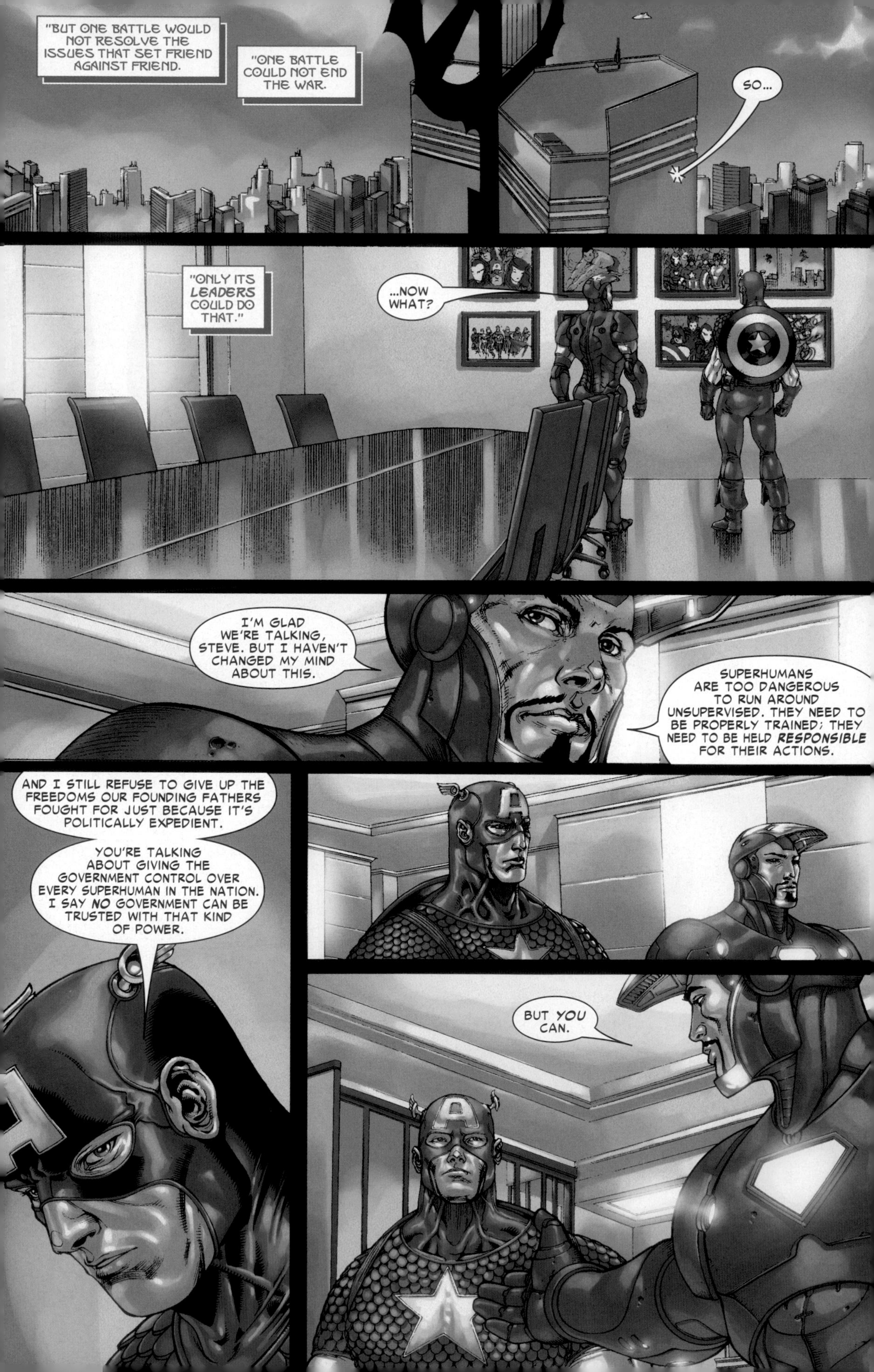
"BUT ONE BATTLE WOULD NOT RESOLVE THE ISSUES THAT SET FRIEND AGAINST FRIEND.
"ONE BATTLE COULD NOT END THE WAR.
SO...
"ONLY ITS LEADERS COULD DO THAT."
...NOW WHAT?
I'M GLAD WE'RE TALKING, STEVE. BUT I HAVEN'T CHANGED MY MIND ABOUT THIS.
SUPERHUMANS ARE TOO DANGEROUS TO RUN AROUND UNSUPERVISED. THEY NEED TO BE PROPERLY TRAINED; THEY NEED TO BE HELD RESPONSIBLE FOR THEIR ACTIONS.
AND I STILL REFUSE TO GIVE UP THE FREEDOMS OUR FOUNDING FATHERS FOUGHT FOR JUST BECAUSE IT'S POLITICALLY EXPEDIENT.
YOU'RE TALKING ABOUT GIVING THE GOVERNMENT CONTROL OVER EVERY SUPERHUMAN IN THE NATION. I SAY NO GOVERNMENT CAN BE TRUSTED WITH THAT KIND OF POWER.
BUT YOU CAN.

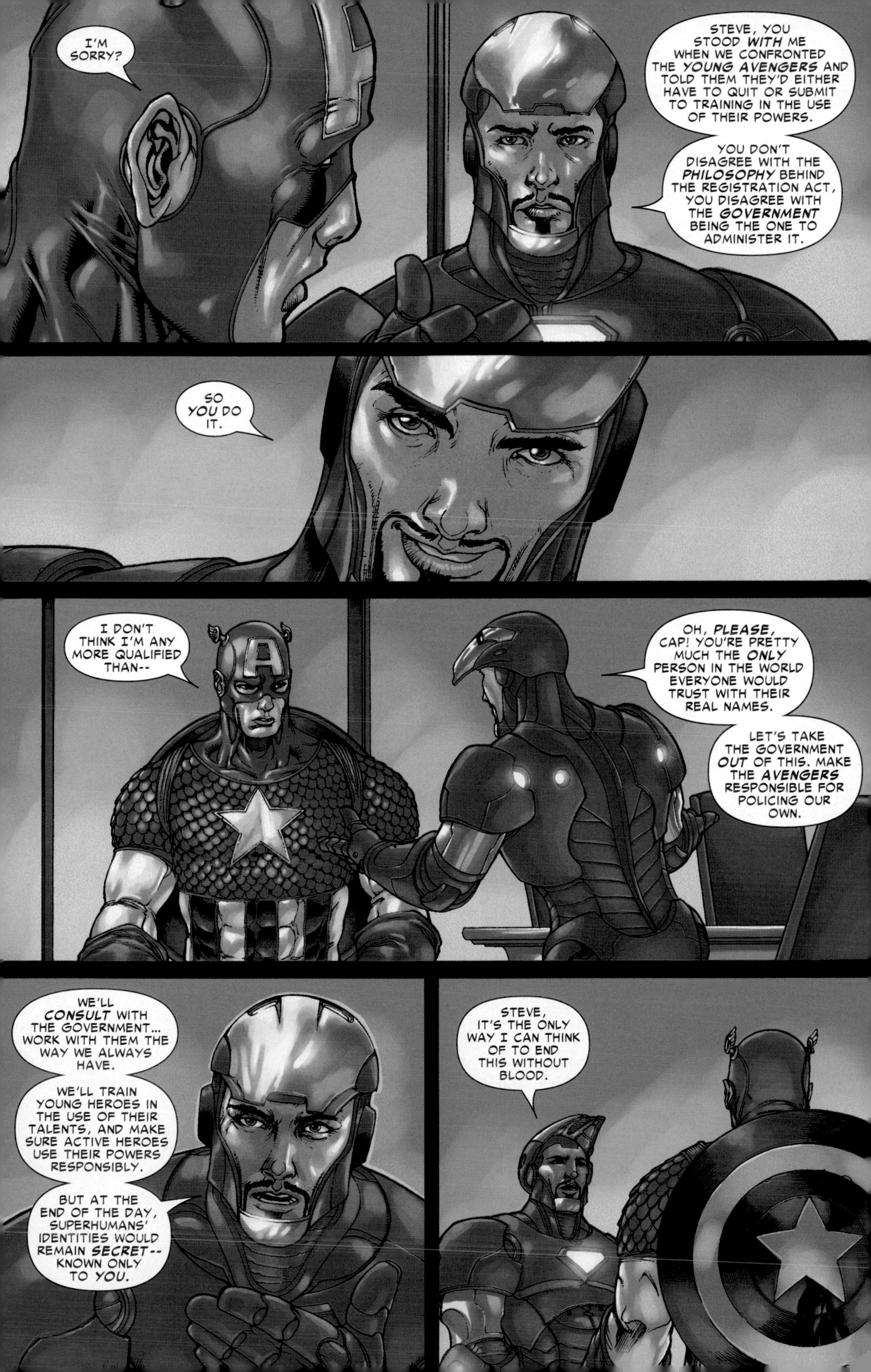
I'M SORRY?
STEVE, YOU STOOD WITH ME WHEN WE CONFRONTED THE YOUNG AVENGERS AND TOLD THEM THEY'D EITHER HAVE TO QUIT OR SUBMIT TO TRAINING IN THE USE OF THEIR POWERS.
YOU DON'T DISAGREE WITH THE PHILOSOPHY BEHIND THE REGISTRATION ACT, YOU DISAGREE WITH THE GOVERNMENT BEING THE ONE TO ADMINISTER IT.
SO YOU DO IT.
I DON'T THINK I'M ANY MORE QUALIFIED THAN--
OH, PLEASE, CAP! YOU'RE PRETTY MUCH THE ONLY PERSON IN THE WORLD EVERYONE WOULD TRUST WITH THEIR REAL NAMES.
LET'S TAKE THE GOVERNMENT OUT OF THIS. MAKE THE AVENGERS RESPONSIBLE FOR POLICING OUR OWN.
WE'LL CONSULT WITH THE GOVERNMENT... WORK WITH THEM THE WAY WE ALWAYS HAVE.
WE'LL TRAIN YOUNG HEROES IN THE USE OF THEIR TALENTS, AND MAKE SURE ACTIVE HEROES USE THEIR POWERS RESPONSIBLY.
BUT AT THE END OF THE DAY, SUPERHUMANS' IDENTITIES WOULD REMAIN SECRET-- KNOWN ONLY TO YOU.
STEVE, IT'S THE ONLY WAY I CAN THINK OF TO END THIS WITHOUT BLOOD.

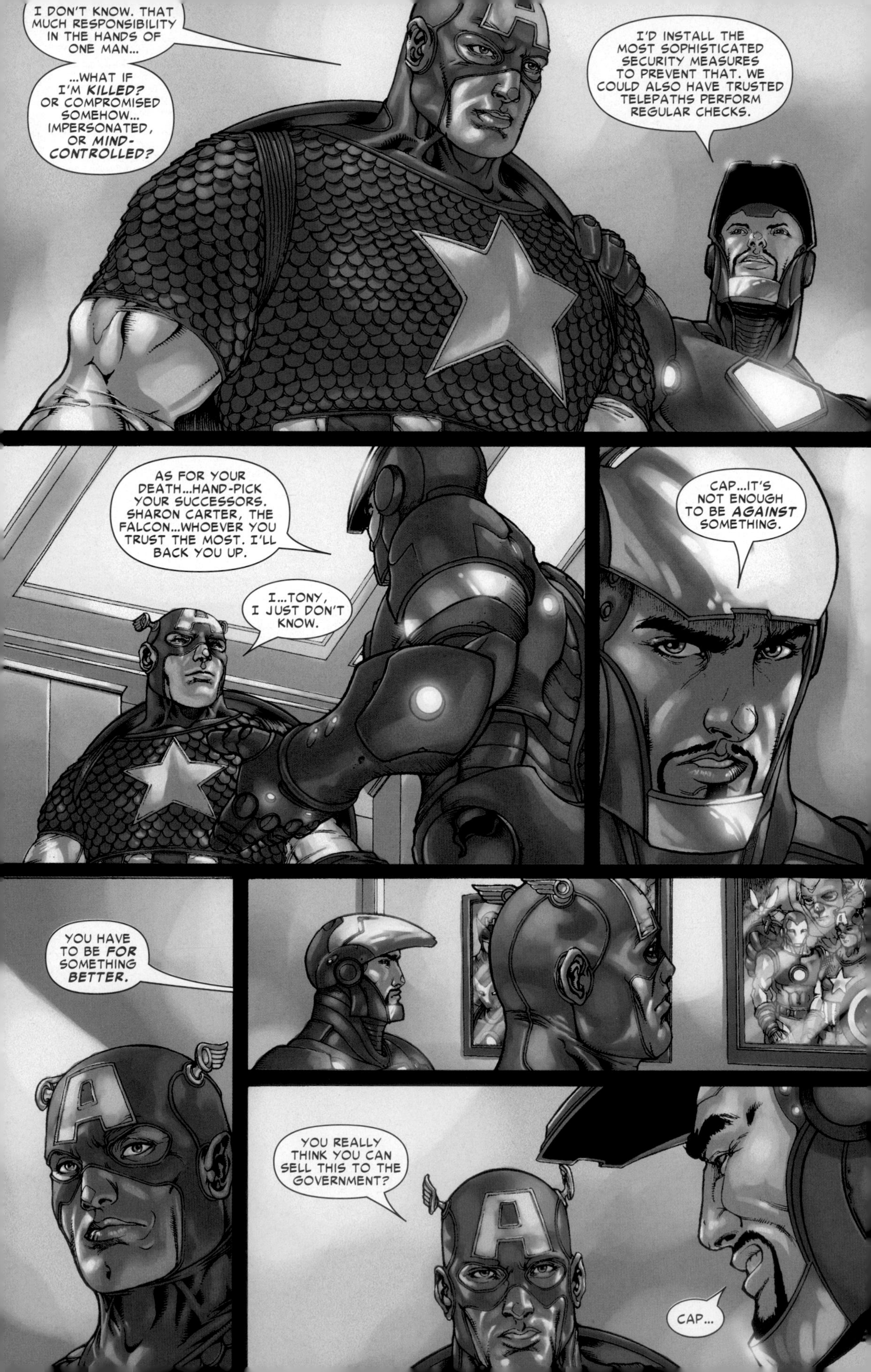
I DON'T KNOW. THAT MUCH RESPONSIBILITY IN THE HANDS OF ONE MAN...
...WHAT IF I'M *KILLED?* OR COMPROMISED SOMEHOW... IMPERSONATED, OR *MIND-CONTROLLED?*
I'D INSTALL THE MOST SOPHISTICATED SECURITY MEASURES TO PREVENT THAT. WE COULD ALSO HAVE TRUSTED TELEPATHS PERFORM REGULAR CHECKS.
AS FOR YOUR DEATH...HAND-PICK YOUR SUCCESSORS. SHARON CARTER, THE FALCON...WHOEVER YOU TRUST THE MOST. I'LL BACK YOU UP.
I...TONY, I JUST DON'T KNOW.
CAP...IT'S NOT ENOUGH TO BE *AGAINST* SOMETHING.
YOU HAVE TO BE *FOR* SOMETHING *BETTER.*
YOU REALLY THINK YOU CAN SELL THIS TO THE GOVERNMENT?
CAP...

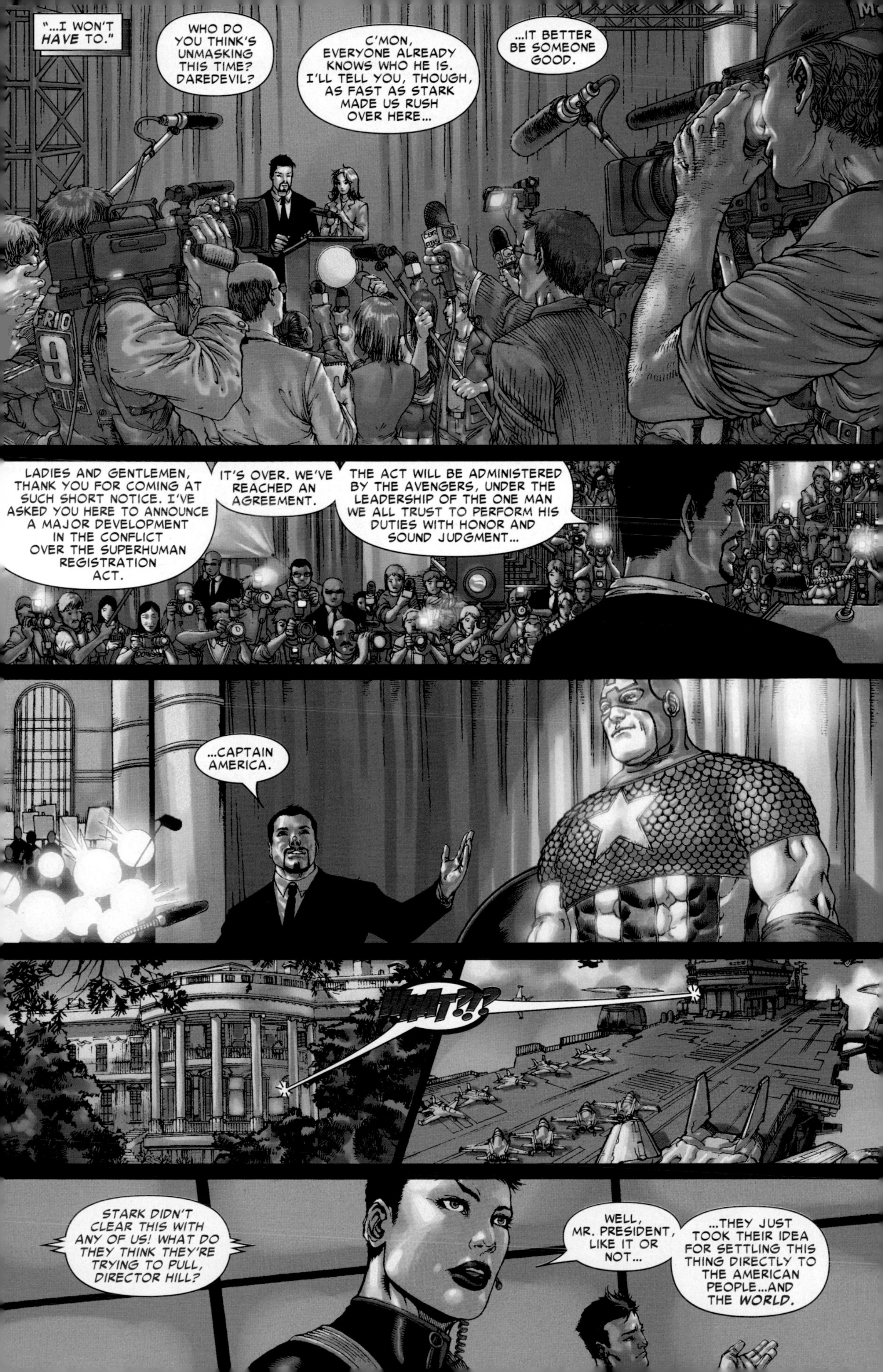
"...I WON'T HAVE TO."
WHO DO YOU THINK'S UNMASKING THIS TIME? DAREDEVIL?
C'MON, EVERYONE ALREADY KNOWS WHO HE IS. I'LL TELL YOU, THOUGH, AS FAST AS STARK MADE US RUSH OVER HERE...
...IT BETTER BE SOMEONE GOOD.
LADIES AND GENTLEMEN, THANK YOU FOR COMING AT SUCH SHORT NOTICE. I'VE ASKED YOU HERE TO ANNOUNCE A MAJOR DEVELOPMENT IN THE CONFLICT OVER THE SUPERHUMAN REGISTRATION ACT.
IT'S OVER. WE'VE REACHED AN AGREEMENT.
THE ACT WILL BE ADMINISTERED BY THE AVENGERS, UNDER THE LEADERSHIP OF THE ONE MAN WE ALL TRUST TO PERFORM HIS DUTIES WITH HONOR AND SOUND JUDGMENT...
...CAPTAIN AMERICA.
WHAT?!?
STARK DIDN'T CLEAR THIS WITH ANY OF US! WHAT DO THEY THINK THEY'RE TRYING TO PULL, DIRECTOR HILL?
WELL, MR. PRESIDENT, LIKE IT OR NOT...
...THEY JUST TOOK THEIR IDEA FOR SETTLING THIS THING DIRECTLY TO THE AMERICAN PEOPLE...AND THE WORLD.

NO DISRESPECT WAS INTENDED, MR. PRESIDENT. BUT LET'S BE HONEST, YOU NEVER WOULD HAVE SIGNED OFF ON THIS IF WE'D COME TO YOU.

YOU'RE DARN RIGHT I WOULDN'T! DIRECTOR HILL AND I HAVE *SERIOUS* CONCERNS ABOUT YOUR PLAN.

FRANKLY, SIR-- AND I INCLUDE IRON MAN AND MYSELF IN THIS--*NO ONE'S* COMPLETELY HAPPY WITH IT.

WHICH IS PROBABLY THE BEST INDICATION WE HAVE THAT IT'S *GOOD.*

THERE ARE THE LATEST POLL NUMBERS. AN OVERWHELMING MAJORITY OF AMERICANS SUPPORT THIS ARRANGEMENT.

WITH ALL DUE RESPECT, SIR, WHAT MATTERS ISN'T WHETHER YOU LIKE IT...

...BUT WHETHER YOU CAN *LIVE* WITH IT.

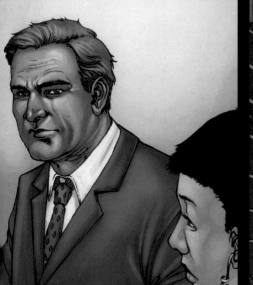

TIMES LIKE THIS I SEE WHAT *CHURCHILL* MEANT WHEN HE SAID DEMOCRACY IS THE WORST FORM OF GOVERNMENT...

...EXCEPT FOR ALL THE OTHERS.

DON'T MESS THIS UP, GENTLEMEN.

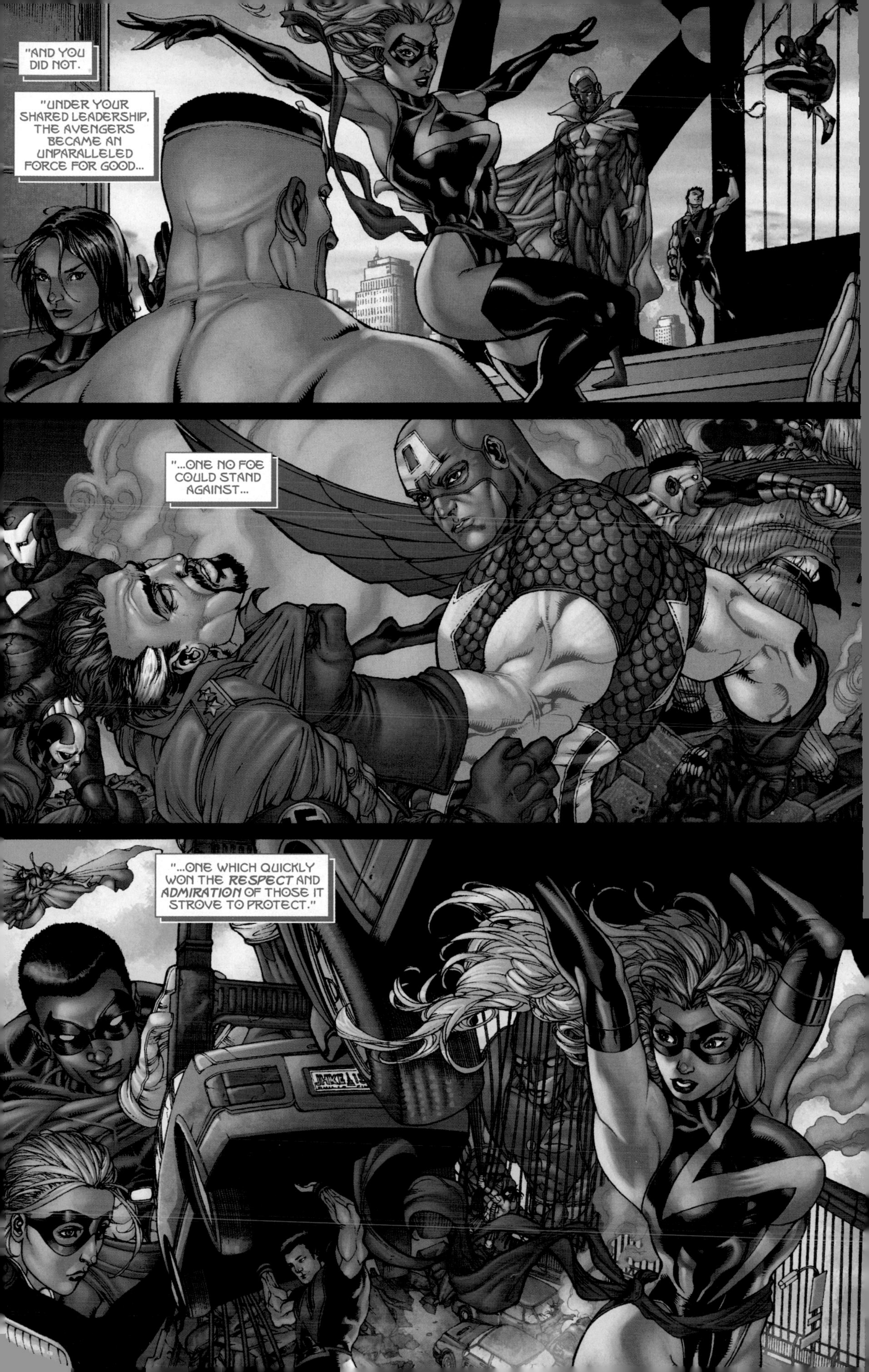
"AND YOU DID NOT.
"UNDER YOUR SHARED LEADERSHIP, THE AVENGERS BECAME AN UNPARALLELED FORCE FOR GOOD...
"...ONE NO FOE COULD STAND AGAINST...
"...ONE WHICH QUICKLY WON THE *RESPECT* AND *ADMIRATION* OF THOSE IT STROVE TO PROTECT."

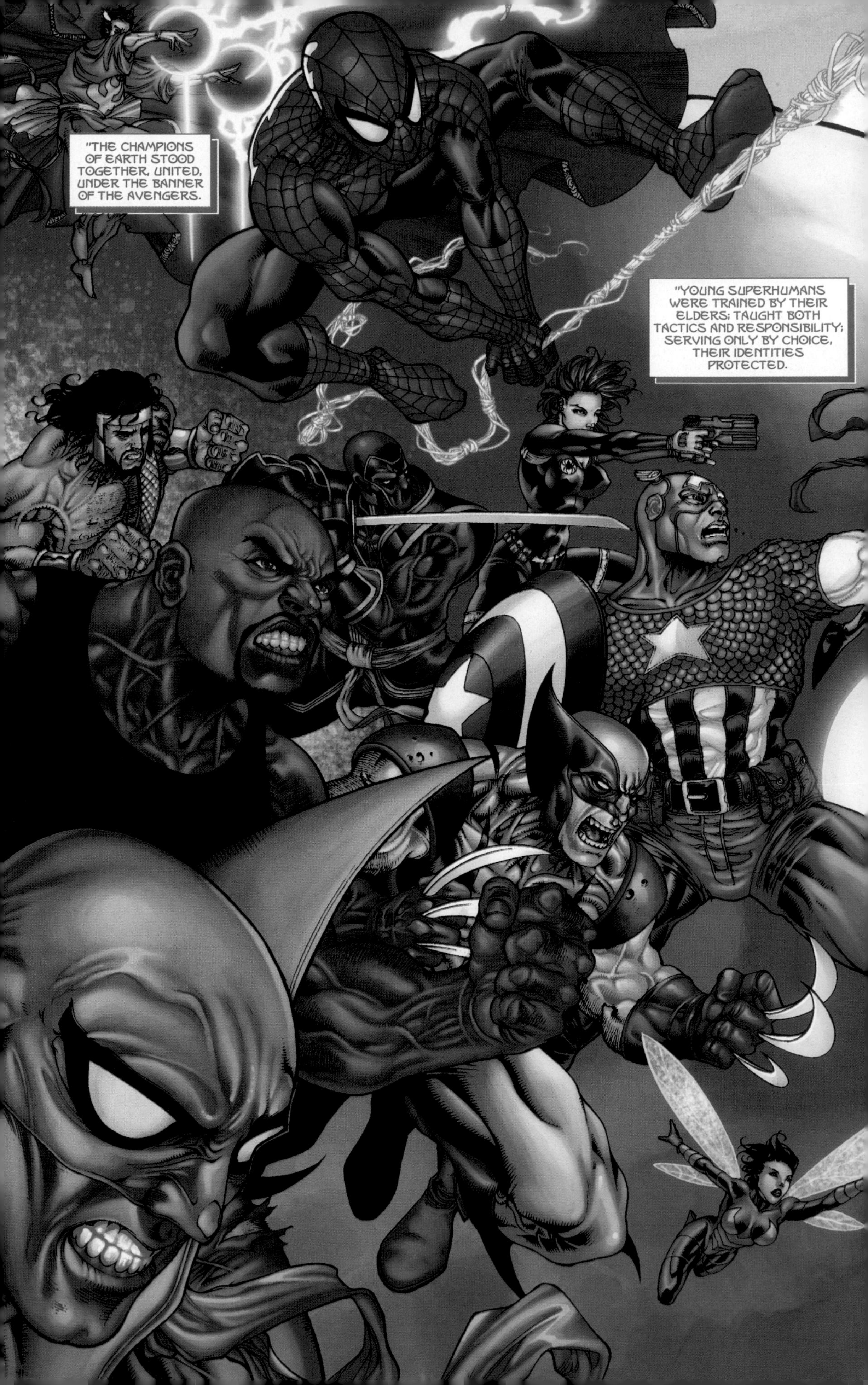
"THE CHAMPIONS OF EARTH STOOD TOGETHER, UNITED, UNDER THE BANNER OF THE AVENGERS.
"YOUNG SUPERHUMANS WERE TRAINED BY THEIR ELDERS; TAUGHT BOTH TACTICS AND RESPONSIBILITY; SERVING ONLY BY CHOICE, THEIR IDENTITIES PROTECTED.

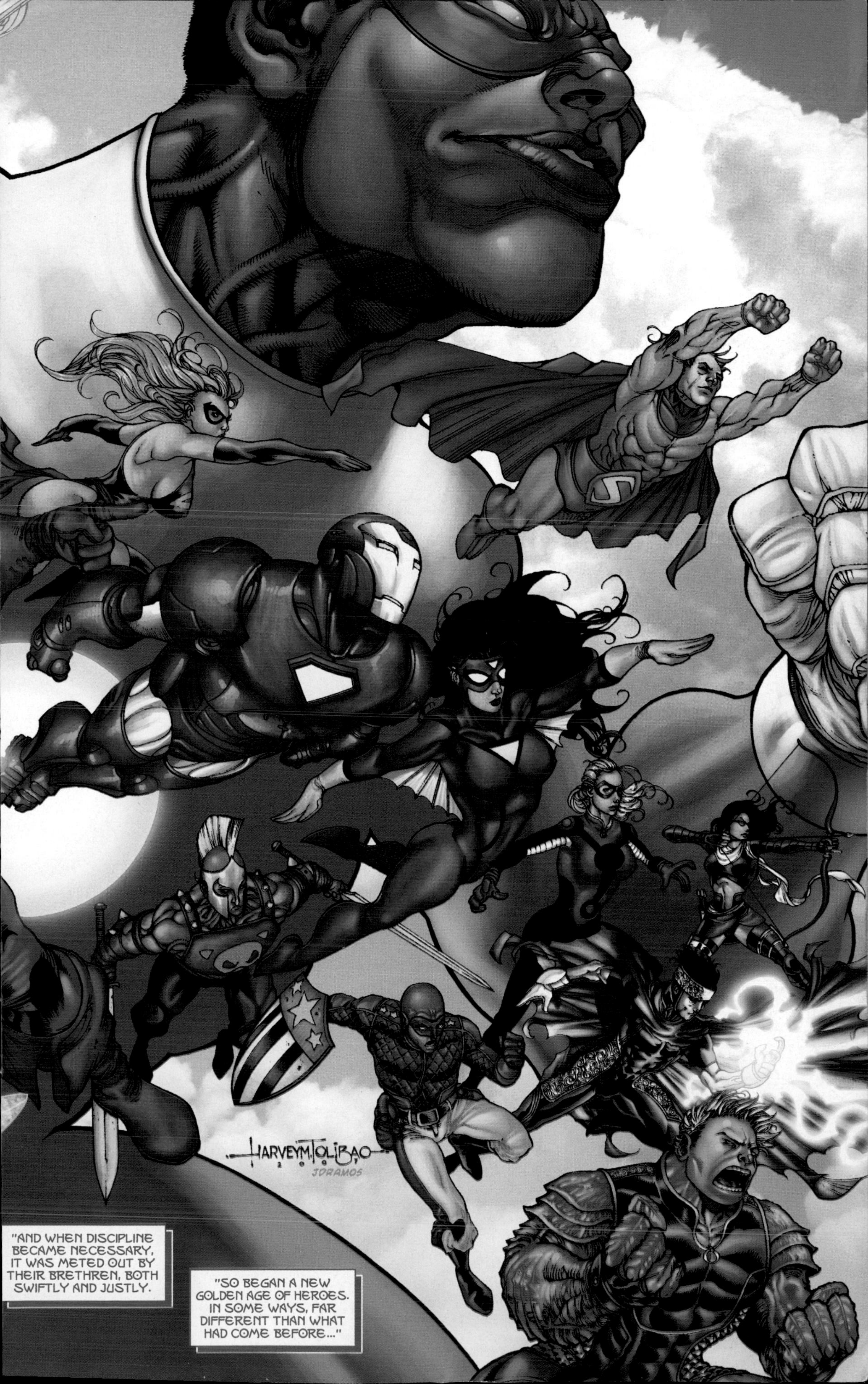
HARVEYM.TOLIBAO
JDRAMOS
"AND WHEN DISCIPLINE BECAME NECESSARY, IT WAS METED OUT BY THEIR BRETHREN, BOTH SWIFTLY AND JUSTLY.
"SO BEGAN A NEW GOLDEN AGE OF HEROES. IN SOME WAYS, FAR DIFFERENT THAN WHAT HAD COME BEFORE..."

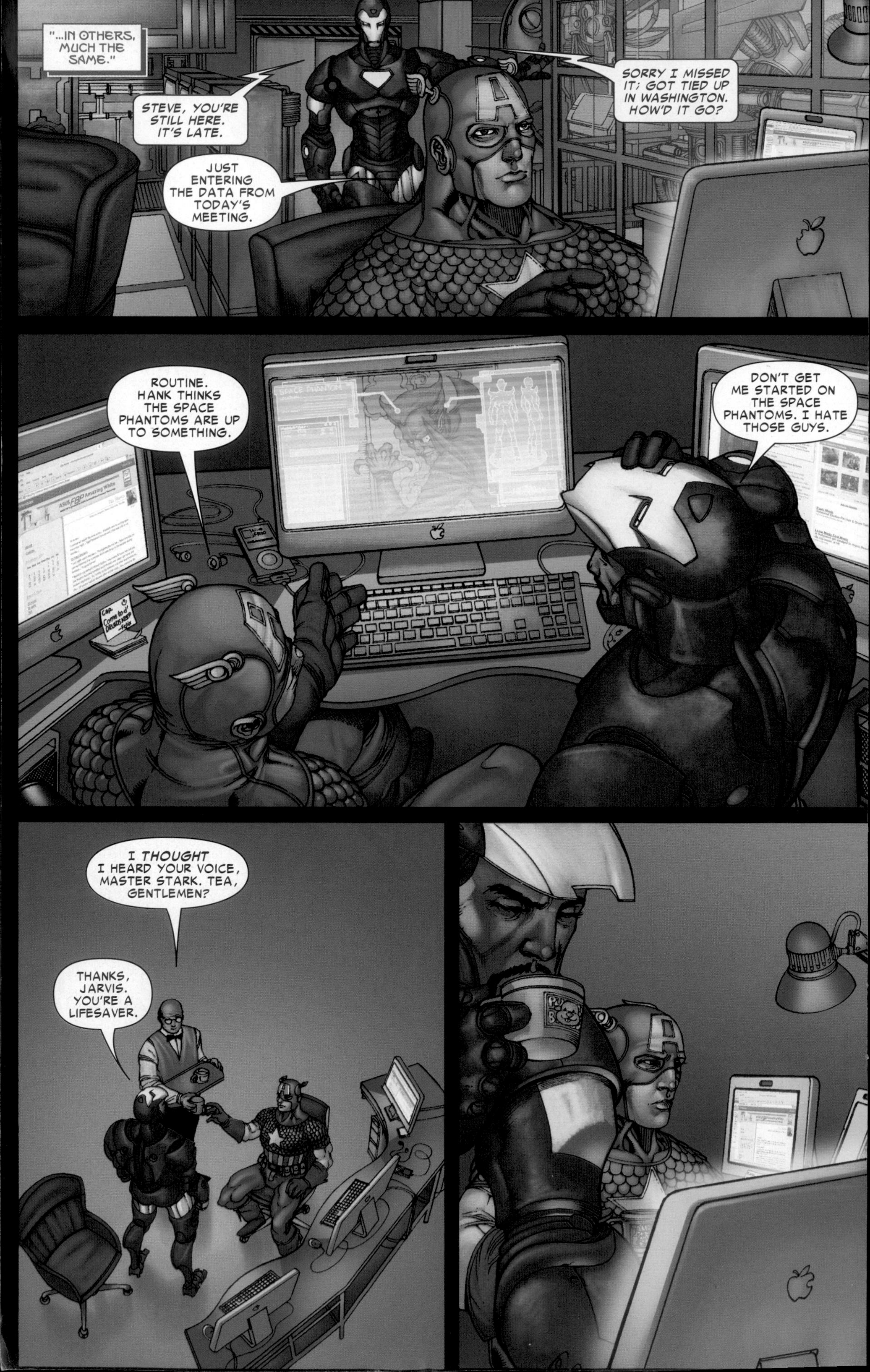
"...IN OTHERS, MUCH THE SAME."
STEVE, YOU'RE STILL HERE. IT'S LATE.
SORRY I MISSED IT; GOT TIED UP IN WASHINGTON. HOW'D IT GO?
JUST ENTERING THE DATA FROM TODAY'S MEETING.
ROUTINE. HANK THINKS THE SPACE PHANTOMS ARE UP TO SOMETHING.
DON'T GET ME STARTED ON THE SPACE PHANTOMS. I HATE THOSE GUYS.
I THOUGHT I HEARD YOUR VOICE, MASTER STARK. TEA, GENTLEMEN?
THANKS, JARVIS. YOU'RE A LIFESAVER.

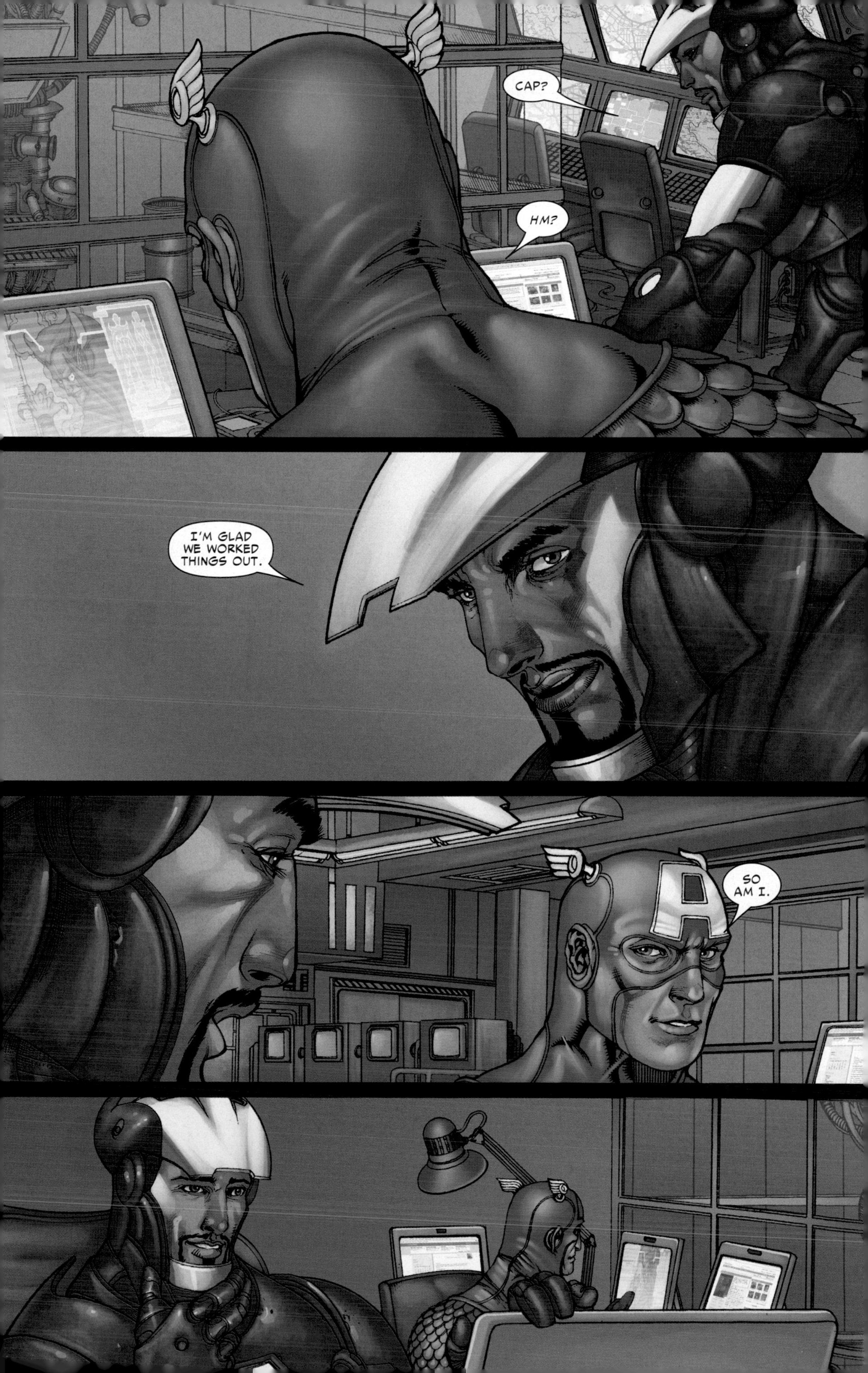
CAP?
HM?
I'M GLAD WE WORKED THINGS OUT.
SO AM I.

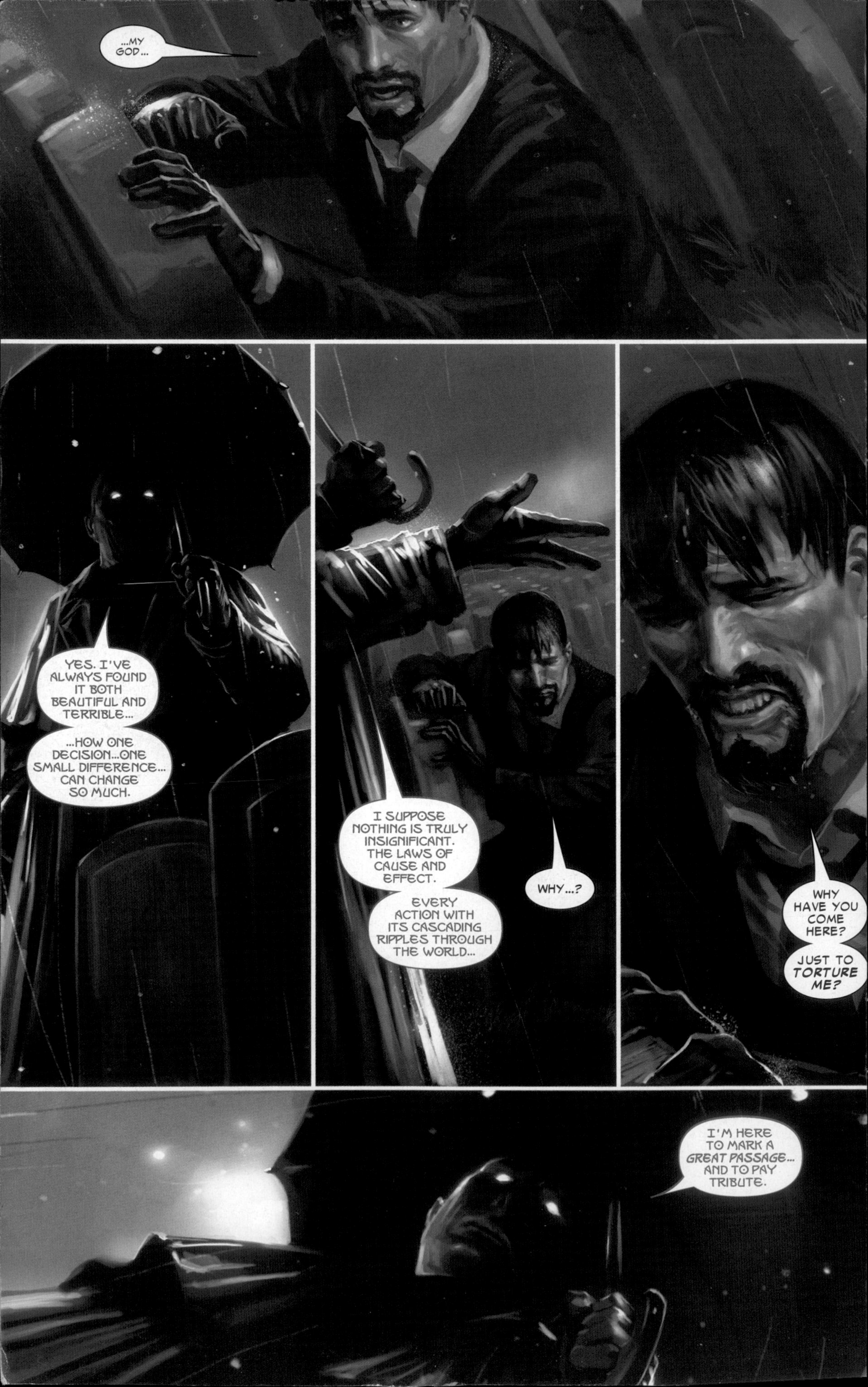
...MY GOD...
YES. I'VE ALWAYS FOUND IT BOTH BEAUTIFUL AND TERRIBLE...
...HOW ONE DECISION...ONE SMALL DIFFERENCE... CAN CHANGE SO MUCH.
I SUPPOSE NOTHING IS TRULY INSIGNIFICANT. THE LAWS OF CAUSE AND EFFECT.
EVERY ACTION WITH ITS CASCADING RIPPLES THROUGH THE WORLD...
WHY...?
WHY HAVE YOU COME HERE?
JUST TO *TORTURE* ME?
I'M HERE TO MARK A *GREAT PASSAGE*... AND TO PAY TRIBUTE.

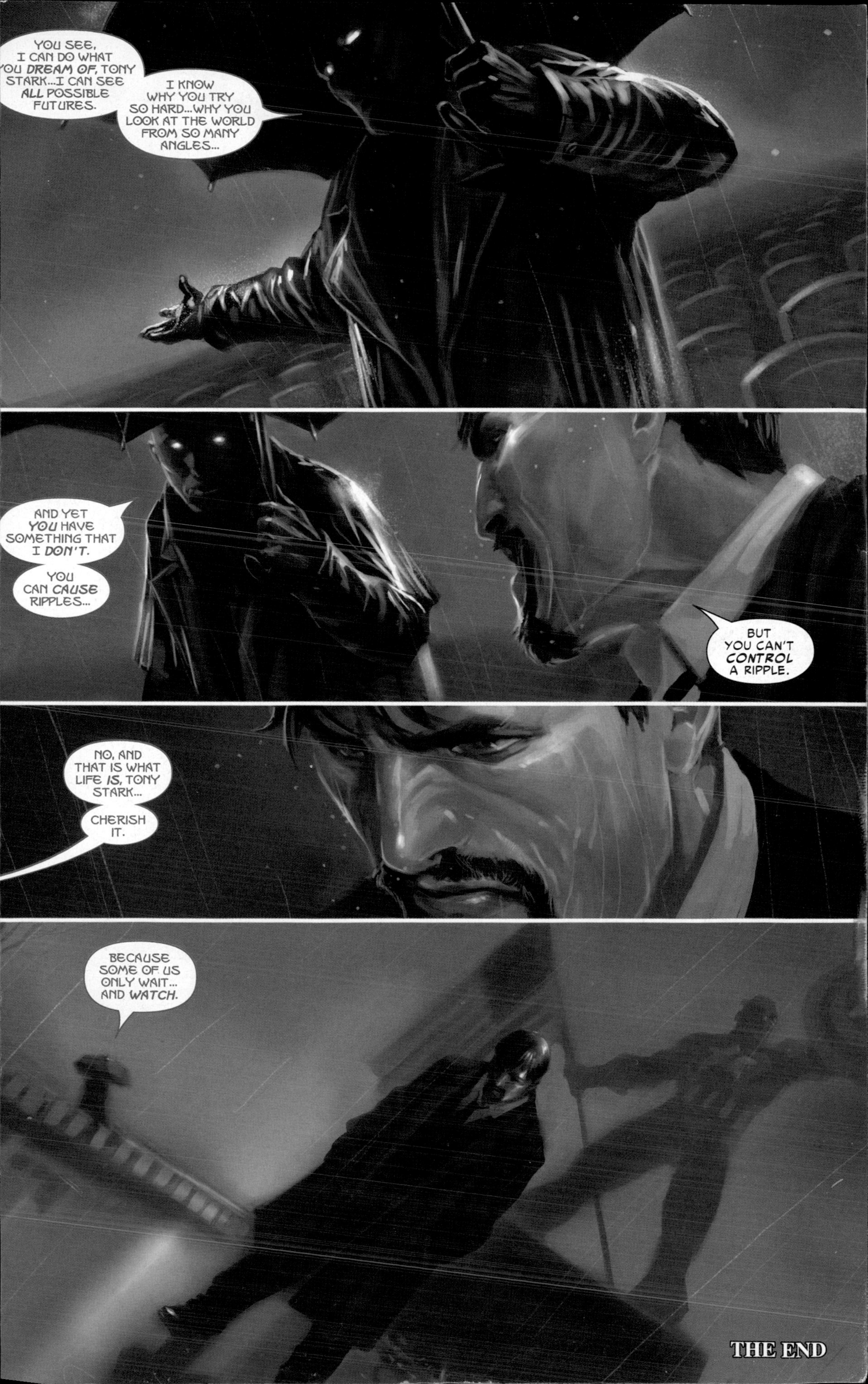
YOU SEE, I CAN DO WHAT YOU DREAM OF, TONY STARK...I CAN SEE ALL POSSIBLE FUTURES.
I KNOW WHY YOU TRY SO HARD...WHY YOU LOOK AT THE WORLD FROM SO MANY ANGLES...
AND YET YOU HAVE SOMETHING THAT I DON'T.
YOU CAN CAUSE RIPPLES...
BUT YOU CAN'T CONTROL A RIPPLE.
NO, AND THAT IS WHAT LIFE IS, TONY STARK...
CHERISH IT.
BECAUSE SOME OF US ONLY WAIT... AND WATCH.
THE END

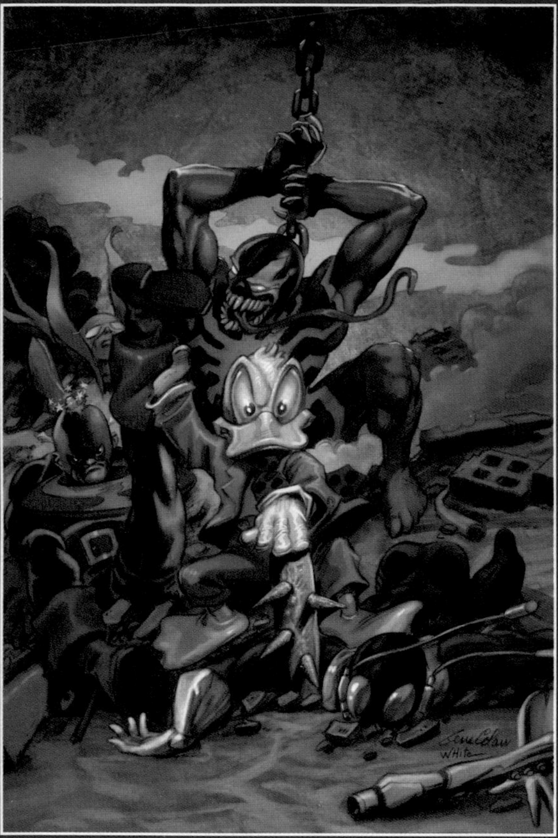

Civil War: Choosing Sides Variant
By Gene Colan & Dean White

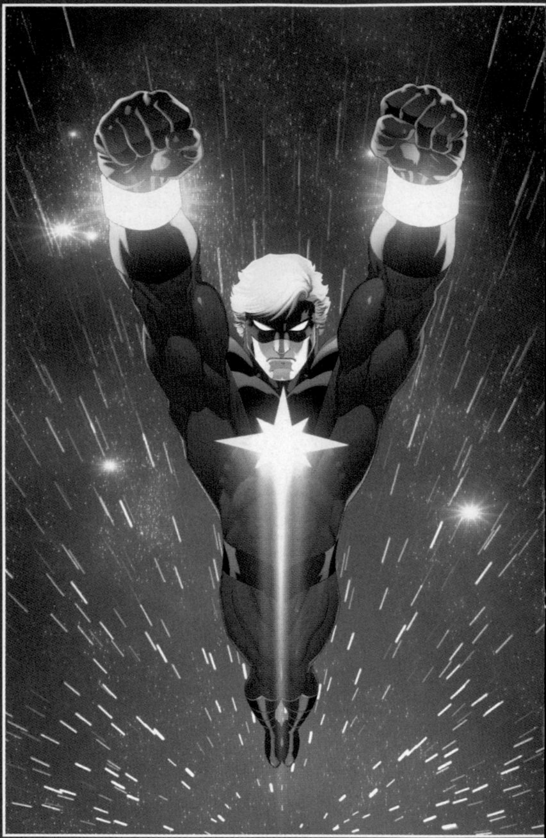

Civil War: The Return Variant
By Ed McGuinness & Dave McCaig

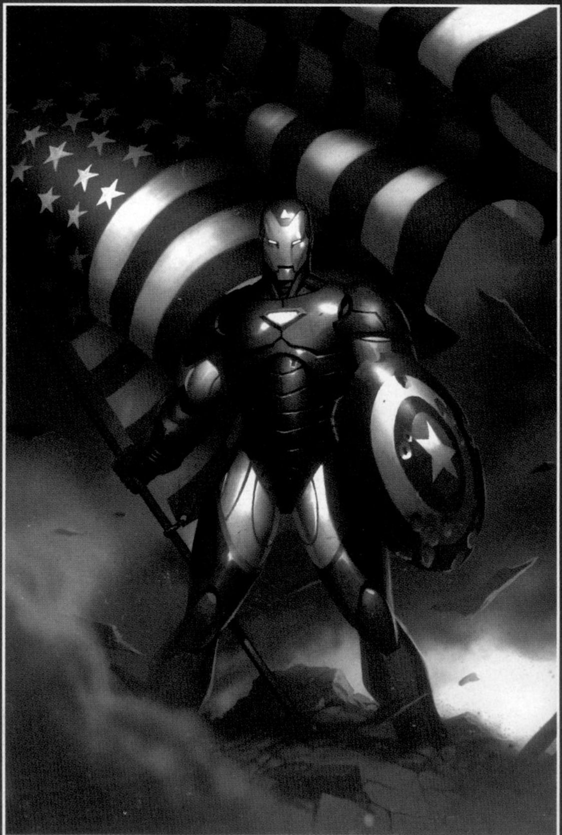

What If? Civil War Variant By Marc Silvestri,
Top Cow & Jelena Kevic-Djurdjevic